THE VIOLENT FACE OF NATURE

SEVERE PHENOMENA
and
NATURAL DISASTERS

THE VIOLENT FACE OF NATURE

SEVERE PHENOMENA and NATURAL DISASTERS

by KENDRICK FRAZIER

WILLIAM MORROW AND COMPANY, INC.

NEW YORK   1979

To Ruth, Chris, and Michele,
who made it possible

Library of Congress Cataloging in Publication Data

Frazier, Kendrick.
    The violent face of nature.

    Bibliography: p.
    Includes index.
    1. Natural disasters. 2. Earth sciences.
I. Title.
GB5018.F7   363.3′4   79-16073
ISBN 0-688-03528-0

Printed in the United States of America.

First Edition

1 2 3 4 5 6 7 8 9 10

PREFACE

Like most people, I am fascinated by the extreme events of nature and the natural disasters associated with them. Fortunately, my experiences with natural catastrophes have not all been in person or I might not be here to write about the subject.

This book's origins go back many years. Images, memories, impressions bubble in the consciousness. Later, when the time seems right, they help shape something more concrete. I grew up in a part of the country, Northern Colorado, subject to frequent storms. Brief-lived thunderstorms were standard summer-afternoon fare. Snowstorms and blizzards gave winter an unmistakably strong identity. Hail's awesome rattle brought anxious fears of farmland ruin. We were far from tornado country, we thought, but one spring day a tornado disposed of the front-porch roof of a neighbor's house two doors away, then skipped two blocks to the high school where, like a giant can opener, it proceeded to rip away the roof of the school bus garage.

In the first week of my first job in journalism, a summer position on a daily newspaper, I reported on the damage dealt the area's sugar beets, corn, and wheat by a sudden hailstorm. I still remember and admire the farmer I interviewed (whom I knew) standing amid the ruin of his corn crop, resolving to persevere against the elements. In a year spent as a wire service reporter, I once worked for 28 continuous hours covering the events of the Platte River floods in Denver in 1965.

Sometime after that, although I hardly mean to imply a causal link, I knew my profession was to write about nature and our efforts to better understand it. I wanted to share with the public some of my sense of wonder about the natural world and the new insights science unveils in probing the mysteries of the earth.

After graduate school, I ended up in Washington, D.C. There, first at the National Academy of Sciences and then for eight very special years at *Science News*, as writer and editor, violent extremes of weather and the subterranean powers of earthquakes and volcanoes were frequently the focus of my attention. Here too grew an awareness of our increasing vulnerability to natural disaster, a concern about extreme natural forces as a problem, and a curiosity about how people respond under the stress of disaster.

It has been said that earthquakes are where geology meets the public. Similar statements can be made about all the kinds of natural forces. They affect every person on earth. They are concrete concerns, not abstract conceptions. They form a very human-oriented subject, and I've tried to bring that out throughout the book.

I regret the public doesn't appreciate the degree to which science progresses in a series of tiny steps (and sometimes missteps), each building on what has been learned previously. For everything new we learn we owe an enormous debt to all who have gone before. In writing a book such as this, especially one that covers such broad territory, the debts one accrues are almost beyond acknowledgment. Although the book is not heavily scientific, I've drawn freely upon the works of many hundreds of researchers, natural scientists, and social scientists. I've benefited from vivid descriptions of disasters by other writers. I visited such places as the National Severe Storms Laboratory in Oklahoma, the National Meteorological Center and National Environmental Satellite Service facilities outside of Washington, the U.S. Geological Survey (USGS) headquarters in Virginia, the Institute for Disaster Research at Texas Tech University, and in Boulder the National Oceanic and Atmospheric Administration (NOAA), the National Center for Atmospheric Research, and the University of Colorado's Institute of Behavioral Science. In all these places I've encountered people helpful beyond my expectations.

Written sources are acknowledged in the bibliography, and to a certain extent within the text, but I want to give special mention to several books. One is Guy Murchie's *Song of the Sky*, a book whose wonder has not been diminished by the years, full of fresh imagery, poetic grace, and lively intelligence. Another is Frank W. Lane's *The Elements Rage*, which so thoroughly explored the ground I now dare to tread. Both have been inspirations. For Chapter 8, Fred M. Bullard's *Volcanoes of the Earth* (University of Texas Press, 1976) proved useful beyond measure, and I gratefully acknowledge his permission to draw upon information within it.

Periodicals that have been especially useful are *Monthly Weather Review*, *Bulletin of the American Meteorological Society*, *Weatherwise*, *Storm Data* (National Climatic Center), *Earthquake Information Bulletin* (U.S. Geological Survey), *Science News*, *Nature*, *New Scientist*, *Scientific American*, *EOS* (American Geophysical Union), and *Natural Hazards Observer* (IBS, University of Colorado).

Perhaps my greatest debt of gratitude is to the scientists and researchers who reviewed chapters or parts of chapters: Charles F. Chappell (Thunderstorms and Flash Floods), Edwin Kessler and Allen Pearson (Thunderstorms and Tornadoes), T. Theodore Fujita (Tornadoes), Marx Brook (Lightning), Neil M. Frank (Hurricanes and Hurricane Vulnerability), Fred M. Bullard (Volcanoes), Bruce M. Bolt (Earthquakes), George Cressman, Duane S. Cooley, Earl Estelle, Frederick G. Shuman, Harry E. Brown, George H. Ludwig, and C. Gordon Little (Forecasting, Prediction, and Warning), Peter L. Ward (Earthquake Prediction), Joseph E. Minor (Wind Engineering and Myths about Tornadoes), Ernst W. Kiesling (Engineering against Tornadoes), and E. L. Quarantelli (Response to Disasters). Their suggestions and comments have been exceedingly helpful. Needless to say, they bear no blame for whatever faults the book may still contain. All responsibility is mine.

Public information officers have contributed all manner of aid. Among them Stanley Eames, Carl Posey, and Louise Purrett-Carroll of NOAA; Don Kelly and Frank Forrester of USGS; and Diane Johnson of the National Center for Atmospheric Research. Photos were graciously made available by them and by Joanne David, NOAA photo librarian in Maryland, and Carolyn Smith of the American National Red Cross photo center in Washington.

Sue Hayes typed each of the chapters as completed and gave needed early encouragement. Julie Houston, my editor at Morrow, was a patient guide and master psychologist of the gentle nudge.

And finally to my family. My wife, Ruth, despite her own busy and important professional life, never lost her warm and supportive spirit which so brightens my life. Our two children,

Christopher and Michele, wise beyond their years, were constant and delightful sources of support and encouragement. Without the loving efforts of all three of them, this book would never even have been started, much less completed. To them it is dedicated.

CONTENTS

Preface   7
Introduction   13

Part I. Severe Phenomena and Natural Disasters

  1. Thunderstorms   21
  2. Tornadoes   46
  3. Lightning   77
  4. Hail   100
  5. Floods   119
  6. Hurricanes   143
  7. Blizzards   167
  8. Volcanoes   190
  9. Earthquakes   219

Part II. Natural Disasters and Society

10. Forecasting, Prediction, Warning   253
11. Modification   278
12. How to Prepare for Disaster   298
13. Our Increasing Vulnerability to Disaster   316
14. Responses to Disaster   337
15. Disasters and the Future   364

Bibliography   367
Index   377

INTRODUCTION

The weather satellite 22,300 miles out in space reveals a beautiful but deceptive picture of earth. The view we see is of a placid world floating peacefully in the blackness of space, patterns of white clouds winding like ornaments across the planet's disk.

But we know how misleading that serene scene can be. Within those clouds, within the rest of the atmosphere so invisible, and beneath the surface of what we think of as a solid planet, lurk awesome energies that need only the proper conditions to unleash their havoc.

The wait need not be long. At any given moment, 1,800 thunderstorms are in progress over the earth's surface. Lightning is striking the earth 100 times each second. If the season is late summer, one or more of the some 50 hurricanes or typhoons that swirl into existence each year is likely to be moving toward a populated coastline. If the time is late afternoon, the odds are good that a tornado is raking across the American heartland; 600 to 1,000 times a year they do so, and in the prime months they can strike with a frequency of four or more a day. Somewhere at any given moment people's homes or crops are under flood waters. Half a billion people live on floodplains, and the crops grown on floodplains supply food for a third of the world's population.

There's no solace beneath the reach of the turbulent atmosphere either. More than 2,000 earth tremors strong enough to be recorded course through the planet every day. Twice a day somewhere in the world earthquakes strike with enough force to damage homes and buildings. From 15 to 20 times a year a quake strikes with enough energy to cause widespread death and destruction. And all the while there are 516 active volcanoes waiting to spring loose their violence. An eruption begins some-where every 15 days.

There is no way to switch off the energy that continually feeds such violence. Storms derive their energy from the life-giving flow of heat from the sun. Earthquakes and volcanoes get their energy from the heat of radioactive decay of the material within the earth itself. This slow but unending release of heat from the interior to the earth's surface amounts to 10 times all the energy used by man. Even then, it is equivalent to only one five-thousandth the energy that the sun delivers to our planet.

Clearly we're talking about forces of nature that dwarf the puny efforts of humankind. A single thunderstorm three miles in diameter may hold half a million tons of water and contain energy equal to 10 atomic bombs the size that devastated Hiro-shima and Nagasaki. Larger ones carry the potential energy of several one-megaton hydrogen bombs. Such comparisons are unsatisfactory both technically and aesthetically, but a single great earthquake of the size that occurs about four times each year releases the energy of a 10-megaton hydrogen bomb, or nearly twice the daily U.S. consumption of electrical energy. A large volcanic eruption produces almost exactly the same amount.

This is a book about the severe forces of nature and the disasters that result when human populations find themselves in the path of the destructive force unleashed. And it is about how human beings—as individuals, families, communities, and gov-ernments—respond to natural disaster.

In one important sense there is no such thing as a natural disaster. A disaster is a social phenomenon. Across our planet for about four and a half billions of years, the forces of nature have shaped, molded, and changed the earth. Oceans have come and gone, continents have assembled and split apart, mountains have grown and eroded. Awesome changes indeed. But what we call a disaster requires the presence of humans, caught up as victims in the violence of nature. A huge volcanic eruption on an uninhabited ocean island may not be a disaster at all. But even a small earthquake beneath a densely populated urban area can be an unmitigated tragedy. A hurricane that sweeps over a coastal fishing village where the storm-wizened residents have taken all possible precautions may cause some destruction. But if the same hurricane strikes a fast-growing Sun Belt coastal city where the new residents have little experience with such storms and ignore the warnings to evacuate, the death toll as well as the property damage could be catastrophic. A once-a-generation flood of a major river could have little ill effect if humans have respected that potential. But when people build their homes and communities on a floodplain, the flood that undoubtedly will come is a disaster. Since populations nearly everywhere are on the rise and people are occupying vulnerable areas to a greater extent, the potential for most kinds of disasters is on a steady increase.

The decade of the 1970s has been plagued by extraordinary natural disasters. The second most devastating earthquake in recorded world history struck in 1976 in China, killing an estimated 700,000 persons. The greatest tornado outbreak in recorded history occurred in 1974 when 148 separate tornadoes in a two-day period ripped across the eastern third of the United States, killing 315 persons, injuring 6,142, and causing $600 million in property damage in 10 states. The Bangladesh storm of 1970 that left 300,000 dead may have been the deadliest tropical cyclone (hurricane) in history. The United States' worst disaster in amount of damage ($4 billion) was the widespread flooding from the rains of Hurricane Agnes in 1972. A series of sudden flood disasters throughout the 1970s made flash floods the nation's number one weather-related killer. Unlike the great pestilences of the past, natural disasters are a phenomenon very much of the present, and certainly of the future. In most instances, their capability for destruction increases as the world becomes more highly developed, heavily populated, and interdependent.

Millions of persons in the United States alone—in fact, more than half the population—live in places that are highly susceptible to natural disasters. But no matter where you live, you are not safe from disaster's reach. Tornadoes have occurred in every state in the union, including Alaska. The devastating effects of hurricanes can extend far inland—Agnes is an example of that. The most prolonged and violent series of earthquakes ever to hit the United States occurred not along California's San Andreas fault as we might suppose but in Missouri, 2,000 miles from the continent's main earthquake belt. Surprisingly, the worst and most consistent killer of all natural phenomena over the long range in this country is not, as we might think, tornadoes, hurricanes, floods or earthquakes, but lightning, which picks off its victims one by one, thus avoiding the attention and national publicity accorded the more mass-destructive hazards. And lightning can strike anywhere. Lightning is not only a solo killer, it is a technological incapacitator. It is capable of knocking out computer systems our society has grown dependent upon or electrical power systems that we can go without even temporarily only at the risk of great social chaos—the lightning-initiated New York City power blackout in 1977, for example.

In the first nine chapters that follow, which comprise the first part of the book, we take up one by one the primary severe natural phenomena: thunderstorms, tornadoes, lightning, hail, floods, hurricanes, blizzards, volcanoes, and earthquakes. You might argue that a book on nature's severe manifestations and their effects on society should deal as well with climate change. That's a timely and significant concern too, but it's a vast subject in itself and it's on a different time scale. The time scale of climate change is decades, centuries, and millennia. With the severe natural phenomena, we are dealing in days, hours, and minutes. The challenge to understanding, the destruction and tragedy and the human response to disasters caused by short-lived natural phenomena should be more than enough to keep us busy here.

Another self-imposed limitation, for practical reasons only, is to confine our focus solely to the violent phenomena of earth and its atmosphere. But we should realize that the forces encountered here have their counterparts elsewhere, some on grand scales. Mars has a volcano that towers 18 miles above the surrounding plain and whose base is as wide as the state of New Mexico. It has occasional planet-wide duststorms. Storms of hurricane violence course through the atmosphere of Jupiter. Soviet and U.S. spacecraft have recently detected probable lightning flashes on Venus. Our Voyager 1 spacecraft has in 1979 detected probable lightning "superbolts" on Jupiter and photographed colossal volcanic eruptions *in progress* on Jupiter's strange moon Io. And far beyond our solar system to the distant reaches of the cosmos almost unimaginable forces are at work in galactic centers and quasars. But it is earth, and its forces and people, that we are concerned with here.

My goal for each of the phenomena is to vividly portray the power and impact on humans of their violence and to sketch the rudiments of what we know about them: their causes, energies, life cycles, and role in nature.

I also report briefly on some of the scientific research underway to better understand these phenomena. I try to provide an up-to-date look at research in progress, a glimpse at the frontiers of discovery. Since the book is intended for the general reader, I've tried to keep technical matters to a minimum.

The final section, chapters 10 through 15, deals with natural disasters and society. Here we come fully to the intersection of people and the severe forces of nature: the forecasting, warning, and prediction of violent events, the efforts to learn how to modify them for human benefit, advice on how you, your family, and your community can become better prepared against the possibility of disaster. I take up in some detail the perhaps surprising fact that the vulnerability of the nation and the world to many kinds of disasters is increasing. And finally, I relate what we know about how human beings respond during them. Here too we encounter some surprises, and some widely held myths.

One theme that may emerge from this book is that for all our self-proclaimed sophistication, modern scientific knowledge, and technological know-how, we are no match for the violent forces of nature. We are better off when we understand and respect the awesomeness of its forces and plan our communities and societies as best we can around the assumption that violent natural events will periodically happen. More wisdom is necessary to respect and to live with nature, not against it. I'm not referring to fatalism. Planning and proper actions save lives.

A second theme is that a greater share of the attention of efforts to prepare for natural disasters needs to be devoted to social, economic, and political—"people"—matters. Ignoring or not fully understanding these human considerations has led some disaster-reduction efforts to failure. In some cases, well-meant but unwise actions can actually lead to increases in the potential for future catastrophe.

One final note. Violent and destructive as they often may be, the extreme events of nature are not unmitigated evils. The hurricanes, typhoons, and tropical cyclones that can visit so much misery on the lands they touch also bring a large percentage of the needed life-nourishing rains to many regions of the world. An afternoon thunderstorm can bring damaging winds and devastating hail; more often it brings welcome and necessary moisture. Volcanoes can kill and destroy; they are also responsible for the existence of most of the oceanic islands of the world and a fair proportion of the fertile soil on the continents. Furthermore, they are the conduits through which escaped outward from the planet's interior the waters and gases that form today's oceans and atmosphere and thus can be said to be responsible for the development of life on earth. No small contribution.

To my mind, the unbounded drama of nature has always proved at least as interesting and stimulating as the fictional dramas of our creative imaginations or the real-life dramas of our everyday lives. Much of that drama is full of majesty and beauty, as when an evening electrical storm sends swords of white light through the black sky. To me, better knowing that majesty is motivation enough to learn more about those severe natural events. But when those same kinds of forces bring death and destruction, we also need to understand why it happens and how to lessen the jeopardy to life in the future. I hope this book brings a better appreciation of both aspects of the violent face of nature.

PART I

SEVERE PHENOMENA
and
NATURAL DISASTERS

CHAPTER 1

Thunderstorms

On the afternoon of June 6, 1977, a series of severe thunderstorms formed across much of the Southeastern United States. The sky darkened and weather conditions worsened throughout the early afternoon. By 3 P.M. the havoc was underway.

Tennessee bore the first wave of this meteorological assault. At Pulaski, in Giles County, one thunderstorm's high winds tore a motel roof off, injuring one occupant. The roofs on several homes and a high school gymnasium were damaged. Trees were uprooted and several power lines blown down.

Twenty minutes later, a tornado swirled out of the clouds and touched down briefly in four places near Fayetteville. The area was open and hilly and only trees and orchards were damaged. At 3:30 another thunderstorm struck Tullahoma. At the airport, part of the hangar roof was blown off, and four airplanes and two other buildings were damaged. An hour later in Chattanooga, high winds clocked at 68 miles per hour at the airport rushed out of a severe thunderstorm and blew down trees and power lines. A seven-year-old boy received electrical burns when he touched a fallen wire. Another person was injured when a section of roofing was ripped from a building and tore through the windshield of his car. Several homes and businesses were damaged. Shortly after five, the winds struck Morristown, in Hamblen County, destroying a house, two barns, and a garage. In nearby Leadvale, the thunderstorm took its first human victim. A carpenter was killed when a house under construction collapsed from the strong winds. In the Sequoyah Hills area of Knoxville, trees and power lines were downed and two barns destroyed.

At the same time, the storm was striking across the border into Western North Carolina. A thunderstorm with strong winds

21

damaged a home, trees, and power lines in the northern part of Yancey County. At Marion, the county seat of McDowell County, strong winds collapsed the roof of a shopping center under construction. Within a space of 15 minutes, three tornadoes touched down in Madison, Buncombe, and Yancey counties. Three campers in a tent were injured by falling tree limbs. Two persons were injured when their trailer was turned over. On Route 2 near Hickory in Catawba County, a man was hurt when strong winds turned over his truck. At the University of North Carolina at Charlotte, an inch of hail fell. Farther east in Sampson County, hail struck a one-square-mile area, causing an estimated $20,000 damage to cotton crops, $7,000 to corn, and $25,000 to tobacco.

The line of severe thunderstorms swept south ahead of an advancing cold front. Moderate-to-extensive damage was reported to trees, crops, and roofs throughout South Carolina as the storm moved down through the state.

As the cold front continued south in the late afternoon hours, the line of intense thunderstorms moving ahead of it stretched across nearly all of Northern Mississippi, Alabama, and Georgia. In Mississippi, the towns of Ilalona, Aberdeen, Clarksdale, Tupelo, New Albany, and Grenada were struck. Roofs were damaged, windows broken, trees felled, and power lines downed. Three persons were injured. In Jackson County, Alabama, mobile homes were damaged. In Northern Georgia, the squall line swept southward producing 50- to 70-mile-per-hour winds, intense lightning, and briefly heavy rains. A woman in Cobb County was killed by lightning while talking on a CB radio in her home. A young man was killed when high winds blew a tree onto the car he was driving. He and his new bride had been returning to their honeymoon cabin in Rabun County. At Lula, a 15-year-old girl was struck and injured by lightning. Several fires were started by lightning. Many power outages were reported.

The worst destruction and the greatest tragedy struck at the eastern end of the storm line, in Virginia. Severe thunderstorms associated with the strong cold front cut a swath of destruction across much of Southern Virginia. In the far southwest part of the state, close to a half million dollars damage was estimated in the Hurley area of Buchanan County alone. Hail larger than golfballs caused great damage to vehicles. Wind devastated houses and mobile homes, leaving four families homeless. Crops were extensively damaged by hail.

The storm's particular fury concentrated on the Tidewater area. Winds gusted in excess of 80 miles per hour. A tornado moving east-southeast touched down two or three times in the Portsmouth-Norfolk, Virginia Beach area. A 14-year-old Virginia Beach girl was struck and seriously injured by lightning in the garden of her home. No trees were nearby. (Police credited the saving of her life to prompt first aid by her father.) In Norfolk, the north wall of a library was blown out, about 50 feet of steel roof of a new recreational center was blown off, several homes under construction were knocked off their foundations, and two large roofs of homes were completely removed. The Navy Operations Base was dealt an estimated $300,000 damage. In Portsmouth, an eight-year-old boy was seriously burned when a power line fell on him, two men were injured when a tree fell on the car in which they were riding, and custodians in two separate schools were hurt by flying debris. Many people received cuts and bruises.

The most tragic event of the day happened not on land but water. Off Norfolk one tour boat reported 100-mile-per-hour

Magnificent creation of nature, a towering thunderhead carries enormous energy soon to be unleashed as rain, hail, wind, and lightning. (NCAR)

winds. Near the Chesapeake Bay Bridge-Tunnel a 42-foot fishing boat was caught in the thunderstorm. The squall line moved in on it; the boat capsized. Twenty-seven persons had been on board. Thirteen of them drowned.

The toll of death and destruction from this one line of intense thunderstorms and its offspring of lightning, hail, and small tornadoes: in seven states in a three-and-a-half-hour period, 16 persons dead, 24 injured, crop damage in the hundreds of thousands, property damage in the millions.

This is not necessarily a typical day of thunderstorm activity in the United States. But with the exception of the tragic multiple-fatality boating accident, it is not all that atypical either. A review of the month's weather for the United States written later for a meteorological publication found that day's death-dealing thunderstorms in the Southeast not unusual enough to mention. And a review of the major severe weather events of the year gave only two sentences to the boating deaths and the damage at Norfolk.

The storm records of almost any day in spring or summer could produce much the same litany of thunderstorm events. It has been estimated that 1,800 thunderstorms are in progress at any given moment around the world, 44,000 of them every day, 16 million every year. Despite its power and drama, the thunderstorm is a common occurrence in nature.

The thunderstorm is, to the eye, a magnificent creation of nature. A peaceful white fluff of cumulus cloud begins to change before your eyes. As more water vapor is drawn up into the cloud and converted to liquid water, it grows tall and turbulent and becomes a boiling caldron, a visible manifestation of energy on an upward path. Parts of it turn dark, and contrasting curves of black and white cloud transferred into cumulonimbus seethe and roll. It towers up toward the stratosphere, into colder and colder air, carrying liquid water which freezes into ice particles. Its top eventually reaches a temperature at which individual parcels of air are no longer warmer than the environment, and its rate of rise slows. As it penetrates into the lower stratosphere the rising cloud top, finding itself cooler than the environment, fans out horizontally to form the familiar anvil of brilliant white cirrus clouds that caps the top of a mature thunderstorm.

Dark swaths of rain wash down out of the lowest part of the storm and powerful downdrafts of cold air rush vertically out of

Dark swath of rain falls from thunderstorm near Columbus, Georgia. (NCAR)

its rearward portions and splash out across the ground to create violent gusts.

Lightning flashes back and forth within the cloud and from cloud to ground, most of it obscured by the cloud mass itself but here and there allowing brilliant white incandescence to reveal some of its hidden and convoluted internal anatomy. Rumbles of thunder echo forth out of the churning mass, a deep primeval sound of nature's overpowering energy.

The force and scale of such a storm is not trivial.

A typical thunderstorm might be three miles across at its base, tower 40,000 feet into the air, and contain half a million tons of condensed water. Huge ones may reach as high as 60,000 feet and spread over 500 square miles. The energy contained within a single thunderstorm is enormous. When water vapor is condensed into water droplets or ice crystals, heat is released. To condense the 500,000 tons of water in a three-mile-diameter thunderstorm causes the release of 300 trillion calories of energy (1.2×10^{22} ergs). This is equivalent to about 100 million kilowatt-hours, or 10 times the energy of the atomic bomb dropped on Hiroshima. A larger thunderstorm might easily contain 10 times as much energy or the equivalent of a two-megaton hydrogen bomb.

Most of the energy in storms goes into overcoming the effects of friction and in heating the air inside and outside the storm system. The energy represented by the actual *motion* of the air, the kinetic energy, is somewhere from a tenth to a hundredth the total amount of energy calculated from the quantity of water condensed. Still, this is a tremendous amount of energy, and it is fortunate that it is released neither all at once nor all in one place. One average thunderstorm contains about 100 times as much kinetic energy as a tornado. This is not as surprising as it may first sound, since thunderstorms spawn tornadoes and so clearly have to be the larger and more powerful. The tornado's destructiveness comes from concentrating its energy in a small area.

A thunderstorm, as are so many of nature's severe phenomena, is the local atmosphere's attempt to reattain stability out of instability, to restore order from temporary disorder. It is an adjustment of the vertical patterns of heat and moisture in the air, a sometimes violent one to be sure, but only a natural result of the unstable conditions that must be brought back into balance. The storm is as much a result of the conditions that lead up to it as it is a cause of the consequences that are felt. From abnormality comes normality. With release of buoyant energy, sometimes violently, the atmosphere is overturned and stability once again reigns.

Most thunderstorms bring positive benefits to humankind. They provide a brief respite from the afternoon heat and, over vast parts of the globe, welcome moisture to water the crops, fill the water holes, enlarge the reservoirs, and wash away dust. They freshen the air and add a vibrant though temporary veneer of glistening moisture to leaves, grass, and grain. To others, less appreciative or living in areas less dependent on additional increments of water as factors in life, they are more a nuisance, a spoiler of picnics, a rumpler of clothes, a hazard to home-bound commuting, a flaw in the fabric of the day. The thunderstorm need not accept praise or offer apology; it is what it is.

Thunderstorms are a worldwide phenomenon, but their geographical incidence varies enormously. If you want to avoid thunderstorms, go to the West Coast of the United States or some high-latitude area such as Alaska, Northern Canada, Lapland, or Northern Siberia. They are rarely seen there. On the other hand, if you want to have thunderstorms as frequent fare, try Central Africa, Central India, Micronesia, Panama, or Central South America. Broad areas in these regions experience thunderstorms 80 days out of the year. If you want to have a thunderstorm more often than that, there is always Kampala, Uganda, where they strike 242 days a year, two days out of every three. If that's still not enough for you, you might try Bogor, Indonesia. Thunderstorms there drench the land and rock the mountain valleys with thunder an average of 322 days a year.

Of course, you don't have to leave the United States to experience relatively high frequency of thunderstorm days. Large sections of Central and Western Florida have 90 to 100 a year. Much of the Deep South and a strip down along the Rocky Mountains in Colorado and Northern New Mexico have 70 to 80 a year. And vast sections of the Midwest and the South have 50 to 60 a year.

A few thunderstorms rise out of the harmless majority to reach far higher scales of energy and violence. In the United States, for instance, there may be 100,000 thunderstorms a year. About 3,000 of them are severe. When one of these thunderstorms coincides in time and place with human beings, the result can be destruction and death. The Chesapeake Bay boat disaster is a tragic example. A similar case happened less than a year later on Lake Martin at Alexander City, Alabama. There, on May 21, 1978, 16 children and two adults were on board a 16-foot pleasure craft on a Sunday outing. A heavy thunderstorm caught the overloaded craft about 100 yards from shore. The strong winds capsized the boat, and four of the children were drowned.

Exactly three weeks later, on June 11, another boating incident in a thunderstorm took an even greater toll. A large group of boys from a private Anglican school in a suburb of Toronto was in the second day of a week-long wilderness trip on Lake Timiskaming, on the border between Quebec and Ontario provinces, when a deadly thunderstorm struck. Three of their canoes were swamped in succession as one tried to rescue the other. Even though all the canoeists were wearing life jackets, 13 of them died in the icy waters, including 12 of the students and one of their schoolmasters. A rescuer said bodies of the victims were found over a 20-mile area of the lake, blown from the scene by raging winds.

Thunderstorms can be remarkably localized. Short intervals of time and of distance can make the difference between safety and disaster, between life and death. On June 24, 1975, Eastern Airlines Flight 66, a Boeing 727 carrying 117 passengers and a crew of seven on a flight from New Orleans to New York City, was approaching John F. Kennedy International Airport for landing. A strong thunderstorm was in progress near the end of the approach path. The pilots of two preceding craft reported that hazardous wind-shear conditions existed on the final approach to Runway 22 Left. Wind shear is noted in many thunderstorms, and it has been a bane to pilots since the days of Wilbur and Orville Wright. It is a condition in which in a very short space the wind completely changes direction so there are oppositely flowing winds adjacent to each other. The shear can be horizontal, vertical, or both.

Eastern 66 had heard the report of wind shear from the previous airliner but not the one from the last cargo plane, a Flying Tiger, whose pilot upon landing urged closing of the runway. While penetrating the thunderstorm between an altitude of 600 and 500 feet, Eastern 66 ran into an increased headwind of about 15 knots. Analysis of the flight recorder shows that at about 500 feet it encountered a strong downdraft of about 16 feet per second. Between 500 and 400 feet the headwind diminished slightly. Then at 400 feet the downdraft increased to 21 feet per second and the headwind decreased by about 15 knots within four seconds. At that point, the craft began to descend rapidly below the glideslope because of the downdraft and the suddenly decreased headwind. The captain reported he had the approach lights in sight, but the crew did not notice that a high rate of descent had developed because of their reliance on visual references which were obscured by low visibility from the storm.

By then, stated the report from the National Transportation Safety Board (NTSB), the high rate of descent had made impact with the approach light towers inevitable. The plane struck a steel light tower less than a half-mile from the end of the runway, rose slightly, then hit several more stanchions. It flipped over and disintegrated. Wreckage was scattered over a marshy area. Some shot across Rockaway Boulevard, although no vehicles were hit. But 113 persons on board the aircraft were killed. It was the worst single-airplane accident in U.S. history.

Both the flight controllers and the crew of Flight 66 had been aware of the thunderstorm activity. Ironically, had they taken action to initiate changes in path or runway, the plane and its occupants might have been spared. The thunderstorm was so localized that, according to the NTSB, at least one of the northwest runways at Kennedy was relatively unexposed to the thunderstorm. Had the airline been diverted to one of those runways, disaster might have been averted.

Later analysis by T. Theodore Fujita, a noted storm researcher at the University of Chicago, discovered that the thunderstorm downdraft encountered by Flight 66 was far from ordinary. In fact, it was so intense, he calls it a "downburst." A downdraft of 20 feet per second is typical at altitudes high up inside a thunderstorm, but it is about 10 times higher than previous estimates for the 300-foot altitudes of an airliner on final landing approach. Fujita and his colleagues have since shown that airliner crashes at Stapleton International Airport in Denver on August 7, 1975, and at Philadelphia International Airport on June 23, 1976, were similarly caused by intense, localized thunderstorm downbursts. Downbursts are particularly dangerous to aircraft taking off or landing, because their downward velocity (defined as at least 12 feet per second) is comparable to the normal rate of descent of a landing airliner. Thus a downdraft suddenly doubles the plane's downward motion. "The most important lesson" learned in their studies, they say, "is that *no one should attempt to fly through the center of a downburst cell.*" (Their emphasis.) The downburst concept is controversial; some meteorologists object that the name implies a distinction from "downdraft" that may not be valid. Plans are underway, however, to equip many airports with arrays of sensors to detect severe wind shear.

Fujita has found dramatic visual evidence of downbursts elsewhere. One of the first was a forest in West Virginia where, in a heavy storm in 1974, 300 trees were blown over in radial directions as if they had been blown outward from a downburst. Then on Independence Day, 1977, a series of tremendous thunderstorms struck across Northern Wisconsin. Aerial surveys and mapping identified a swath of damage 17 miles wide and 166 miles long caused by no fewer than 25 downburst cells. A subsequent request for other evidence of downbursts by the director of the National Weather Service turned up a total of 13 other areas of recent downbursts.

In 1978, Fujita began leading a cooperative research program continuing through the spring of 1980 called Project Nimrod that used satellites, airplanes, helicopters, and ground radar southwest of Chicago to study the thunderstorm downburst phenomenon. The project has shown that downbursts, now defined as strong downdrafts that induce an outward burst of damaging winds (generally 40 miles per hour or greater) on or near the ground, are far more prevalent than expected.

Thunderstorms require three conditions for their creation. The first is a local atmosphere that is unstable. The second is something to set off that instability. The third is sufficient moisture to ensure that cloud droplets will form in the rising air. It all sounds simple enough, but if one of these needs is missing, there will be no thunderstorm. Puffy, white, fair-weather cumulus clouds may spring into view and rain may fall. But the towering, swirling cumulonimbus cloud will not form. No flash of lightning will be seen or rumble of thunder heard.

An unstable atmosphere is one in which the air temperature decreases with height very rapidly. As balloonists, mountain climbers, and pilots long ago learned, the air is usually cooler at successively higher levels above the ground (at least up to the stratosphere). This rate of temperature drop varies with conditions. When the rate is higher than normal—when the difference between temperatures near the ground and higher in the atmosphere is especially great—the first stage is set for thunderstorm growth.

Take, to begin with, a small parcel of air. (Meteorologists are always talking about "parcels" of air.) If something causes it to be lifted, it will rise into the air and cool at a certain rate, called the adiabatic rate. The question is whether it will become colder or warmer than the air around it. If it becomes colder than its environment, it will decelerate and then sink to a level where its density is the same as the surrounding air. This is the situation with a stable stratification. The air at a particular altitude is warm enough that the parcel of rising, cooling air is no longer warmer than its environment and so loses its ability to rise any further.

If, however, the air temperature decreases rapidly with height, producing an unstable atmosphere, the rising parcel of air will find itself remaining warmer than the air around it. It will remain buoyant like a hot-air balloon. Even though it cools as it rises higher, it will remain warmer than the surrounding air. It will continue to accelerate upward, carrying with it a supply of energy in the form of water vapor, waiting to be unleashed at some eventual altitude where finally it becomes cooler than the environment. Multiply this process by millions of similar bubbles of rapidly rising warm, moist air and the makings of the thunderhead, or cumulonimbus cloud, are underway.

A way to imagine it visually is to think of a pan of water on a hot burner. When the heat reaches the lower levels, they become energetic. Bubbles rise rapidly and soon the whole mass of fluid is in violent vertical motion. This is the transport of heat by convection, the same thing that happens to form clouds and create thunderheads. The motion is an attempt by the system to spread out the heat more evenly, to reduce the intense differences in temperature from top to bottom, to bring an unstable situation into equilibrium.

With the atmosphere, as with the water on the stove, most of the instability is usually created by heating at the bottom. The afternoon sun warms the ground, and the air nearest the surface is heated and becomes buoyant. (The atmosphere itself is nearly transparent to solar radiation and therefore tends to be heated directly by sunlight to a relatively smaller degree.) This type of thunderstorm is frequent over land in the afternoons during spring and summer. Spring is an especially likely season because the temperature of the atmosphere near the ground is rising in response to increasing amounts of solar radiation as days lengthen and the sun climbs higher in the sky.

Sometimes the temperature difference between the lower and higher levels of the atmosphere can be intensified by cooling from above; cold air may be brought in horizontally from another area by winds. Also, if the upper air is especially dry, it contains less moisture and therefore less heat and cools more rapidly than it otherwise would. Thunderstorms resulting from high-level cooling are usually high level themselves, with bases one or two miles above the ground. These kinds of thunderstorms are common, for example, just to the east of the Rocky Mountains. Cooling from above also takes place over the oceans by nighttime radiation of heat upward into space from the large quantities of moist air. The frequent result is early morning thunderstorms at sea. If it weren't for this mechanism, fewer thunderstorms would occur over the oceans because the surface-water temperature remains nearly constant.

Sometimes, both heating from below and cooling from above occur simultaneously. This is the usual case when thunderstorms are intense and generate attendant tornadoes, hail, and high winds.

Still another way the atmosphere can be made convectively unstable is to bring about differential cooling by lifting an entire layer of air. If conditions are right (dependent upon the vertical distribution of moisture), the top will cool faster than the base. Thus, lifting will bring about a trend toward instability. This kind of lifting occurs along warm and cold fronts and along mountains. It can also occur when air converges toward a central, local, low-pressure area and is forced to ascend.

Frequently, most of the vertical section of air above a region is unstable and conducive to thunderstorm formation. But somewhere within this deep layer of unstable air lies a thin layer of stable air, an inversion where temperature rises rather than drops with increasing height. This can act as a lid over the low-level unstable air and prevent or delay the release of convection that leads to thunderstorms. In these cases, the lower level air, even though it may be moist and light (contrary to our intuition, moist air is lighter than dry air), needs an extra boost to get it up through that inversion barrier. That boost can be supplied by additional strong solar heating as the ground warms up during the afternoon. Or the lift may be supplied by mountains

Thunderhead building behind a herd of peacefully grazing Colorado cattle. Such scenes frequently change quickly to the violence of a severe thunderstorm. (NCAR)

which may force flowing air upward like a wedge. Often, in potential severe-thunderstorm conditions, converging air rises and cools, lifting and dissipating the inversion and releasing the instability suddenly and explosively.

So there are many ways and places thunderstorms may spring into being. The afternoon thunderstorms that frequently drench the Florida Peninsula may be brought about as the sun warms the land faster than the surrounding water, drawing sea breezes onto the land to converge and lift the mass of warm air. The storms that drop afternoon moisture over the Rocky Mountains may have been triggered by the presence of the mountains themselves, which not only warm up faster than the surrounding air at the same altitude but also mechanically lift the air up to unstable levels. The line of thunderstorms that brings rain and possibly strong winds across two or three states in the Midwest may have generated initially along a convergence line where northerly moving warm air confronts a southeastward-advancing cold air mass.

Whatever the initiating mechanisms, the warm, moist air begins to rise, in a natural attempt to get above the cooler, heavier air surrounding it. Within this updraft, air rushes up past the condensation level where the water vapor it contains condenses to form visible liquid water droplets. A cumulus cloud begins to form. Drier air may enter the cloud from the sides, causing cloud parcels to cool by evaporation. This evaporation of cloud adds to the humidity of the environment, creating a more friendly situation for the next-arriving bubbles of cloud air. Time-lapse photographs have shown a series of forming and then vanishing cumulus clouds, each one growing taller and bigger than its predecessor. Soon, several of the clouds merge to form a cloud large enough to grow into the mature thunderstorm stage. High-level winds near cloud top may create a chimney effect sucking still more air upward. As the cloud enlarges, the updraft may now be protected from the evaporative cooling occurring on the outer edges of the cloud. The air in the updraft is now rushing upward at great speeds, propelled by the energy released in the condensation process. When water evaporates from your skin it draws heat away and your skin feels cooler. Just the opposite happens when water vapor condenses into water droplets or ice particles. When water condenses, it adds heat to the cloud parcel. This heat provides the principal source of energy for the development of the cloud. The release of heat keeps it growing. Now the cloud particles are growing by colliding and combining with one another. They become rain, snow, or hail. Many times, all three may be forming at different levels in the same cloud. They will stay within the cloud until they become heavy enough to overcome the force of the updraft or until they are thrown out of the updraft by turbulence. When that point comes, precipitation falls.

Now the cloud is in its mature stage. It is a full-scale black-and-gray cumulonimbus, a dark mass of rolling energy, towering into the lower reaches of the stratosphere, where its top spreads out to form the glistening white anvil of ice crystals. The large number of falling raindrops now drag the air downward, and the air on the fringes of the storm cools by evaporation. Air accelerates downward creating a downdraft, another vertical chute in the air parallel to the earlier updraft. This couplet of updraft and downdraft is known as a thunderstorm cell. Each cell may be several miles in diameter, and a large thunderstorm may contain many of them. A series of these cells comes into being, survives for perhaps 20 or 30 minutes, and then dies. New cells replace old ones. The storm may continue this way for an hour or more, a dynamic, almost organic entity. It was the growth and life cycle of these cells that led pioneer thunderstorm researcher Horace R. Byers, whose research program discovered them, to propose an almost animal-like analogy. These cells grow, fuse, and multiply, Byers explained, "in much the same way as the growth of masses of certain kinds of bacteria."

Within the cloud, updrafts and downdrafts are, for a time, in simultaneous existence. Tremendous wind shears and turbulence rock through the storm. On the ground directly below the storm, rain can now be quite heavy, and out of the downdraft strong gusts of cold wind rush out in different directions across the terrain. Lightning issues forth from the cloud, and the storm is now in its most violent stage. Under certain conditions, tornadoes may drop down out of the storm.

But the storm cell's lifetime is short. Even now it has begun to die. The downdraft begins to move under and dominate the updraft, cutting off the cell's supply of moisture and energy. New cells may form where the cool downdraft air lifts the warm unstable air ahead of the dying cell, and the process repeats. Eventually, the atmosphere is overturned in the area as the supply of warm, buoyant air is eliminated. Whatever downpour, violence, and destruction the storm may have brought, it eventually brings about its own demise. The changes the storm produces eventually destroy the buoyant energy on which its life depends. Nature has once again come into balance.

Some of the more severe thunderstorms are not the single isolated variety brought about by uneven heating of the ground, but the more organized lines of thunderstorms consisting of individual cells strung out along several hundred miles. They are called squall lines, and they are generated and maintained by especially favorable large-scale weather patterns. Often, they are the forerunners of cold fronts. The earlier-described series of thunderstorms that struck across the southeastern states on June 6, 1977, is an example of this type of storm. Unlike the isolated storms, squall-line thunderstorms can move rapidly eastward or southeastward and last for several hours. Some of the most intense squall lines in the world occur over the Great Plains. They often produce quite harsh weather, and tornadoes more than occasionally are one of the products. They occur when warm, moist air, usually brought northward from the Gulf of Mexico by the clockwise circulation around a high pressure center, comes into contact with the cold, dry air moving in from the Northwest with a cold front. The warmer air is forced upward ahead of the cold front. Thunderstorm squalls can form parallel to and ahead of the entire line of contact. As they move forward, they are fed by warm, moist air streaming northward ahead of the line. The squall lines may move east or southeast from 10 to 40 miles per hour, thus crossing vast areas of land and affecting potentially millions of people. The movement of the cells and the increase of winds with height allow the rain to fall out of one side of the storm rather than uniformly throughout its area. This enables the updraft and the downdraft to co-exist without interference and allows the whole system to organize and stay alive.

Meteorologists have also identified the concept of a supercell thunderstorm. A supercell storm is an isolated large thunderstorm dominated by a large single cell where updrafts and downdrafts co-exist for long periods. Often a supercell storm runs out ahead of a squall line. It gets first crack at the moisture in the air and doesn't have to fight for it. This makes it a much more efficient energy releaser. Being in advance of the other thunderstorm cells, it is not obstructed by clouds, it builds up more quickly, and its updraft is more intense.

Tremendous amounts of precipitation can be produced in squall-line storms, and their rapid motion can often take people by surprise. The results can be disastrous. April 4, 1977, will be best remembered in severe storm annals for the powerful tornado that raked across the Birmingham, Alabama, area, killing 22 persons and causing $15 million damage. But the same storm system that spawned the tornado produced a fast-moving line of moisture-laden thunderstorms. A Southern Airways DC-9 carrying 85 persons crashed that day while attempting an emergency landing on a highway near New Hope, Georgia. Sixty-three of those on board and nine others on the ground died when the aircraft struck several cars and a gasoline station.

Investigation by the National Transportation Safety Board showed that the aircraft had flown in heavy rain and hail for about two and one-half minutes before its engines went dead. It concluded that extremely heavy rain and hail had caused a "total and unique loss of thrust" in both engines. The exact intensity of the rain and hail was not known. But the board said tests showed that engine rotational speed would be lost at that low thrust if water was ingested fast enough that the ratio of water to air was greater than 14 percent. So much water was in the engines that the compressors stalled and the blades broke. The engines, in effect, drowned in the intense rain. Officials found fault with flight dispatchers for not adequately monitoring the area of very strong and intense rainfall earlier identified by the National Weather Service and for not alerting the crew to the hazards. The abnormally high speed of advance of the line of thunderstorms, 70 miles per hour, was one of the problems. Warning procedures have less tolerance when things are moving quickly.

The usual concern of thunderstorms to pilots is not the rainfall but the sudden, often violent shifts in the winds. In the 1920s and 1930s, a number of pilots of adventuresome spirit, inquiring mind, and possibly less than good sense flew directly into the heart of thunderstorms. The stories of those experiences are more emotional than reliable, but they all told of violent shaking, out-of-control vertical excursions of great speed and extent, fear about the survival of the plane and themselves, and the exhilaration of coming out of it alive.

Sometimes they didn't. Just before World War II, five German pilots at a glider meeting in the Rhön Mountains soared into a thunderhead and were soon swept upward with great violence. They all bailed out and opened their parachutes amid the enormous turbulence. It was a mistake. The tremendous updrafts caught the parachutes and carried the men upward amid a barrage of hail until they reached freezing levels. They kept rising until they were frozen stiff, possibly reaching 30,000 feet and 30-below-zero temperatures. They literally became human hailstones, and they had been blown up and down many times before the storm released them. Only one of the men landed alive, and he lost three of his fingers and much of his face before he was dismissed from the hospital.

One pilot told of flying into the front part of a thunderstorm over Western New Jersey. "Before I knew it I had gained 4,000 feet. I shut my engine off and dived at 100 miles per hour—and I was still going up."

One man who parachuted through a thunderstorm and lived to tell about it was U.S. Marine Corps jet pilot William Rankin. At an altitude of 47,000 feet—nine miles above the earth—the engine of his single-seat fighter failed. He ejected, and his preset parachute did not open until he had fallen to an altitude of 10,000 feet. Normally, the descent from that altitude to the ground should have taken about 13 minutes. Rankin, however, got caught in the turbulence of a thunderstorm, and his journey took nearly three-quarters of an hour.

I was blown up and down as much as 6,000 feet at a time. It went on for a long time, like being on a very fast elevator, with strong blasts of compressed air hitting you. Once when a violent blast of air sent me careering up into the chute and I could feel the cold, wet nylon collapsing about me, I was sure the chute would never blossom again. But, by some miracle, I fell back and the chute *did* recover its billow.

The wind had savage allies. The first clap of thunder came as a deafening explosion that literally shook my teeth. I didn't hear the thunder, I actually felt it—an almost unbearable physical experience. If it had not been for my closely fitted helmet, the explosions might have shattered my eardrums.

I saw lightning all around me in every shape imaginable. When very close, it appeared mainly as a huge, bluish sheet several feet thick. It was raining so torrentially that I thought I would drown in midair. Several times I held my breath, fearing that otherwise I might inhale quarts of water.

By the end of World War II, experiences of pilots had produced a list of generally accepted facts about thunderstorm flying. One of the most basic was to pass to the right of the storm in the Northern Hemisphere, to the left in the Southern Hemisphere to avoid headwinds. (This is because winds swirl counterclockwise around low-pressure storm centers in the Northern Hemisphere, clockwise in the Southern.) Another was that if possible it was better to fly over the storm than under it. Beneath thunderstorms, violent updrafts and downdrafts and heavy rain and hail could be encountered. Twenty thousand feet was found to be the average height of greatest danger, but some storms towered three times that high. A wide hole with clear sky and land showing was usually a safe channel through the storm. In contrast, a thin-appearing part of the cloud might or might not herald a safe passage; often the cloud closed in around you.

Modern thunderstorm research might be said to have begun in 1946 when the U.S. government organized the Thunderstorm Project. Four agencies joined in this scientific assault on the secrets of thunderstorms. Horace Byers, a widely respected meteorologist from the University of Chicago, was put in charge. He and his associates organized a three-dimensional network of monitoring stations to track and probe every aspect of particular thunderstorms. Radiosonde balloons were sent up into them, and flying weather stations aboard sturdy, twin-fuselage P-61 Black Widow night interceptor aircraft penetrated into thunderheads at preassigned times and levels. The aircraft, many of them manned by experienced crews just back from the war, made 1,363 penetrations of 76 separate thunderstorms. They encountered downdrafts as fast as 79 feet per second (54 miles per hour) that dropped them 2,000 feet and updrafts as great as 84 feet per second (57 miles per hour) that lifted them 5,000 feet. They were struck by lightning 21 times and battered by hail on 51 penetrations. An array of fixed stations on the ground recorded the storms' outpourings of rain and wind, and radar was used for the first time not only to seek out the storms and monitor their progress but also to record precisely the positions of the airborne monitoring stations within the storms. Out of it all came much of the modern understanding of the thunderstorm, including the concept of the cell structure of the storms.

Today, a new array of sophisticated instruments is at the disposal of atmospheric scientists to study the many remaining unknowns about thunderstorms. Among them are microwave

radio beams, meteorological towers, color-display conventional
radar, Doppler radar (more about that in Chapter 2), acoustical
sensors, and satellites.

The satellite photos you see on your evening television weather
programs are taken from 22,300 miles out in space by two satellites in stationary orbit around the equator called GOES-West
and GOES-East. (The acronym stands for Geostationary Operational Environmental Satellite.) Under normal conditions, each
takes a picture every 30 minutes. But under severe weather
conditions they can be instructed to increase that frequency to
every 15 minutes. Meteorologists can obtain smaller-than-usual
views, or sectors, 1,000 miles on a side of a region afflicted by
potential heavy storms. The imagery from these satellites has a
resolution of one-half mile, a high-quality view that gives a
unique ability to continuously monitor the conditions that lead
to thunderstorms. A whole variety of phenomena important in
initiating and maintaining convection is readily detectable. Previously, the forecaster could only try to infer the presence of
these phenomena from larger-scale patterns. Now he can see
them.

The research meteorologists can make movies using GOES

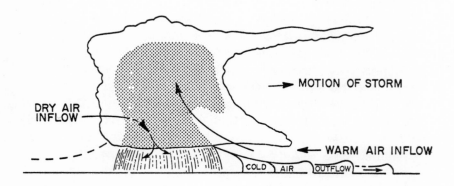

Cross section of thunderstorm. (NATIONAL SEVERE STORMS LABORATORY)

pictures. One important new finding to come out of analysis of these movies is that there is little, if any, random aspect to thunderstorm development. The meteorologists can see that convection is usually organized into lines. These convective lines seem to be quite important in producing subsequent thunderstorms. The place where two convective lines merge, for instance, often marks the location of intense convective development. Under the right conditions that activity will be severe.

The boundaries of clouds produced by thunderstorms are also easily detected in the photos. These boundaries, called arc clouds, can be dramatic in appearance. As the name implies, they have a curved front face. This white mass of organized cloud can sometimes be seen to move rapidly forward across the terrain. On the ground, the phenomenon is known as a gust front, the forward edge of wind from the thunderstorm's downdraft splashing out across the ground ahead of the rest of the storm. Violent gusts of wind are often felt as the gust front passes. The ability to monitor these gust fronts by satellite is relatively new. Where the gust front boundary intersects another boundary of convective activity, severe weather often breaks out. I have seen one such movie of a gust-front thunderstorm with its arc line clouds moving over the region where Missouri, Kansas, and Oklahoma meet on April 24, 1975. The energy contained within this system was immense and when it came into contact with another line of convection, the gust front underwent explosive development. It rapidly expanded, quickly extending over a much greater area. From these space views, it looks something like a time-lapse movie of a flower opening, except that you know that the unfolding is releasing violence, not revealing beauty. According to Edward Ferguson, manager of the Satellite Field Services Station for the National Oceanic and Atmospheric Administration in Kansas City, "tremendous thunderstorms" hit such cities as Joplin and Neosho, Missouri, that day as that system passed over. Just after darkness fell, a tornado spun out of the storm and passed through Neosho, killing three persons and injuring 122.

Another case was the intersection of an arc cloud thunderstorm in Southeast Oklahoma on May 26, 1975, with a stationary cold front. Precisely where they intersected, according to James F. W. Purdom of NOAA, intense thunderstorms broke out. A similar case occurred over central Texas on May 25, 1976, where a thunderstorm arc merged with the boundary of a stationary front. A large thunderstorm complex developed, and where the merger point moved eastward along the arc into the Abilene area four tornadoes struck, causing considerable damage to farms and homes.

James J. Gurka of the National Environmental Satellite Service in Washington, D.C., has used satellite photos to identify no fewer than four types of cloud patterns associated with thunderstorm gust fronts. He found that his Types 1 and 2, patterns with especially deep convection near or along the leading edge of the gust front, can produce wind speeds considerably greater than the speed at which the arc itself is moving. Three of the four cases with arc speeds of 40 miles per hour had maximum wind reports of 58 miles per hour or greater.

All this leads to the conclusion by Purdom that high-resolution satellite imagery is helping to open the door for a new era in meteorology on the scale that produces severe thunderstorms.

In addition to watching for places where lines of convective activity intersect, those who analyze satellite imagery know that a clue to strong thunderstorms is a cumulonimbus cloud that towers well above other clouds. In fact, it has been shown that one measure of thunderstorm intensity is the number of overshooting

Series of severe, rapidly developing thunderstorms over Missouri and Oklahoma seen by satellite, April 24, 1975. Center storm produced destructive tornado at Neosho, Missouri. (JAMES F. W. PURDOM, NATIONAL ENVIRONMENTAL SATELLITE SERVICE)

cloud tops, where built-up tops of thunderstorms protrude above the anvil of cirrus. These high cloud tops can be seen as dots in the satellite photos, little puffs that stand out above the rest and betray their potential for destruction. Satellite infrared images can be used to determine the temperatures of thunderstorm clouds. Since high clouds are usually colder, $-65°$ C ($-85°$ F) at the tops of some thunderstorms, this information can be used to pinpoint high-towering and possibly dangerous thunderstorms.

Of course the traditional ways of studying thunderstorms have not been abandoned. The aptly named Project Roughrider is still sending aircraft into the heart of thunderstorms to see what makes them tick. A sturdy F-4C Phantom jet is now used, and J. T. Lee, director of the aviation turbulence program for the National Severe Storms Laboratory in Norman, Oklahoma, reports that more than 1,000 penetrations have been successfully made. Few parts of a thunderstorm are now off limits to such a solid research aircraft, says Lee, but he has on display on a cabinet in his office a section of a wing from one aircraft that had the misfortune to pass through a part of a thunderstorm where intense hail was plummeting down on everything in its path. Dents as wide and nearly as deep as a fist in the metal of the wing serve as a reminder of the violence within such a storm.

The Project Roughrider aircraft is now being directed into higher regions of thunderstorms, but in the previous several years it was used to fly into and along the gust fronts that rush out along the ground at relatively low altitudes. This information can then be correlated with data taken from the ground to provide a profile of a gust front's passage.

Thunderstorms are a phenomenon of beauty, power, strength, and intricacy, with direct impacts on humanity in vast segments of the world. But there still may be another, almost cosmic, importance to thunderstorms, an intriguing possibility that has come to the fore only in the late 1970s. It is based on a certain amount of evidence and a considerable amount of scientific speculation. If it is borne out, however, thunderstorms may be shown to be a long-sought link, a physical mechanism, to explain how short-term variations in the behavior of the sun can affect weather and atmospheric circulation on earth.

Scientists have long pondered how certain statistical associations between observed changes in solar activity and weather changes on earth could be explained. Drought cycles in the

Western United States seem statistically to be related to the 22-year magnetic sunspot cycle, for instance. And the passage of the earth every week or so through a new sector of the interplanetary magnetic field as the field rotates with the sun seems to be correlated with changes in atmospheric vorticity and therefore storminess in the Northern Hemisphere. Hundreds of such statistical correlations have been identified, and some of them are quite solid. But in science, merely showing that two occurrences seem to be related is not completely satisfactory. A physical link, a direct cause-and-effect explanation of how the one change could bring about the other, is needed.

Thunderstorms could be an essential part of the connection. The idea begins with the concept credited to the great English physicist C. T. R. Wilson half a century ago that worldwide thunderstorm activity is, in effect, a direct-current generator, causing current to flow through what might be called the atmospheric electrical "global circuit." (The specific electrical manifestations of thunderstorms, lightning and thunder, are the subject of Chapter 3; here we are considering their electrical properties in a wider, more general perspective.) If thunderstorms were to stop, the electrification of the atmosphere would quickly decay. It persists because thunderstorms occur somewhere at all times. Conduction currents can flow in the atmosphere because it is ionized, meaning atoms in the upper atmosphere are caused to be electrically charged. That conductivity is mostly maintained by ionizing cosmic radiation from space, but it is augmented in the stratosphere at times of high solar activity by particles and X-rays from the sun.

Now these solar-modulated variations in the amount of ionizing radiation above thunderstorms change the storms' electrical resistance. Thunderstorms are in effect a valve regulating the flow of current in the entire global circuit. So an increase in solar-caused ionization over thunderstorms would cause a worldwide increase in electric field intensity, and this would explain why measurements of electrical fields have been reported to be higher at times of solar flares.

In addition, greatly increased sun-caused ionization could cause an increase in thunderstorm activity. This could be brought about directly and locally by increased ionization above individual large cumulonimbus clouds. Also, more thunderstorms worldwide would be indirectly initiated by the increased intensity of the electric field, near developing cumulus clouds. Some correlations between thunderstorm activity and both solar flares and sunspot cycles have been reported.

Since thunderstorms are such a powerful force in the earth's weather (they bring almost all the rainfall in many parts of the world) and, as we have seen, release vast amounts of energy, an increase in their numbers at certain times could affect other parts of the weather system as well.

So thunderstorms could be the electrical link between the sun's variations and earth's weather, a connection, if confirmed, of possibly far-reaching consequence. This kind of mechanism was proposed independently in 1978 by Ralph Markson of the Massachusetts Institute of Technology and J. W. Follin, Jr., of Johns Hopkins University, based on data and ideas from a number of scientists in the past few years. The first part of the link—the increase in earth's electric field caused by solar activity—seems to be on fairly firm ground; the connection to increased thunderstorms and world weather changes is more speculative but nevertheless appealing.

Thunderstorms, as if they weren't already interesting and powerful enough, thus may be even more important and significant than we thought. And all this before even considering, in the following chapters, their dramatic offspring of tornadoes, lightning, and hail.

CHAPTER 2

Tornadoes

Early on the morning of April 2, 1974, weather forecasters at the National Severe Storms Forecast Center in downtown Kansas City were watching with increasing concern a low-pressure center over the Southern Rocky Mountains. All signs indicated that this area of low pressure and its trailing cold front would intensify and move rapidly eastward during the next 24 to 36 hours. As early as the day before, Allen Pearson, director of the center, had become concerned about the possibility of a major outbreak of bad weather when the cold front moved into the Midwest and came into contact with warm, moist air from the Gulf of Mexico. He and his associates dug out the weather maps for the Palm Sunday outbreak of April 11, 1965, which had spawned 46 tornadoes and killed 256 persons. The similarities were not comforting.

During the day of April 2, the disturbance moved across the Rocky Mountains into Eastern Colorado and Western Kansas and continued to deepen as it advanced eastward at 35 miles per hour. "It looked like it would be fairly strong," recalls Pearson. "So I did something I'd never done before. I sent out on the internal teletype circuit a notice to alert all the weather radar stations in the central region to get any needed repair and maintenance work done." The southern region stations were similarly alerted. The severe storms center also asked for additional weather balloon releases that day. The Kansas City field service station requested that the ATS-3 satellite be operated on April 3 in a "severe weather mode," enabling more frequent photographs from orbit.

It was clear that the developing storm system had the potential to produce violent thunderstorms and tornadoes the next day. But the precise location and timing were not yet evident. The expanding and deepening low was now an egg-shaped area 1,000 miles across, and strong southerly winds began to develop over the lower Mississippi River Valley in response to it. During the night of April 2–3, these winds brought warm, moist maritime air streaming northward toward the lower Midwest and Ohio Valley states. The conditions were set for disaster.

At 4:19 A.M., April 3, a carefully prepared and considered 24-hour weather outlook was transmitted from Kansas City. It was 19 minutes late because of the issuance of early-morning tornado watches. It warned: "SCATTERED SEVERE THUNDER-STORMS EXPECTED TODAY AND TONIGHT FROM NORTHEAST TEXAS ACROSS ARKANSAS, SOUTHEAST MISSOURI, ILLINOIS, INDIANA, OHIO, WEST VIRGINIA, KENTUCKY, TENNESSEE, WESTERN VIR-GINIA, WESTERN NORTH CAROLINA, EXTREME NORTHWEST SOUTH CAROLINA, NORTHERN AND CENTRAL ALABAMA, NORTHERN AND CENTRAL MISSISSIPPI, NORTHERN HALF LOUISIANA, AND NORTH-WEST GEORGIA. STRONG LOW PRESSURE AREA EXPECTED INTO NORTHWEST MISSOURI BY 0000Z [6 A.M. CDT] WITH COLD FRONT SOUTHWARD THROUGH EASTERN ARKANSAS AND LOUISIANA. STRONG SOUTHERLY WINDS WITH COOLING ALOFT EXPECTED TO GIVE SEVERE THUNDERSTORMS . . . WITH ACTIVITY SPREADING EASTWARD DURING THE PERIOD."

The area of the outlook covered practically all the tornado and thunderstorm activity that broke out in the next 24 hours. "By our standards," recalls Pearson, "this was an outlook for very severe weather." But just how severe, no one could have known.

For that afternoon and into the morning hours of the next day, the largest outbreak of tornadoes on record raked across 13 states. One hundred forty-eight tornadoes swept across towns, rural areas, and cities. Several of the tornadoes were among the most powerful ever seen. Whole communities, such as Xenia, Ohio, Brandenburg, Kentucky, and Guin, Alabama, were nearly wiped out. When it was over, 315 persons were dead and 6,142 injured. More than 9,600 homes had been destroyed and 27,590 families had suffered losses. In the 10 states declared disaster areas by the President, property damage was placed at $600 million.

Although it was a horrible toll, at least one tornado outbreak caused more deaths—the tri-state outburst of March 18, 1925, when eight tornadoes struck Illinois, Indiana, and Missouri, killing 792 persons and injuring 13,000. But in total number of

Brandenburg, Kentucky, shattered by one of the strongest tornadoes of the April 3, 1974, superoutbreak. Thirty-one of the community's 1,673 residents were killed. (AMERICAN RED CROSS PHOTO BY JACK SHERE)

tornadoes, total path length (an incredible 2,598 miles), and total damage, the onslaught of the 1974 tornadoes was more extensive than any previously known. It truly deserved the label "superoutbreak" affixed later by meteorologist T. Theodore Fujita, who studied it in detail.

The havoc began in St. Louis, where hail struck, causing $30 million damage. Around 2 P.M. CDT tornadoes touched down in Tennessee and Georgia. Within 10 minutes two more had hit in Illinois, and by 2:20 two more had struck and caused deaths in Indiana. The tempo was quickening. Between 3 and 10 P.M., Pearson recalls, "My sole job was to try to keep track of the reports coming in. We knew we had a helluva thing going on." At one time, 15 tornadoes were on the ground simultaneously. Tornado warnings were being issued as fast as they could be processed. (Some 150 tornado warnings plus 28 Severe Weather Watches covering nearly the entire area from the Gulf of Mexico to Canada and from the Mississippi River to the East Coast were issued that day.)

One of the worst tornadoes bore down on Brandenburg, Kentucky, a small farming community with a population of 1,673 atop a pair of hills on the banks of the Ohio River. It was peaceful and quiet, and the residents liked its closeness, intimacy, protectiveness, and permanence. "It was a Mark Twain town," said one of its citizens. "It was Hannibal, Missouri, all over again, and I was Tom Sawyer. I loved it." All that was soon shattered.

One man was fishing when the tornado struck. He said he saw houses, autos, and bodies "come flying over and into the water."

"If I live forever, I will never see anything so horrible as this again," said Paula Wright, a 21-year-old housewife. She and her nine-year-old brother were in their apartment in an old two-story house when the tornado swept along the river's edge. Thirty seconds later, five persons in the house, including three children, were dead. Mrs. Wright and her brother found themselves somehow unhurt but trapped in the wreckage. The infant daughter of one of the dead women was later found to have been plucked from the house by the wind and deposited at the bottom of a hill 200 yards away.

Thirty-one inhabitants of the tiny town were killed, nearly 2 percent of its population, the greatest per capita loss of any community hit by the superoutbreak. Two hundred seventy others were injured. Mayor H. M. Ross estimated that 75 percent of the town was a total loss. One of the town's two funeral homes was destroyed, and two refrigerator trucks had to be put into service as morgues, where survivors came to try to identify relatives. Many of the bodies were badly mangled.

Standing on a hill amid the wreckage that had been his home, county lawyer Ellis Blake cried: "My God! My God! What has happened to my town!"

Another town that suffered human loss all out of proportion to its population was Guin, Alabama, a community of 2,200 some 70 miles northwest of Birmingham. Coming from the southwest, as all the tornadoes did that day, a funnel developed first over Northeastern Mississippi, touched down, crossed the Alabama border, and continued on toward Guin, 28 miles away. By then it had grown into an especially powerful and long-lasting tornado. It struck Guin, and as it passed through it left behind 30 persons dead and 280 injured. Even that was not the end of the tornado, which continued on toward Huntsville to become one of three tornadoes that day with path lengths longer than 100 miles.

Xenia, Ohio, a city of 27,000, was directly in the path of one of the afternoon's superpowerful tornadoes. The record of destruction wrought there will forever be remembered in tornado annals. The tornado churned northeast through the heart of the city for perhaps four minutes on a path 2,000 to 3,000 feet wide. Thirty-four persons were killed, 1,150 injured. Nearly 3,000 homes and stores were damaged or destroyed, and property damage totalled $75 million.

Tom Waters was one of many Xenia residents who saw it coming. Waters had heard the tornado watch being broadcast on the radio. He kept an eye on the warm sky, and soon saw it, about a mile away. "It was a real dark mass of clouds going round and round. Then all of a sudden it must have touched down—there was a whole mess of confetti going up from the ground. A warm rain started, and I knew it was time to go."

Waters rushed into the house, and just then the wind hit. He and the others in the house got down on the floor of the kitchen. "Then all the windows went all at once. You could hear them breaking all over the house. Then all I could hear was the wind. Mud and glass was flying around and hitting everybody. The wind went on and on and on. . . ."

It took about five minutes for the wind to die down. He and his family crawled out and looked around. There were no roofs, and almost no second stories left on any of the many houses he could see from his backyard. Two large, three-story brick schools looked like bombed-out ruins. His truck had been lifted from the driveway, hurled over his sportscar, and rammed into a tree, which was uprooted. The truck lay on top of the tree on its side, five feet up in the air. A neighbor's garage was gone, leaving the car inside it undamaged, except for a cracked windshield.

Charles Wood emerged from under a bedroom mattress after the brick wall of his house fell on him. "I just happened to look out the window," he recalled. "It was just like the tornado in the *Wizard of Oz*. It was about a mile away. I continued to watch it and then it seemed to split up, fan out at the bottom, just like it was sweeping. I watched it till it got one block away. Then I knew it was going to hit. It sounded like three huge locomotives. . . ."

After the wall came down on his mattress shelter, Wood looked up through an opening into the middle of the storm. "It was all smoky but churning. It was just like looking into the jaws of hell."

As tragic as it was, the Xenia tornado could have been worse had it occurred two hours earlier. Five of the 11 schools in Xenia were in the direct path of the tornado. Three of the schools were almost completely destroyed. The other two were damaged extensively. The time of the strike was about 4:40 P.M., and 5,000 students and teachers were out of school. It has been estimated that had it struck before school had let out, without well-executed tornado plans and prior drills, hundreds might have died.

One person who was still inside school was Ruth Venuti, an 18-year-old senior at Xenia High School. She had stayed after school waiting for a friend to drive her home, and was standing by a doorway facing west. The time was about 4:20. About 4:25 she looked out the doorway and saw a black cloud about a block long and perhaps two and a half miles from the school. Lightning within the cloud was becoming intense, and it began changing from a vertical to a more horizontal position as she watched. Then, just north of its center, the cloud seemed to shrink into a column. It became grayish-white. "I realized it was a tornado when I saw the air currents begin to swirl."

Knowing that the school's drama cast was rehearsing in the auditorium at the opposite end of the school, she rushed there to warn them. English teacher David Heath at first thought it was a joke. He and the class ran to the front doors nearest the auditorium. "We saw what looked to be a column of dirt or smoke swirling around," recalled Heath. "We couldn't see anything that resembled a clearly defined funnel cloud. It appeared to be between 100 and 200 yards away. Then cars parked in front of the school began to bounce around. It was beyond belief." They all ran toward the center hall of the school. The lights went out just as they all turned the corner and crouched against the walls on both sides of the corridor.

"The impact of the wind was immediate, with no build-up. The first thing I heard was the sound of shattering glass." Heath compared the sound of the tornado to "a noise like the clattering of a thousand sets of Venetian blinds, along with tremendous crashing and grating sounds." Large pieces of dirt and wood were flying down the corridor. Several sections of lockers were pulled from the wall and thrown to the floor.

Heath says there was a momentary calm, as in the eye of a hurricane. Then the wind hit again with seemingly greater force. They were all hit with dirt, broken glass, and mud. The air pressure kept changing constantly in the building.

"My ears hurt a lot, and I was constantly swallowing to make them pop. I had no idea how long the winds pelted the building, although it was probably about a minute. It seemed like an eternity. Finally, it stopped, and there was total silence."

The group rose from its crouched positions and began to survey the destruction. No one in the school was killed or even seriously injured. They went back to the auditorium where they had been rehearsing. The roof had collapsed and was resting on the auditorium seats. A school bus was lying upside down on the stage.

"When we went outside the school," says Heath, "the park across the street looked like a part of a planet that had burned up years ago. Then I turned around, and was completely stunned. The entire top floor of the high school was missing. Rubble was everywhere. Fountains of water were streaming up from where the second-floor chemistry labs had been. It was then I realized just how bad the tornado really had been." Heath credits the warning Ruth Venuti had given him and his students with saving them from death or injury.

Charles Sanford of Xenia is a native of Oklahoma where, he said, people learned how to live through tornadoes. When he heard of the tornado warning, he went through his house and broke every window and opened every door. Tornado experts don't advise this extreme action, but his was the only house on the block that did not have large chunks of its roof or exterior walls blown away.

One family pushed down the last remaining wall of their laundry shed to find an empty sock driven three inches into the ground. Their clothes dryer was somehow full of dishes, and an open box of laundry soap sat completely undisturbed on the washing machine where they had left it.

There were other oddities as well. At Mt. Gilead, 90 miles northeast of Xenia, a man reported finding a gift catalogue addressed to a Xenia man. A woman there told the sheriff she had found mail addressed to Xenia on her property. Canceled checks from two Xenia banks were found in bundles as far as Cuyahoga Falls, 200 miles away.

At Louisville, Kentucky, where a 21-mile-long tornado killed two persons and injured 228, schoolchildren were also spared. All the students at Dunn Elementary School outside of Louisville had just gone home when the twister hit, ripping off roofs and knocking down walls. The engine and transmission of a car parked in front were torn out and carried 60 feet.

At least 20 schools in Indiana, Ohio, Kentucky, and Alabama

alone were severely damaged in the outbreak. In almost all cases, the tornadoes struck when school was out for the day.

Although later study teams found few concerted efforts in schools to prepare students for tornadoes, the twisters produced two dramatic examples where education and preparedness in schools did save lives. In Hanover, Indiana, a high school physics teacher had spent the last 25 minutes of his class on April 2 discussing tornado safety. He cited the danger of being in a vehicle hit by a tornado and suggested taking cover in a nearby ditch or ravine. The next day, a Hanover school bus was on a collision course with an approaching tornado. One of the students who had been in the physics class convinced the driver to stop and everyone headed for a ditch. The bus was demolished. None of the passengers was injured.

At Monroe Central High School, east of Muncie, Indiana, students were dismissed early when a tornado watch was issued for the area. The teachers who remained posted a lookout, and when the tornado was seen they went to a predetermined central hallway. The school was destroyed, but the interior hallway remained intact and no one was injured.

Immediately after the outbreak, Pearson, under a long-stand-

THE FUJITA—PEARSON TORNADO SCALE

F INTENSITY	P PATH LENGTH		P MEAN WIDTH	
F0 Light Damage	P0	less than 1 mi.	P0	less than 0.01 mi.
F1 Moderate Damage	P1	1.0–3.1	P1	0.01–0.03
F2 Considerable Damage	P2	3.2–9.9	P2	0.04–0.09
F3 Severe Damage	P3	10–31	P3	0.10–0.31
F4 Devastating Damage	P4	32–99	P4	0.32–0.99
F5 Incredible Damage	P5	100 or longer	P5	1.0 mile or wider

The intensity, path length and width of tornadoes are rated on a scale developed by T. Theodore Fujita and Allen D. Pearson. Five tornadoes in the superoutbreak of April 3–4, 1974, had an intensity of F5. Three had P5 path lengths. Eight had P5 path widths.

ing arrangement with disaster researchers, called T. Theodore Fujita of the University of Chicago. Fujita quickly organized an aerial survey team to study the entire damage area, which extended from Central Alabama to the Great Lakes and from Central Illinois to Virginia. Fujita is a seemingly tireless investigator of tornadoes. He studies them not only in the laboratory where he has built equipment to simulate their winds but also from the air where he manages to extract an extraordinary amount of information and insights from photographs of their damage paths. Pearson jokingly refers to Fujita as "the perfect Japanese tourist—always flying around with a camera in his hand." He is a prolific and imaginative scientist, and sometimes it seems difficult to pick up a meteorological journal without finding in it a new report by him on tornadoes. If Horace Byers deserved the nickname Thunderstorm Byers in the late 1940s, Ted Fujita might well be called Mr. Tornado in the late 1970s.

Fujita, with Allen Pearson, has devised a now widely used scale for rating a tornado's intensity. The Fujita-Pearson Tornado Intensity Scale is a six-point system. F0 is "light damage."

No fewer than six of the tornadoes on the afternoon of April 3, 1974, were rated at F5. The Brandenburg, Guin, and Xenia tornadoes were all F5s. But three others also caused "incredible damage." The Sayler Park Tornado that touched parts of Indiana, Kentucky, and Ohio, ending just outside of Cincinnati, killed three persons and injured 210. The Depauw Tornado in Indiana killed six and injured 76. And the First Tanner Tornado in Northwestern Alabama, not far from the Guin killer twister, killed 28 and injured 260.

This supports the view that most tornado deaths and damage are caused by only a few extremely destructive tornadoes. Although eight out of 10 of the tornadoes in the superouterbreak were of intensity F3 or less, eight out of 10 of the deaths were caused by tornadoes of intensity F4 or F5.

From his aerial studies, Fujita produced an extraordinary map of the April 3–4 superoutbreak. (Although most of the damaging tornadoes hit on the afternon of April 3, a few continued to form in the early morning hours of April 4.) It shows an incredible series of 148 wiggly but almost parallel paths trending southwest to northeast over 13 states. The varying lengths and widths of the lines outline each tornado's area of damage. Numbers along the path lengths give the tornado's intensity at

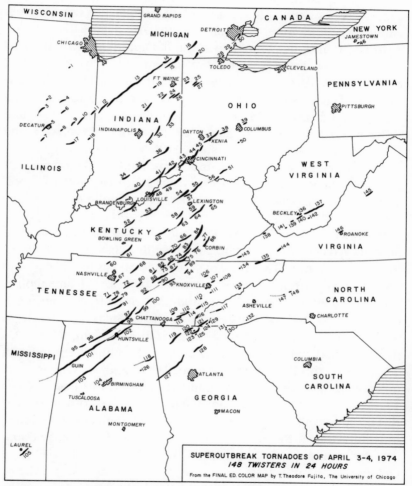

Paths of the 148 tornadoes on April 3–4, 1974. (T. THEODORE FUJITA)

various points. Where the numbers increase toward 4 and 5, one can chillingly imagine the human tragedy on the ground.

Three-quarters of the people injured in the superoutbreak were in houses and buildings. Perhaps not surprisingly, 17 percent were in mobile homes, which unless tied firmly down are one of the most dangerous places to be in a tornado. Seven percent were in automobiles, and the final 3 percent, another chilling statistic, were "en route to shelters."

In addition to its magnitude and toll of destruction, the superoutbreak produced many peculiarities. Six cities were hit twice by tornadoes: Etowah, Tennessee (3:00 and 5:30 P.M.); Livingston, Tennessee (7:30 and 11:30 P.M.); Cleveland, Tennessee (3:05 and 5:05 P.M.); Tanner, Alabama (7:00 and 7:30 P.M.); Harvest, Alabama (7:15 and 7:45 P.M.); and Huntsville, Alabama (10:55 and 11:05 P.M.).

Two different tornadoes hit the same house in Southern Tennessee. The first one, the Harmony Tornado, took off the roof. The second one, the Second Tanner Tornado, took the whole house away.

One twister, the Windsor Tornado, crossed the international boundary twice from the United States to Canada and back to the United States. The Depauw Tornado deposited a car into the basement, after blowing away the two-story frame house. The Brandenburg Tornado crossed the Ohio River causing a significant fall and subsequent rise of the water level.

The longest-track twister, the Monticello Tornado, left a 121-mile diagonal path across almost all of Northwestern Indiana. The widest, the Frankfurt Tornado, left a path of damage five miles wide near Stamping Ground, Kentucky. It is one of the widest tornado tracks ever documented.

The path of the Guin Tornado in Alabama appeared distinctly in pictures taken by NASA's Earth Resources Technology Satellite, 600 miles above the earth. The path was still visible in October, six months later.

The Obey River (Tennessee) Tornado descended into a 1,000-foot-deep canyon with its full strength and then climbed to the top of the cliff on the other side. The Blue Ridge (Georgia) Tornado moved over the 3,300-foot Betty Mountain, the highest of all tornado paths. This ability of tornadoes to cause continuous damage up and down steep slopes, across mountaintops and through deep gorges was one of the surprising scientific findings from study of the superoutbreak.

Termed the worst series of storms and the most significant meteorological event in 50 years, the 1974 superoutbreak tornadoes understandably have attracted widespread scientific interest. One of the more significant findings has helped put the final kibosh on what Joseph E. Minor of Texas Tech University has called the myth of astronomical wind speeds in tornadoes. There has been a growing consensus among meteorologists and engineers who work with tornadoes that ground-level windspeeds in tornadoes rarely exceed 250 to 275 miles per hour. Nevertheless, some professionals and many laymen had vastly higher conceptions. As recently as 1972, technical literature contained reports of maximum windspeeds of 500 miles per hour or more. Some even speculated that tornado winds blow at the speed of sound. Some basic reference books contributed to the perpetuation of the belief in such excessive speeds. The 1973 edition of Encyclopedia Britannica, Minor points out as an example, assesses tornadic windspeeds as being "on the order of 100 to 500 miles per hour." Minor was part of a group from Texas Tech University's Institute for Disaster Research that studied the engineering aspects of the April 3–4 tornadoes at the request of the Committee on Natural Disasters of the National Academy

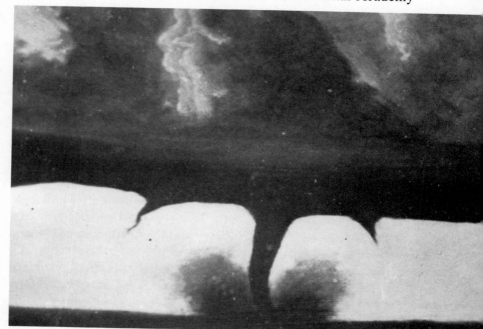

The first known photograph of a tornado, taken 22 miles southwest of Howard, South Dakota, on August 28, 1884. (NOAA)

of Sciences. They devoted considerable attention to calcula-
tion of maximum windspeeds. The maximum windspeeds in the
tornadoes that were most intense (such as those that hit Xenia
and Brandenburg) were in the range of 200 to 250 miles per
hour. These two storms in particular seemed to be as intense as
any previously studied storms on record. The investigators
found no evidence in the documented damage that windspeeds
in the April 3–4 tornadoes exceeded 250 miles per hour.

Edwin Kessler, director of the National Severe Storms Laboratory, says the previous accounts of excessively high windspeeds of 300 to 400 miles per hour or more were a result of
speculation filling in for an absence of scientific evaluation. In
a significant portion of the cases, exaggeration or incomplete-
ness in reporting has essentially been proved. In others, he says,
it appears that observations under stress by untrained observers
were honestly erroneous. "There are today less than a half-dozen
apparently thoughtful observations of tornado effects that support winds in excess of about 250 miles per hour. All are rather
questionable on one basis or another."

Engineering analyses have shown that the incredible damage
from strong tornadoes can easily be inflicted by maximum winds
below 250 and usually below 200 miles per hour. In fact, much
tornado damage is now believed caused by winds around 100
miles per hour.

Direct measurements of windspeeds inside tornadoes are understandably lacking. But in recent years, the widespread availability to the public of motion picture cameras coupled with
great public interest in tornadoes have led to an outpouring of
movies of tornadoes. For many years, according to Kessler, a
film of the 1957 Dallas Tornado was the only film from which
extensive estimates of tornado speeds could be prepared. Now
there are at least a half-dozen more films suitable for photogrammetric analysis. These studies show maximum winds near
200 miles per hour in the tornadoes striking Union City, Oklahoma (May 24, 1974), Xenia, Ohio (April 3, 1974), and
Great Bend, Kansas (August 30, 1974). The first windspeed
estimation using Doppler radar yielded a maximum figure of
200 miles per hour for the Stillwater, Oklahoma, Tornado of
June 13, 1975.

Related to the misconception about extremely high winds
within tornadoes is the somewhat exaggerated emphasis by
many laymen and some professionals on "explosive decompres-

sion" as a tornado passes over a building. The presence of a slight reduction in pressure when a tornado passes over undoubtedly plays a role in causing some structures to fail. But most tornado researchers now feel this effect has been greatly overemphasized. Instead, the worst effect of a tornado on a building is due to the blast of wind from the tornado, especially from that portion of the tornado whose rotary windspeeds are augmented by the speed of the tornado's forward motion. Take, for example, a tornado rotating at 150 miles per hour and moving forward at 50 miles per hour, as some can do. Objects that come into contact with the right side of the counterclockwise-turning tornado, as seen looking in its direction of forward movement, are subject to a blast of 200-mile-per-hour winds.

As did the 1974 superoutbreak, most tornadoes in the United States approach from the southwest. This is because most tornadoes form in the moist flow ahead of an advancing low-pressure center, and this flow is almost always southwesterly. This has helped give rise to considerable confusion over the safest place to be in a building in event of a tornado. A widely held notion that the southwest corner is safest is wrong. Minor calls it "a classic example of the manner in which tornado stories are passed about in seeming disregard for scientific fact." The notion apparently had its origin in the rural areas in the Midwest where it was correctly noticed that tornadoes usually came from the southwest and also that the southwest corner of basements were often free of debris after a tornado. S. D. Flora reported this observation in 1953 with a technical explanation that a southwest-approaching tornado would cause debris to be blown away from the southwest corner of the basement. Somehow, however, says Minor, this rational observation by Flora, which was specifically limited to the basements in rural areas, got translated to first floors of houses and buildings. Even in the mid-1970s, directions incorrectly favoring the southwest corners of a house without a basement were still in print.

In fact, on above-ground floors, the side facing an approaching tornado is the most dangerous place to be because it will receive the maximum impact. "Time and time again," reported James J. Abernethy, a member of the group of engineers and architects who studied the effects of the April, 1974, tornadoes on buildings, "we found windows and walls on the south and west sides pushed in, not out, while if a north wall failed it usually fell outward. But such failures were rare. We also frequently

Violent tornado churns up road near Dallas, Texas, April 2, 1957.
(NOAA)

found window glass imbedded in interior walls of south- and west-facing classrooms, again illustrating the extreme danger of remaining in such areas. Windows on north-facing rooms were often intact."

Most recent observations support the idea that for homes and buildings with no basements, the safest place to be during a tornado is in a small interior room with non-load-bearing walls on the lowest floor. Time and time again pictures of otherwise devastated buildings show such interior rooms relatively intact. For schools, study of the 1974 tornadoes showed that interior corridors that open only to the east or north, where wind forces are smaller, are the safest areas other than basements. Corridors in line with the tornado's travel can act as wind tunnels for glass and debris and be incredibly dangerous. Nevertheless, even they are somewhat safer than the rooms on either side. Other places to avoid in schools and other large buildings are gymnasiums, cafeterias, and auditoriums. The free-span roofs over such large expanses are often destroyed by a combination of aerodynamic lifting of the roofs by the wind passing over the buildings plus a ballooning effect of internal pressure from air rushing in through openings in windward walls.

Although tornadoes occur in many parts of the world besides the United States, especially Australia, the American Midwest has more tornadoes than anywhere else in the world. Geography has determined that. The Gulf of Mexico provides a plentiful supply of warm moist air from the south. Upper-level air from the west is often dry because it has been lifted by the Rocky Mountains and already dropped its moisture there. The dryness of this upper air allows it to cool readily, causing the whole depth of the atmosphere to became unstable. All this unstable air can easily be made to rise by the cold fronts that frequently come in from the north and northwest. Also, some mechanical rising is imparted by the gentle upward slope of terrain northward from the Gulf. All these conditions conspire to produce the lines of severe thunderstorms that can in turn produce tornadoes.

The worst times for tornadoes are the spring and early summer months. The area where tornadoes most frequently form early in the season is the lower Gulf states. Over the months, it gradually moves northward as warm Gulf air penetrates farther and farther inland to do battle with cold air from the north. The center of maximum frequency is over the Gulf states in

February and over the Southeast Atlantic states in March. In May, it moves into the Southern Great Plains states and in June into the Northern Great Plains, Great Lakes states, and even into Western New York. After June, there is no more cold air intrusion to speak of and tornado frequency falls off, reaching its lowest level in mid-winter.

The details of tornado formation are not fully understood. The rotary motion of a tornado vortex may be due to the combined efforts of thermal and mechanical forces. The violent updraft in a thunderstorm can cause a corresponding fall in surface pressure, and this can initiate rapid convergence of low-level air toward the center of the updraft. Just as an ice skater increases the speed of her spin as she draws her arms in closer to her body, the air rushing in toward this updraft is given greater rotary velocity as it moves closer to the center. If this rotary motion is strong enough, it becomes the vortex of a tornado.

Many tornadoes appear to get their start from a parent tornado cyclone. Often now called a mesocyclone, this is a rotating thunderstorm, or a rotating portion of a thunderstorm. It may range from a half-mile to five miles in diameter with winds of 20 to 100 or more miles per hour.

The distinctive funnel is initially composed of condensed water vapor and is itself a cloud. Its formation depends not only on swirling motions but also on proper moisture conditions. So, contrary to common belief, damaging tornado winds can be raking across the ground, even though a visible funnel doesn't extend all the way down. As it picks up dust and debris, it takes on the characteristic dark color. Rare tornadoes that have descended over snow-covered terrain have been observed to be snowy white.

Funnels vary greatly in size and shape. Some can be very tightly formed and walled. Others can be ragged and irregular, suggesting especially strong turbulence. They can come straight down out of the sky or snake across the ground diagonally. They can range in width from less than 50 feet up to, in rare instances, a mile (remember the 1974 Frankfurt Tornado) or more.

One classic tornado photograph, taken on a farm near Jasper, Minnesota, on July 8, 1927, shows a narrow, whiplike funnel, a beautifully defined silver-gray sliver extending horizontally far out beyond its parent cloud, then curving down to the ground to create a formidable spray of black earth and debris. Pictures

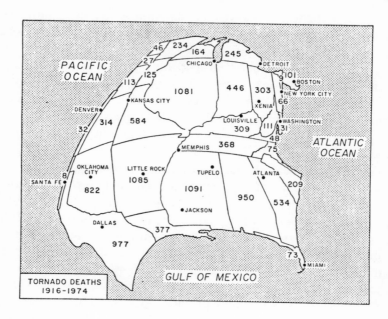

Map of the United States prorated by tornado-related deaths. (T. THEODORE FUJITA)

of irregular tornadoes such as the one that devastated Xenia in 1974 show only an indistinct but ominous mass of dark dust in motion around and above the houses and streets.

Despite their prevalence in the Central United States, tornadoes have hit all 50 states, including Alaska. Over the past 25 years, the greatest numbers have occurred in Texas and Oklahoma, although in recent years there seems to have been a shift eastward. Tornadoes in the Southeast tend to kill more people than those in the Great Plains and Midwest. Pearson says this may be because tornadoes in the Southeast are usually obscured in clouds and heavy rain and therefore are not detected nearly as early as tornadoes in the plains, which often can be seen from miles away. Another factor, he says, is that while most tornadoes elsewhere happen in the few hours before sunset, those in the Southeast show less pronounced predictability of time. They can occur any time of the day, and some strike in the night.

A usual year will see somewhere from 600 to 1,000 tornadoes striking the United States. Pearson says the modern average is around 850. Fujita and Pearson have produced a color-coded map showing the locations and intensities of 19,189 known tornadoes across the United States for the period 1930–74. The record year for tornadoes was not the year of the superoutbreak but ironically, just the year before, 1973. That year 1,107 tornadoes hit, giving 1973 the label Year of the Tornado. Forty-six states had tornadoes that year (all but Alaska, Rhode Island, Utah, and Washington). "The 1973 tornado season," announced the National Severe Storms Forecast Center, "can only be described by liberal use of superlatives. It had the most, lasted the longest, and involved more states . . . than any year since tornado records began."

The mathematical chance of a tornado striking a specific location in any one year is quite small. Even in the areas most frequently subject to tornadoes, the probability of a tornado striking a given point is less than 0.04, or less than once in 250 years. In the far western states, where tornadoes are rare, the probability is close to zero. None of that is of course consolation to the home or community that, against the odds, is struck. And as we've seen with the six towns that were hit twice by tornadoes on April 3, 1974, tornadoes provide no immunity to once-hit areas. Some part of Oklahoma City has been hit by tornadoes 32 times since 1892. And Codell, Kansas, was struck three successive years, in 1916, 1917, and 1918. All happened on May 20.

After the force of the winds themselves, the next most dangerous aspect of a tornado is the barrage of objects and debris it hurls through the air.

Dramatic examples of the ability of tornadoes to turn normally earthbound objects into powerful airborne missiles abound. These missiles can range in size from gravel to truck trailers. The most prevalent are pieces of timber. They can vary from splinters to laminated beams or arches from the roofs of auditoriums or gymnasiums.

Willis L. Moore, then chief of the U.S. Weather Bureau, visited Saint Louis the day following the great tornado of May 27, 1896. He saw a two-by-four wooden plank that had been embedded in a steel bridge. The two-by-four had been blown through solid iron five-eighths of an inch thick. Its end protruded several feet through the hole it had gouged.

In the Tri-State Tornado of March 18, 1925, a grain binder was blown a quarter of a mile, a railroad bridge was lifted off its supporting piers and abutments, and a large touring car was blown 225 feet.

In Sioux Falls, South Dakota, a tornado in 1932 was reported to have caused a six-inch-wide flange beam to perforate a 14-inch-diameter tree. Allen Pearson and Joseph A. Miller reported that in a tornado that hit Clarendon, Texas, in 1970, a wooden splinter had perforated a steel-pipe gate post one and a half inches in diameter.

A certain amount of caution is necessary in assessing anecdotal missile reports. James R. McDonald of Texas Tech University notes that under the right circumstances, automobiles, vans and buses, and semi-truck trailers can become airborne. But more often, he says, they are tumbled or rolled by the tornado rather than carried through the air. McDonald has documented the case of a 41-foot-long, 26,000-pound cylindrical fertilizer tank found approximately three-fourths of a mile east of its original location after the May 11, 1970, Lubbock Tornado. Investigation could not positively establish whether it had been airborne or rolled and tumbled part of the way. But it had to cross a four-lane highway and an access road, and there was no damage to any structures along the path. (That tornado, incidentally, caused $135 million damage within the city of Lubbock and put a small but permanent twist in a downtown Lubbock high-rise office building.)

After the Union City, Oklahoma, Tornado of May 24, 1973, a 10-foot-long, 2,000-gallon gasoline storage tank was found half a mile from where it had rested on a pedestal. Study showed that it had been airborne for 1,300 feet and then bounced to its final position. Some steel I-beams were carried 160 feet, and a car engine was carried 1,000 feet.

Investigation into the case of three 40-passenger school buses found in the woods at the top of an embankment near an elementary school outside of McComb, Mississippi, after a tornado in 1974 confirmed that the buses had indeed become airborne.

After the 1974 Xenia Tornado, investigators found a 20-foot-long open-web steel joist on a hillside. Its source could not be found anywhere within a 300-foot radius. The same tornado deposited two 40-foot-long truck trailers on the roof of a bowling alley. They had traveled about 150 feet.

In 1931, a Minnesota tornado carried an 83-ton railroad coach and its 117 passengers 80 feet. In 1975 a Mississippi tornado carried a home freezer more than a mile.

Joseph E. Minor says that although many dramatic missile events have been documented, others have proved to be overstatements of actual phenomena. He puts in this category reports of locomotives being turned around and houses being moved while intact. Other strange phenomena are also often reported but there are none, Minor says, that can't be explained by currently held concepts about the behavior of materials. The straw-through-a-plank phenomenon is one of these. It sounds strange. But it has been frequently observed by scientists and engineers and it violates no known principles.

Water has been "blown" from ponds during passage of a tornado, but Minor says there is no substantial evidence that a tornado can move a significant amount of water through any type of a "sucking" mechanism. To move water through a lowering of pressure in the tornado core, the outside diameter of the tornado would have to be smaller than the body of water affected, as in the case of a soda straw. Thus, most swimming pools could not be so affected other than through the wind blowing water out. Also, the drop in atmospheric pressure from the passage of a tornado is currently considered to be one-fifth of an atmosphere at most and probably much less. This pressure drop, he says, could not be expected to move very large quantities of water.

The often-reported chicken-defeathering phenomenon from a tornado's passage can also be easily explained as a wind-induced, rather than a "strange phenomenon"-induced action, he says.

Nevertheless, the power of a large tornado is very real. The 1896 Saint Louis Tornado was the first great tornado to strike a major American urban area in modern times. It hit at 6:10 in the evening of May 27, smashing into tenements, residential sections, a poorhouse, an insane asylum, a hospital, the armory, and the Saint Louis Exposition buildings. It crossed the riverfront area, damaging warehouses. As it skipped across the Missouri River, it smashed 16 steamships and other small craft to bits, then headed into East Saint Louis, on the Illinois side. The death toll in the sister cities was 300, and damage reached at least $12 million.

The monster Tri-State Tornado of March 18, 1925—the most deadly of the eight that day—will forever be remembered. It started at one o'clock on a Wednesday afternoon as an amorphous black mass over Reynolds County, Missouri, and began a nearly straight line path of destruction traveling 57 to 68 miles per hour. During one short section it moved at 73 miles per hour. In Murphysboro, Illinois, 152 city blocks—60 percent of the town—was destroyed. Two hundred thirty-four persons were killed. At West Frankfort it killed 148 persons and ruined the largest coal mine in the United States. On it continued, still with no one warning the communities in its path. Town after town was hit before it finally came to an end outside of Princeton, Indiana, 219 miles and three hours 18 minutes after it had begun. The death toll was 689, the worst single twister in U.S. history.

On April 5–6, 1936, a series of twisters sliced through Mississippi and Georgia. At Tupelo, Mississippi, later to become famous as the birthplace of Elvis Presley, a tremendous tornado eradicated 15 blocks of the town's best residential section, destroyed its reservoir of drinking water, and mangled much of the business area. At least 216 persons were killed, and nearly 1,500 injured. At 8:45 the next morning, two tornadoes spun through Gainesville, Georgia. A large part of the business district was destroyed, and then fires broke out. Fire trucks were hindered from reaching the blazes by the rubble from the tornadoes, and rescuers trying to extract victims from the debris had to race the flames. The tornado killed 203 persons, and injuries from all causes totaled 934. The town's three biggest cotton mills had to be used as morgues. Gainesville, incidentally, is another city that has suffered multiple tornado strikes. A twister in 1903 claimed 28 lives and one in 1944 took 44.

Whole towns have almost been totally wiped out. A tornado that hit Udall, Kansas, May 25, 1955, killed 80 and injured 270 of the town's population of 610. Of the 187 houses, 170 were destroyed and 16 were damaged beyond repair. One escaped untouched.

Several cases are on record of persons looking up into the center of a tornado and living to tell about it. One of the most famous is that of Will Keller, a Greensburg, Kansas, farmer. In his wheat field just destroyed by a hailstorm on June 22, 1928, Keller and his family saw a tornado coming and ran to their storm cellar. As he was about to close the door, he turned around and looked. Seeing it start to rise off the ground as it neared, he kept his position and watched.

Steadily the tornado came on, the end gradually rising above the ground. I could have stood there only a few seconds but so impressed was I with what was going on that it seemed a long time. At last the great shaggy end of the funnel hung directly overhead. Everything was as still as death. There was a strong gassy odor and it seemed that I could not breathe. There was a screaming, hissing sound coming directly from the end of the funnel. I looked up and to my astonishment I saw right up into the heart of the tornado. There was a circular opening in the center of the funnel, about 50 or 100 feet in diameter, and extending straight upward for a distance of at least one half mile, as best I could judge under the circumstances. The walls of this opening were of rotating clouds and the whole was made brilliantly visible by constant flashes of lightning which zigzagged from side to side. Had it not been for the lightning, I could not have seen the opening, not any distance up into it anyway.

Around the lower rim of the great vortex small tornadoes were constantly forming and breaking away. These looked like tails as they writhed their way around the end of the funnel. It was these that made the hissing noise.

I noticed that the direction of rotation of the great whirl was anticlockwise, but the small twisters rotated both ways. . . .

The opening was entirely hollow except for something which I could not quite make out, but suppose that it was a detached wind cloud. This thing was in the center and was moving up and down.

On another occasion, a motorist traveling with his wife was caught in a tornado. The windshield and windows broke. He bent down for protection, but during a slight lull he looked up and saw boards, branches of trees, and a boulder floating round the car. This apparently was when the eye of the funnel was directly overhead. Then the winds hit again, and he and his wife were thrown out of the car.

No tornado has ever been so systematically observed as the one that hit Union City, Oklahoma, on May 24, 1973. The events began at 3:45 that afternoon. In the darkened radar room at the National Severe Storms Laboratory in Norman, Oklahoma, a thunderstorm that had grown explosively was under observation. The tornado intercept coordinator had just hung up the phone when it rang again. An excited member of the laboratory's tornado intercept team reported that a large tornado was touching down to his west. The team was just south of the

Scenes like this, a neighborhood converted to rubble, are repeated each tornado season in the United States. In Wichita Falls, Texas, Julie Shults (foreground) is joined by her parents and others as they remove personal property from homes destroyed by tornado which ripped through here, April 11, 1979. Tornadoes hit the Texas-Oklahoma border late on April 10, killing at least 56 people and injuring nearly 1,000. (UPI)

small farming community of Union City, 29 miles west-north-west of the laboratory. Other sighting reports quickly came in. Word swiftly spread, and laboratory personnel rushed to the building's observation platform, where the tornado was visible in the distance. The anvil of the parent thunderstorm stretched over the laboratory and and far to the east and southeast. In the next half-hour, a team of meteorologists managed for the first time to seek out and photograph the life history of a tornado. In the meantime, all the laboratory's sensors covered the storm.

The life-history observations came from the tornado intercept team. Daniel Purcell of NSSL describes the life cycle he and his colleagues recorded. It is probably typical of many tornadoes. Traveling in a truck to the site of the thunderstorm, they saw a characteristic wall cloud forming. A wall cloud forms beneath the parent thunderstorm and is often the progenitor of tornadoes. The wall cloud began to rotate slowly, and some short-lived funnel-like protrusions formed beneath. The bottom edge of the wall cloud went through rapid changes in form as moist air was drawn up through its base into the storm's rotating updraft. Soon a short, smooth funnel appeared beneath the wall cloud. This first stage of the tornado, labeled the organizing stage, lasted 10 minutes. During most of that time the funnel remained aloft. The lower two-thirds of the funnel, Purcell says, appeared and disappeared in a ghostlike manner. But surprisingly the tornado produced a continuous damage path as it passed over five farmsteads.

Once the funnel remained on the ground, the tornado was in its mature stage. The funnel began to widen rapidly while moving east-southeast about 30 feet per second. At maximum, the funnel width was 1,900 feet at the base of the cloud and 500 feet at 500 feet above the ground. The damage path also reached its maximum width of 500 feet. The tornado's shape was like a broad, truncated, inverted cone. The wall cloud had by this time become indistinct. A barn and a two-story farmhouse were hit by the tornado during its mature stage and completely destroyed. An eyewitness claimed that the house as a whole was lifted 15 to 30 feet before it disintegrated.

As the tornado began its shrinking stage it entered Union City. A large bend developed in its middle, and it turned sharply southeast. As it passed through the middle of town, it shrank rapidly. In fact, it changed so much that the many people who took shelter there thought what they saw entering and leaving were two separate tornadoes. There was complete destruction along the damage path. Twenty homes and 18 mobile homes were destroyed. An additional 43 homes and several stores and churches were damaged, some heavily. By now its speed of movement had increased to 50 feet per second (34 miles per hour).

As it passed through wheat fields southeast of town, its damage path narrowed. One farm family realized that the funnel was curving toward them and tried to outrun it in their car. It overtook them and rolled the car over, causing minor injuries. When they crawled out of the car, they found that their home nearby had disappeared. Only a bare concrete slab remained.

After hitting the farm, the tornado entered its decaying stage. The bottom third of the funnel temporarily evaporated after hitting the farm, although the vortex remained in contact with the ground. At the same time, it began bending rapidly into a serpentine shape, with a contorted, rope-like structure.

The entire lifetime of the Union City Tornado spanned 26 minutes. During all stages, the damage path bore a remarkable resemblance to funnel width at 1,800 feet elevation. The townspeople had had ample warning and had seen the tornado coming. Concludes Purcell: "When it was all over, the people of Union City and Canadian County knew that they had been visited by one of the most intense tornadoes anywhere during 1973."

One doesn't have to actually see a tornado to learn a lot about it. The ground marks left by tornadoes are strong clues to the forces at work. Like the meteorological Sherlock Holmes he is, Fujita and his colleagues have made quite a science of it.

"Tornadoes," says Fujita, "are like criminals who cannot get away without leaving behind their fingerprints at unexpected locations."

Out of his studies in the 1970s, Fujita has documented his concept of multiple "suction vortices" within large tornadoes. A suction vortex is a small, fast-spinning column of air within a tornado itself. It is like a mini-tornado within the main one. It is usually less than 30 feet in diameter. A large tornado can have perhaps four or five suction vortices. Each vortex has its own rotation in addition to its rotary movement with the overall funnel.

The effects of suction vortices have long been commented on, without anyone realizing what they had noticed, says Fujita.

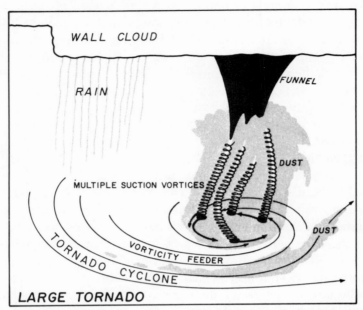

Model of a large tornado with multiple suction vortices. (T. THEO-
DORE FUJITA)

They can account for the rather erratic damage people often notice left behind by tornadoes, including such comments as, "My
house was badly damaged but the wind did not touch my neighbor's. . . ." In fact, says Fujita, in large tornadoes three scales
of motion act in concert: the tornado itself, the parent rotating
tornado cyclone that spawns it, and also the suction vortices
swirling with the tornado.

Suction vortices are hidden inside the huge column of dust
around the funnel and are rarely seen. But, as Fujita says, the
swirl marks they leave in open fields are their footprints, which
disclose their secrets.

From his aerial photographs of different types of peculiar
ground marks left by some tornadoes, Fujita has identified six
different types of suction vortices. The most common orbits
around the tornado core and leaves looping or scalloping marks.
But others can spiral in toward the core, producing crescents or
spirals, or wobble around the center or stray around the outside,
leaving distinctive lineations.

The swaths left by suction spots are visible only from certain
directions relative to the sun, and that is why they had not been
photographed in the past. But Fujita has now accumulated an

impressive collection of photos of suction swaths. Many of them were produced by tornadoes in the 1974 superoutbreak, such as giant looping marks across a field near Home Lake, Illinois. A tornado that nearly wiped out Magnet, Nebraska, on May 6, 1975, left quite dramatic ones.

Suction vortices are features of powerful tornadoes. Several photos of the early stages of the killer Xenia Tornado clearly show helix-shaped condensation funnels followed several seconds later by a small, violent suction vortex near the ground. Fujita's chart of the suction-vortex paths from the 1970 Lubbock Tornado reveals that 26 of the 28 deaths in the city occurred within the suction swaths.

Pearson says he believes there are about 10 regular tornadoes for every one that has multiple-suction vortices within its funnel. But these large, multiple-vortexed tornadoes may often be the biggest killers.

Another peculiar type of twister has recently been documented by Fujita and Pearson—anticyclonic tornadoes. Practically all tornadoes are thought to swirl cyclonically (counterclockwise in the Northern Hemisphere, clockwise in the Southern Hemisphere). A tornado's vorticity field is seemingly too small to be significantly affected by the earth's rotation. But tornadoes form within the parent swirls embedded inside large cyclonic wind systems, and these of course are given their counterclockwise (north of the equator) direction of rotation by the Coriolis effect of the earth's rotation.

In 1977, however, Fujita and Pearson identified 29 anticyclonic (clockwise) tornadoes that occurred during the 27 years from 1950 to 1976. Examples include the Three-Farm Tornado in Iowa on June 13, 1976, which left behind a large hay field swept by strong winds of clockwise curvature. An apparent anticyclonic tornado that hit Silverton, Texas, on June 22, 1975, destroyed a farmhouse, killing a family of three, and deposited debris from the swept-free foundation in a pile 70 feet to the northwest. Some wreckage was found as far as 400 yards to the northwest. Most of the anticyclonic tornadoes identified were in the United States, but at least one was in Japan and two in the Soviet Union. Often they happened in conjunction with regular tornadoes. "As a matter of both scientific interest and public safety," concludes Fujita, "it should be recognized that anticyclonic tornadoes may develop in the vicinity of a cyclonic tornado."

The most exciting and significant new advance in tornado research and detection has been the validation of a technique called Doppler radar. Under development throughout the 1970s, the high hopes atmospheric scientists and severe storms forecasters have held for it now appear about to be fulfilled. In 1978, the National Oceanic and Atmospheric Administration announced that Doppler radar had detected tornadoes in severe thunderstorms in Oklahoma more than 20 minutes before they became visible to ground observers and had added at least 10 minutes to the lead time possible in tornado warnings.

"Doppler radar is a real breakthrough in the area of severe storms investigation," says Edwin Kessler. "It provides a new dimension in observation unobtainable only a few years ago."

With the technique, storm observers can for the first time, in effect, see inside a thunderstorm and measure the velocities of rain particles, and therefore of the winds within it. The rotating mesocyclone that is often the mother of tornadoes can be detected this way as well as at times a distinctive wind-velocity "signature" of a tornado itself.

Doppler radar draws on a familiar effect first explained by the Austrian physicist Christian Doppler in 1842 but something so common we've all seen (or at least heard) manifestations of it. It's what accounts for the changing pitch of the horn of a car, truck, or train as it passes us. As a train approaches, more and more sound waves from it are jammed into each second of time. We hear that as an increasingly higher frequency or pitch. The reverse happens as it recedes from us. Fewer sound waves are now being received each second and we hear that as an increasingly lower frequency or pitch. A similar thing happens with light or radio waves. If a radar beam is bounced off a particle moving toward the antenna the return beam will be detected as a higher frequency than if the particle is stationary. If it's moving away from the antenna it will be detected as a lower frequency. The radar's computer then takes this information and calculates wind velocities toward and away from the observing site. This information can then be displayed in a variety of interesting and colorful ways on display screens.

The weather radars used by your local weather service office or television station are not Doppler, but conventional, radar. They show areas of high reflectivity (precipitation or ice crystals) within a storm but not velocities.

Just outside the modern, low-slung building of the National

Severe Storms Laboratory on the north edge of Norman, Oklahoma, is a domed structure that houses the Doppler radar antenna and the electronic equipment that is causing all the excitement. In the darkened room beneath the antenna, researchers scan the Doppler reflections from thunderstorms for the telltale signs of tornadoes.

Before the observers are display screens showing the Doppler information on thunderstorms over Central Oklahoma. One shows the relative intensity of the storm, arbitrarily color-coded into 10 colors ranging from cool to hot to indicate increasing echo intensity. Next to it is a screen showing the pattern of velocities within the storm, color-coded into as many as 15 shades of red (approaching winds) and blue (receding).

On a separate black-and-white console to the left, the velocity data are plotted as a series of arrows whose directions, lengths, and widths vividly portray to the observers the intensity, velocity field, and turbulence within the storm. The display can focus in on different horizontal and vertical segments of a large storm. On this screen the observers watch for a counterclockwise swirl of arrows. That would be the sign of a tornado mesocyclone, the larger parent circulation of a tornado.

On the color-coded velocity display they watch for a distinctive couplet pattern, a small area of intense blue directly adjacent to a small area of intense red. This would be an indication that within a very small area winds of high velocity are moving in opposite directions. This is what you would expect if you were seeing the two opposite sides of a tornado. If this "tornado vortex signature" is detected aloft near the center of the parent mesocyclone, it signals that a tornado is forming. If seen at zero-degrees elevation as well as at higher levels, there is a high probability that a tornado is on the ground.

This tornado vortex signature was first discovered in the Union City Tornado. From 1973 to 1976 it was found 10 more times by NSSL's Doppler radar, and eight turned out to be definitely associated with tornadoes or funnels.

In 1977, the Severe Storms Laboratory, the National Weather Service, the Air Weather Service, and the Air Force Geophysics Laboratory began a cooperative two-year experiment to test the tornado-warning capabilities of the experimental Doppler radar at Norman in actual operational use. The results of the first year of the project, headed by Donald W. Burgess, were very encouraging. Twenty-four mesocyclones detected resulted in 23 verifications of severe weather. Of the 24, 12 had at least one associated tornado.

It turned out that when Doppler radar detection was used, advisories were forwarded to the Weather Service about 23 minutes ahead of conventional sightings. Actual tornado warnings were sent out an average of 10 minutes before the tornadoes were detectable by conventional means.

After the season was over, the success of the Doppler technique was compared with the normal Weather Service detection and warning methods, which are based on a combination of conventional radar and visual sightings from the public. This analysis showed that the probability of detecting a given tornado was 94.4 percent with Doppler and only 69.4 percent with normal methods. Another important measure was that the false-alarm rate with Doppler was only 24.4 percent while with the normal methods it was 73 percent. Overall, a measure called the "critical success index" gave Doppler a .723 rating (1.0 is perfect) compared with a .242 for conventional techniques. No wonder the scientists were pleased.

So the future of detecting twisters by Doppler radar seems bright. Many weather scientists want to see an operational system of Doppler installed across the most tornado-prone areas of the United States in the 1980s. It already seems to be significantly better though somewhat more expensive than the conventional radars now in use. The next few years of research and the decisions of government agencies will determine its future. But the chances are good that if you live in a state frequently subject to the wrath of tornadoes, you may be receiving significantly improved warnings, courtesy of Doppler radar, by 1985.

CHAPTER 3
Lightning

The lightning and thunder bursting out of a thunderstorm are wonderfully spectacular. If the thundercloud itself is pure magnificence in form and shape and its whirling progeny—the tornado—is concentrated power and destruction, the electrical offspring—lightning and thunder—are indeed awesome, a sensual light-and-sound show as only nature can stage it.

Nearly everyone has a favorite memory of a dramatic electrical storm. My own comes from a nighttime drive across Nebraska a few years back. The display began shortly after darkness as we drove eastward. In the typical electrical storm, the flashes are usually concentrated in a few particular areas of the sky at any given moment. As the storm progresses these locations may move. This one seemed to light up the entire sky. With almost unceasing action, the lightning bolts slashed their intricate patterns of brilliant incandescence across the black sky. To the right, to the left, directly overhead, behind, far down the road, the show surrounded us, nature's own Cinerama-Sensurround making puny by comparison the most creative efforts of any Hollywood special effects whiz. On and on the storm continued, etching multi-fanged lines of incomparable variation and beauty. I suspect we may have been just keeping pace with the motion of the storm, because as the miles rolled on, the drama continued around us, our moving front-row seat never falling behind the action on the stage. In our glass-enclosed cubicle, safe and secure, we were privileged witnesses to this dynamic spectacle, and as we rolled along it sometimes seemed as if we were the only persons to be seeing it in its true scale of beauty and wonder.

The vivid display of lightning has blotted out any memory of strong thunder. As dramatic as the storm was, I cannot be

Near Miami Beach, Florida. An excellent example of a lightning flash with all forks or branches traced through the surrounding clouds. Usually the majority of a flash is obscured by the clouds. (NOAA)

sure that, during the 45 minutes to an hour we were beneath it, the lightning and thunder were literally continuous. But some intense storms do produce almost continuous lightning and thunder for considerable periods. A storm over London during the night of August 2, 1879, is said to have produced continuous thunder for 20 minutes. And Frank W. Lane tells of a storm in Hertfordshire, England, during the night of June 12, 1964, in which thunder was timed that lasted continuously for 28 minutes. During a great thunderstorm in England in July, 1923, 6,924 flashes were recorded over London alone, including 47 in one minute. A great storm over Pretoria, South Africa, on Christmas Day, 1923, produced 100 flashes a minute for more than an hour.

Such frequencies need not be surprising. In the roughly seven seconds it takes you to read this paragraph, lightning will have struck the earth some 700 times. This estimated 100-times-a-second rate of discharge worldwide represents something like 4 billion kilowatts of continuous power.

But make no mistake about it; lightning is far more than dramatic display, atmospheric fireworks. It can be a dangerous killer, and often is, far more often than many people realize. When a tornado, flood, or hurricane strikes, it gets enormous news attention. Reports of death and damage are flashed across the nation and around the world. A particularly bad killer-storm can cause fatalities by the dozens and injuries by the hundreds, and these understandably stick in the public's mind, overshadowing the fact that these multi-death occurrences are, for all the tragedy they cause, relatively infrequent.

Lightning, in contrast, picks off its victims by ones or twos, and that doesn't make the national news. In fact, it usually is worth only a few paragraphs in the local newspaper, in the same way that the death of one or two persons in an automobile accident seems to be of only local concern despite the horrible cumulative toll of highway fatalities nationally, while the occasional crash of an airliner gains public attention all out of proportion to the relatively small role of airplane crashes in accidental-death statistics.

Hurricanes kill an average of 54 persons a year, floods 90, and tornadoes 132, according to a 34-year compilation of storm deaths in the United States published in 1976. Over the same period, lightning killed 6,928 persons, an average of 204 a year. And it is generally concluded that the lightning-fatality figures are conservative. The statistics-gatherers may miss many deaths. Others are not included under lightning deaths by the Public Health Service (PHS) if there was a secondary cause of death, such as a fire resulting from lightning. One National Weather Service observer estimated that to one year's total of 124 lightning fatalities reported by the PHS should be added 87 deaths due to lightning-caused house and apartment fires. Still, this would not include those who die of lightning-caused forest fires or of electrocution by lightning-downed power lines. Lightning is, without a doubt, a big killer, the greatest cause of death among all types of storms.

The toll of lightning victims during just one recent summer month (August, 1977) reminds us how susceptible we can be. Most of the victims were working or playing outdoors when struck. This is typical of lightning deaths. A 33-year-old man was helping 12 other persons pull weeds and clean out trees on a hillside area of a fruit tree nursery in Wartrace, Tennessee, when lightning struck and killed him. Three men in Tuscarawas County, Ohio, were out hunting frogs when lightning struck, killing a 30-year-old man and injuring the other two. On Lake Lanier, Georgia, a woman riding in a boat operated by her husband was killed by lightning and three other persons injured. In Albuquerque, New Mexico, a man was struck and killed by lightning in a city park. In Ruidoso, New Mexico, a woman riding a horse on a mountainside was struck.

A lifeguard in Rye, New York, was killed by lightning as he was running from the beach area to the clubhouse. Two people picnicking in a park in East Meadow, New York, were struck and killed. During a thunderstorm at Lee Center, Oneida County, in Central New York, lightning struck a tree and traveled along the ground to a camping area. Two teenage boys died of electrocution and two others were injured. In Lucas County, Ohio, a 48-year-old Toledo man was struck and killed while playing golf. A Boy Scout attending the Jamboree in Maraine State Park in Eastern Pennsylvania was struck while running between camp sites. He died in the hospital four days later.

Many of the victims had taken shelter under trees, a natural but deadly inclination. One was a man fishing alone at a farm pond nine miles east of Holdenville, Oklahoma. Strong winds and rain came up and he took shelter under a large tree. Lightning struck the tree and jumped to the man, killing him. Four members of a Harriman, Tennessee, family sought shelter from a thunderstorm under a tree near a lake. Lightning struck the tree knocking all four of them several feet. Three members of family recovered, but the fourth died 11 days later. She had never regained consciousness. In Wayne County, West Virginia, a man was killed by lightning while standing near a tree. In Northern Texas, a Mexican national laborer working on a ranch near Bonham sought refuge from a thunderstorm in a pecan orchard. A lightning bolt struck a tree and then hit him in the back of the neck. It traveled down through his body, burning holes in his clothes, knocking the soles of his shoes off, and killing him instantly.

Others were close to shelter. A man in Onway, Michigan, was struck and killed while in his backyard feeding his dogs. In Hampshire County, Massachusetts, a young man was killed when lightning struck him as he stood in a barn hayloft doorway.

Being inside was no guarantee of safety. In Prospect Park, New Jersey, a man was working under a car in a garage when lightning hit a nearby tree, passed into the garage, and struck the car, killing him. In Brick Township, New Jersey, a lightning bolt passed through a bathroom window and struck and killed a man who was shaving. Nearby and almost at the same time, a second man was killed by lightning when he left his car to aid several boaters.

In Magnolia, Arkansas, fire sparked by lightning destroyed a home and killed a 19-year-old man inside. And on Chicago's South Side, lightning touched off an explosion in a grain elevator. Two men were killed in the explosion and two others injured in the resulting fire.

But the most tragic event of all happened in Buck Creek, Iowa. There lightning struck a CB antenna mounted on the roof of a house, starting a fire. Six persons inside the house were engulfed by flames and killed.

The toll in just that one month in just one country: thirty persons dead.

Some of the close calls are instructive. Safety advisories always caution people not to talk on the telephone during a severe electrical storm. Here are examples why. Lake Placid, Florida: A woman suffers injuries when lightning strikes while she is talking on the telephone. The phone is knocked from her hand. She is dazed for several minutes and suffers a circular white burn where the receiver touched her ear. Prince Georges County, Maryland: Lightning strikes a utility pole and travels into a house, sending a jolt of electricity through the telephone receiver. A man talking on the phone is shocked but fortunately not injured.

Other communications equipment is just as dangerous. Melbourne, Florida: A woman holding a radio microphone in an office is injured when a lightning bolt apparently travels down the antenna. Her left hand and shoulder are numb for several hours. Such incidents are common. These three examples are taken from a 13-day period in 1977. Statistics show that there were 66 casualties, including nine deaths, in lightning-related telephone incidents from 1968 to 1976.

A new but related hazard is the CB radio. In the four years since they have been in wide use, reports of deaths and injuries from lightning striking persons using a CB radio have begun to show up. In the eight years prior to 1975 only two persons were reported injured in lightning-related CB and other radio equipment incidents. In 1975 and 1976 six persons were injured and two killed. In 1978, fortunately, there were no CB-related lightning casualties, but one boy was killed when lightning struck the antenna of a portable radio he was carrying and three persons were injured by lightning while using stereo equipment.

Still, lightning most often strikes down a person who is outdoors. Recent studies show that lightning victims are more and more likely to have been participating in some form of outdoor recreation when hit. In the 1950s and 1960s, one of every four persons killed by lightning were outdoor recreationists. For the eight years through 1976, that figure climbed to well over 40 percent. This seems to be due to the rising proportion of the population taking part in outdoor recreation. The greatest risk is to those taking part in water activities. Of every 100 persons killed by lightning during outdoor recreation, 38 are engaged in water activities, 16 are camping or picnicking, 14 are playing golf, nine are at athletic events, and two are riding horseback.

Lightning deaths are clustered most heavily in the summer months of June, July, and August, when thunderstorms are frequent and outdoor activities at a high. Florida by far outranks all other states in lightning deaths and injuries, undoubtedly due to a combination of its high frequency of thunderstorms, proximity to bodies of water, and relatively heavy population. Pennsylvania, New York, Ohio, Michigan, North Carolina, Mississippi, Louisiana, Arkansas, and Oklahoma are also relatively

high-risk areas. Lightning casualties are uncommon in California, Nevada, Washington state, and the Dakotas.

Unique with the lightning hazard is the relatively high probability of death if struck. Persons caught in hurricanes, tornadoes, and earthquakes are very likely to survive. But with
lightning, for every two persons injured, one is killed. No other
natural hazard has such a high death-to-injury ratio.

Sometimes the probability of survival depends on the excellent
general health of the victim. An example is the case of a sixteen-
year-old boy struck by lightning at a golf course in Tarpon
Springs, Florida, on August 10, 1977, while running for cover
during a thunderstorm. A bolt of lightning struck the golf umbrella he was holding, entered his right hand, and passed through
his body. The umbrella ended up in shreds, and the boy's golf
shoes were completely ripped apart. He received second-degree
burns on both feet and burns on his neck and body. He had to
have six stitches in his right hand. The doctors who attended
him stated that his pulse rate increased to 200 beats per minute
and that an older person might not have been able to stand such
a strain on the heart.

On August 26, 1978, a 25-year-old Greensboro woman received a direct lightning strike at Atlantic Beach in Carteret
County, North Carolina. Her heartbeat and breathing stopped
for several minutes. The skin around her neck was scorched
where lightning struck her necklace, there were burns on her
head, stomach, legs, and right foot, and her heart tissue was
burned. She lay in a coma for 18 hours. Yet she recovered completely.

Some persons have foiled the odds by being struck twice and
surviving. Hardly anyone has survived a third strike. The most
phenomenal case on record is that of Roy C. Sullivan, a retired
Shenandoah National Park ranger who lives in Waynesboro,
Virginia. Sullivan has been struck by lightning seven times. For
good reason, he's known in Virginia as the human lightning rod.
He still bears scars on his right arm and leg from the first strike,
which happened in April, 1942, while fleeing a fire tower during
a thunderstorm. He was struck again in July, 1969 (lost eyebrows), July, 1970 (left shoulder burned), April, 1972 (hair
set on fire), August, 1973 (knocked 10 feet out of his car and
hair set on fire again), and June, 1976 (injured again but recovered). The seventh time, in June, 1977, happened while he

was fishing and put him in the hospital with chest and stomach burns. He said afterward he hopes it's the last time. "You can tell it's going to strike," he says, "but it's too late. You can smell sulfur in the air, and then your hair will stand up on end, and then it's going to get you. You don't have time to do anything." I have never heard a satisfactory explanation for lightning's attraction to Sullivan.

Lightning has produced many freakish actions. Lane recounts a case of lightning setting fire to a building and then striking a nearby fire alarm which summoned the fire department to extinguish the blaze. A farm laborer was carrying a pitchfork over his shoulder when lightning tossed it 50 yards and twisted the tines like a corkscrew. Two young girls were standing next to a reaping machine when lightning tore their clothes and boots off, leaving the girls naked, but except for being embarrassed, unharmed. A soldier was in his sleeping bag when the metal zipper was welded shut by a lightning strike. After a storm at Great Yarmough, England, in 1958, lightning reportedly caused a clock to stop and then a few minutes later start again in the wrong direction.

Livestock are frequent victims of lightning, far more often than are humans. One reason is that their four legs span more ground and thus they receive a greater shock than do we two-legged humans. Another is that during storms cattle and sheep tend to cluster together and a lightning charge is passed from one animal to another. I never realized how common livestock lightning fatalities were until I perused a few monthly reports of storm events relating significant strikes. Take one brief summer period. Newton, Alabama: 17 Angus calves killed by a bolt of lightning. Fayette, Alabama, 24 Jersey cows. McHenry County, Illinois, 12 cows. Camden, South Carolina, 11 cows. Lorida, Florida, 21 milk cows at a dairy farm killed instantly when lightning struck a barbed wire fence near where they were standing in a pasture. Grangeville, Idaho, 7 cattle killed by a bolt of lightning. Eastern Pennsylvania, 16 cows killed by lightning strikes. New Prague, Minnesota, 10 cattle killed by a lightning bolt. All these incidents happened during an eight-week period in July and August of 1977. It amounts to a lot of lightning-killed livestock.

The most notorious livestock-killing lightning bolt struck in Wasatch National Forest in Utah on July 22, 1918. It struck dead a flock of 504 sheep. A photograph of that scene shows an almost continuous mass of sheep bodies spread across a broad, sparsely wooded hilltop.

Seldom are human beings struck down by lightning in large numbers. But there are a few extraordinary cases on record. The French astronomer Nicholas Camille Flammarion told this amazing story, from more than a century ago:

> Mr. Cardan relates that eight harvesters, taking their noonday repast under a maple tree during a thunderstorm, were killed by one stroke of lightning. When approached by their companions after the storm had cleared away, they seemed to be still at their repast. One was raising a glass to drink, another was in the act of taking a piece of bread, and a third was reaching out his hand to a plate. There they sat as if petrified, in the exact position in which death surprised them.

One of the worst cases of multiple human fatalities in the United States directly from a lightning strike happened on July 12, 1961. Nine tobacco workers ranging in age from 13 to 70 had taken shelter in a tobacco barn three miles south of Clinton, North Carolina. Lightning apparently struck a metal heating system against which they were leaning. Only one of the nine workers survived.

The worst death toll in the world from a single lightning bolt happened when lightning hit a hut near Umtali, Rhodesia, December 23, 1975. Twenty-one persons inside the hut were killed.

On July 31, 1949, lightning struck a baseball diamond at Baker, Florida, during a game. The bolt dug a ditch 20 feet long in the infield, killed the shortstop and first baseman, fatally injured the second baseman, and injured 50 persons in a crowd of 300 spectators. On September 7, 1970, lightning struck a school football field at Saint Petersburg, Florida, during a game. Two players in the huddle were killed and 21 other players injured.

Lightning has been implicated in several tragic aircraft accidents. The crash and fire of the zeppelin Hindenburg in 1937 occurred when an electrical storm was nearby, and may well have been caused by static electricity igniting the craft's hydrogen when landing lines made contact with the ground. The explosion of a jet liner near Elkton, Maryland, in 1963 killing all 81 on board is attributed to lightning igniting residual fuel vapor in one of the outboard wing tanks as the plane passed through a tremendous thunderstorm.

Most people realize that lightning is a major cause of forest fires—at least 7,500 a year in the nation as a whole, or an average of 20 a day. Such fires destroyed 2 million acres of forest in California and Alaska alone during July and August of 1977. But lightning has also caused many damaging industrial fires, such as the disastrous oil fire at San Luis Obispo, California, on April 7, 1926. The fire lasted five days, spread over 900 acres and burned nearly 6 million barrels of oil. In another lightning-triggered blaze on July 1, 1933, 300,000 barrels of oil were destroyed at the Texas Oil Co. plant in Elizabeth, New Jersey. A spectacular oil fire was started by lightning on July 5, 1900, at the Standard Oil refinery at Bayonne, New Jersey, on Newark Bay. The column of smoke rose to 13,000 feet during the three-day blaze, and oil was burning on the waters of the bay.

The most costly lightning stroke in the United States is considered to be the one that hit an ammunition magazine at an army arsenal in Northern New Jersey on July 10, 1926. It set off a series of explosions. All buildings within 2,700 feet were destroyed and 16 persons were killed. Debris fell as far as 22 miles away. Property damage from this single lightning bolt was placed at $70 million.

The susceptibility of today's interdependent technological society to lightning was dramatically brought home to millions of people on the night of July 13, 1977. At 8:37 P.M. lightning from one of a series of thunderstorms that had been sweeping through New York State struck an electrical transmission tower in Westchester County and short-circuited two 345,000-volt lines. There quickly followed a series of equipment malfunctions and at least one serious error by a system operator. When a second lightning bolt knocked out two more lines of the same voltage at 8:55 P.M., the electrical system serving New York City cascaded toward collapse, and by 9:36 P.M. the New York City metropolitan area was plunged into darkness. Subways halted. Elevators stopped. Air conditioners went off. Power was completely restored only after 24 hours. In contrast to the blackout of 1965, this night of darkness stimulated widespread looting and destruction in several areas of the city.

An extraordinary case of a lightning bolt nearly incapacitating one of the most complex technological systems ever built happened November 14, 1969, in Florida. This time the target was not on the ground but in the air, rising like a rocket. In fact it *was* a rocket, a Saturn 5, and in a capsule at its top were nestled the three Apollo 12 astronauts, lifting off for the moon. Less than half a minute after the 11:22 A.M. launch, with Apollo 12 barely a mile and a half above the earth, a brilliant bolt of electricity appeared between the rocket and the ground. Virtually all the electrical equipment in the spacecraft suddenly shut down. Row upon row of abruptly opened circuit breakers glowed ominously green. The vital inertial platform, heart of the Apollo guidance system, began drifting. "I don't know what happened here. We had everything in the world drop out," Apollo 12 Commander Charles Conrad radioed to the ground. Fortunately, within three minutes the crew managed to get all the circuits back in operation, and they went on to a successful landing on the moon. But the incident brought about a series of measures to mitigate lightning hazards in space launches and stimulated broad new programs of lightning research.

Lightning is such a powerful and transitory phenomenon that it poses formidable obstacles to our attempts to better understand it. With the spectacular violence it unleashes from the heavens, no wonder the ancients viewed it in supernatural terms, a manifestation of the gods. The divine origin of lightning is a part of the mythologies of Indian, Greek, Roman, Egyptian, Japanese, Chinese, and Tibetan cultures and of many tribal societies as well.

The Roman poet and philosopher Lucretius 2,000 years ago set the stage for modern understanding of lightning by casting aside superstitious views about its origin. In a series of remarkable observations published in his *The Nature of the Universe,* he correctly concluded that lightning is associated with unstable air conditions, that it forms in clouds of great vertical depth, that it is a consequence of a sudden release of stress, and that lightning and thunder are created in the same instant within the cloud. He thought that the heating effects of lightning were caused by friction, but then he didn't know about electricity.

And that brings us to Benjamin Franklin. When I was a youngster, I suspected that the tales of Franklin and his lightning studies and his kite were in the same category as the stories about George Washington and the cherry tree and never telling a lie— one of those charming legends or exaggerated half-truths our elders like to have us believe about our forefathers so that we'll be sure to see them as larger than life. But in fact, Franklin did carry out the first systematic scientific investigation of lightning, and he did prove that it is an electric discharge or giant spark. He was, and still is, internationally respected as a first-rate creative and innovative scientist (although the word hadn't been invented then). His lightning rod eventually liberated an age from the helplessness of watching churches and houses destroyed and ships sunk by the sudden flash of lightning from the sky. And, although he carried out many other elegant electrical experiments as well, he did on that day in June, 1752, in the pivotal demonstration, fly a kite in a thunderstorm. Extending a short length above the top of the kite was a metal wire. At the bottom of the kite twine he attached a metal key. A brief length of silk ribbon insulated him from the key.

Joseph Priestley, later himself to become a renowned chemist, got the details from Franklin in London:

> . . . At length, just as he was beginning to despair of his contrivance, he observed some loose threads of the hempen string to stand erect, and to avoid one another, just as if they had been suspended on a common conductor. Struck with this promising appearance, he immediately presented his knuckle to the key and the discovery was complete. He perceived a very evident electrical spark.

Franklin's demonstration that lightning was an electrical discharge was a scientific sensation. Because of that, his lightning rod, and his other electrical experiments, he went on to receive virtually every honor that could be bestowed by his contemporaries. (The marvel is that Franklin was not killed during his kite experiment.)

One of the long-recognized fundamental properties of a thundercloud is that its uppermost part tends to be positively charged, the lower part negatively charged. (There is also often a small area of positive charge within the large area of negative charge at the base of the cloud.) To this day, scientists are arguing about what exactly accounts for this distribution of charge within a storm. We'll get to that in a few moments.

As a thunderstorm moves over the landscape, its negatively charged base induces a positive charge over the ground below and extending out for several miles beyond the storm. This induced positive charge follows the storm like an invisible electrical shadow. The stronger the cloud's charge, the stronger the induced charge below. The potential difference may reach as much as 100 million volts. The positive ground current flows up high objects such as trees, hills, and buildings in an effort to establish a connection with the opposite charge in the cloud above. Air, being a poor conductor, however, discourages the connection. Until something else is done, no current can flow.

What is done is invisible to the eye. The charged cloud sneakily finds a way to gradually lessen the electrical separation between it and the oppositely charged ground. Guy Murchie has compared this process to an ancient army crossing a small stream. The first soldier picks up a small rock and throws it into the water on the opposite bank. Other soldiers join him, and soon the stones have formed a jetty, getting larger and growing back toward the soldiers as they continue throwing stones. As soon as the jetty has become a causeway, the soldiers all rush over (like lightning) to the opposite side.

In much the same way, early electrical action prepares the atmosphere and forms, in effect, a bridge for the main surge of current to suddenly rush across.

First a small amount of current advances downward toward the ground. This pilot leader blazes the path for a larger but as yet still invisible series of charges that proceed downward in steps. One proceeds several hundred feet, pauses, then another follows down the path and extends it a few more hundred feet. Step after step the charges proceed downward. This step leader, as it is known, repeats the sequence perhaps as many as 40 times until a conductive path of ionized (electrified) particles is near the ground. Discharge streamers on the ground, usually from some high point, extend upward to complete the conductive channel between the cloud and ground.

With the circuit completed, a tremendous surge of electricity, called the return, or main stroke, leaps upward along the channel at speeds of one-third to half the speed of light. The enormous energy released causes the surrounding atoms and molecules in the air to glow, and this light brilliantly illuminates the previously formed, descending, step leaders. It is the illumination coming from this intense, upward return stroke lighting up the downward-pointing zig-zagged step leaders that we see as lightning. Thus, although the main electrical surge in a cloud-to-ground lightning flash is upward, our eyes perceive it as downward because the step leaders are pointing downward. The process is a curious trick on our senses, a turning of our perceptions upside down. (The rarer ground-to-cloud-initiated lightning produces step leaders pointing upward, branching toward the sky like a tree.)

Once the return stroke has firmly established the electrical path and itself dissipated, dart leaders may fork down out of the cloud to initiate usually three or four secondary return strokes (the most ever recorded is 26) along the same path. These continue until the electrical difference between the cloud and ground has diminished and brought the opposing sides back into temporary balance.

The whole process from initiation of a pilot leader until fade-away of the final secondary return strokes may last a second. The visible discharge (the flash) itself, including the return strokes, lasts about two-tenths of a second, and the separate strokes within a discharge have faintly luminous phases each lasting several thousandths of a second and separated by intervals of a few hundredths of a second. The eye can just perceive such individual strokes, and that is why lightning appears to flicker.

The heat generated by a lightning stroke can be as great as 30,000° C (50,000° F) or five times the temperature of the surface of the sun. The sudden expansion of the surrounding air because of this intense heat creates a sound wave which we hear as thunder. A nearby strike of lightning produces a sharp crack of thunder. More distant strikes produce the distinctive low rumble of thunder. The lower pitch is due to the attenuation of higher frequencies. The rumbling results from the sound reaching you at slightly different times because of both the differing distances from you to parts of the lightning channel and the reflection of the sound waves off clouds, hills, and buildings.

Probably everyone has estimated the distance of a lightning flash by the interval until thunder is heard. (I'm often surprised at how close it turns out to be.) For all practical purposes, the lightning is seen at the moment it occurs, but the sound travels just a little more than 1,000 feet a second. So, if thunder is heard five seconds after the lightning is seen, the lightning struck about one mile away. (In a distant active storm, it is often difficult to tell which rumble of thunder is associated with which flash of lightning.)

We all have been startled by a tremendous crack of thunder from a nearby lightning strike, but there is no reason to fear it. If you heard the thunder, the lightning has already struck.

The lightning stroke between cloud and ground described so far is what we all tend to think of as a typical lightning discharge. Yet, flashes within clouds are about five times more frequent. Most of the light from these lightning flashes is obscured by the clouds, so we usually don't think of them as being so dramatic. Even a cloud-to-ground lightning stroke, recent research is showing, takes place mostly within the cloud itself. The visible part we see descending down out of the cloud base is only a portion of the total stroke.

Lightning can take several forms other than the streak or forked lightning typical of cloud-to-ground flashes or the sheet lightning that illuminates large areas in cloud-to-cloud discharges. I do not recall ever seeing ribbon lightning, and I feel I've missed something. Ribbon lightning is streaked lightning whose conductive channel is blown sideways by the wind during a multiple-stroke flash. Each successive stroke might occur three feet farther to the right, for example, and the whole appearance is as if a camera has been moved sideways while taking a picture of a single stroke. Beaded or chain lightning appears as an interrupted stroke.

Ball lightning is the least understood and most controversial.

An 18-stroke lightning flash, the multiple strokes revealed by horizontal motion of the camera during flash. (MARX BROOK)

Its highly sporadic occurrence doesn't make it amenable to controlled observation. A few scientists even doubt its existence,
feeling that many reports are due to optical illusions produced
by normal lightning. Undoubtedly, some reports of ball lightning are exaggerations or otherwise unreliable descriptions of
less exotic phenomena. The general view, however, seems to be
that ball lightning occurs, but so rarely and unpredictably that
scientific study of it is next to impossible.

Ball lightning seems to be less rare in Europe than in North
America (a reverse of the situation with tornadoes). One such
case in Paris, on July 5, 1852, was the subject of sworn statements to the French Academy of Science. In a fourth-floor
apartment, a tailor was waiting out a severe thunderstorm. A
short time after he heard a loud thunderclap, the wooden frame
closing the fireplace for the summer was pushed out. Then a
fiery ball about the size of a man's head emerged from the opening and began moving about the room, a few inches from the
floor. It was glowing brightly but gave off no heat. It approached
the tailor's feet which he raised up to let it pass. He watched it
move slowly about the room then suddenly rise about a yard
off the floor and become elongated. It then flew to the hole in
the wall where in the winter the curved stovepipe of the fireplace entered the chimney. For the summer the stovepipe had
been removed and the opening covered with heavy wrapping
paper. The ball entered the hole, causing the paper to be peeled
off in the process, rose up the chimney and exploded. The top
portion of the chimney was destroyed.

Another case was related by a New Jersey man recalling an
incident that happened to him at a boys' camp in Chicopee,
Pennsylvania, in 1925 or 1926. He was sitting on his bunk next
to an open window during a thunderstorm when suddenly he
saw coming directly toward him a yellow ball of fire about the
size of a basketball. As he saw it heading toward his window
he pulled his head back in time to watch it pass through the
window and right past his head, go through the cabin and out
the opposite window. There was no damage and no noise.

Some scientists have spent a lifetime in lightning research
and have never seen ball lightning. But a few reports of ball
lightning have been made by scientists. Two of the most significant were by J. Durward, one-time deputy director of the
British Meteorological Office. In Scotland in the summer of
1934, he and his son saw a ball of fire about a foot across move

out from among some pine trees. It moved toward them and struck an iron gate post while the boy had his hand on the latch. The boy yelled in pain and his arm was so numb that he could not lower it for several hours. Four years later in a BOAC flying boat flying through a dark raincloud over France, Durward saw what appeared to be a ball of fire enter the cockpit window, which the pilot had left open because of the poor visibility. The ball passed through the cockpit so close to the pilot that it singed his eyebrows and burned holes in his safety belt, passed on into the rear passenger cabin and loudly exploded.

All in all, ball lightning seems to consist of a large amount of electrical energy concentrated in a small volume. It remains stable only a short time, prefers to follow electrical conductors (although that's not always the case), and often ends in a loud but harmless explosion. Without systematic observations, a good scientific understanding of ball lightning is elusive. Few scientists hold much hope that the situation will soon improve.

The processes that electrify a thunderstorm itself are also still far from understood. Most theories of cloud electrification are intimately tied to the process of precipitation, but exactly what happens is not at all clear. Very likely a combination of circumstances and effects are at work.

Theories of thunderstorm electrification are in quite a tangle. A wide variety of competing ideas are hotly (or at least warmly) debated, speculation often substituting for an admitted scarcity of hard information. There is no consensus view. It's an area, says one scientist, "where there are as many theories as there are investigators."

Marx Brook, a veteran lightning researcher at the New Mexico Institute of Mining and Technology in Socorro, feels the immediate need is to forget about theorizing, which he considers premature for now, and get on with collecting the kind of hard data that's been missing. It is not an easy task. The thunderstorm is a hostile environment for study, and its electrical properties are difficult to monitor in any instantaneous "snapshot." Progress is, however, being made.

Brook and colleague Paul R. Krehbiel have been using arrays of as many as 10 electric field-charge antennas placed around thunderstorms in New Mexico and Florida to measure with reasonable accuracy the three-dimensional positions and magnitudes of the sites of negative charge within the cloud that serve as sources of cloud-to-ground lightning flashes. They have found that the flashes almost always originate within one particular temperature level of the cloud. Ninety-five percent of all the flashes whose sources have been calculated originate in the cloud layer that is between $-10°$ and $-20°$ Celsius (roughly equivalent to $+15°$ to $-5°$ Fahrenheit).

This may seem like a fairly broad temperature range, but it represents only a small proportion of the total thundercloud. The part of the cloud that is between $-10°$ and $-20°$ C is a layer only a little more than a mile thick out of a total cloud height from top to bottom of six to 10 miles. It's a fairly small horizontal slice of the cloud. Hardly any cloud-to-ground lightning flashes originate above or below that layer, Brook and Krehbiel have found.

Now, the remarkable thing is that this finding holds true of summer storms in both New Mexico and Florida, even though cloud conditions in the two areas are considerably different. New Mexico summer thunderstorms have higher bases, and only a relatively small section of the lower part of the cloud is warmer than freezing ($0°$ C). Florida thunderstorms tend to extend down quite close to the surface, and a very large section of their lower part is warmer than freezing. Still, the negatively charged area that serves as the source of cloud-to-ground lightning lies between $-10°$ and $-20°$ C in both types of clouds, even though it is higher above the cloud base in the Florida thunderstorms.

Other remote-sensing studies of lightning have shown much the same results. Lightning research led by W. David Rust at the National Severe Storms Laboratory in Oklahoma using radio triangulation (lightning discharges produce crackles on the radio) has shown that clusters of lightning activity are tied to this temperature level. David Proctor in South Africa has shown that the sources of lightning flashes there are at $-10°$ C or colder. Arthur Few, in Texas, has recorded the sounds picked up by an array of microphones and also finds the charge confined to that same temperature layer.

The identification of this $-10°$ to $-20°$ region as the source of lightning charges is "a very significant result," says Brook. "It eliminates some ideas. Any theories now have to explain why the lightning originates in one region only and why the cloud boundaries don't make any difference—why it doesn't matter how much cloud there is above or how much warm cloud below."

Lightning over Rio Grande Valley of New Mexico. (MARX BROOK)

What's so special about −10° to −20° C? Water droplets in a cloud continue in liquid form below normal freezing temperatures if they have no particle around which to condense. In this state they are known as supercooled. Droplets can remain supercooled down to a temperature of about −10° C. Below that they begin to freeze spontaneously. So lightning seems to have its origin at the level where droplets are making the transition from liquid to ice, and where there is an abundant mixture of supercooled water, graupel (soft hail), and probably some snow in co-existence. This fits with most precipitation-linked theories of thunderstorm electrification. This water-graupel-snow mixture would be available for the interactions that produce electrical charge.

The New Mexico group has also designed rapid-scan radars that can locate sources of precipitation within a thunderstorm more accurately than normal weather radar. They spin vertically four times per second and get a complete picture of the sky overhead every 15 seconds. Using an array of such radars in association with other monitoring equipment, they have shown that with the −10° to −20° region the negative charge source for lightning seems to coincide with vertical shafts of precipitation.

This was true, for instance, of an unusual lightning flash that struck a weather tower at the Kennedy Space Center in Florida in 1976 under the instrumental scrutiny of lightning experimenters from half a dozen universities and agencies working together in a still-continuing project known as Thunderstorm Research International Program (TRIP). The charge source for the three-stroke flash not only originated in the $-10°$ to $-20°$ layer but also coincided with a vertical shaft of precipitation inferred to be graupel or hail. This particular flash became the most comprehensively studied single lightning flash ever. (Among other things, the first stroke had a peak current of between 150,000 and 640,000 amps and the second stroke, between 200,000 and 870,000 amps. Previous studies indicate that peak currents in the range of 200,000 amps occur less than 1 percent of the time; 30,000 amps is more typical.)

Lightning research using a variety of ground-based remote sensors is now attempting to relate lightning production to the other dynamic events going on inside a thunderstorm. Rust and NOAA physicist William L. Taylor in Oklahoma are tracing the lightning bolt back to its origin with the storm by sensing the radio-frequency signal emitted along each branch of the lightning stroke.

They have found quite a distinction between intracloud and cloud-to-ground lightning. Cloud-to-ground discharges are associated with radio impulses that are confined to a relatively small region of the storm. The impulses associated with intracloud lightning are produced at much higher rates and are located throughout a large horizontal extent of the storm. "We've found that lightning formation is an extremely long, horizontal process," Rust says, "especially in the big storms we get in Oklahoma, where the whole electrical web of a lightning stroke can be tens of kilometers long." Since a kilometer is more than six-tenths of a mile, he's talking about quite a broad distance.

Their results also confirm that the lightning we see, the cloud-to-ground discharges, are, says Rust, "really a very small part of the overall lightning activity in a storm."

In late 1978, Rust and colleague Edwin W. Szymanski reported that the National Severe Storms Laboratory's powerful Doppler radar had detected lightning echoes as far away as 110 miles, and that didn't seem to be the limit. Radar detection of lightning at such distances is still another new aid that may help unravel some of lightning's hidden mysteries.

In the summer of 1979, scientists in the TRIP research project planned to gather in New Mexico and concentrate a formidable array of radio, acoustic, and Doppler radar remote sensors together with aircraft on a single isolated thunderstorm. The goal was to obtain for the first time a detailed description of the electrical and dynamic evolution of a storm. Then perhaps some of the uncertainties about what creates lightning could be resolved.

Satellites too have recently shown their value in charting lightning. Satellites were responsible for the detection of unusually intense lightning strokes called superbolts. Superbolts are lightning flashes over 100 times more intense than typical lightning.

Superbolts were discovered by Air Force Vela satellites. Four of the satellites are equally spaced around the earth so that all the earth's surface is in view at all times. Their primary mission is to detect nuclear explosions, but the Vela optical sensors record thousands of lightning flashes each year. B. N. Turman of the Air Force Technical Applications Center reported to the American Geophysical Union in 1977 that Vela sensors had recorded a few such signals so extremely bright that he said they deserve the description "superbolt."

A typical lightning bolt has an optical power of about 1 billion watts. The superbolt flashes radiate 100 billion to 10 trillion (10^{11}–10^{13}) watts. They are quite rare. Combined with other information, Turman says, the observations indicate that about two lightning flashes in 1,000 exceed 100 billion watts and perhaps five flashes in 10 million exceed 3 trillion watts.

These tremendous lightning flashes have been seen scattered about the world but they seem to be especially concentrated over the North Pacific off the coast of Japan. Winter storms over this area are noted for very intense but infrequent lightning discharges, and studies indicate that the flashes originate not in the lower, negatively charged regions of the clouds but in the high-altitude positive layers. These storms form as the air leaving Siberia is rapidly heated by the warm sea, and the upper, positive layers are blown far forward of the main body of the storm, allowing them to discharge directly to the ground.

A program using a satellite to map for the first time worldwide lightning activity is now underway by Turman and Bruce

C. Edgar of the Aerospace Corporation in Los Angeles. For this they are using a lightning detector aboard an Air Force DMSP Flight 2 meteorological satellite, in orbit since July, 1977, 500 miles above the earth. The satellite's polar (north-south) orbit is such that it is always passing along the length of the boundary between day and night on earth. So it sees lightning occurring at dusk during half its orbit, lightning occurring at dawn on the other side of the earth during the other half. As the planet turns beneath it, the satellite eventually scans the whole globe.

The first such global view was for August-December and was reported in 1978. Over land, it reveals much more lightning at dusk than at dawn. This is expected, since most thunderstorms over land come about from convection caused by afternoon warming of the surface.

The reverse was true over the oceans. Lightning is far more prevalent at dawn than at dusk. This is presumably due to thunderstorms formed by radiative cooling of the atmosphere over the oceans during the night. Most, but not all, dusk lightning over the oceans seems to be associated with weather over nearby land masses.

In general, there is far less lightning over the oceans than over land, although significant pockets of lightning activity do show up over the oceans.

Regions of highest lightning activity identified by the satellite correspond closely with those areas classically regarded as lightning capitals of the world. Among them: the Southeastern United States, the Gulf of Mexico, Central America, Central Africa, Southeast Asia, India, and Southern China. Lightning maps produced from the satellite data are filled almost solid with symbols for lightning over those areas. Edgar notes that over the Southeastern United States and Gulf of Mexico there is little dawn-dusk variation in amount of lightning. He speculates that this is probably because the warm Gulf waters can maintain through the night thunderstorm activity started over land regions during the day.

Between August and November, the satellite reveals a dramatic shift of lightning activity from the Northern Hemisphere to the Southern Hemisphere. This is apparently due to the change of seasons. As fall thunderstorms fade out in the Northern Hemisphere, spring storms in the Southern Hemisphere get underway. The satellite lightning maps show this shift clearly, a unique and strikingly visual way of following the change of seasons. The previously strong Gulf of Mexico activity at dusk has now diminished to near nothing. Lightning activity is now particularly strong over Central South America, Southern Africa, and Australia at dusk and over the far southern ocean regions at dawn.

From all these satellite observations, Edgar has tried to do rough estimates of the global frequency of lightning. The satellite sees only about the brightest 8 percent of lightning flashes in its field of view. If you then further assume that clouds obscure five to 10 flashes for every one detectable, the rate calculated from satellite data agrees roughly with the estimate of 100 lightning flashes per second over the earth first cited more than half a century ago but still, says Edgar, largely untested. "However," he cautions, "such calculations [from the satellite data] are purely speculative until accurate ground-satellite coordinated observations now in progress can be evaluated."

Nevertheless, the space-borne observations are giving the first global snapshots of lightning. Thus from far above where the ancients thought Thor split the thunderclouds with his hammer and Zeus hurled down thunderbolts in anger, we now have our own silently circling sensors continually charting the brilliant flashes of energy that humanity has long treated with awe. Our understanding may be greater than that of our ancient ancestors, but we nevertheless share with them the same sense of mystery and much the same vulnerability to the sudden and sometimes terrible violence of lightning.

CHAPTER 4

Hail

Hail, the sudden scourge of farmers round the world, deals its devastation to families by ruining their livelihood. Unlike drought or plagues of insects, the assault is not gradual. The *blitzkrieg* of hail is over in minutes. What moments before was a healthy crop of wheat or corn or cotton or soybeans soon to yield a bountiful harvest to support a family over the coming year is now a pulverized mass of battered vegetation, suitable only for plowing under and starting over. A year's work and hopes destroyed in a few minutes' violent outpouring of stones from the sky.

To my mind, no one has described the dread and tragedy of hail better than the late Hal Borland, recalling the hailstorms of his boyhood on a farm on the high wheat plains of Eastern Colorado:

> The heartbreaking thing about hail is that it wipes you out in the passing of a cloud. . . . It waits till you've built big hopes and dreams, then wipes them out in one devastating stroke.
>
> Hail waits till the wheat is tall and golden with ripeness, the heads full and the kernels fat, the wealth right there, only a week or two away from harvest. You can almost hear the dollars clinking in your pocket. Then that greenish cloud comes and the air turns cold as November and the lightning rips the sky apart. Between lightning flashes it is as dark as dusk. It starts to rain, slashing rain, and you stand in the doorway and watch the dark rain turn to a white curtain coming across the fields. You hear it coming and you know nothing in God's world can stop it. It comes across the wheat fields

A Colorado hailstorm dropping a wide swath of hail. On the ground farmers can only wait and hope this one misses them. (NOAA)

with a deafening roar and across the farmyard and on across the fields beyond. And when it has passed, you go out and walk across the yard, the ice crunching underfoot, hail sometimes the size of peas, sometimes big as hens' eggs. You see but don't notice the chickens stoned to death. You see the broken windows and the splintered shingles on the roof, and you don't notice them either. You are looking at the devastated fields, the beaten, ragged wheat fields now covered with hail, devastation that came and passed, ruin complete, in 10 minutes. Half an hour ago you had a half-section of wheat—320 acres—ready to harvest and haul to town. Now you haven't got a penny. . . . You are broke and in debt. . . . You've got a leaky roof and broken windows. And a wife who says, "I don't see why we keep on farming when things like this happen. I so hoped this year—" And she begins to cry. You are filled with weariness, bone tired, and there's a nauseating gripe in your belly, a wrenching at your heart. You can already taste the mush and beans you'll have to live on next winter. But you'll try again. You know that. You'll go to the bank and try to get another loan to pay for seed wheat, pledging your land because there's nothing else left to pledge, not one blessed thing.

That's hail. That's what hail does to a man.*

Hail is a fickle and mercurial foe. Your crops may be spared, your neighbor's in the next section over ruined. Your time may come next year, in 10 years, or never. You have no way of knowing. Every hailstorm is followed by anxious comparing of reports. Who got hit, who didn't. And if you were missed again, you feel a thankful tug in your heart, and you give perhaps a silent prayer of gratitude that it wasn't you.

Hail, like lightning, is an underrated hazard, but for a different reason. While lightning singles out widely scattered, individual victims for death, thus avoiding the attention drawn to multiple fatalities, hail rarely takes lives, instead visiting its destruction upon the crops necessary for life. In both instances the effects are tragic, but neither gets too much publicity: it is death tolls that take the headlines.

Not that hail doesn't at times kill. Hailstones described as "as large as cricket balls" fell over the Moradabad and Beheri districts of Northern India, near New Delhi, on April 30, 1888, killing 246 persons. Many died instantly. Others were battered down by the huge chunks of ice, became buried by the hail drifts, and died of cold and exposure. More than 1,600 cattle, sheep, and goats were killed.

An eyewitness to this hailstorm said it came with a terrific wind that blew away verandas and caved in part of his roof. "The walls shook. It was nearly dark outside, and hailstones of an enormous size were dashed down with a force which I have never seen anything equal." All the windows and glass doors of the house were broken. The destruction was confined to a fairly small area of six or seven miles around Moradabad. "Men caught in the open were simply pounded to death by the hail. Fourteen bodies were found in the race course."

A severe hailstorm in the western part of Hunan Province in Southeast China on June 19, 1932, killed some 200 persons and injured thousands.

A dispatch from a correspondent from *The Times* of London and reported in the journal *Nature* in 1936 told of a deadly hail-

* Passage abridged from pp. 79–80 in *Country Editor's* Boy by Hal Borland (J. B. Lippincott). Copyright © 1970 by Hal Borland. Reprinted by permission of Harper & Row, Publishers, Inc.

storm that pelted an area of Northern Transvaal on February 1
of that year. Nineteen members of the Barolong tribe were killed.
"About three inches of rain fell in a few minutes, and then came
the hail, which consisted of jagged lumps of ice. In 30 minutes
the hail was lying everywhere to a depth of three feet and in
some cases the dead natives had to be dug out of it. There were
many cattle killed, which the natives afterward dragged away
on sleighs. Whole crops were obliterated, and there are said to
be over 1,000 native families afflicted in the area."

Hailstones the size of hens' eggs killed six children and injured
10 others at Klausenberg, Rumania, on May 1, 1928. A hailstorm in the Siatista district of Greece on June 13, 1930, killed
22 persons. And at Rostov, Russia, on July 10, 1923, hailstones
said to have weighed between one and two pounds killed 23
persons and many cattle. Most of the victims were peasants who
had rushed out into the fields to try to save their cattle.

In view of such fatal maulings, the account in the Book of
Joshua (10:11) of a fatal hailstorm does not seem so farfetched:
"As they ran from Israel . . . the Eternal rained huge hailstones from heaven upon them . . . they died of these. Indeed
more died by the hailstones than at the hands of Israel by the
sword."

A similar severe hailstorm is described in Exodus (10:24):
"The Eternal rained hail on the land of Egypt, most fearful hail,
such as never had been seen in all Egypt ever since it was a
nation. The hail struck down all that grew in the fields and broke
all the trees."

Devastating hailstorms have figured prominently in several
more recent events in history. One of them took a direct toll of
death of man and beast and brought about a peace accord. In
May of 1360, the army of Edward III was situated between
Chartres and Paris getting ready to renew war on France. An
incredible hailstorm struck. Hailstones the size of "goose eggs"
crashed down. "It seemed," reports the chronicler Sir John Froissart, "as if the world were to come to an end. Giant hailstones
killed men and horses, and even the most courageous were terrified." The *Old Chronicle* says the "hailstones [were] so pro-
digious as to instantly kill 6,000 of [Edward's] horses and 1,000
of his best troops." These numbers are suspect, but the impact on
King Edward is not. He was so affected that he vowed he would
conclude a peace. The result was the treaty of Brétigny.

More than four centuries later, on the morning of July 13,

1788, two great hailstorms began in Southwest France and swept nearly 500 miles to the northeast in parallel bands about 12 miles apart. Some 1,039 communes were affected by the hail. Crops were greatly damaged, and the harvest was ruined. The resulting food shortage was a factor in causing the French Revolution in 1789.

The United States has also had hail fatalities. On May 8, 1784, "a most extraordinary shower of hail," with "pieces of ice measuring nine inches in circumference" struck the area of Winnsborough, South Carolina. According to a dispatch in the *South Carolina Gazette*, "It killed several Negroes, a great number of sheep, lambs, geese, and the feathered inhabitants of the woods without numbers." Trees were stripped of their leaves and even their bark. "But what is still more astonishing," said the dispatch, which was dated 46 days after the event, "there are at this time many wagon loads of hailstones unmelted, lying in the hollows and gullies on the Wateree."

The most recent known hail fatality in the United States was on May 13, 1930, when a 39-year-old farmer was caught in the open during a hailstorm near Lubbock, Texas, and died of his injuries.

Humans usually have access to shelter, but animals are more vulnerable to the onslaught of severe hail. An analysis by a U.S. Fish and Wildlife Service biologist of the effects of a violent hailstorm that left a five-mile-wide path of destruction along a 150-mile-long strip of Alberta Province, Canada, on July 14, 1953, found that the storm had killed at least 36,000 ducks and ducklings as well as thousands of songbirds, hawks, owls, and other birds. Hundreds of the ducks died of crushed skulls and many had their upper mandibles torn away. Four days later, another hailstorm swept through the same area, this time killing an estimated 27,000 ducks and ducklings.

Hogs, calves, squirrels, lizards, rabbits, chickens, and other small animals are occasional victims of hail, and cattle and horses are often injured, sometimes fatally. On July 15, 1978, more than 200 sheep were killed in three counties of Montana by baseball-sized hail from an intense storm.

Animals have also been known to become involved in hail in another way. Take this report of an unusual hailstorm at Dubuque, Iowa, on June 16, 1882. According to the report in the *Monthly Weather Review*, "for thirteen minutes . . . the largest and most destructive hailstones fell that were ever seen at this place." They measured one to 17 inches in circumference, and the largest weighed one pound, twelve ounces. A number of persons were cut and bruised by falling hailstones and one florist lost 2,387 panes of glass. But the extraordinary item was this: "The foreman of the Novelty Iron Works, of this city, states that in two large hailstones, melted by him, were found small living frogs."

Other small animals have also been reported found inside hailstones. An account in the same journal of a hailstorm at Vicksburg, Mississippi, on May 11, 1894, tells of a small gopher turtle entirely encased in ice that fell with the hail. A one-and-a-half-inch carp was found inside a hailstone in Germany. The apparent explanation for such occasional supposed findings is that local whirls or gusts carry objects from the earth's surface up to the cloud region, where they become involved in the hail-forming process.

The force of hail can occasionally do dreadful things even to the metal-skinned birds man has built to fly through the clouds. In 1959, a Strategic Air Command B-52 bomber got caught in the hail-producing region of a severe thunderstorm. Baseball-sized hailstones shattered the windshield, tore off the radome, hammered the leading edges of the wings nearly flat, and punctured holes in the wings and engine coverings, sending pieces of metal into the jet turbines. The electrical system temporarily failed, and the giant aircraft went out of control. The crew readied to bail out, but the plane quickly passed through the storm. The struggle with the elements had lasted 47 seconds. The pilot then managed to land the plane with its nine-man crew safely at Carswell Air Force Base outside of Fort Worth, battered but intact.

Hail itself can come in a remarkable variety of shapes. Most hailstones are spheroidal or irregular. But hailstones have been found in the shape of disks, saucers, doughnuts (with holes), stars, tears, acorns, hourglasses, rhombohedral crystals, pyramids, and cones. The pyramids and cones apparently are parts of complete spheres of ice that may burst or become split up into segments in their fall through the air. One observer estimated that 24 of the "perfect pyramids" he found after one storm would fit together to make a sphere.

The key characteristic of hail is its enormous variability, in size, time, and space. Storm researcher Stanley A. Changnon, Jr., of the Illinois State Water Survey shows a picture of hailstones

Airliner after flight through hailstorm. (NOAA)

of a dozen different sizes found from one storm in Colorado and on a surface no larger than the average kitchen floor.

Hailstones range from the size of grapeshot to grapefruit. Occasionally, bigger ones fall. Until 1970, the largest hailstone documented in the United States was one that fell at Potter, Nebraska, on July 6, 1928. It was 17 inches in circumference and weighed 1.51 pounds. But on September 3, 1970, a fierce storm battered the town of Coffeyville, Kansas, with numerous stones larger than grapefruit. One huge one was preserved in a freezer and then sent to the National Center for Atmospheric Research in Boulder, Colorado, for scientific study. It measured 17.5 inches in circumference and weighed 1.67 pounds. Study of thin cross sections of the Coffeyville hailstone by Charles and Nancy Knight carried out in a special cold room at NCAR confirmed it to be one single hailstone, displaying growth layers roughly analogous to the rings of a tree. It was estimated that because of its size it must have fallen at nearly 100 miles per hour.

Probably the most hail-prone region of the world is the Kericho and Nandi Hills area of Kenya in East Africa. Hail falls there an incredible average of 132 days a year. This also hap-

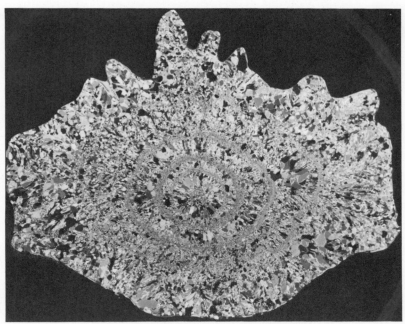

Cross section of record-breaking Coffeyville, Kansas, hailstone photographed in polarized light. (NCAR)

pens to be the area of Kenya's lucrative tea plantations, and these severe and localized hailstorms cause serious damage to the tea crops. In late 1978, Russell C. Schnell of the National Oceanic and Atmospheric Administration Laboratories in Boulder and his wife Suan N. Tan-Schnell reported that the hail-tea link apparently is not coincidental. Their studies show that organic litter from the tea plants on the ground between the rows of tea trees contains dustlike particles of just the right size to serve as the nuclei, or seed, around which hailstones can easily grow. These tiny particles, they showed, are easily churned up into the atmosphere by the activities of the hundreds of tea pickers employed in the estates. This, then, may be a case of organically induced hailstorms. As the Schnells suggest, the tea may be producing the "seeds for its own destruction."

Hail is a worldwide phenomenon, but according to Changnon the climatology for hail is more thoroughly defined for the United States than for any other nation. The findings clearly demonstrate the extreme variability of hail in all scales, whether for one point or the continent, for one minute or 50 years.

The principal hail area of North America exists along and to the lee of the eastern Rocky Mountains, stretching from New Mexico up to Montana. This area averages more hail days, more hailstorms, more and bigger hailstones, and thus a greater hail intensity than any other area in the continent.

Hail is also a problem in the Northwest where specialty crops such as tree fruits are especially vulnerable, in the Midwest grain belt, and in the central section of the East Coast, also because of specialty crops. In the Upper Midwest, hail occurs where large-scale hail-producing weather conditions are prevalent and where the Great Lakes affect hailstorm development.

The greatest frequency of hailstorms is centered roughly at the area where Wyoming, Colorado, and Nebraska meet. Here, hail falls an average of nine to 10 days a year, and the area is sometimes referred to as Hail Alley. It's not surprising, then, that the early westward-bound pioneer settlers along the California Trail from 1846 on frequently reported in their diaries undergoing barrages of hail along the Platte River in what is now Southwestern Nebraska. Eastern Colorado gets hail seven days a year, Northern New Mexico six, and upper Michigan and parts of Utah five.

But it is the intensity of hail that causes the damage. Intensity depends on the number of stones, their sizes, and the wind. Here too national variations are enormous, and Eastern Colorado finds itself bearing the brunt of the onslaught. Changnon and G. E. Stout have found that hailstorms during the peak of the loss season in Eastern Colorado produce hail that is 18 times more intense than the typical crop season loss storms in the Midwest. Intensity decreases very rapidly away from the Great Plains.

Hailstone size is a prime factor in intensity. "Look at these variations," says Changnon. "An Illinois hailfall averages 24 stones in a square foot and only about 2 percent of these are over a half-inch in diameter. In Northeastern Colorado, a hailfall averages 202 stones per square foot and more than half of these [51 percent] are larger than a half-inch."

I grew up in Northern Colorado on the edge of this high-intensity Hail Alley, and the sudden rat-a-tat-tat of white hail crashing down on everything out of a ragged-bottomed, grayish-green thundercloud was a commonplace occurrence. To the sugar-beet, corn, and dryland wheat farmers in the area it was an especially unwelcome sight and sound, but we townspeople, dependent on a healthy farm economy, were also affected. When local farmers were "hailed out" it was a sure sign that business in town would suffer. I remember one particularly severe storm that not only caused great crop damage but also left every roof in town in ruin. Homeowners and insurance companies, along with my first car, took a battering in the storm, but it was a bonanza to anyone who could pick up a hammer and do roofing work that summer.

The time and season of high hail activity vary also. Close to the Rocky Mountains hail most often falls from noon to 3 P.M. About 100 to 200 miles to the east hail is most prevalent from 3 to 6 P.M., and still farther east, around Kansas City, 6 to 9 P.M. is the most likely time. The pattern of time suggests a west-to-east sequence of storm activity. The Midwest has a high point from 2 to 5 P.M. and a secondary peak in the dark of night from midnight to 3 A.M. East of the Great Plains hail is more likely in the spring, but in the lee of the Rocky Mountains it strikes most often in the summer.

On virtually every day from April through October there is some degree of hail loss occurring in the United States. The annual toll is enormous: an average of $773 million to crops and

Hail damage to corn, Boone County, Iowa. Crop damage by hail in the United States now runs at about $1 billion a year. (NOAA)

$75 million to property (the 10-to-one ratio has shown up in several studies) for a total of $848 million. The figures increase as prices increase each year.

Few crops are spared. Soft fruits, tobacco, and beans are especially vulnerable. Nationwide, 7 percent of the plum crop, 5 percent of the dry beans, and 5 percent of the rye is lost to hail each year, but particular areas suffer far greater shares of the losses. Twenty percent of the apples grown in Utah are lost to hail each year as are 19 percent of the peaches in Texas and 18 percent of the dry beans in Nebraska. In the mountain states 13 percent of the fresh tomatoes grown each year are ruined by hail.

The large grain crops suffer the greatest total dollar damage, however. More than $100 milion worth of wheat, about $75 million of corn, and $55 million of soybeans are destroyed by hail each year in the United States. It all amounts to a hail loss of 2 percent of the nation's entire crop production. Something less than one-fourth of it is covered by insurance. The loss in foodstuffs available to an ever-growing world population is staggering. And the trend in damage is upward.

Crops aren't the only victims. Homes and automobiles can

suffer tremendous beatings from hail. In Colorado and Wyoming, the 1978 hail season was the worst in memory. More than a dozen major hailstorms pummeled the populous eastern foot-hills of the Rockies from Southern Colorado to Northern Wyoming. An estimated 75,000 homes and 60,000 vehicles were damaged. Insurance claims for property damage alone from hail in the two-state area totaled at least $100 million, compared with a typical year's losses of $1 million to $3 million. An insurance executive called it one of the costliest insurance catastrophes of the decade. "You could almost call it a quiet catastrophe. It has received little attention outside the communities involved. Hail doesn't have as much sex appeal for the news media as other types of natural disasters."

One of the more costly series of hailstorms in the United States swept across North-central Illinois on June 19–20, 1964. Three squall lines moved through within 18 hours dumping hailstones from half an inch to four inches and causing crop and property damage totalling $9.2 million in more than 50 counties. Another especially costly one moved through Southeast Iowa on August 18, 1925, completely destroying the corn crop in its path. At the time, damage was estimated at between $2.5 and $5 million.

A tremendous four-day multi-state hail outbreak raked almost the entire Central United States, July 21–24, 1962. This series of storms shows that hail need not always be localized. The outbreak began on the first day with a line of hail through North Dakota and Minnesota and another through Eastern Nebraska and Western Iowa as a result of the combined action of a cold front approaching from the northeast and at least one squall line south (ahead) of the front. Hailstones 4½ inches in diameter pelted Nebraska. The next day, the combined influence of the approach of the cold front and the frontal low produced a colossal band of hail losses through Minnesota, Iowa, and Northern Illinois. Over the next two days, Pennsylvania, Virginia, Kentucky, Georgia, and the Carolinas were badly hit, and new losses were suffered in Minnesota and Montana. Each of the first three days, the storms dropped hail four inches or more in diameter. In four days the storm raked across 31 states, causing more than $1 million damage each day, with a four-day total of $7 million.

The greatest property damage from a hailstorm in the United States, according to David M. Ludlum, a noted chronicler of weather events, occurred across a path from Wichita, Kansas, eastward into Missouri on June 23, 1951. Not counting damage to crops, property damage in Wichita and nearby El Dorado was estimated at $12.75 million. Two years later, another fierce hailstorm hit the Wichita area and caused $9.1 million damage.

One of the most well-documented hailstorms passed over an array of instruments of the Illinois State Water Survey on May 15, 1968. A typical hailstreak (the path along which hail is dropped) is perhaps half a mile wide and five miles long. In this storm, one super hailstreak was spread across an area 19 miles wide and 51 miles long. At one particular moment, hail was being dumped along a streak 19 miles wide and 10 miles deep that was moving forward at 35 miles per hour. The largest stones were 2¼ inches in diameter. The scientists calculated that this storm produced 82 million cubic feet of ice.

A greater hail accumulation was left behind by a severe hailstorm at Seldon, Kansas, on June 3, 1959. Hail fell for 85 minutes. When it was over, an area nine miles by six miles was covered by hailstones to a depth of 18 inches. An aerial view of that white-covered scene makes it look as though a mid-winter blizzard had hit.

Hail on the ground tends to be swept downhill into drifts by the rain. One storm in Washington County, Iowa, in 1897 left piles six feet deep. Snowplows sometimes have to be called out in summer to clear the highways. That very thing happened in June, 1978, along Interstate 25 in Northeastern New Mexico, when snowplows had to be used to clear off six inches of hail.

Even in late summer, accumulations of hail sometimes melt slowly. Ludlum tells of a storm in Maryville, Missouri, on September 5, 1898, that deposited 12 inches of hail on the ground and blocked fields with ice for two weeks. Ice cream was made from ice picked up off the ground four weeks afterward.

The ruined crops, broken roofs, shattered windows, and drifts of hail along fields and roads are the visible, ground-level manifestations of turbulent hail-forming processes going on invisibly in the thunderclouds above. Thunderstorms almost always generate hail, but fortunately for us most of it melts before it reaches the ground. The storms where hail does reach the ground cause enough damage as it is.

Hail is formed when small embryonic ice pellets remain for a sufficient time in an area of supercooled water, the section within a thunderstorm where the water is below freezing temperatures but still in liquid form because of the absence of nuclei around which to freeze. The hailstones grow as water droplets strike the ice pellets and freeze to them. To grow into hailstones, the ice pellets usually must remain among the supercooled water for at least several minutes. That task is seen to by the strong up-drafts found within the thunderstorm. The hailstones grow until they are either tossed out of the updraft or until they become too heavy for the updraft to support. Then, downward they drop, in a race against melting that reduces some of their size as they pass through the above-freezing lower atmosphere.

Occasionally, the hailstone growth process is repeated several times as the stones are sent up and down past the freezing level by successive updrafts and downdrafts. The partial melting and new freezing produces hailstones with laminations of ice of vary-ing textures and appearances.

From 1972 to 1976, scientists from the National Center for Atmospheric Research, a dozen universities, federal agencies, and private groups carried out the National Hail Research Ex-periment (NHRE) over a 5,000-square-mile wheat-farming area of Hail Alley in Northeastern Colorado near the Wyoming and Nebraska borders. It was reminiscent in a way of the Thunder-storm Project of the 1940s. Two NCAR Queen Air aircraft, a University of Wyoming Queen Air and an NCAR Sabreliner were sent above and around hailstorms. An armored T-28 from the South Dakota School of Mines and Technology, and even a research sailplane, the *Explorer,* were sent directly into hail-storms. Dual-wavelength conventional radar and three Doppler radar units probed areas of hail within the storms. A network of weather stations, rain gauges, and hail pads recorded the storms' outpourings. Time-lapse photos automatically recorded the growth of hailstorms from six locations. And four ground ve-hicles chased hailstorms and collected hailstone samples. It was one of the most complete networks of sensors ever applied to the study of major storms.

The main goal was to determine the potential for using cloud seeding to reduce hail, and particularly to give a full test to a Soviet model of hail growth and artificial suppression. Random experimental cloud seeding was carried out. The scientists found no significant effect—either suppression or enhancement—at-tributable to the seeding. The conclusion of the hail suppression part of NHRE was that more knowledge of the detailed physical processes of severe convective storms was needed before further suppression experiments could be carried out. Also it seems likely that Northeastern Colorado hailstorms may be different from those described by the Soviet researchers.

The field experiments did, however, provide a detailed picture of the structure of an evolving hailstorm.

The majority of hailstorms in the North American continent appear to be of the ordinary multicell variety. These are the thunderstorms consisting of a sequence of evolving cells each of which may go through a life-cycle resembling that first described in the Thunderstorm Project by Horace Byers and his associates in 1949 (see Chapter 1). Each new updraft cell in such a storm is seen first as a discrete, newly growing cumulus cloud. During an effort known as Project Hailswath in the mid-1960s, these became known as feeder clouds. But as a scientific group that summarized NRHE's studies of hailstorm structure points out, this term can be misleading. As they put it, "The clouds do not *feed* the mature hail cloud but rather grow and *become* the mature hail cloud." Therefore, they refer to them instead as daughter clouds. Those who have previously described these daughter clouds "consider them to be one of the most striking visual phenomena associated with Great Plains thunderstorms."

The daughter clouds begin forming at distances as great as 15 to 20 miles away from the hailstorm core. Each cloud grows rapidly as it approaches the main cumulonimbus (thunderstorm) cloud mass. In an eastward-moving storm the merger usually takes place on the southwestern side of the main cloud mass and occurs 15 to 40 minutes after the initial formation of a daughter cloud. On radar, an echo usually appears in a daughter cloud just before it merges fully with the main cloud mass. Soon after the merger, a burst of heavy rain or hail usually reaches the ground.

Inside the storm, it is necessary that the hailstones grow in an updraft having a velocity comparable to the fallspeed of the stones at each stage of their growth. The problem is that in the early stages, when the hailstone is still quite small, its fallspeed is low, and too strong an updraft will whisk it upward out of the supercooled zone of the cloud before it can grow to a large size. In most hailstorms, this problem seems to be solved by having the small embryo hailstones grow in an updraft whose intensity is developing with time. The young daughter clouds are the ideal place for this early growth because they do not develop into strong updrafts until some time later.

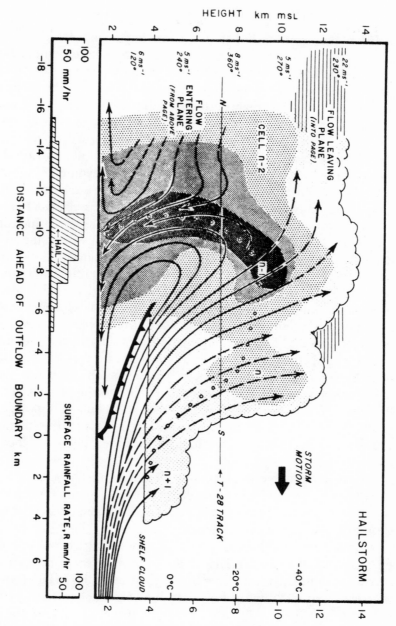

Schematic model of a hailstorm showing a sequence of evolving cells. This is both an instantaneous "snapshot" of four different cells at the same moment and a portrait of how each cell evolves. Each cell begins as a daughter cell (n+1) at front of storm, on the right, and develops into more mature stages (n and n-1) as it moves toward the storm's interior. There it drops its load of hail and then dissipates. Open circles represent trajectory of hailstone during its growth. (K. A. BROWNING ET AL., MONTHLY WEATHER REVIEW)

Inside the storm itself, here is what is happening. Imagine you are seeing a hailstorm in cross-section. It is moving to your right. Air feeding the updraft is entering low on the right, from the front of the storm, whooshing transversely up through it and leaving it as an anvil high on the left, out the rear. At the front of the storm, at the far right, a small daughter cloud has just merged with the main cloud mass and become a fledgling storm cell. Small ice pellets, the embryos that will grow into hailstones, are forming from small cloud particles in this young fledgling cell. Farther inward to the left is a second, more mature storm cell. Here, hailstones are growing to sizes that will eventually reach the ground approximately half to two-thirds of an inch in diameter. But they are still essentially balanced within the updraft. They are being kept aloft without much change in altitude.

Still farther to the left is a third cell, the main one at the moment. Here the concentration of particles is at a high point. Precipitation loading and temperature effects now come into play, and the lower portions of the updraft are quickly converted into a downdraft. The hailstones cascade rapidly to the ground. Combining their own maximum air speed of 75 feet per second with a typical downdraft velocity of 33 feet per second, the hailstones descend from the cloud four miles to the ground in as little as 200 seconds (an average speed of about 72 miles per hour). For about 120 of those seconds they will have been falling below the freezing level, so melting shrinks their diameter about 10 to 15 percent.

To complete our cross-sectional picture of the hailstorm, we need to mention one more cell, the fourth one, at the far left or rear of the storm. This is an old cell, now depleted of its energy, soon to dissipate into nothingness.

This picture of a hailstorm can be viewed in two ways. It is an instantaneous view, a snapshot, of four different cells at a given moment, each in a different stage of evolution. But it also portrays how each individual cell evolves. Each of the cells begins as a daughter cell on the far right at the storm's front and develops into more mature stages as it moves to the interior of the storm, dropping its load of hail and then dissipating. It truly is, as Horace Byers first noted, almost an organic entity. During their growth, most of the hailstones probably will have remained within the same updraft cells as the cell moved through the storm system.

In the case study from which this hailstorm view is portrayed, the growth of the hailstones from embryos less than a quarter of an inch to stones nearly three-quarters of an inch across is believed to have occurred as they were carried more or less horizontally relative to the storm system through a distance of nearly four miles at air temperatures between $-5°$ and $-20°$ F. This gave them a growth period of about 12 minutes. Previous studies have shown that's easily enough time to account for the growth observed under the moisture conditions at the time.

Some uncertainties still surround the early stages of growth, but what is now clear is that the embryos originate in the young daughter clouds, that they grow into hailstones while suspended at high levels after the updraft has become strong, and that they follow a generally horizontal and slightly upward trajectory rearward through the hailstorm until they fall through the downdraft.

This view of a typical evolving hailstorm comes from Keith A. Browning, who served as chief scientist for the National Hail Research Experiment during a one-year leave from the British Meteorological Office, and numerous colleagues from the National Center for Atmospheric Research, National Oceanic and Atmospheric Administration, and the South Dakota School of Mines and Technology.

There's another type of hailstorm that's not typical. And that is fortunate. It's called a supercell storm. Most hailstorms go through the succession of stages of cell growth just described, but a supercell hailstorm manages to attain a semi-steady structure with a large updraft and downdraft co-existing and feeding on each other for long periods. They are much larger and more powerful than the usual multi-cell storm, and produce uncommonly large hail. It is now becoming clear that they cause the major share of hailstorm damage in the United States.

The embryo in a supercell storm grows in one organized recirculation under the influence of mid-level winds flowing around the storm. It apparently develops during an ascent on the edge of a steady updraft where the vertical velocity is relatively weak. Then after it grows larger it gets carried around to the inflow side of the main updraft and enters the core of the updraft at a low level. Here, it is recycled many times to reach an exceptionally large size.

Study shows that supercell storms are the probable culprits in especially heavy hail damage. The supercell storm is only one extreme of a spectrum of storm types, so for one study a more general category of storms called "severe right-moving" (SRM) was specified. This category includes all supercell storms and some thought to be supercells but not strictly identifiable by radar and other clues. They are called "severe right-moving" because supercell storms tend to drift toward the right in the prevailing wind field.

These rightward-veering monsters, it turns out, cause a disproportionate share of the damage. Hailstorms on the 13 days of most damaging hail out of 509 hail-damage days across Central Oklahoma over an eight-year period caused 37 percent of the total crop losses. And on those 13 days, SRM storms caused two-thirds of the crop damage.

One area near Norman, Oklahoma, suffered three damaging hailstorms during the study period. One straight-line storm lasted about a half-hour, covered 12 miles and caused $17,000 damage. Another lasted 45 minutes, covered 36 miles and caused $177,000 damage. But an especially long-lived storm lasted an hour and a half, veered sharply to the right, spread hail over a total distance of 55 miles, and caused an estimated $377,000 damage. It was classified as a "severe right-moving" storm—probably a supercell.

It now appears that when conditions favor the development of SRM storms, hail damage is likely from other types of hailstorms as well. These rightward-curving supercell storms may simply be the most violent manifestation of generally strong hail conditions, another tragic example of natural violence carried to the extreme.

CHAPTER 5

Floods

"I'm stuck. I'm right in the middle of it. I can't get out. . . . Tell them cars to get out of that low area down below. As soon as the water starts picking up . . . [static] . . . high ground. . . ."

Those were the last words spoken by Colorado State Patrolman Hugh Purdy. The date: July 31, 1976. The time: 9:15 P.M. The place: On U.S. Highway 34 about one-half mile east of the tiny mountain settlement of Drake, Colorado, in the Big Thompson Canyon.

Purdy's mangled body was later discovered eight miles downstream from this point. His car was an almost unrecognizable mass of mud and twisted metal, a bent steering wheel here, a crushed metal wheel (tires ripped away) there, a section of seat upholstery springs sticking up out of the ball of wreckage.

Purdy had driven up the canyon to try to determine the location of the headwaters of a flash flood rushing down through its narrow confines. Instead, the flood found him. He was the first victim to be identified of the almost inconceivable barrage of water that roared down through the canyon that night. Before the night was out, 139 persons were dead. Many of them were visitors to this picturesque canyon, slicing through the brown granite of the Rocky Mountains and linking the plains to the 7,500-foot-high resort community of Estes Park at the foot of Rocky Mountain National Park. It was a flash flood whose magnitude no one could have anticipated. Never in recorded history had anywhere near that much water come through the canyon.

Its timing could hardly have been worse. A midsummer Saturday evening, the peak of the vacation period, in a scenic area that draws visitors from all over the world. In addition, it was the eve of the 100th anniversary of Colorado's statehood, so for the state's residents it was a three-day weekend. The canyon was filled with campers and vacationers, its campgrounds and tidy little motels and cabins occupied by 2,000 to 3,000 visitors and summertime residents.

Few of them could know of the extraordinary series of meteorological events that had caused a series of tremendous, moisture-laden thunderstorms to become almost anchored in place over the headwaters of the canyon and its tributaries. In a typical July, these mountains would receive a total of two inches of rain the entire month. The plains below average about 13 inches of precipitation the entire year. This night, within a small oval-shaped area over the Front Range of the Rocky Mountains near the head of the Big Thompson Canyon an incredible 10 to 12 inches of rain fell, most of it in the four hours between 6:30 and 10:30 P.M. At one location, near Glen Comfort, scientists estimate that seven and one half inches of rain fell in the one hour and 10 minutes between 7:30 and 8:40. An estimated 50 million tons of water were dumped by the rains, mostly in the area between Estes Park and Drake. Even the meteorologists watching the developing storm and predicting some flash flooding couldn't anticipate that kind of deluge.

Waters bursting through this narrow part of the Big Thompson Canyon on the night of July 31, 1976, obliterated U.S. Highway 34 like an explosion, according to an eyewitness, and swept away a 110-ton, 9-foot-diameter water siphon that crossed the canyon at this point 15 feet above the highway. (GREELEY TRIBUNE PHOTO BY MIKE PETERS)

Rube Seilback and his party were probably the last westbound travelers to make it up the canyon that night. A long-time resident of Loveland, below the mouth of the canyon, he was familiar with its twists and turns. He was determined that they attend the final performance of some favorite entertainers at the Gaslight Inn in Estes Park. Two miles outside of Drake the first rains hit, a cloudburst. "The windshield wipers even at top speed could do nothing with the pouring rain," Seilback recalls. Despite great uneasiness and suggestions to stop, they went on. Water by now was pouring over the highway. The last two miles were a nightmare. In at least two places the pavement had been washed away. They had to dodge mud and rock slides and obstacles of water, boulders, and splintered trees. Rivers of water cascaded down normally dry ravines. "The mountainsides seemed like they were all water," Seilback reports. Finally, they emerged to the safety of Estes Park.

Then the storm really struck. According to Seilback, "It hit about 9 P.M. and I never saw such a downpour or such spectacular lightning, or such earthshaking thunder. The clouds seemed to be circling around, and some out-of-state guests were sure we were in for a tornado. After about an hour, the rain gave way to marble-sized hail. Then it rained again, hard."

A young couple already in Estes Park were equally lucky. They were attending a dinner-theater play at the Stanley Hotel. The noise of the thunder and the downpour became so intense that they couldn't hear the performance, and they decided to leave and drive home back through the canyon. But authorities had just barricaded the road, and they were diverted to a longer, but safe, way out of the mountains.

In the canyon itself, the waters were rising with astonishing speed. Much of the canyon is narrow and granite-walled, with room only for the highway and the normally modest river beside it. Nearly everyplace where the canyon widens were homes, cabins, small motels, campgrounds, and restaurants. There was nowhere else for the water to go.

Wayne Link, of Marysville, Kansas, on vacation and ailing from the flu, was at the Cedarmont Motel, six miles east of Estes Park, while his wife and three children were in Estes Park. He says that while he was asleep on the second floor, he heard "the river roaring louder than usual" and grabbed a flashlight.

"It was pitch dark, no light anywhere." Pointing the flashlight, he saw water running level with the motel's second deck and a car's roof lodged against the building. He kicked out a window and scrambled up the canyon wall. Within one or two minutes, he saw the motel swept away.

Seven miles farther down the canyon, Mr. and Mrs. H. L. Huggins of Redfield, Iowa, stopped to register at the Waltonia Motel. Huggins had retired the week before, and they were on a leisurely vacation in the Rockies with their new car. The motel manager warned them to get to higher ground. As they drove away, "the car went right into a mountainbank," says Huggins, "and we waded in water up to our waist. Then, of course, the car went on. All our belongings, everything." They struggled up a hillside. Says Mrs. Huggins: "We sat there and watched the whole motel go."

Jerry Alanko was rousted from his house near Estes Park by a deputy sheriff and told to warn all the people he possibly could. Then he joined the rescue efforts. "There were cars floating by, and people inside the cars were waving flashlights for us to help them. There was nothing we could do. You just had to watch them nosedive."

Dewey Salgren of Drake, where the main and north forks of the Big Thompson River converge, watched one man help his wife to a higher cabin across the road and return to his own cabin only to disappear. The neighbor who had taken in the man's wife went out on the porch to call him back, but the porch washed out from under him, and he was saved only by grabbing some chokeberry bushes near the house.

John B. Hennessey of Denver, with his wife and neighbors, was running to high ground when he saw a man across the canyon waving at him. "He was on his patio. He was yelling over for us to get out. I think he was telling us to get out. I couldn't hear him very well. Then, the wall of the patio caved in and he and the whole thing went in [the river]."

At the settlement of Cedar Grove, James Stengel thought he heard calls of help above the noise of the maelstrom and the hiss and clank of shattered propane tanks. The calls seemed to be coming from a tree surrounded by water. He had no rope but he took his home's coaxial TV cable, cut a length of it with some rocks, tethered one end to a sturdy gatepost on the edge of the seething waters, and worked his way out through the waist-deep water to the dimly seen cottonwood tree. There he secured the cable and managed to bring back to safety a woman and her husband whose house had been swept away and who had taken precarious refuge in the tree. "I doubt that we could have hung on much longer," said the rescued man, D. R. Pulliam.

The strangest sounds that night were of huge boulders, crashing against each other like marbles. "Boulders bigger than a car would be thrown up out of the water and against another boulder," said one witness. "They sounded like thunder and shook the ground."

"It was like an abyss out there, as if we were sitting in on the end of the world," recalled Dale Greer. "The river sounded like wind and storm . . . maybe sort of as if this were accompanied by grinding and crashing boulders. Then there was the propane hanging over like fog. You could see it in the eerie lighting from distant lightning; sense it constantly in your nostrils."

Greer, staying with his wife at the Big Thompson Trading Post and Indian Village as guests of its owners, the Howard Carmans, had driven his jeep down behind the building to see how the water was rising at the garage on the lower level. "I bet no one ever backed out of anything as fast. The water was at the garage. By the time I had backed out and up to the top level the water was there with me too. I would say the river came up 13 feet in less than two minutes."

The Greers and Carmans were only a quarter of a mile downstream from the ill-fated Covered Wagon Restaurant. They probably heard the last screams of those inside as it was swept down the river.

Guests at the Palisades Motel, across the river from the restaurant, watched the restaurant tragedy. "The people in the restaurant began screaming and scrambling . . . trying to get out," recalled Douglas Magill of Mishawaka, Indiana. "Within seconds, the restaurant, still full of people, plunged into the river. It was some sort of a dream. It wasn't really happening." But it was.

First the crest took a footbridge, then the house next to the restaurant. Then the restaurant and an office on the road were gone. "We heard screams and that was all," recalled Ann Dauth. "The cafe had dinner guests in it besides the managers and help —just the peak of the tourist season."

Mrs. Dauth also saw the water wash away a trailer, five cars, and a motor home. "We saw children's faces looking out of the motor home with a look of disbelief. Also people in the cars. Two cars lodged against our pine trees near the road until the trees went too. The motor home took our bridge."

Shattered homes, broken trees, and rock and mud debris in aftermath of Big Thompson flood. (GREELEY TRIBUNE PHOTO BY MIKE PETERS)

Three miles downstream, 14-year-old Cindy Miller had just gotten home from working at the Covered Wagon Restaurant. Worried about those still inside, she called her friend Stannis Bashford, still on waitress duty there. Stannis described cars and propane tanks rushing past as the waters surrounded the building. Suddenly, Cindy became hysterical and came away from the telephone screaming. The call was broken off by the washing away of the restaurant. The seven persons inside were gone.

Cindy's own fight for life was not yet over. Her father ushered the family into the pickup. Seconds after they passed over the bridge connecting their place to the road, the bridge collapsed. They sped down the canyon ahead of the advancing water.

"We raced into the narrows," Adam Miller recalls, "where the banks strained against the swollen river, or submitted to the angry water in places. We splashed our way through the blackness, looking desperately for the opening to safety." They eventually made it to high ground at the mouth of the canyon, where it narrows. There at the Dam Store they watched as wildly careening propane tanks, cars, campers, and trailers rushed past.

At one point, they saw an ambulance speeding into the canyon run into a wall of water and smash against the canyon walls.

Inside the ambulance, emergency medical technicians John McMaster and George Woodson watched the enormous wave crash toward them. The wave swept underneath the vehicle, lifting it an estimated 15 feet up the canyon wall.

"I knew I was dead, that was it," McMaster recalls. His wife, Dee, was monitoring the radio from the ambulance company headquarters in Loveland when the last transmission from ambulance 716 was heard: "We're caught in the narrows. . . ." Her husband's voice was "hysterical." It was the last she heard for five hours.

McMaster and Woodson somehow managed to get out of the ambulance window, grab onto the rock, and scramble partially up the canyon wall. Woodson says he looked back and saw the ambulance slam into the canyon wall and buckle in two with all lights shining straight into the sky. They spent most of the night in a V-shaped wedge on the canyon wall, Woodson on a ledge, McMaster clinging below to a rock where he had fallen, half in the water. All the time they could hear Mrs. McMaster's frantic calls for them on their packset radios but their answers couldn't be heard in Loveland. After 2 A.M. when the water dropped somewhat, they climbed around the cliff onto a ledge where their radio transmissions could be heard. "When we heard that voice, it was the most wonderful thing in the whole wide world," says Dee McMaster. They were rescued by helicopter after daylight.

Radios brought many less-happy messages that night. At one point, John Englebert, a Larimer County Sheriff's operations officer, heard a woman's voice on the sheriff's radio network. "She was screaming that her boyfriend had just been washed away, but we have no idea who she was or where she was."

Walter A. Skowron was with friends and relatives from New York and Boston at his cabin on the North Fork of the Big Thompson just south of Glen Haven. When electricity went out during the torrential downpour, they listened to the CB radio in one of their vehicles. "All we heard were stress and panic calls —calls from people camped along the river. Since CB reception is limited in the mountains, we knew those calling out were close by. 'I'm trapped in my van with my wife and two children,' said one. 'For God's sake, help us!' Then, 'Oh. . . .' And then, silence. Calls of terror, calls of panic, calls of pain. We'll hear them forever."

The Fred Woodrings of Estes Park started down the canyon about midnight to try to make contact with their son and to reach a Canadian family, the Dave Broughtons, stranded at a motel in the canyon. The water was too much and they radioed on their CB that they were turning around. Suddenly, Mrs. Woodring's voice burst over the radio: "My God! It's the end of the world!" Then silence. Their son and the Broughtons had heard the transmission. The next day the Woodrings' vehicle was found buried in mud and gravel. Mrs. Woodring's body was inside. Her husband's was found later downstream. "If only they hadn't come down the canyon to get us," Broughton lamented.

One well-known landmark at the "Narrows," at the mouth of the canyon, was a nine-foot-diameter water pipe that stretched between the canyon's walls 15 feet above the highway. Large enough to drive a car through, the Big Thompson River Siphon was part of a vast water project that brings water from Colorado's Western Slope through the mountains to the reservoirs of the populous Eastern Slope. The siphon weighed 110 tons and was full of an estimated 490 tons of water running through it at the rate of 500 cubic feet a second. As the peak of the flood erupted through the Narrows, debris plunging down the river crashed against the siphon's supports. The north end of the steel pipe tore loose, releasing still more water into the torrent, and with a deafening crash the huge mass of steel was crumpled and carried 200 yards downstream where it slammed into a house.

About the same time, the highway just inside the Narrows exploded, according to a State Patrol officer, Captain W. E. Thomas, "sending 10- or 12-foot chunks of asphalt high in the air."

Near the same spot, propane tanks smashed into the nearby power station. "Electricity was arcing in a tremendous display of man-made lightning," said Thomas. "It was high in the towers so it didn't ignite the heavy layer of propane gas that clung to the ground."

A short distance farther downstream, in what had been an attractive mountain park, an entire hydroelectric plant serving the city of Loveland was washed away, leaving only a foundation and some machinery.

Of the 139 persons who perished in the flood, the bodies of some were not found until days or even weeks later, buried deep in the mud and debris scooped out by the catastrophic deluge. Temporary morgues were set up in an abandoned hospital and in a meat-packing company's donated refrigerator trucks. Since most of the bodies were mangled and stripped of all clothing and

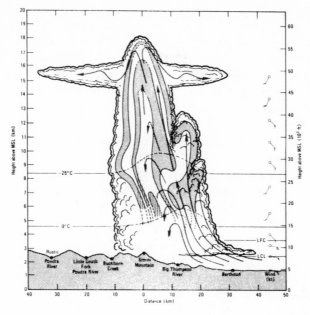

Model of one of the initial cells of the thunderstorm complex that dropped 12 inches of rain at the head of the Big Thompson Canyon on the evening of July 31, 1976. (MADDOX, CARACENA, HOXIT, AND CHAPPELL)

many of the victims were travelers, the job of identification was especially difficult. Two hundred hours of long-distance calls were made to relatives, dentists, and physicians of missing persons to obtain detailed descriptions. Donated computers were used to process the information.

It was the worst natural disaster in Colorado history and, with the exception of the very similar Rapid City flood of 1972, the worst single flood in the United States since 1937.

Later analyses showed that 240 times the average amount of water rushed down the main Big Thompson Canyon that night. Property damage totaled $35.5 million.

But statistics cannot portray the extent of the tragedy to the canyon. It had been a scenic attraction, a haven from the summer heat and workaday concerns of persons from all walks of life, a home to some and a retreat to many, a place to trout fish in a rushing, bubbling stream, and a route to the highest national park in the United States. Within a flash, all that was wiped out.

I have been through the Big Thompson Canyon many times. By coincidence I was in Colorado the weekend before the flood and drove through it with my family to Estes Park on a relaxing Sunday excursion. All was in place, the highway hugging the canyon's brown granite walls, the well-kept little homes, cabins, and motels, the vacationers enjoying themselves, and the spar-kling river itself, beautiful but small, hardly what easterners would call a river at all, water splashing over its boulders, fisher-men casting into its deep, cold pools.

I was back again in mid-October on the first weekend the canyon was reopened to the public after the disaster. The con-trast was shocking.

The canyon walls were there, but much of everything else was gone. The homes and other buildings, many of them, had van-ished. Only bare concrete slabs revealed their former existence. The upstream sides of all trees anywhere near the river that hadn't been ripped away were battered to shreds, their lower 10 or 15 feet of branches and bark stripped away. A temporary road had been put back into service with surprising speed, but the river—that was the saddest. The river bed had been scoured out; it now looked more like a ditch or canal than a typical Rocky Moun-tain trout stream. Amazingly, all the sturdily built concrete and steel bridges were still intact, the waters having passed over them (the flood had deposited a house on top of one bridge), but dozens of private bridges to homes and cabins had been swept away. Incongruously, some homes near the river remained untouched, the rampage of water apparently having been chan-neled safely past them by particular twists and turns of the can-yon's walls.

The Big Thompson Canyon is now coming back to life. The river's not quite the same except where some scenic-minded workers have left boulders in the river bottom to break up the smooth flow of water. The scars are fading, but the memories of the tragedy remain.

And here and there is a new kind of warning sign. A stylized picture shows waves of water lapping at the ankles of a man scurrying up a pine-covered slope. Exclaims its message: "CLIMB TO SAFETY IN CASE OF A FLASH FLOOD." Authorities say if more persons had heeded that kind of advice on the night of July 31, 1976, the human tragedy of the Big Thompson flood would not have been so great.

According to George P. Cressman, Director of the National Weather Service from 1966 to 1979, flash floods have in recent years become the number one weather-related killer in the United States. Over the long-term average, lightning has killed more people than any other type of severe geophysical event. But in the last decade, flash floods have become a far worse problem than before, and they have now taken over that dubious honor.

In May of 1978, Cressman and other weather scientists pointed out that since 1968 the annual average death toll from flash floods in the United States has risen to about 200. This is more than double the rate of the 1960s and more than triple that of the 1940s. Property damage from flash floods is now running at more than $1 billion a year.

Floods are the most widespread natural hazard, and every state has been affected. The Federal Disaster Assistance Administration reports that 85 percent of all Presidential declarations of major disasters currently are associated with floods and flash floods.

The increased toll from flash floods is due to nature, performing as it usually does, colliding with an increased and more urbanized population settling and occupying sites that are ready targets for floods. In the countryside, as evidenced in the Big Thompson, the increased use of mountainous areas and narrow canyons for recreation purposes is exposing growing numbers of unwary visitors to flash floods.

The list of danger spots is growing. By latest count, more than 15,000 U.S. communities and recreational areas were identified by the Flood Insurance Administration as prone to flash floods.

The problem has gotten so bad that the American Meteorological Society in 1978 urged a concerted effort by federal, state, and local officials to reduce the losses from flash floods, "the nation's number one natural disaster."

They called for improved forecasts and warnings, increased regulation of flash-flood-prone areas, certification of dam safety, better information on maximum precipitation and runoff, and programs of public awareness and community warnings. "The death toll and property damage from flash floods can be significantly reduced if positive action is taken," said the meteorological society statement. In 1979 an intensive program to accomplish these goals was proposed to Congress by the government.

Scientists from the National Oceanic and Atmospheric Administration in Boulder, Colorado, have shown that flash floods frequently have almost frighteningly similar circumstances and causes. The Rapid City, South Dakota, flood of June 9, 1972, was in many ways almost a twin to the later Big Thompson flood. Both storms developed when strong low-level winds from the east pushed moist, unstable air masses upslope into elevated mountainous terrain. Uplift of the air by the mountains released the instability. The winds at high altitudes were very light and this served to keep the storms from drifting away. They remained nearly stationary, pouring extraordinarily high quantities of water over the same drainage area.

The Rapid City flood had its genesis in an almost stationary group of thunderstorms that formed over the eastern Black Hills of South Dakota near Rapid City. The rainfall amounts were similar to those above the Big Thompson Canyon in 1976. Nearly 15 inches of rain fell in about six hours near Nemo, South Dakota, and more than 10 inches fell over a 60-square-mile area. As in Colorado, the resulting floods were the highest ever recorded in the state.

The cultural circumstances of the two disasters were similar too. The Big Thompson flood happened in a popular vacation area on the first day of a busy three-day summer weekend, on the eve of Colorado Day. In South Dakota, June 9, 1972, was the first day of one of the early weekends of the summer season in Rapid City. The first of the year's expected 6 million visitors to the Black Hills were looking forward to the start of the Dakota Days celebration.

When the thunderstorms over the eastern Black Hills opened up, the deluge was almost unbelievable. A previous analysis of 132 heavy rainstorms over the Northwestern Great Plains during the past century shows that only 10 dropped 10 inches or more of rain in six hours. Only two exceeded the 15-inch, six-hour precipitation of the Black Hills storm.

The water rampaged down Rapid Creek, Boxelder Creek, Battle Creek, and two dozen other streams. Coming off the slopes of the Black Hills, the flood peak traveled the 22 miles between Deer Creek and Rapid City in about three and a half hours.

Rapid City Mayor Dan Barnett, concerned about the dam straddling the man-made Canyon Lake above one of the city's best residential sections, called together an inspection group. The group got a call from a man upstream above the dam saying he had seen a wall of water coming down the creek. It would hit the lake in about 20 minutes.

The mayor called the local radio stations to issue a warning to abandon the area at once. He called the National Guard to get the people out. He even drove through the city, horn honking and lights flashing, and ran up and down the creek to warn people. Many failed to heed the warning.

"They wouldn't listen," he exclaimed afterward.

"When we heard the warning, we thought he was kidding," said one survivor. "We just sat there, and pretty soon this big bunch of water came down the creek. We ran next door and suddenly the water was up to my neck. The top of a house came floating by and we grabbed on to that. A little way downstream we got off and climbed on the roof of a neighbor's house."

The floods in the Rapid City area struck quickly and viciously but did not last long. The flood peaks were sharp. In Rapid City, Rapid Creek went over its banks at 10:15 P.M. It was back within its banks before daylight, devastation done. At one point, the floodwaters rose three and a half feet in 15 minutes.

"The people were crying and screaming for help," said one eyewitness. "You could just see the people floating around, just before your eyes. Some going under . . . some floating in a car or in a house. . . . It's just terrible."

"Our daughter just floated away," one father said later. "She tried holding on to a tree, but she just floated away."

Cars were stacked up piggy-back by the torrent, and roads and bridges, as well as mobile and permanent homes, were swept away.

Campers in the nearby Black Hills were taken by surprise.

"Tom heard water coming in the cabin," one young survivor recalled. "He woke us all up. We couldn't open the cabin door to get out because of water outside. I kicked out a window, and right then a car smashed into it. We all grabbed a mattress and floated in the water . . . and the cabin started floating downstream. It went at least a mile and then one wall of the cabin broke away from the rest of it. I'd given myself up for dead. I thought this was it." For three of the six companions of this boy it was. They perished.

In addition to the 237 persons killed in the flood (some 10 percent of them tourists from 13 states and France), more than 3,000 were injured. Eighty blocks of buildings along the creek bank were knocked out. Thirteen hundred homes and 5,000 automobiles were destroyed. The total damage was in excess of $160 million. According to the National Flood Insurance Association, only about one-half of 1 percent of the damage to homes and businesses was covered by insurance.

Cars stacked by the Rapid City flash flood. (NOAA)

The Rapid City and Big Thompson floods aren't the only ones that have features in common. It turns out that there are similarities among many flash flood disasters. Robert A. Maddox and Charles F. Chappell of the NOAA laboratories in Boulder have studied 150 significant flash flood events beginning with the Rapid City disaster in 1972 through the floods in Kansas City, Missouri, that killed 25 persons in September, 1977. The floods occurred in most states from Connecticut, Maryland, and South Carolina to Texas, Nevada, Idaho, and California.

Flash floods are distinguished from general river flooding by the very rapid rise in the run-off water level with the flood usually occurring within a few hours of the rainfall that causes it. The affected area is limited and is frequently restricted to a single stream or drainage basin.

Flash floods over the Eastern and Central United States tend to occur at night, while those over the western states tend to strike during the afternoon. What's responsible for the noctural focusing and intensification of the storms over the eastern two-thirds of the country isn't yet clear, Maddox and Chappell say, but it obviously exacerbates the forecast and warning problem. Not only are the potential victims often settled in for the night, but weather forecast offices and local agencies responsible for warnings have fewer people on duty.

July is clearly the predominant month for flash floods, accounting for about a fourth of all occurrences. The warm season period, April through September, accounts for nearly 90 percent, consistent with their origin in convective storms.

Flash floods are likely to be created by heavy thunderstorm rains in a region where there is unusually high moisture throughout a thick layer of the atmosphere. Usually, wind velocities change very little from the top to bottom of the storm. Frequently, new storms or storm cells repeatedly form and move over the same area, supplying a continuing source of new moisture to drench the watershed.

The storm's towering cumulonimbus clouds reach more than six miles above the ground's surface. And a small-scale pressure system, some 300 miles in extent, frequently helps trigger, focus, and sustain the storms.

"In many cases," says Chappell, "the typical flash flood thunderstorm is entirely different from other severe thunderstorms. They grow in an entirely different environment, and they may not appear on radar in the same manner."

One of the findings of study of the Big Thompson disaster, according to Chappell, was that the thunderstorm that caused the deluge was far more tropical in its characteristics than is usual for storms at mid-latitudes. In most thunderstorms over the United States, large parts are below freezing temperatures, and the rain forms by an ice process. In the Big Thompson storm, Chappell explains, much of the cloud was above freezing, and the rain formed by a warm-cloud collision and coalescence process in the lower part of the cloud. With so many of the precipitation particles forming in the lower part of the cloud and quickly falling out, the higher portion of the storm was weaker than it would have been under more normal circumstances, considering the tremendous amount of precipitation in the cloud. Thus, the radar, far out on the Eastern Colorado plains at Limon and for that reason able to see only the top of the storm, greatly underestimated the amount of precipitation in it.

From then on, everything clicked steadily toward disaster.

"Almost everything about the Big Thompson storm conspired to make it very efficient as a rainmaker," says Chappell. "There were very strong winds feeding in at the bottom but much lighter winds at the top. So the storm had very strong easterly winds laden with high moisture content feeding into it; yet because of the light winds aloft it moved very slowly.

"The atmosphere was very unstable, but it needed a kick to set it off. The foothills provided it, and also tended to help lock the storm in one place. A whole series of thunderstorms were formed."

They just stayed there and dropped their tons of water. "The key to understanding flash floods," says Chappell, "is to learn what mechanism locks the storm into place and causes individual storm cells to repeatedly affect the same area." Chappell heads a meteorological research program that he hopes will lead to a better understanding of flash flood situations and possibly to better flash flood forecasts and warnings.

With the Big Thompson flood, the mountains provided the necessary lift to kick off the atmospheric instability. With the Johnstown, Pennsylvania, flood of August 19, 1977, the cold downdrafts from previous thunderstorm activity provided the lift. As with other disastrous flash floods, those over the mountainous areas of South-central Pennsylvania that night resulted when meteorological processes combined to focus successive convective rains over a relatively small area. In this case, a mound of cool outflow air from previous thunderstorms was overrun by warm, moist air intruding from Ohio. The previously rain-cooled air lifted the new warm air, triggering new thunderstorms, and the boundary of the previous outflow focused the thunderstorms and their heavy rains over a fairly small region.

Johnstown is hardly a stranger to flash floods. The most famous and one of the most devastating floods in U.S. history struck there in May of 1889 when the South Fork Dam broke after a week of torrential rains, sending the waters of the overflowing Conemaugh Lake Reservoir into the valley below. Twenty-two hundred persons perished and a fourth of the buildings of Johnstown were wiped out. Ninety-nine entire families were killed. Ninety-eight children lost both parents.

The flood of 1977 was not of that scale, but it was bad enough. Eight to 12 inches of rain fell in the Johnstown area during the night of July 19–20. There was major flash flooding along the Conemaugh River and its tributaries. During the early morning hours, several earthen dams failed, compounding the flooding. Seventy-six persons were killed, and nearly 2,700 injured. Estimates of damage exceeded $200 million.

As with intense thunderstorms or tornadoes, the impact of a

flash flood depends largely upon the extent of development and population density of the area affected. In fact, the actual damage and destruction associated with flash floods is as much the result of topography and population density as it is of the amount of rain. More than 12 inches of rain fell in Northeast Maryland during the early morning hours of June 28, 1975, causing considerable flooding, but the damage was less than $5 million and there were no reports of deaths or injuries.

As with other types of disasters, the way humans respond to it can often determine how great the tragedy will be. On September 12, 1977, two distinct episodes of heavy rain struck Kansas City, Missouri. Between midnight and 6 A.M., more than six inches of rain fell. That evening, from 7 to 9 P.M., more than five more inches plunged down over the city. Twenty-five persons died in the resulting flash floods, but there is evidence that many went to their deaths unnecessarily.

"A lot of people who died didn't have to die," an exhausted policeman told a *Chicago Tribune* reporter afterward. "They could just have walked away from it. They didn't." In most areas the flood was not sudden. No wall of water came crashing down over victims. In the Country Club Plaza shopping area along the banks of Brush Creek where many of the dead were found, the water rose rapidly but not so quickly as to explain all the deaths.

"Anybody who turned to walk to high ground [only two blocks away] could have made it with little more than wet shoes," the policeman explained. "They didn't walk."

Witnesses told of one man in a black Mercedes who drove up behind a string of flood-stalled cars, some of which were in window-deep water. He pulled around them and drove on into the water. He, his wife, and their two children drowned. Similar reports have come out of other flash flood disasters.

Some persons ran to save their cars, even while other cars were floating past them. Others ran into underground parking garages, apparently not stopping to think that was the first place the water was going.

Sometimes a well-intended attempt to flee tragically backfires. When seven inches of rain sent flash floods rolling through homes and businesses of Rochester, Minnesota, on July 6, 1978, three elderly patients and a nurse's aide at a nursing home got into an elevator to go up and escape the rising floodwaters on the first floor. The floodwaters short-circuited the elevator and instead sent it down, into the flooded basement. All four were trapped inside the elevator and drowned.

Before moving on to floods of the less sudden variety, I must briefly mention the most colossal flash flood ever documented by man. It dwarfs any other flash flood ever described. It happened in what is now the United States. In fact, it was responsible for carving the strange and unique scarred topography today covering 15,000 square miles of the northwestern part of the nation.

In Eastern Washington state, the land is marked by deep scars cut into bare, black volcanic rock. Something incredibly violent has gouged out the rock. Everywhere there are channels, deep basins, ledges, ragged buttes, cliffs, alcoves, immense ridges of gravel, and giant ripple marks. Yes, ripple marks. In the 1920s, a University of Chicago geologist named J. Harlen Bretz dubbed this region the Channeled Scablands, and proposed the idea that its enormous erosional features were the result of a sudden and gigantic flood. The idea was controversial for some time, but now it is generally accepted that the Scablands were carved by a flood of unprecedented proportions.

The exact date of what scientists now call the Great Spokane Flood is unknown. But it was sometime between 18,000 and 20,000 years ago during the last Great Ice Age. Whether any humans witnessed it or were swallowed up by its violence we cannot know for sure, because the earliest confirmed evidence for the presence of man in the region, at the Marmes site in Southeastern Washington, has been dated at about 10,130 years ago, some millennia after the flood. But we can try to put ourselves into the skin of some possibly still earlier Ice Age hunter, and imagine the incredible spectacle that lay before him. (He would have had to have been on very high ground indeed!)

It was a time of great glaciers, and lobes of ice stretched down across North America blocking rivers and forming lakes. The largest such lake formed in the Pacific Northwest during the Great Ice Age was Glacial Lake Missoula. Like a giant cork, glacial ice had plugged the Clark Fork Valley, northeast of present-day Coeur d'Alene, Idaho, near the Montana border. The resulting Glacial Lake Missoula at its highest level covered an area of 3,000 square miles and contained 500 cubic miles of water—half the volume of present-day Lake Michigan. Its depth was nearly 2,000 feet, more than twice as deep as Lake Superior. Wave-cut shorelines of this lake are still visible high on the mountain above Missoula, Montana. Where the University of Montana stadium now stands, the lake had a depth of 950 feet.

Meltwater from surrounding glaciers caused the lake level to steadily rise, and the waters eventually reached the lip of the ice dam and began to overflow. The subsequent details are unknown, but the cascading waters probably cut deep into the ice dam until one day a great breach opened. The lake waters rushed through, and with what must have been a tremendous roar, the entire ice dam gave way. The lake waters were released.

The lake drained at a rate unmatched by any flood known. The current through the narrow parts of the Clark Fork Canyon is calculated to have reached 45 miles per hour. The maximum rate of flow is estimated to have been nine and a half cubic miles per hour, or about 10 times the flow of all the rivers of the world. The Amazon, the world's largest river, flows at 6 million cubic feet per second, but the flow of this flood was an almost unimaginable 386 million cubic feet per second—65 Amazon Rivers suddenly unleashed on the landscape to the south and southwest.

Across a ridge north of Markle Pass, Montana, a cascade of water 800 feet deep scoured away the ridge crest. Boulders were tossed about like pebbles. The nicks and chips gouged out of them as they crashed together are visible today. Ripple marks —giant gravel ridges, some of them 20 to 30 feet high, two miles long and 200 to 300 feet across—were formed in many places. They are clearly visible in aerial photographs.

Where the flood reached the broad, southwestward-sloping fields of lava that covered much of Eastern Washington, the water gained further downhill momentum. Its tremendous volume, velocity, and turbulence removed the overlying soil and tore loose 30-foot blocks of columnar basalt, tossing them about like matchsticks. Canyons, cataracts, and depressions as much as 200 feet deep were gouged out, many of them the site of present-day lakes.

Three giant rivers raced across the lava. The easternmost was 20 miles wide and 600 feet deep. The middle one was 14 miles wide. The westernmost one carved out Grand Coulee, a canyon 50 miles long and as much as 900 feet deep, and exposed the granitic rocks that are now the foundation for the Grand Coulee Dam.

All three torrents raged simultaneously, crisscrossing and

spawning dozens of tributaries. One carved away 150 to 200 feet of soil and left a wild wasteland of contorted mesas, ridges, and depressions.

On southwestward the waters flowed. Temporarily impounded behind the barrier now called Horse Heaven Hills into a lake 600 feet deep, they then wedged through the narrow opening of Wallula Gap and raced on to the Portland area, leaving behind giant icebergs and rock debris.

How long did the inundation last? At maximum flow through the ice dam, Glacial Lake Missoula could have drained in a little more than two days. The maximum rates probably weren't sustained, however, and a realistic estimate is that from the moment the ice dam broke until the scabland streams returned to normal flow the elapsed time was about one month. A month of the greatest flash flood ever known, its work of sculpting the earth's surface still clearly apparent 20,000 years later.

Since the advent of civilization, humankind has been subjected to floods more than any other kind of natural disaster. The Biblical flood of Noah, is, to consider nothing else, an apt symbol of the centuries of continuous misfortunes due to floods. It has been estimated that they account for 40 percent of all

Artist's conception of the devastation wrought by the raging flash flood at Johnstown, Pennsylvania, in 1889. Ninety-nine entire families perished. (AMERICAN RED CROSS)

the world's natural disasters. They do by far the greatest damage.

In the United States, nearly every community has some kind of flood problem, chiefly resulting from inadequate drainage systems for runoff water produced by heavy rainfall from storms. Overflowing rivers and streams cause significant flooding in about half the communities and over at least 7 percent of the land area of the nation.

The majority of these flood disasters come not with the sudden shock of the flash flood, catching its victims by surprise. Instead, they are marked by the slow, steady, inexorable rise of the river, relentlessly swelling to its banks, then spreading over the land, the human inhabitants first attempting futilely to somehow barricade its reach, then fleeing in helplessness as the water reclaims, if only temporarily, the floodplain land. Rivers turn to seas, houses turn to islands, crops turn to mud, communities stick up halfway above the water's surface, as though some madman developer built on the bottom of a rising reservoir.

This is the way the Mississippi Valley looked in the spring of 1927. Breaking all previous water level records, the Mississippi River spread out over 18 million acres of land from Southern Illinois to Southern Louisiana. A National Geographic Society staff member described the scene he flew over: "A vast sheet of water as yellow as the China Sea at the mouth of the Yangtze stretched practically from southeast Missouri down to the Atchafalay Basin of Louisiana. This sea is about 1,050 miles long and in places over 50 miles in width. Over 750,000 people normally live within its limits. . . . You see the roofs of their houses, the smokestacks of their sawmills, their church steeples, the tops of their shade trees, and lines of telegraph poles sticking up from the water."

One and one-third cubic miles of water a day was flowing past Vicksburg, Mississippi. Relief boats floated among the tree tops. A steamboat captain found his landmarks obliterated and lost himself and his craft in a flooded forest. New Orleans saved itself from total inundation by dynamiting some of its levees so the river would flood its bayou islands instead. All along the river, death came when levees holding back the river broke.

Three hundred thirteen persons were killed, and 637,000 were left homeless. Damage was $300 million. Secretary of Commerce Herbert Hoover was put in charge of rescue and rehabilitation operations. Boats were commandeered, tent cities set up. This was before the time of vast federal largess, and

Rescue during flash flood, Montgomery County, Maryland, July 15, 1975. (NOAA)

Hoover raised relief money through charity drives. His efficient efforts, it is said, helped land him in the White House.

Even more disastrous in the number of human lives lost were the Ohio River Valley floods of 1913. Winter rains had saturated the ground, and when more rains came in late March, the worst floods in Ohio and Indiana history spread over the land. Dayton was turned into a lake. People sought safety by walking like high-wire daredevils on telephone and electric lines. Wire and rope were strung between poles, trees, and other high objects to give victims caught in the water something to cling to. Seven hundred thirty persons lost their lives. The flood led to a major effort of channel clearing and dam building, a pioneer flood-prevention effort paid for by the people of Dayton.

The Kansas-Missouri floods of June and July, 1951, were the first billion-dollar floods in U.S. history, but fortunately, the loss of life was not proportionately high. Only 28 persons died.

The floods from Hurricane Agnes (demoted to tropical storm status as it moved far inland) in 1972 spread from Virginia to New York, killed 117 persons, and resulted in the most costly natural disaster in U.S. history. Damage was estimated at $3.1 billion. The entire state of Pennsylvania was declared a disaster area. No one who lived in the Middle Atlantic States in late June and early July that year will forget the way the skies opened up (15 inches of rain at several locations) and river basins large and small soon went awash with raging, turbulent waters, exceeding all previous levels at many points. The Susquehanna, the Monongahela, the Delaware, the Allegheny, the Rappahannock, the Potomac, the Patuxent, the Occoquan, the Chowan, the Roanoke—the rivers with rhythmic names from America's Indian past surged with another kind of rhythm then, a churning, debris-laden turbulence that swept around, past, or through everything in its path.

In Washington, D.C., where I then lived, Rock Creek Parkway, a pleasant, winding, forested route to downtown and government offices, was turned into a raging river. Water from the Potomac and the Tidal Basin lapped up over Independence Avenue, and sandbag barriers were stretched across 17th Street just west of the Washington Monument, evoking a curious image of the nation's capital under siege.

Other cities were not so lucky. The Susquehanna River flood was the worst since 1784. Such Pennsylvania cities as Harrisburg, Wilkes-Barre, Wyoming, and Kingston were inundated. In Southern Virginia, flooding on the James River south of Lynchburg was the greatest known since at least 1870, and much of the capital city of Richmond was buried under water.

England and Europe have had their share of floods. The greatest British inland flood was in North Devon, around the town of Lynmouth, on August 15, 1952, following nine inches of rain. Water-logged ground was underlain by rock that prevented absorption. Little rivers usually having only a few inches of water carried torrents tens of feet deep. Rocks and boulders were gouged out. One huge boulder was found in a hotel basement. Telegraph poles, trees, and automobiles were carried out to sea. A string of 17 consecutive bridges was taken out. A car still with its lights on was seen being swept along beneath the water's surface, like a weird submarine. The landscape was vastly altered, and 93 buildings were destroyed. Thirty-four persons lost their lives.

Along the Hwang Ho (Yellow) River in China, the most flood-prone river in the world, the waters have periodically inundated the land for 40 centuries. The most lethal flood in recorded world history struck there in the fall of 1887. The river overflowed 70-foot-high levees in Honan Province. Eleven cities,

300 villages, and 50,000 square miles of crop land were flooded to depths of 20 to 30 feet. An estimated 900,000 people were killed and 2 million made homeless.

In Northern China, in 1939, some 500,000 persons drowned in extensive flooding. Famine resulting from the floods may have cost an additional several million lives. Several hundred thousand may have died in China's Shantung Province in April, 1969, when storm surges raked the coastline and pushed flood tides up the Yellow River Valley.

The tragedy of flood has plagued humankind since the dawn of recorded history. With the continuing spread of a growing population into the world's floodplains, authorities see little hope in abating the tide of destruction. Floods seem likely to hold forever their record as the world's most widespread, prevalent, and damaging type of natural disaster.

CHAPTER 6
Hurricanes

In 1900, Galveston, Texas, was an attractive and fashionable city, a thriving center of commerce, and the fastest growing port in the United States. The 27-mile-long barrier island on which it was situated was jeweled with beautiful beaches on the Gulf of Mexico side, and rich Texans had built fabulous homes, some worth in excess of a million dollars. It was the fourth wealthiest city per capita in the United States.

Then came the hurricane of September 8, a day never to be forgotten. The storm had been rambling around in the West Indies for some days. It initially seemed to be moving north toward the Florida Keys, and from there might be expected to veer up the Atlantic Coast toward the Carolinas. Even if it were to head northwest toward Galveston, there would be little real concern. Hurricanes had swept toward Galveston before but had almost always veered to the northeast and spared the island. Besides, the hurricane of 1875 and the storm of 1887 had been withstood.

On September 4, the U.S. Weather Bureau decided the hurricane could go either way and issued warnings for both the East Coast and the Gulf Coast as far west as Galveston. On September 6, the hurricane was confirmed to be in the Gulf. Still, no one could say where it would strike land. To Isaac M. Cline, chief of the Weather Bureau in Galveston, the signs pointed to Galveston as the prospective target, but the information was too incomplete to make an official warning. He did understand the island's vulnerability, however—the highest point in the city of Galveston was only 20 feet above sea level. To the few persons who called, he suggested that, if they had a sturdy house well away from the beaches, they stay put; other-

The destruction of Galveston, the nation's worst natural disaster.
(AMERICAN RED CROSS)

wise, get to the mainland. But not even he could know the force of this storm.

At 4 in the morning on the 8th, a Saturday, a driving rain squall hit. By 10 A.M. the winds had reached such a point that the bay area began to flood. Ships were being battered against the wharves. As the winds mounted, spectators, still not appreciating the danger, stood on the beaches to watch the approaching storm. Cline and his brother Joseph hitched horses and rode to the beaches to warn them. Most people ignored them. Storm-warning flags hoisted to the top of the Levy Building in downtown Galveston were soon ripped away by the winds, which reached hurricane velocity by mid-afternoon. When the winds reached 84 miles per hour, the Weather Bureau anemometer was torn away. Their roar grew steadily worse.

The city's electricity went out, and a steamship torn from its moorings crashed through all three bridges to the mainland, trapping the islanders within the center of the hurricane's violence. The island was now awash.

The Clines rushed to evacuate their families. From 3:30 till 7:30 the waters rose steadily. At that moment, recalled Isaac Cline, there was a sudden rise of about four feet in four seconds.

"I was standing at my front door, which was partly open, watching the water which was flowing with great rapidity from east to west. The water at this time was about eight inches deep in my residence, and the sudden rise of four feet brought it above my waist before I could change position."

The water rose five more feet in the next hour, bringing a high tide more than 20 feet above normal on the south side of the city. Houses were torn from their foundations and turned into giant battering rams. A mass of splintered cottages and debris two stories high was pushed four to six blocks inland by the waves.

Among the first to die were three citizens toasting the storm at a table on the first floor of Rietter's Saloon on Strand Street. The roof collapsed, crushing them. Others were saved when the bar caught the roof and flooring.

A dozen artillery soldiers at Fort Crockett were killed when their barracks building caved in. The company commander saved himself and his family by taking refuge behind a bolted steel door in a small steel room beneath a 10-inch gun emplacement. At the Catholic Orphanage Asylum, 15 Sisters of Charity attempted to save the one hundred children there by linking them with ropes. But the building collapsed on them. Only two small boys among all those inside survived. Fifty persons died inside city hall, where they had taken refuge. Scores were crushed when the Rosenberg schoolhouse fell. Inside St. Mary's infirmary, only eight of 100 persons survived.

Most of the dead, however, were killed by the collapse of their own houses. Most of these homes were weakly built of cedar posts, brick columns, and brick foundations imbedded only a few feet in the sand.

Weatherman Cline's house collapsed, and his wife was drowned. He, his youngest child, his brother, and some other survivors drifted about in the waters for hours. Hundreds of others were adrift also, clinging to whatever debris was available. Many were killed by timbers and roof tiles turned into flood-and-wind-propelled missiles.

At about midnight the winds subsided, the rain slackened, and the waters began falling back.

Dawn broke on Sunday to a scene of utter devastation.

"About 3,000 homes, nearly half the residence portion of Galveston, had been completely swept out of existence," Cline wrote later. "Where 20,000 people lived on the 8th, not a house remained on the 9th, and who occupied the houses may, in many instances, never be known."

An estimated 6,000 persons were dead, a weather catastrophe of proportions never before or since equaled in the United States.

Rescuers coming over from the mainland found hundreds of bodies in the bay "floating around like cordwood." Former State Senator Wortham described the scene: "Great piles of human bodies, dead animals, rotting household furniture, and fragments of houses themselves are piled in confused heaps right on the main streets of the city."

The water-logged ground could not be used for burial. In fact, the storm waters had dislodged caskets from existing cemeteries. Attempts to make trenches for the dead were unsuccessful. A heat-wave immediately after the disaster compounded the danger, causing the piled-up bodies to swell and blacken and hastening decomposition. The threat of disease loomed. A plan to tow the corpses out to sea on barges failed when all the bodies washed back to shore with the tide.

By now, the situation was desperate, and only one choice was left. Shallow trenches were dug and lined with wood. Corpses and debris were piled into them together and set afire. The funeral pyres burned over Galveston all week, an acrid and gruesome conclusion to the worst natural disaster ever to beset the United States.

"Hurricane" derives from the Spanish *huracán*, which in turn probably comes from the Mayan storm god, *Hunraken*, from the Quiche god of thunder and lightning, *Huraken*, and from many other Caribbean Indian terms for evil spirit, big wind, and other similar forces. *Hurricane* is the name used for the storms spawned in the Western Atlantic Ocean and Caribbean Sea. The same storm is called a *typhoon* in the Western Pacific, a *tropical cyclone* in the Indian Ocean, a *baguio* in the Philippines, and sometimes a *willy-willy* in Australia. Different names for the same vast whirling force, both a bringer of needed rains and a dealer of death and destruction.

That the Caribbean Indian names have come down to us through the Spanish is not surprising. Often the fleets of early Spanish sailing vessels carrying goods and gold between the New World and Spain were caught in hurricanes, and many a ship with its crew and cargo was sent to the bottom.

One of the earliest such losses on record was that of the Spanish fleet of 30 caravels carrying gold in July, 1502. A storm-wizened Christopher Columbus, newly arrived at Hispaniola on his fourth voyage, cautioned the fleet not to set sail but was ignored. He himself took shelter at anchor in an island cove. A hurricane caught the vessels off Mona Island, Hispaniola. Twenty of the ships sank outright, and only one made it to Spain. Five hundred men were lost.

In 1555, the New Spain Flota of 20 ships was struck by a hurricane five days out of Veracruz on a voyage to Havana. Only two of the vessels reached land, and those survivors were massacred by the Indians.

A one-month period in 1559 was particularly devastating. On August 20, a Spanish expedition from Veracruz seeking to colonize Florida was caught in a hurricane in what is now known as Tampa Bay. Fifteen hundred men were crammed aboard 13 caravels. Every ship was either broken apart or grounded, and 600 of the men, mostly soldiers, were killed. Then on September 19, a 13-vessel fleet under the command of the Governor of Florida was smashed in half by a hurricane in the Bay of Santa Maria, and several hundred more lives were lost.

In August of 1591, only three years after the destruction of the Spanish Armada in the English Channel, the Spanish treasure fleet, making its annual run from Havana to Spain, was caught in the worst of four hurricanes that struck the Western Hemisphere in a month's period. A dozen of the vessels and 500 Spanish soldiers and sailors went to the bottom, and Spanish seapower had been dealt another brutal blow.

The losses had not ceased, however. In September, 1600, 1,000 men were lost when the Spanish flota was raked first by a hurricane off the coast of Villa Rica and later by another storm on the voyage to Veracruz. In September, 1622, a dozen vessels in the Armada de Tierra Firme and the Tierra Firme Flota were wrecked by a hurricane in the Florida Keys, and several thousand lives were lost. Still another eastward-bound Spanish flota, this time of 19 ships, was struck by a hurricane one week out of Veracruz in October of 1631, with the loss of 300 lives. And on November 1, 1643, the Spain-bound flagship of the Spanish silver fleet foundered on a reef in a hurricane north of Hispaniola. Of the 514 persons aboard the huge vessel, 324 died.

Reading through this litany of destruction of early Spanish vessels by hurricane, I marvel at the resiliency, aided and abetted by the lure of New World wealth, that enabled Spain to persevere as a world maritime power as long as it did.

Early English colonists in the New World soon learned the might of the hurricane. On July 25, 1609, a hurricane scattered a fleet carrying settlers to the new English colony of Jamestown. The flagship eventually foundered on a reef at Bermuda and was not heard of again for 10 months, when its passengers and crew sailed into Jamestown in a small boat built from the remains of the ship. Accounts of the adventures of these people, first published in England in the fall of 1610, served as the inspiration for William Shakespeare's beautiful play *The Tempest.*

The early English colonists in New England, even as far north as they were, were not spared from the hazard of the hurricane. The great storm of 1635 was impressive enough to be described in William Bradford's history of Plymouth plantation, in Governor Winthrop's journal, and in the diary of the Reverend Richard Mather, ancestor of the famous Mather family.

This description is from Bradford's chronicle (I have modernized the spelling and syntax):

On the 15th of August, came such a storm of wind and rain as none living in these parts, either English or Indians, ever saw. . . . It began in the morning, a little before daylight and grew not by degrees but came with violence at the beginning. It blew down sundry [Bradford then specifies 211] houses, and uncovered others. Diverse vessels were lost at sea, and many more were in extreme danger. It caused the sea to swell (south of Plymouth) above 20 feet, and made many of the Indians climb into trees for their safety. It took off the boarded roof of a house on the plantation at Manamet and floated it to another place, the posts still standing in the ground. If it had continued long without the wind shifting, it is likely it would have drowned some part of the country. It blew down many hundred thousands of trees, turning up the stronger by the roots and breaking the higher pine trees in the middle. Tall young oaks and walnut trees of good size were wound like a wreath, very strange and powerful to behold. The signs and marks of it will remain 100 years in these parts where it was sorest.

The storm of 1635 leads a list of four great storms that have hit New England, one in each century since settlement. The others are the gale of 1723 (chronicled by Cotton Mather in a paper to the Royal Society in London), and the hurricanes of 1815 and 1938.

Oliver Wendell Holmes was a six-year-old boy in the storm of 1815, and to the more conventional description he later wrote he added whimsical mention of one particular loss:

> It chanced to be our washing-day,
> And all our things were drying
> The storm came roaring through the lines,
>   And set them all aflying;
> I saw shirts and petticoats
>   Go riding off like witches;
> I lost, ah! bitterly I wept,—
>   I lost my Sunday breeches.

The hurricane of 1938, a whirling mass 240 miles across, struck with furious rapidity. Moving northward at 50 miles per hour, it quickly sliced a path of destruction across Long Island, then smashed into Rhode Island, Connecticut, and Massachusetts. It derailed the Long Island Express at East Hampton and twisted the tracks into loops. At West Hampton it left 19 people dead. In New England it brought tides 17 feet above normal, drowning many who underestimated its power. Airborne spray covered windows and killed vegetation as far as 22 miles inland. In New London, Connecticut, the naval anemometer recorded 98-mile-per-hour winds before the wind cups blew away. Near Boston, the anemometer at Blue Hills Observatory registered 180 miles per hour before it blew off. Thirty passengers and crew aboard the Bridgeport-Port Jefferson ferry, its engines put out by the storm, spent a night of darkness on the helplessly drifting vessel, but were rescued the next morning.

New London was in the direct path. Destruction was terrible, and then fire broke out, reminiscent of the horrible day during the Revolutionary War when the British under Benedict Arnold burned the city. Small sea vessels of every description littered the streets. A training ship, the barkentine *Marsala*, was lodged against a railroad trestle, and the lighthouse tender *Tulip* was atop railroad tracks. At Stonington, Connecticut, the passenger train *Bostonian* was brought to a halt first by a cabin cruiser on the tracks and then a house. The tracks farther ahead were washed out, and passengers spent 20 hours inside the train in isolation.

As in the 1815 storm, Rhode Island was the worst hit. Winds of 121 miles per hour pushed the waters of Narragansett Bay into the business section of Providence, where within half an hour Union Street was under six feet of water, sending people struggling for their lives to whatever safety they could find. Great waves washed right through coastal villages, wiping out people and property alike. Ten women attending a church social at Misquamicut were washed out to sea when the building collapsed and were never again seen. Lighthouses, built to withstand the sea's full fury, were downed.

By 7:30 in the evening, Rhode Island lay isolated and in ruins, electrical and telephone lines down, transportation links severed, even its geographical boundaries altered by the force of the storm.

Telephone communications between Boston and New York were routed through London. A U.S. Navy battleship carried mail between the two cities.

The hurricane, the worst in more than a century in New England, left more than 600 dead and caused more than $300 million damage. In addition to the deaths and the damage to property, millions of New England's beautiful trees were blown down by the wind, and forests throughout the region suffered extensive damage that only decades could heal.

One of the greatest hurricanes on record had an influence in altering American history, although it hit not on the mainland of North America but in the West Indies. Known now as the Great Hurricane of 1780, it struck the island of Barbados with frightful force. The devastation was complete. Not a tree or a building was left standing and 6,000 inhabitants were killed. It then slammed into the island of Saint Lucia, and destroyed a British fleet anchored there, altering the naval balance of the American War of Independence. It went on to hit Martinique with similar force. Nearly 20,000 persons were left dead by the storm.

A hurricane is a child of the tropics, a whirling mass of energy formed when circumstances of heat and pressure nourish and nudge the winds over a large area of ocean to wrap themselves around an atmospheric low with particularly high energy.

Hurricane Gladys photographed by Apollo 7 astronauts in 1968. The spiraling might of a hurricane releases more energy in one day than the United States uses electrically in one year. (NASA)

It is a heat engine generated and maintained by the energy of condensation of rain within its saturated spiral clouds. Like other storms that may bring destruction, the hurricane has no innate malevolence. It is a natural atmospheric process, nature's way of releasing heat that builds up in the tropics. The violence hurricanes inflict may strike our hearts with fear, but the rains they and less powerful tropical storms bring are essential to successful agriculture in parts of the world. Japan, for instance, gets a fourth of its rainfall from typhoons.

A hurricane is by definition a rotating wind system (whirling counterclockwise in the Northern Hemisphere) formed over tropical water and having wind speeds of 74 miles per hour or more. Thus the distinction between a hurricane and a tropical storm (winds from 39 to 73 miles per hour) and a tropical depression (winds of less than 39 miles per hour). *Tropical cyclone* is the general term for all such cyclonic (rotating about a low) circulations originating over tropical waters. In the twentieth century, an average year has seen eight tropical cyclones whirling out across the Atlantic, with five of them becoming hurricanes. In the typical hurricane, the entire spiral storm system is at least 1,000 miles across, with hurricane-force winds over a diameter of 100 miles and gale-force winds extending beyond to a diameter of 400 miles.

The energy contained within such a hurricane is on nature's grand scale. A typical hurricane liberates heat from the condensation of moisture at a rate of about 100 billion kilowatts. So in a single day, a hurricane produces the equivalent of 2.4 trillion kilowatt-hours. By comparison, the total electrical consumption across the entire United States in the year 1977 was 2.13 trillion kilowatt-hours. Thus, in one day an average hurricane releases more energy than the nation uses electrically in a whole year. To express it in more violent terms, the condensation energy released by a typical hurricane in one day is equivalent to the explosion of 2,000 one-megaton hydrogen bombs.

The transfer of this thermal energy to mechanical energy (wind) is very inefficient, about 3 percent. Nevertheless, that is sufficient to produce and maintain winds of up to 200 miles per hour, although winds of about 130 miles per hour are more typical. And by one estimate an average hurricane squeezes out 200 billion tons of water a day as rain.

Couple all this with a lifetime of hurricanes that is measured in days and weeks rather than hours or minutes (Ginger in 1971 lasted 20 days as a hurricane, 31 days as a tropical cyclone) and it is easy to see why hurricanes deserve being called the greatest storms on earth. No other storm combines size, duration, and violence more destructively.

Most of us who have never been in a hurricane have the image of hurricane-force winds bending rows of beach-side palm trees back toward the land, an assault of wind that seemingly only the most sturdy buildings can withstand. The pictures of the action of rain-soaked wind are vivid indeed. Yet the direct action of the wind is not the biggest killer in a hurricane. Hurricane winds do much damage, but most of the victims of hurricanes die by drowning. And most of the flooding comes not from the intense rains but from what is known as the storm surge. The winds and low pressure around the hurricane eye tend to raise the level of the ocean one or two feet. When this dome of water, perhaps 50 miles across, moves into shallow coastal water, the decreasing water depth transforms it into a storm surge that can rise high above normal sea level, bringing the seas well inland.

The National Weather Service estimates that storm surges

Hurricane winds battering coastline. (NOAA)

cause nine of every 10 hurricane fatalities. Depending on the strength of the storm and local bottom conditions where the surge comes ashore, the storm surge may cause the sea to rise as much as 20 feet higher than normal. The storm surge is superimposed on normal astronomical tides. In turn, wind waves are superimposed on the storm surge. The worst circumstance is to have the storm surge (it is not, by the way, a "tidal wave") strike the coast at the time of high tide. Much human activity and development along coastlines takes place at elevations less than 10 feet above sea level and still more at less than 15 feet above sea level. A hurricane storm surge of 15 feet accompanied by a two-foot high tide would raise the water 17 feet above mean sea level. When that happens near any populated area (as we've seen with the inundations of Galveston in 1900 and Providence in 1938), disaster is inevitable.

Storm surges can reach almost unbelievable proportions. During Hurricane Camille in August, 1969, one of the strongest U.S. hurricanes of this century, the storm surge that demolished buildings and inundated Pass Christian, Mississippi, was estimated to have been 25 feet high, according to the National Oceanic and Atmospheric Administration. One hundred fifty-two persons in Mississippi and Louisiana lost their lives in that hurricane. Among them were 23 of 24 persons at Pass Christian who refused to evacuate and held a "hurricane party" instead. The three-story apartment building they were in was obliterated by the storm surge, leaving nothing but the foundation. The one survivor spent a fearful time being buffeted about in the debris-strewn waters before eventually being swept into a tree top, where she was found and rescued the next morning.

Hurricane storm surges have been responsible for many of the most deadly disasters in the United States. A storm surge in the Louisiana bayou country in October of 1893 killed 2,000. One on Lake Okeechobee in Florida in September of 1928 broke the dikes and left 1,836 victims. Hit still again were Florida, in 1935, with a loss of 400 lives, and Louisiana, in 1957, with a toll of 390.

People of other nations have suffered even worse. More than 5,000 Japanese were killed in 1959 when a typhoon sent the waters of Ise Bay onto land. The Ganges-Brahmaputra delta at the head of the Bay of Bengal is one of the most susceptible areas in the world. In October, 1737, a cyclone raised the sea waters 15 feet and drowned 300,000 people. That same area has had killer cyclones and coastal inundations for centuries. The earliest record of one was written in 1584. In 1965, two separate cyclones in May and June killed at least 35,000, and in December a third killed an additional 15,000.

In November of 1970, disaster struck again. Even by standards of previous cyclone disasters, this one was awesome. A tremendous cyclone swept over the offshore islands located to the south of what is now called Bangladesh, then East Pakistan. According to M. Aminul Islam of the University of Dacca, "The cyclonic storm of November 12–13, 1970, could be regarded as unprecedented in world history in terms of damage caused." It was the greatest natural disaster of the 1970s prior to the Chinese earthquake of 1976. A brief look at the circumstances shows not only the power of the hurricane and its storm surge but also the way in which nature, geography, culture, traditions, and social systems sometimes combine to make for tragedy.

Bangladesh is one of the more densely populated nations of the world—1,400 persons per square mile. Food supply is an acute problem, and farmers are faced with either feeding their families from even smaller plots of land or moving to new areas. Faced with hunger, many have spread out onto the flat lands of the delta. The land there is fertile and ideal for rice cultivation. But it is also at great risk from coastal storms, and much of it has been settled only in the past 60 years. Some land was reclaimed from the sea by the government, with great engineering and agricultural effort and international assistance. New populations were officially encouraged to occupy these regions. Most of the people live in bamboo and straw houses perched on mounds to keep them above the waters of the summer monsoons.

The cyclone of 1970 was first identified by satellite on November 9. It was subsequently tracked by radar as it moved up the Bay of Bengal, but no monitoring aircraft were available for flights to determine its precise intensity.

At about 11 P.M. on November 12, it slammed into the coast. The worst had happened—the peak of the storm surge nearly coincided with high tide. Along the eastern coast of Bhola Island, the waters reached a maximum of almost seven meters (23 feet) above mean sea level. Throughout the low and nearly flat region, the storm surge combined with rapid overflow of the rivers from intense rainfall to produce cyclone flooding of enormous proportions. The depth of the inundation ranged from 10 to 30 feet.

The fierce winds continued inland, and by morning at least 225,000 persons were dead. Other estimates range from 300,000 to 500,000. No one will ever know the exact total. Many victims were migrant laborers, and in the aftermath, little could be done but quickly bury the bodies. Most of the victims died when the land they were on suddenly became the sea. On some islands, all the inhabitants perished. Later study showed that most of those who survived the inundated areas did so by climbing trees. Those who were too young or slow or weak to do so perished. The government had issued warnings of the cyclone, but the communications system and social organization necessary to get the messages to the people and have them act was woefully inadequate.

The case of the village of Char Jabbar was perhaps typical. The village had been linked to the mainland in 1964 by an 11-mile embankment, which brought new settlers into the village. Scientists later reported that if adequate warning had been given, transportation prepared, and evacuation plans made in advance, the villagers could have escaped along the embankment, which was overtopped by the cyclone waters but not washed away. The villagers reported that the warning of the cyclone never reached Char Jabbar. The telegraph office was 16 miles away. Radios were scarce, and the radio station goes off the air at 11 P.M. anyway. No motorized transportation was available. Families were reluctant to leave their homes or to subject women members, accustomed to seclusion, to the public exposure of evacuation and community shelters. It is estimated that of the 18,000 regular residents of the village, 6,000 died.

Throughout the affected area, it was estimated that the massive storm surge brought death to 17 percent of the population. Eighty-five percent of the families had their homes destroyed or seriously damaged, and 600,000 were left homeless. A million head of livestock were destroyed, and an estimated 800,000 tons of rice growing in the paddies were swept away. The indifference of the central government of Pakistan, far away on the other side of India, to the suffering and the halfhearted rescue and relief efforts fomented social disorder. Rebellion and bitter civil war soon followed, leading to the establishment of the new state of Bangladesh, a troubled nation born out of disaster.

India has often borne the brunt of the great cyclones whirling up through the Bay of Bengal. On November 19, 1977, a cyclone crashed into a 250-mile stretch of coastline of Andhra Pradesh State north of Madras. A storm surge estimated at 18 feet swallowed up at least a score of villages. Twenty thousand persons were killed, and an estimated two million left homeless. One report described the scene at the coastal district of Divi Taluk as "hell on earth." Thousands of bloated human corpses and animal bodies were strewn about. The army was called out to bury the dead, clear debris, and disinfect villages and water supplies.

Seen from the remote-control safety of our orbiting weather satellites, the storms that cause such human grief when their paths cross populated land are beautifully organized entities, their tightly wound graceful spirals belying the destructive force hidden within. In a case of different scales of nature seeming to imitate each other, they bear a remarkable resemblance to astronomers' photos of distant spiral galaxies whirling timelessly in the blackness of space.

This organization is a product of many forces cooperating to shape what would ordinarily be towering linear bands of cumulonimbus thunderstorms into a rotary form that feeds on itself and the ocean's heat to grow into a mighty system of whirling energy. Required first are weeks of high summer sun, heating the ocean surface and enriching the humidity by evaporation. This is why hurricanes tend mainly to form in the late summer, after the sun has had time to warm the tropical ocean to temperatures of 80 degrees Fahrenheit or more. A weak disturbance in the easterly tradewinds—perhaps an easterly wave, or low pressure trough—slowly drifts westward across the Atlantic, maybe from the mainland of Africa. A portion of this disturbance organizes low-level circulation into an area of weak convergence, drawing in air near the surface. As the air flows together, it rises and cools by expansion, and this triggers intense thunderstorms and rainfall. Most play themselves out quickly, and are heard of no more.

But if the air is especially humid and the water warmer than normal, the cumulonimbus clouds can moisten and warm the air to quite high levels. Since warm air weighs less than cool air, this produces a fall of pressure at the surface. And where there is a lowering of surface pressure, the winds that were converging there intensify. They respond to the increased difference in pressure by accelerating toward the area of low pressure.

The effect of the earth's rotation helps nudge these inward flows into a counterclockwise rotation (in the Northern Hemisphere). The principle of conservation of angular momentum, by which the product of the rotational velocity of a flow and its distance from the center of rotation must remain constant (the same principle governs the speed of a spinning figure skater), causes the winds to flow faster and faster as their distance from the center grows smaller. Once started, this intensification may proceed rapidly.

The inflowing air cannot reach all the way into the center because to conserve momentum would require higher speeds and therefore higher kinetic energy (which is proportional to the square of the windspeed) than is available from condensation heating. This limits the penetration of inward flow. Instead of going farther toward the center, then, the air turns and whirls upward. Here in this 10-mile-thick inner spinning ring of towering clouds and rapid upward motion known as the hurricane's eyewall, condensation and rainfall are intense, and the winds are at their most violent.

Harbored within the eyewall is the calm eye of the hurricane, usually 10 to 20 miles across, protected from the inflowing winds and often free of clouds altogether. Here surface pressure

Three tropical storms line up in perfect order across the eastern Pacific on September 26, 1976. On the left, Hurricane Kate; in the center, a tropical depression; on the right, a tropical depression that four days later became Hurricane Liza and smashed into LaPaz, Baja California, causing great damage and killing more than 100 persons. (NOAA)

drops to a minimum, and winds subside to less than 15 miles per hour. High up in the eye temperatures may be 20 degrees F warmer than the surrounding air. Although its role in legend and fiction is perhaps overplayed (remember in *Marooned* the last-minute launch of a manned rescue rocket from Cape Kennedy during a moment of respite from a hurricane as the eye passed overhead?), the calm eye is no myth. But the period of grace it grants is short-lived. Soon, because of the hurricane's motion over the ground, the far eyewall now accosts the surface, this time of course with winds from the opposite direction.

The upward spiraling air in the hurricane's eyewall eventually reaches the top, about 40,000 feet high, wrung dry of its moisture and cooled by the cold upper atmosphere, and now flows outward away from the storm center. In a reverse of its inflow acceleration, as it moves further from the center its rotational velocity decreases, and soon it merges with the large-scale circulation of the tropics. The cycle is complete. The air flows into the hurricane at its base, rises up through its thickness, and passes back out and away from the storm at the top. Out beyond the eyewall, the hurricane forms into characteristic spiral rainbands, alternate bands of rain-filled clouds.

Within the hurricane's core on the surface beneath, the air pressure drops, as though part of the atmosphere has suddenly disappeared, and the degree of fall is one measure of a storm's intensity. A normal reading of the air pressure at sea level is 1013 millibars, or 30 inches of mercury. The lowest pressure ever recorded in a tropical cyclone was 886.7 millibars (26.19 inches) in a typhoon east of Luzon, the Philippines, in 1927. About a dozen North Atlantic hurricanes in this century have produced pressures as low as 927 millibars (27.37 inches of mercury). The only one to reach below the 900-millibar level was the hurricane that struck the Lower Matecumbe Key of Florida in September, 1935. The pressure there dropped incredibly to 892.3 millibars (26.35 inches of mercury). The force of the storm matched the pressure drop. At a place called Camp Number Five were housed 716 bonus army workers, down-and-out World War I veterans who had marched on Washington to appeal for a bonus for their service in France. They had been sent to Lower Matecumbe Key ostensibly to build a government road but more likely to be kept out of sight. As the storm approached, a rescue train was sent to try to evacuate the men but was blocked by water washing over the tracks. One hundred twenty-one of the veterans and 279 local residents were killed in the storm.

One of the persons who waded through mangrove swamps to help look for victims was Ernest Hemingway, who lived nearby. Later Hemingway, who blamed an indifferent federal government for the men's deaths, wrote scathingly of the experience:

And the wind makes a noise like a locomotive passing, with a shriek on top of that, because the wind has a scream exactly as it has in books, and then the fill goes and the high wall of water rolls you over and over and then, whatever it is, you get it and we find you, now of no importance stinking in the mangroves . . . You're dead now, brother. . . .

Hurricanes generally move along their path at speeds of less than 20 miles per hour, especially in their formative stages. On rare occasions, such as the New England Hurricane of 1938, one will turn into a speedster and race along at up to 60 miles per hour.

Hurricanes are born imbedded within the easterly tradewinds, so they have an initial westward-moving flow. If they drift far enough northward, they can be caught by the prevailing westerlies of mid-latitudes and sent back to the east or northeast. Their direction is also affected by other large-scale weather conditions. A southeastward-advancing coldfront, for example, can stall a northwestward-moving hurricane off the U.S. coast and perhaps nudge it back out to sea. But generalizations about hurricane direction are risky. Their paths can be as erratic as a fly avoiding a flyswatter.

If the conditions of warmth and humidity are sufficient, a hurricane can change course often enough and last long enough to turn any weather forecaster or coastal resident into a nervous wreck. An average mid-season storm lasts 12 days, but Hurricane Ginger in 1971 lasted from September 5 to October 5, traveled halfway across the Atlantic twice, and crossed over its own path twice (one loop was within the other) before going ashore in North Carolina and back out to sea from Virginia. Forecasters issued 88 hurricane advisories during its existence. Hurricane Ginny in 1963 looped back over itself twice also. Hurricane Faith in 1966 started near West Africa, moved westward across the Atlantic to near the Windward Islands, then turned northeastward to eventually reach far beyond the Arctic Circle.

Once a hurricane moves over the mainland, its supply of evaporated water from the ocean surface is cut off and its power eventually diminishes, but often not before it dumps enormous quantities of rain on the land below. The floods mentioned in the previous chapter when the remnants of Hurricane Agnes dropped up to 17 inches of rain over the Eastern United States are one result. Hurricane Diane in 1955 caused little damage along the coast but the floods its rains brought to Pennsylvania, New York, and New England killed 200 persons and caused $300 million additional damage. Hurricane Camille in 1969, after its destructive attack on the Gulf Coast, dropped up to 27 inches of rain on the mountainous areas of Virginia on August 19–20, and the ensuing floods killed an additional 112 persons and brought its total toll of damage to $1.42 billion— until Hurricane Agnes, the most costly disaster in U.S. history.

Scientists used to think that friction with the rougher surface as the storm moved onto land helped contribute to the hurricane's dissolution, but that idea seems to have run into some trouble by a series of computer experiments done by scientists

Hurricane Agnes advancing inland, June 19, 1972. The rains of this storm resulted in the most costly natural disaster in the nation's history. (NOAA)

of the National Oceanic and Atmospheric Administration and announced in August, 1978.

Scientists of NOAA's Geophysical Fluid Dynamics Laboratory ran three experiments using numerical models to simulate three different conditions. In one, the simulated land was rougher and dryer than the ocean, as it is in reality. In the second, the "land" was rough but as wet as the ocean. In the third, land surface was as smooth as the ocean but evaporation was eliminated.

The greatest drop in the resulting simulated winds happened in the first situation, when the land was both rough and dry. The third situation, totally smooth land, also caused the winds to drop. But when, in the second experiment, oceanic evaporation rates were continued over the land and only the roughness of the land surface was increased, the model hurricane actually intensified in force. Apparently, the rougher texture of land can augment the storm if enough moisture is present.

The study confirms that the main effect of land in diminishing a hurricane's intensity is to cut off its supply of energy from the evaporation of warm sea water.

Computer portrayals of the behavior of hurricanes are one

Hurricane Anita from satellite, September 1, 1977: A powerful hurricane and a bonanza to science. (ROBERT S. SHEETS, NATIONAL HURRICANE & EXPERIMENTAL METEOROLOGICAL LABORATORY)

of the main tools modern atmospheric scientists have at their disposal to study the inner workings of these tropical storms. Here, numerical data set within complex equations of the atmosphere and set to flow within the electronic circuitry of the computer play out scores of hypothetical storms with their imaginary winds and deluges. Within a storm, a single condition, such as temperature of the sea surface, can be varied and the results examined to follow the effect on the growth and life-cycle of the storm. As with all such numerical simulations of the complex workings of flows in nature, inaccuracies are introduced both by our imperfect grasp of how one condition affects another and our inability to measure the conditions within a storm at every single point at every moment. But these numerical simulations are becoming increasingly sophisticated, and they have become an indispensable complement to the direct study and monitoring of hurricanes from land, sea, air, and space.

Numerical models have, for example, shown that the release of heat within the secondary clouds of the hurricane's spiral rain-bands out beyond the eyewall contributes more to the storm's energy than was previously thought. Computer models have given clear indication that the amounts of heat and moisture the hurricane picks up from the ocean's surface are critical to the development of intense storms.

Flights by highly instrumented aircraft—flying weather stations—into hurricanes gather crucial data to help form a more complete picture of storm conditions. In late August, 1977, Hurricane Anita formed in the Gulf of Mexico. With winds of 172 miles per hour and a central pressure of 926 millibars, the fourth lowest recorded in the Gulf this century, Anita was a strong hurricane. About 100,000 people were evacuated from the coast and offshore oil rigs, but its landfall was in a sparsely inhabited area of the Mexican coast and damages and deaths were light. But the storm was a bonanza to science. Three missions carrying the latest radar equipment, instruments, and computers flew into the storm, and, according to the chief of the Hurricane Group of the National Oceanic and Atmospheric Administration, collected as much information as was gathered in the previous five years. Separate radar units in the nose, belly, and tail of the aircraft provided a three-dimensional picture of the storm. Laser particle counters on the wings counted and analyzed the tiny ice crystals and water droplets in the clouds.

SAFFIR/SIMPSON HURRICANE SCALE

Category	Central Pressure (millibars)	Winds (mph)	Surge (ft)	Example
1	980 or more	74-95	4-5	Agnes 1972 (Fla. coast)
2	965-979	96-110	6-8	Cleo 1964
3	945-964	111-130	9-12	Betsy 1965
4	920-944	131-155	13-18	Donna 1960 Fla., Carla 1961 Tex.
5	less than 920	more than 155	more than 18	1935 Storm on Fla. Keys

The way storm surge, wind, and other factors combine determines the hurricane's destructive power. To make comparisons easier— and to make the predicted hazards of approaching hurricanes clearer to emergency forces—hurricane forecasters use a disaster-potential scale, which assigns storms to five categories. Category 1 is a minimum hurricane; Category 5 is the worst case.

All the information was analyzed by a computer able to handle more data than previous equipment.

In addition, a research ship of Texas A&M University, the *Gyre,* measured ocean conditions before and after the storm, and one of the NOAA flights through the storm dropped expendable instruments into the ocean that measured water temperatures at various depths and then radioed back this water-column temperature profile. The storm also passed over three automated scientific buoys that measured changing air and sea conditions. Anita thus became the first hurricane in the Gulf for which detailed data exists immediately before and after its passage. All these measurements produced what scientists later called possibly the most complete set of direct observations of a hurricane drawing its energy from the warm sea.

Out of all this study came an interesting conclusion. It turns out that there was a warm eddy of water in the Gulf, a slowly rotating, 150-mile-wide pool of water about a degree warmer than the surrounding Gulf water. It appears that as tropical storm Anita intensified into a hurricane, it drew part of its power from this warm pool of water. It then left these waters cooler by several degrees, having extracted their heat and, in effect, turned it into the rotating mechanical energy of the hurricane.

The warm eddy had been discovered in the Gulf by NOAA scientists a month before the storm, and its existence there was confirmed by the *Gyre* on August 28 as the storm developed. The data seem to show that as what was first a tropical disturbance moved toward the center of the warm eddy it intensified steadily to tropical storm strength. Then, about 18 hours later, as the storm passed the western boundary of the eddy, the storm's central pressure began dropping rapidly. Anita reached hurricane force a short time later. In other words, the passing of the storm over the area of warm water seems to have helped energize it to hurricane force.

Drained of its extra heat by the passing of the storm, the warm eddy was left seven degrees Fahrenheit (four degrees Celsius) cooler after Anita's passage. The eddy's thermal structure was drastically altered down to depths of 600 feet. In addition, throughout a large part of the Gulf of Mexico, surface water temperatures were decreased by an average of nearly four degrees Fahrenheit.

The warm eddy implicated in the hurricane's intensification appears to have broken off from the Gulf of Mexico Loop Current, NOAA oceanographer John Proni reported. It is now certain that scientists will be watching for such warm pools in the paths of future developing tropical storms. Perhaps that way they may be able to better anticipate whether a storm is likely to intensify into a hurricane. At any rate, the observations dramatically confirm the degree to which a hurricane is the product of the interaction of a disturbed tropical atmosphere and a warmer-than-usual sea.

For the origin of the atmospheric disturbances that can lead to Atlantic hurricanes, scientists are more and more looking eastward to Africa. An African birthplace of many of these disturbances has been suspected for some time, but recent analyses of data gathered in an international scientific effort known as GATE, for GARP Atlantic Tropical Experiment, have pointed the meteorologists' finger toward that continent with unprecedented certainty. (GARP itself stands for a larger scientific effort called the Global Atmospheric Research Program.)

One set of studies found a close relationship between disturbances in large-scale easterly air currents and the smaller-scale lines of showers over the tropical ocean, some of which lead to tropical storms and hurricanes. The studies verified the belief that the large weather patterns control the development of clouds and that the heat released in the clouds, as water vapor condenses and falls as rain, produces a feedback effect that intensifies the bigger weather patterns. These large-scale and small-scale processes interact over the tropical ocean, and this storm-brewing cooperation needs to be properly represented in computerized weather forecasts to better anticipate hurricanes.

These studies, led by Richard J. Reed of the University of Washington, confirmed that the large-scale disturbances form over Africa in the region just south of the Sahara. They start as an instability in a narrow east-to-west jet stream that forms in the area between June and September as a result of the great temperature contrast between the hot desert and the cooler, more humid region to the south. The research shows that the disturbances generated over Africa have long lifetimes. Many of them cross the Atlantic, and according to Reed, about one of every 10 develops into a hurricane in the Western Atlantic or Caribbean.

A Florida State University meteorologist, T. N. Krishnamurti, has carried out computer simulations that verify the African connection. About 55 of the atmospheric disturbances over West Africa slip westward into the Atlantic each hurricane season. Using data gathered in GATE, he has carried out computer simulations showing that a knowledge of the temperature over North Africa, especially the desert areas, is crucially important for realistic prediction of disturbances over the ocean. In fact, he reported that he cannot simulate hurricanes in his model unless he includes the effect of temperature from over the West African land mass.

So a hurricane that may wreak havoc and destroy lives in a barrage of rain, wind, and seawater on the coast of one continent seems to have its origins in conditions over the desert wastelands of another continent, 5,000 miles away. It is another example of the interdependent linkages of nature and of both the subtlety and the vast scale of the forces that sometimes merely bring life-giving moisture and other times culminate in tragedy.

CHAPTER 7

Blizzards

The blizzard strikes amid the gray skies of winter, when the pace of life is already slowed by the frozen land, long cold nights, and days of short-lived sun. Like the hurricane, whose late-summer assault is accomplished by wind, rain, and the surge of high seas, the blizzard too strikes with a triad of powerful weapons from nature's arsenal: wind, snow, and cold.

The wind again, yes, the wind, that ever-present, wall-rattling wind, carrying in inseparable bondage sheets of hard-driven snow. Everywhere and from every direction the snow, the ubiquitous snow, not the gentle geometrical flakes and silently accumulating crystalline cover of the normal mid-winter snowfall with its picture-postcard scene of tranquility, but snow charged with the fierce energy of the wind, blown out of the sky and off the land, stinging exposed skin with its icy pellets, sweeping past and through everything in its course until it wraps itself up against some unmovable obstacle, its drifts altering for days the topography of the landscape and all normal patterns of life.

And the cold, that penetrating cold, that wind-amplified cold that jars your teeth and face, takes away your breath, brings quick-frozen tears to the eyes and numbness to the ears, filters through your clothing and seeks out the slightest crack in your shelter, sucking away precious warmth from body and home.

The term *blizzard* (origin uncertain) is generally applied to any storm in which there are strong winds, falling or blowing snow, and cold. Meteorologists consider blizzard conditions to be present when the wind exceeds 30 knots (35 miles per hour), the temperature is well below normal, and visibility is no more than one-eighth of a mile. A severe blizzard condition exists when the winds exceed 40 knots, the temperature is below 10 degrees Fahrenheit, and visibility is essentially zero in the blow-

ing and drifting snow. But those who are in one need no defini-
tions to tell them that a blizzard has hit.

The blizzard strikes its blow individually and collectively, society and community no less a victim than the individual. Whole
towns, cities, regions, portions of entire nations can be frozen
in its grasp, virtually all activity brought to a halt, the complex
workings of our interdependent civilization failing to function
for a time under the strain of the elements. New social patterns
are for a while brought into play, families and neighborhoods
once again the important units, the transportation that powers
our mobile society temporarily curtailed. A blizzard can bring
us into touch with ourselves again. It can also bring hardship,
misery, and tragedy.

Over the decades and centuries, bitter blizzards and harsh
winters have shaped our history. The years 1717, 1778, 1780,
1857, 1864, 1888, 1899, 1918, 1936, 1940, 1949, 1958, 1966
and 1969 are among those known in parts of the United States
for especially harsh blizzards or bitter-cold winters.

Yet never since records have been kept have two winters in
succession had the combined one-two punch of the winters of
1977 and 1978. Vicious blizzards and pervasive, long-lasting,
record-setting cold across vast sections of the East and Midwest
during those winters rewrote the weather record books.

One might have guessed it was going to be an unusual winter
when, on January 19, 1977, for the first time in recorded history,
snow fell in Southeastern Florida. The farthest south snow had
been observed previously was a line between Fort Myers and
Fort Pierce during the notorious cold wave of February, 1899.
The events started the day before when a line of light snow
started moving down through Northern and Central Florida behind an advancing cold front. At 6:10 A.M., on January 19,
West Palm Beach reported its first snowfall on record. From
8:30 to 9, snow fell at the Fort Lauderdale/Hollywood International Airport in Northern Dade County. Snow was soon
spotted on radar in the Miami area, and numerous reports of
snow around Miami came in from the general public, including
one report from Miami Beach. No snow was reported at Miami
International Airport, the official observing station, but snow
was seen as far south as Homestead in Southern Dade County,
about 23 miles south of the airport.

The snow was a phenomenon, a strange and wondrous sight.
People came out and pointed to the skies, and a hardware store

A tramped-out SOS in snow tells pilot this South Dakota farm family isolated by blizzard needs help. Blizzards bring normal routines of families and communities to a halt. (AMERICAN RED CROSS)

jokingly put out a sign advertising snowshovels. The wire services spread the news to the world, and *The Miami Herald* bannered it the next morning: "SNOW FALLS ON S. FLORIDA." It would be forever known, as another headline stated it, as "THE DAY IT SNOWED IN MIAMI."

The cold wave that struck South Florida that night was one of the worst of the century. Although mild by northern standards, it served to typify this winter of anomalous cold. Freezing temperatures covered the entire mainland peninsula, and all-time record lows were set at Miami Beach (32 degrees Fahrenheit), West Palm Beach (27 degrees), and Naples (26 degrees). Some of the farming areas of Dade and Broward counties had temperatures as low as 20 degrees, and despite near-heroic efforts, citrus and vegetable crops suffered extreme damage. Eighty percent of the orange crop was damaged, sending citrus prices upward. The crop damage in Dade County alone was estimated at $100 million, and President Carter declared 35 counties in Florida disaster areas.

To the north, states of the Midwest and the Northeast, which are used to fierce winters, were, even by their standards, having a bad time of it.

The circulation around a huge low pressure area that filled almost the entire Northern Pacific Ocean created a ridge of high pressure in the atmosphere over Western North America and a deeper than normal trough over the eastern part of the continent. This pattern formed early in the fall of 1976 and continued with practically no change or weakening until the latter part of February, 1977. The high-pressure ridge pushed the prevailing westerlies up into a far northward loop where they picked up cold Arctic air and swooped down with it across the Eastern United States. "True, this is a frequent occurrence in winter," one National Weather Service forecaster reported later, "but what made the difference this season was its dogged persistence." In early January, the situation became even worse when an enormous blocking high-pressure area formed over the Arctic Ocean and displaced the polar vortex south of its position to Southern Canada. The result of all this was to put the entire Eastern United States into a deep freeze. Across large sections of the country, the thermometer plunged down well below freezing and stayed there, as though time itself had been frozen into immobility.

January, 1977, became the coldest single month in the Eastern

United States since formal weather records have been kept. In most places, mean temperatures for the month were 12 to 18 degrees lower than normal. In Waterloo, Iowa, the mean temperature for January was a tenth of a degree below zero, meaning the thermometer was below zero more often than not. Across Iowa, Missouri, Illinois, Indiana, Ohio, and Pennsylvania, January was the coldest month on record, with mean temperatures of 3.4 degrees in Dubuque, 8.5 degrees in Peoria, 9.2 degrees in Fort Wayne, 9.6 degrees in Toledo, 12 degrees in Cincinnati, and 11.4 degrees in Pittsburgh. New York City had its coldest winter in 41 years. At upstate cities such as Albany, where temperatures did not reach record lows, the almost steady flow of cold winds caused the wind-chill temperatures to plummet far below those of the "record" cold year.

As if the record-setting cold weren't enough, in the closing days of January a savage blizzard began raging across the frozen central states and into the East. Large parts of the country became paralyzed by the storm, whose blinding snow was driven into drifts by winds up to 60 miles per hour. Coupled with the near-zero and sub-zero cold, the blizzard brought the wind-chill temperatures, the effect of the cold on exposed skin, down to 40 to 70 degrees below zero. Factories, schools, and stores closed. Hundreds of thousand of workers from Wisconsin to Georgia were laid off. Transportation came to a virtual halt. The Ohio, Mississippi, Illinois, Allegheny, and Monongahela rivers froze, stranding barges carrying fuel oil and worsening already bad shortages of fuel for heating. Ships were stalled among ice floes on the Great Lakes. Amtrak canceled 12 of its trains running between New York-Chicago, Boston-Chicago, and New York-Kansas City. All roads were closed near Toledo. Fifty emergency shelters were opened in Western Pennsylvania. In Indiana, a fleet of 23 snowmobiles was dispatched from Rensselaer to rescue 400 travelers stranded in cars and three buses on Interstate 65. The National Guard was called out.

Buffalo, New York, caught the full force of the blizzard. Buffalo is situated at the east end of Lake Erie. Like Watertown, New York, at the east end of Lake Ontario, the Buffalo area is periodically buried under what meteorologists call lake-effect snowstorms. These are intense, local snowfalls to the lee of the Great Lakes that result when cold Arctic air picks up large amounts of moisture as it passes over the lakes. Single-storm snowfalls of three feet or more are common. But this season's lake-effect snowfall had not been equaled in the history of recorded meteorological observations. Early in the season 40.5 inches of snow fell on Buffalo in a four-day storm ending December 2. By the time the late January blizzard hit, Buffalo had already had 12.5 feet of snow for the season, triple the normal amount for the date. The temperature had not risen above freezing since before Christmas.

The blizzard struck the Buffalo metropolitan area at 11:30 A.M. on January 28, a Friday. This time it was not so much the snowfall (only 12 inches of new snow fell during the blizzard) but the wind that did the damage. The thermometer stood at 10 degrees below zero, and winds of 68 miles per hour with gusts up to 80 miles per hour sent the wind-chill temperature plummeting to 60 degrees below. These tremendous winds picked up the snow deposited from previous storms on the ice-covered surface of Lake Erie and blew it, together with the new snow, straight into Buffalo. Visibility was near zero. Snowdrifts towered as high as 25 feet. Thousands of cars and many single-story buildings were buried. Buffalo was now isolated by the storm, cut off from train, bus, and airplane service. The city was paralyzed. Roads were clogged with buried cars; even snowplows were disabled. Thousands of stranded people who had tried unsuccessfully to make it home after the storm hit took shelter in

Volunteers look for persons trapped in cars buried in Buffalo, N.Y., blizzard, February, 1977. Buffalo had 53 consecutive days of snowfall. (AMERICAN RED CROSS PHOTO BY SMITH)

public buildings, factories, supermarkets, and hotels. Three hundred workers stayed overnight in city hall. Three thousand workers stayed at the General Motors radiator plant. Eighteen hundred Ford employees were marooned at a stamping plant at Lockport, south of Buffalo. Two hundred persons stayed overnight in the lobby of the *Buffalo Evening News*. About 100 persons stayed in a state office building. All hotel rooms had been quickly snatched up. At the Sheraton Hotel near the airport, people slept in the corridors and in the lobbies on couches, billiard tables—anywhere they could find an empty spot.

One man who had been trapped for two hours inside his car near a downtown office building used as a refuge, stumbled into the shelter: "It only took me five minutes to walk to this building, but I thought I wasn't going to make it. I almost froze."

Others weren't so lucky. By Saturday, six persons had been found frozen to death. One of the bodies was found in a car by a Buffalo State College professor who despite having a four-wheel drive jeep reported he had gotten stuck twice trying to reach the car.

By noon Saturday, more than a day after the blizzard began, workers had managed to clear a few of Buffalo's main streets and some of the stranded began to inch their way home. An editor for the *Buffalo Courier-Express* found that his normal 20-minute drive home to Grand Island took five hours. The storm had defeated his newspaper's efforts to get out its Saturday edition, its first such failure in 147 years. But it did publish the Sunday and Monday editions. The *Buffalo Evening News*, which does not publish on Sunday, managed to get out abbreviated Friday, Saturday, and Monday editions.

Over the weekend, National Guard bulldozers and tanks joined in trying to cut through the drifts. Army helicopters had arrived from Fort Dix, New Jersey. Drifts were so high that three reindeer at the Delaware Park Zoo in Buffalo were able to climb up on them, leap over the fence, and escape. (They were captured within an hour.) Police answered looting calls by snowmobile. A man in suburban Amherst used a snowmobile to carry maintenance workers to apartment houses so they could keep furnaces and water heaters running.

Still the blizzard raged on, and on Monday Buffalo remained an isolated city. The snowplows found their attempts to keep major thoroughfares open a losing battle. A few cars trailed along behind the plows, but most vehicles were encased in giant lumps of snow. No trains had come or left since Friday. At Buffalo International Airport, no commercial flights were moving, although a few private airplanes were managing to get in and out. One passenger on an arriving private plane said it was like "descending into a scene of desolation . . . like a scene at the South Pole. Nothing was moving. Everything was dark gray."

Department stores and most other commercial establishments as well as government offices and schools were still closed. An estimated 200,000 employees were at home. A few grocery stores, restaurants, and fuel delivery companies were operating, but shortages of gasoline, fuel oil, bread, milk, cereal, and meat were developing. One store was reported selling milk at $2.50 a half-gallon, but reports of neighbors sharing food and other necessities were common. Visitors to the hospitals volunteered to make beds and help feed patients.

On Tuesday, Buffalo saw its first sun in a week and the snow and wind dropped off considerably. The temperature rose to 22 degrees and snow-removal crews worked round the clock. Most businesses and public transportation were still closed down. Milk was in short supply, but, ironically, dairy farmers at the south end of the county had to dump milk because their trucks couldn't get through the drifts to deliver it in Buffalo. In Buffalo itself, most roads were still impassable.

On Thursday, the relief effort from the outside began in earnest. Massive amounts of men and snow-clearing machinery were flown in from military bases and New York City. Giant C-5A transports landed on the now cleared airport runways bringing tractors, plows, trucks, and ambulances. A ban on automobile travel was lifted but quickly reinstated when streets became clogged by workers trying to get back to their jobs, many for the first time in a week. On Friday, Chip Carter, the President's son, flew into Buffalo. He brought no word of federal disaster aid to the city, which did not have the budget to cope with the extraordinary expense of snow removal, but he was obviously surprised by the magnitude of the storm's impact. "I'm a little shocked— very shocked," he said. "I've never seen so much snow in my life."

The next day, despite more snow and wind, came the news Buffalo area officials had feared they might never hear. President Carter had decided to designate nine upstate counties, including Buffalo, a major disaster area. It would mean there would be federal money to help the counties and municipalities pay for the huge cost of digging out from beneath the storm. (Blizzards are unique among nature disasters in that the costs of recovery must be borne almost entirely by local governments.) It was the first time in the history of the United States that an area had been declared a federal disaster area solely on the basis of the volume of snow it had received.

The area's residents were now emerging from their long period of isolation. They were treated to the sights of orange snow blowers from New York City and blue snow equipment from Nassau County on Long Island helping clear their streets and return their city to normalcy. Snow flurries still fell, but the siege was over. And at the railroad switching yards, dozens of gondola cars were being loaded with snow and dispatched to points south, a shipment no one was sorry to see go.

Twenty-nine persons had lost their lives in the storm, nine of them stranded in automobiles. The Environmental Data Service estimated that the total economic loss to the Buffalo area in storm damage, snow removal costs, lost wages, and lost production was $250 million.

When the winter ended, Buffalo residents could recount their adventures and, like all persons who revel in surviving through the rigors of nature's onslaughts, take pride in the records that were set. For the winter, for example, Buffalo had 199 inches, nearly 17 feet, of snow, outstripping the previous high amount of 124 inches which had stood for 67 years. And its 53 consecutive days of observed snowfall exceeded the previous record by 23 days.

Towns to the lee of Lake Ontario in New York State had had even greater amounts. Other record-breaking seasonal snowfall totals included Boonville with 346 inches, Barnes Corners with 370 inches, and Old Forge with 408 inches. Topping it all was the community of Hooker, which recorded an incredible 466 inches—almost 39 feet—of snow, the largest amount of snow ever observed to the lee of any of the Great Lakes.

The 1977 winter was so cold that scientists of the National Oceanic and Atmospheric Administration later found that it had cooled the Gulf Stream system far more than usual, leaving the Northwestern Sargasso Sea chilled as much as 300 feet deeper than in moderate years.

Everyone who perseveres through a particularly savage winter has certain memories. Washington, D.C., had its fifth-coldest January on record. Apart from the three-figure heating bill for

January (high heating bills posed an economic problem for millions of Americans that winter), I particularly remember the sheet of compacted, solid ice that covered my front yard and sidewalks, created when a frozen rain was followed by the deep freeze. Every evening for more than a week I worked to try to chip the ice from the sidewalks, but it would not break away in pieces. Every square millimeter had to be tediously chiseled away.

A more pleasant memory is of the extraordinary experience my two children and I and hundreds of other Washingtonians had of going down to the banks of the Potomac River just south of Memorial Bridge and walking across the frozen river from the District of Columbia to Virginia shores and back again. It was one of the few times this century the river had frozen over at Washington.

After the rigors of the winter of 1977, few could expect that the winter of 1978 could be even more extreme. But in many areas in the eastern two-thirds of the nation it was. Many records set in 1977 were broken by the blizzards and frigid blasts of 1978. New record-cold winter average temperatures were established at such widely scattered places as Galveston, Saint Louis, Cincinnati, Nashville, and Concordia, Kansas.

The winter of 1978, despite some similarities to the previous winter, resulted from somewhat different conditions. One sign of this was that the major drought in the West in 1977, caused by the same high pressure ridge responsible for the fierce winter in the East that year, was ended in early 1978 by record rains and floods in California and abundant snow in the mountains of the West. Both winters did have high pressure in the West and low pressure in the East combining to pump cold Arctic air down across the Eastern United States. But the high pressure area was farther north and east in Canada. The jet streams were more intense, farther south, and less convoluted in 1978. Instead of one steady flow of cold air, the 1978 storms alternated at intervals of about five days, every time bringing blasts of cold and snow with them.

And what a series of storms it was. No fewer than five major storms swept northeast up through the Midwest and into the Northeast between January 7 and January 27, followed at the end of the first week in February by still another storm along the Middle and North Atlantic seaboard. Some areas had barely dug out from one blizzard when they were hit by another.

When the storm of January 19 and 20 struck, it was already the fourth major snowstorm of the month in the eastern half of the nation. Up to 18 inches fell in Ohio, New York City had its worst snowstorm in nine years (13.6 inches in midtown Manhattan), and Boston broke what was then its all-time 24-hour snowfall record with 21 inches. In Connecticut, the strain of the snow, ice, and water caused the roof of the $70 million Hartford Civic Center Coliseum to collapse hours after 5,000 spectators at a basketball game had left. In Central New York State, where up to two feet fell, stores, industries, offices, and schools were closed, and heavy snow loads collapsed roofs of barns, garages, showrooms, and recreational halls in many areas. Traffic in New Jersey was at a virtual standstill. In New York City skiers glided past buses and taxis, offices were closed, and the stock market opened late. In Pennsylvania, where a foot or more of snow fell, hangar roofs at airports in Pittsburgh and Russellton collapsed, along with the roofs of 15 to 20 barns and numerous other structures such as warehouses and fairgrounds buildings.

That storm, however, turned out to be merely a prelude to the tremendous blizzard of January 25 to 27. It came up out of Texas, and raged through Kentucky, Illinois, Wisconsin, Indiana, and Ohio. Strong winds combined with 14 inches of snow brought immense drifts across Illinois, and in Chicago, O'Hare International Airport had to close for only the third time in its history. One woman died of exposure as she attempted to walk from her stalled car to her home in rural LaSalle County, and another died of exposure in a snowdrift in Lawrenceville.

On Interstate 57 near Ashkum, Illinois, the bodies of a young couple were found in their drift-surrounded car. Authorities said rescuers on snowmobiles had earlier checked the car but the couple had declined to accompany them, preferring to try to wait out the storm in their car. In Wisconsin, the storm described as the Blizzard of '78 came with 25- to 35-mile-per-hour winds gusting to 58. Drifts of five to 15 feet quickly stranded travelers, many of whom had ignored no-travel warnings. Through Southeast Wisconsin, travelers filled up schools, churches, motels, and restaurants. The University of Wisconsin suspended classes at its Madison and Milwaukee campuses, and the Milwaukee airport closed, stranding additional travelers. In rural Oshkosh, a 27-year-old woman died after losing her bearings while traveling by snowmobile through zero-visibility conditions to a neighbor's home. The blocked highways forced farmers to dump hundreds of thousands of pounds of milk, even while snowmobilers were transporting groceries and milk to communities isolated by the enormous drifts.

In Indiana, Indiana University closed for the first time in 158 years. Near Roachdale, volunteers dug through drifts as tall as locomotives to rescue 60 persons stranded on an Amtrak passenger train for 16 hours. A one-year-old boy in rural Newcastle died of exposure after the furnace in his family's mobile home went out and the mother, her efforts at finding other shelter stymied by the deep drifts, turned back to find the door frozen shut. By the time she managed to get back in, her son was dead.

Ohio caught the full force of the storm. It was the worst blizzard of the century in the state. The 10 inches or more of snow that fell was blown into 25-foot-high drifts by winds that averaged 50 to 70 miles per hour and gusted to 100. Visibility was near zero, and the night of the 26th temperatures dropped to below zero.

"Ohio is in trouble tonight," cried its governor, James A. Rhodes, who called the situation a dire emergency and the greatest disaster in Ohio history. "All Ohioans are united in their determination to help their fellow citizens who are in danger tonight." He said his office was receiving 25 calls every five minutes, "Cries of mercy—they want help and you can't get to them." He feared for what rescuers would find when they reached stranded homes and vehicles. Some 150,000 homes were without electricity because of downed power lines, and the power company advised their residents "to contact friends and relatives who have heat and try to get to their homes before dark." Two thousand National Guardsmen were called out to help people stranded in snowdrifts, but Guard officials said half of the Guardsmen themselves had to be rescued from drifts.

The governor's forebodings were justified. Fifty-one persons died in the storm in Ohio alone. Two persons died beneath structures blown down by the winds or collapsed by the snow. Thirteen were found frozen in stranded vehicles, and 13 more were found frozen in unheated houses. Twenty-two died while walking outdoors seeking help, either from homes with no heat or from stranded vehicles. And there were several freak deaths. A man froze walking to a doctor's appointment, another man froze while working on a chicken coop, and a woman froze while walking her dog.

Ohio was also the scene of a remarkable survival story. A

42-year-old trucker, James Truly, of Cleveland, was hauling a load of steel from Cleveland to the Northern Ohio city of Mansfield in the early morning hours of January 25 when he got caught in the blizzard on Ohio State Highway 13. The engine stopped. He tried to reach someone on his CB but got no answers. The snow was blowing so hard he couldn't see so he decided to stay in the cab. He climbed up into his bunk, crawled under his one blanket, and fell asleep. When he awoke, he found that the truck was covered by a snowdrift. He could see nothing; it was totally dark. It was then that he prepared for a long stay. "I prayed and I hoped I would come out of it. All I could do was wait." He had a hard hat and could open his window enough to fill it with snow. He ate snow, slept until he got too cold, woke, ate more snow, and slept in an endless cycle. He lost track of what day it was. Finally, late on the morning of January 31 a rescue team led by Truly's brother, Don, spotted a radio antenna sticking up from the snow and started digging. James had been found. "They came beating on the top of the roof and I beat back," he said. "I thought, 'Thank God.' " Truly was taken to a hospital where doctors found him in amazingly good condition for someone who had spent six days buried beneath the snow.

The winter's furies were not over. On February 6 and 7, a giant blizzard moved up from the Carolinas and paralyzed most of the Middle and North Atlantic seaboard under the heaviest snows in decades. New York City, hardly yet recovered from the 13-inch snowfall of January, found itself buried under nearly 18 inches of snow, the most to hit the city in 31 years. A thousand cars were abandoned on the Long Island Expressway. Providence, Rhode Island, had a record 27 inches of snow, and the 26 inches of snow in Boston broke the record set in the January storm just 18 days earlier. Winds up to 100 miles per hour whipped the snow into huge drifts and battered coastal cities with hurricane-like effect. Once again schools, offices, and industries were closed down, and the mounting costs of snow removal caused great hardships at all levels of government. President Carter ordered federal troops airlifted to the snow-struck regions, but they had no place to land.

In Massachusetts, the February storm was, according to the Environmental Data Service, one of the three most intense and persistent winter storms on record. Some reports called it the worst winter storm in New England history. Even before snow began to fall, winds were gusting to 65 miles per hour.

A pair on skis surveys the thousands of cars stranded by drifting snow in the southbound lane of Route 128, a beltway around Boston, February 9, 1978. (UNITED PRESS INTERNATIONAL)

Driven by the winds, the snow stung like pellets and blew into huge drifts. Then it began accumulating at the steady rate of two inches per hour. All travel quickly came to a halt. Boston's outer circumferential artery, Route 28, was jammed with 3,000 cars, most of them buried up to the level of their windshields. Helicopters and snowmobiles had to be used to rescue travelers from that freeway, and it took National Guard snowfighting troops three days to get it reopened to traffic. Logan Airport in Boston was closed for the longest period on record as it took nearly a week to get its runways cleared.

The cold and drifts took numerous lives. One was that of a 10-year-old boy in Uxbridge, Massachusetts, near the Rhode Island border, who struggled through the snow but fell short of his front door by a few steps. Despite a widespread search in which poles, sticks, and shovels were poked into snowdrifts in the neighborhood in an attempt to find the missing boy, his body was not discovered until February 27, three weeks after the storm, when a mailman noticed part of his mitten exposed in a melting snowdrift.

The storm moved very slowly just south of New England because of a combination of surface and upper atmosphere circulations. This persistence, coupled with a fairly large astronomical tide, brought one of the several highest tides on record. All along the Massachusetts coast, houses took a beating from the hurricane-force winds and high seas. Many were smashed by tides three to five feet higher than normal. Coastal residents dubbed the storm "the white hurricane." Thousands of people were forced from their homes, many of them waiting to leave until the waters started smashing their windows and breaking in the doors. At Rockport, where old-time residents expressed amazement at the power of the water that came crashing over a 20-foot-high breakwater, a 150-year-old landmark, a lobster shack dubbed Motif #1, was destroyed. The picturesque red shack on a stone quay had been painted by artists 10,000 times or more and photographed by tourists millions of times as the quintessential New England coastal scene.

There was tragedy at sea. The 45-foot pilot boat *Can Do* went out to check on a Greek oil tanker being battered by the waves off Salem. The 30-foot waves crashed through the boat's pilothouse windows and finally sunk the vessel, killing its four crewmen.

In New Hampshire and Maine a weather summary termed the

Tremendous force of storm is shown in this photo made early on February 8, 1978, as heavy surf pounded this beachfront property in the Peggotty Beach section of Scituate, Massachusetts. (UNITED PRESS INTERNATIONAL)

blizzard "one of the monster storms of the century." The powerful winds and high seas destroyed homes, businesses, and seawalls and put Route 1A under four feet of water. Thirteen to 20 inches of snow was measured along the New Hampshire coast, and the winds drove them into mountainous drifts that paralyzed traffic. In Maine, coastal areas were heavily damaged. Lighthouses had to be evacuated, and offshore islands such as Matinicus and Monhegan reported damage to wharves and buildings that had weathered a century or more of storms. Tides at Portland reached 14.3 feet, thought to be the highest in a century. The coastal battering was described as awesome, and it was accompanied by heavy snow, blizzard conditions, and huge drifts.

Even the storm-wizened residents of coastal New England will long remember the storm of February, 1978. For that matter, the entire winter of 1978 will long be remembered by the tens of millions of persons caught up in its throes throughout the Midwest, the Great Lakes, and the Northeast. When it was all over, it turned out that while January of 1977 still stands as the coldest single month in the United States since formal weather records began, the winter of 1978 as a whole was even colder across the Eastern United States than was the bitter winter of 1977. Robert C. Quale of the National Climatic Center in Asheville, North Carolina, had reported in late February of 1977 that the '77 winter "may well wind up being the coldest since the founding of the Republic." He says now that although records before 1890 have to be treated with caution, that dubious honor now has to go to the winter of 1978. It, he says, was marginally colder in the East than was the winter of 1977— snow cover was more extensive too. Satellite photos issued by the National Oceanic and Atmospheric Administration showed that 72 percent of the land mass of North America was covered by snow during parts of January, 1978, two percentage points greater than in 1977 and the most extensive snow cover in the 12 years since satellites have made the measurements.

Which winter was actually "worse" is a matter of definition. Quale says that while the winter of 1978 was marginally colder, he believes the winter of 1977 had a somewhat greater impact on the nation because that winter was preceded by a cold fall that greatly exacerbated fuel shortages when the bitter cold came. A warmer fall before the winter of 1978 allowed fuel supplies to be stockpiled. Also, he says, the area of greatest cold in the winter of 1978 was displaced slightly farther west from its position a year earlier and this means it affected a smaller proportion of the nation's total population.

While the relative magnitudes of the winters of 1977 and 1978 can be debated, what is certain is that, as a pair, those winters are the two coldest consecutive ones on record in the United States. "The winters of 1904 and 1905 were a cold pair as were the winters of 1856 and 1857," he says, "but they weren't quite as bad a combination as the winters of 1977 and 1978."

These two harsh winters in a row helped accelerate an already identifiable trend of migration from the Northeast and Upper Midwest to the "Sun Belt" states of the South and Southwest. The oil crisis of 1973 and the rising fuel prices following it had already helped nudge thousands of families into a decision to move to warmer climates with their smaller heating requirements. Following both the winters of 1977 and 1978 many a family newly arrived in a Sun Belt state gave among their primary reasons for leaving a desire to get away from the harsh winters and high fuel bills of their previous locale. The winter of 1979, which was also harsh, especially in Illinois and adjacent states, didn't help matters any.

Most climatologists, however, do not see any special long-term portent in having two, or even three, especially cold winters in a row. It seems to be part of the natural variability of weather and climate. No one contends, however, that fuel costs will change in any direction but up or that northern states will not always have the greater necessity for heating. So a southward migration trend away from the land of northern winters is not all that difficult to understand.

The full economic impact of a damaging winter is difficult to measure, but it can be enormous. Workers are laid off because of fuel shortages, or blizzard-blocked transportation. The purchasing power of each citizen is reduced because of the higher food and fuel costs. The funds and savings required to pay for these costs are not available for investment to increase future production. The foreign trade deficit increases to pay for the costs of importing oil. For the cold winter of 1977, the Commerce Department estimated that the cost to the nation was $3 billion in lost economic growth and $5 billion in extra fuel bills. An estimated $2 billion of those additional fuel costs were borne by the 41 million households east of the Mississippi in the month of January alone.

The real problem, though, is not severe winters, which we have to expect every so often, but all the factors that make society more vulnerable to them such as ever-greater population, our dependence on a highly efficient transportation system that is easily disrupted by heavy snows and blizzards, and steadily rising fuel costs. Perhaps little can be done to ease that vulnerability. But people and institutions need to prepare better for the inevitability that periodically a particularly rough winter will hit.

Obviously, there is nothing new about hazardous winters. In America, the Indians had had thousands of years of experience in coping with them before Europeans arrived. The first English encounter with them in America dates to 1607, the same year the first successful colony at Jamestown was established. That year another group of Englishmen attempted to found a colony in Sagadahoc County, Maine, but they failed when harsh snowstorms brought death to about half of the settlers and caused the other half to return to England.

In 1778, the third year of the Revolutionary War, English troops and Hessian mercenaries, who were not used to bitter, howling winter snowstorms, were caught in New England's worst blizzard in three decades. Their encampments were trapped in the drifts and cold, and many of the men froze. Long-time American residents of Rhode Island and Massachusetts were used to them and stayed inside wherever possible, but the intensity of this blizzard was such that many a poor soul caught outside when the storm started never made it to shelter. A trip to the barn to usher in stray livestock was fraught with peril. Many a bizarre death was reported. At Boston Neck, a team of oxen and a man were found frozen to death standing upright in the road.

The ill-fated Donner party, late in getting under way toward California in 1846 and besieged by difficulties crossing the mountains and desert of the Great Basin, was caught in a heavy early winter snowstorm in the closing days of October on the eastern flank of the Sierra Nevada and had to hole up in make-shift shelters for the winter while a series of blizzards raged around them. The tragic story of the struggle by those starving men, women, and children, who eventually had to resort to eating the flesh of the dead among them in order to survive, has become a part of our history and folklore.

One of the worst snowstorms in United States history was the catastrophic blizzard of 1888. On March 12 an eastward-moving heavy snowstorm collided over the Northeast with an advancing front of warm, moist air that had come up from the South and was carrying gale-force winds. The result was a raging blizzard that brought 40 to 50 inches of snow and drifts 30 to 40 feet high to Southeastern New York State and Southern New England. Dozens of trains were marooned, 200 vessels were sunk, grounded, or wrecked, and electrical and telephone wires throughout the Northeast were downed. From Washington, D.C., to Philadelphia, New York, and Boston, a quarter of the country's population was suddenly immobilized. In Middletown, New York, residents had to tunnel through the snow like miners, shoring up their snow-covered passageways with timber. New York City was paralyzed, a bustling city turned into a frozen Arctic landscape. Two hundred persons died in the city alone, and 200 other victims were claimed in other parts of the Northeast. In the days after the storm, sleighs scurried over snowbanks at the second-story level of New York's brownstones. In Danbury, Connecticut, the blizzard was called "a night of horror—the worst storm that has ever blasted this town. . . . The tempest's roar made hearing impossible. The winds howled and screamed all night." Roofs were crushed, smokestacks snapped. The town was transformed into a white wilderness. Passenger trains were trapped all over New England. The passengers on one New Haven train faced their ordeal by feasting on pies, oysters, and sausage. Passengers of other trains were at the mercy of nearby farmers, some of whom supplied food for free, others charging outrageously high prices. The storm became a legendary event for those who experienced it. People named their babies Snowdrift, Snowdrop, Storm, Blizzard, or Tempest. Organizations were formed to annually commemorate the storm, and as late as 1941, one of these clubs, "The Blizzard Men of 1888," was still meeting to compare stories.

Except for the lake-effect snowstorms, the heavy snowstorms and blizzards of winter are brought by the passage of extra-tropical cyclones, the name meteorologists give any large-scale circulation around a low-pressure area in the mid-latitudes. The bitter, cold winds and heavy snows of an intense snowstorm are favored by the presence of strong north-south temperature contrasts and the fast eastward-racing jet streams of winter. A weak low-pressure center moving up from the South may intensify when it comes into contact with a trough in these fast upper-level westerlies. At the same time the amplitude of the westerlies increases; the trough deepens, and the following ridge builds. The northward-advancing low carries with it moisture from the Gulf of Mexico or the Atlantic (or for Far West storms, the Pacific) that soon comes into conflict with the cold air mass to the north. The warm, moisture-laden air from the South glides up over the cold air mass. The ascent cools the warm southern air, and the abundant moisture it carries condenses out in the form of snow. When the moisture is sufficiently high and the pressure in the cyclone is especially low, very heavy snow and strong winds can result, and soon the towns and communities in the path may be ravaged by a full-scale blizzard.

Although predicting the amount and exact location of snowfall is still a difficult forecasting problem, the signs of an impending snowstorm are there for anyone to see long before the storm arrives. The weatherwise observer can recognize them for himself, as in this description:

Great snowstorms in the eastern United States usually give the alert individual warning of a day or two. First the brilliant cerulean skies of a mid-winter cold snap give way to high, delicate cirrus clouds which streak in from the southwest and entangle the sun in a web of icy fibers. The barometer, which has been rising for several days, hesitates, and then slowly begins to fall. Flags which have been rippling from the north now hang limp, and smoke from the fireplace, refusing to rise, drifts slowly westward. The thermometer climbs sluggishly from the teens into the more moderate twenties. . . . Twelve hours later, the signs are even more legible. The halo around the moon disappears in a thickening mass of clouds. The barometer, as if making up its mind, falls more rapidly, and bare trees begin to sway in the increasing northeast wind. In another six hours, the first tiny snowflakes flutter across the landscape. The clouds lower, and soon thick-falling snow reduces the lights from nearby houses and street lamps to hazy patches of luminescence. The snow falls heavily. . . .*

If now the wintry triumvirate of heavy snow, high wind, and cold conspires in simultaneous assault, a blizzard then rages over the surface. The impact depends on the strength and depth of these elements, the breadth and timing of their attack, and the number, vulnerability, and preparedness of the people in its path. The blizzard may be only a temporary inconvenience, a pause in the normal human routine, an unscheduled winter vacation from school and work. Or, as we've seen, it may bring full-scale disaster, with the deaths and the disruption of the social fiber that too often accompany the other violent forces of nature.

No account of major blizzards or extraordinary periods of cold is complete without at least passing reference to the year 1816, the famous Year Without A Summer. In that year the problem was not so much a cold winter but an abnormally cold summer. It was preceded by a late and cold spring and followed by an early and cold fall, so the frigid summer of 1816 brought widespread hardship and misery. From June 6 to 9 frost occurred every night from Canada to Virginia. Ice was an inch thick on standing water in Vermont. Everywhere, people shivered, broke out their winter clothing, and watched helplessly as their gardens and crops blackened in the cold. Newly shorn sheep died, and millions of birds perished. A light snow in much of New England and Western and Northern New York

---

* Anthes, Panofsky, Cahir, and Rango, *The Atmosphere*, 2nd ed., Charles E. Merrill Publishing Co., 1978, reprinted by permission.

State on June 6 was followed by moderate to heavy snow in New England on June 7 and 8. In Vermont there were drifts 18 to 20 inches deep. "It was indeed," as an account in a Danville, Vermont, newspaper put it, "a gloomy and tedious period."

A man in Plymouth, Connecticut, found the events still vivid in his mind 44 years later in 1860: "I well remember the 7th of June . . . dressed throughout with thick woolen clothes and an overcoat on. My hands got so cold that I was obliged to lay down my tools and put on a pair of mittens. . . . On the 10th of June, my wife brought in some clothes that had been spread on the ground the night before, which were frozen stiff as in winter."

Just after things warmed up enough for farmers to replant, a new outbreak of cold came at the end of the first week of July, killing corn and vegetables. Cool weather came again on July 18, and in August two more severe frosts hit. Travelers between Boston and Albany, New York, reported corn in most low-lying areas was destroyed. Then on September 27 a widespread killing frost destroyed all hopes for salvaging anything of the corn-growing season.

A history of Madison County, New York, described the "cold season" of 1816:

There was frost in every month. The crops were cut off, and the meagre harvest of grain was nowhere near sufficient for the needs of the people. The whole of the newly settled interior of New York was also suffering from the same cause. The inhabitants saw famine approaching. . . . Every resource of sustenance was carefully husbanded; even forest berries and roots were preserved. The spring of 1817 developed the worst phases of want. In various sections of the county families were brought to the very verge of starvation. . . .

The cold was not local but worldwide. Throughout the Northern Hemisphere, the weather was abnormally cold. In England it was almost as cold as in the United States, and 1816 was a famine year there and in Germany and France. Actually, the year 1816 was just one of a famous series of cold years from 1812 to 1817. Everywhere, temperatures were lower than usual, and in the United States the depression of summer temperatures was the lowest on record.

The cause of all these anomalously cold seasons is generally considered to be a series of three especially intense volcanic eruptions. They started with Soufrière on Saint Vincent in 1812, then Mayon in the Philippines in 1814, and concluded with the worst, the explosion of the volcano Tambora on the island of Sumbawa in Indonesia in April, 1815. It is still today considered to be, in total volume of matter discharged, the greatest volcanic eruption of modern times. Scientists estimate that Tambora ejected an incredible 35 cubic miles of rock, dust, and debris. This matter created a thick layer of volcanic dust in the atmosphere that girdled the globe and persisted for several years, screening out a portion of the sunlight that would normally heat the surface and causing the frigid summer and famines of 1816. So it is apparent that even events in the boiling chambers deep inside the earth can influence the weather on the surface. And it is to the force and violence of the volcano, the link between the atmosphere and those molten subsurface cauldrons, that we now turn our attention.

CHAPTER 8

Volcanoes

Let's begin by dispelling some misconceptions about volcanoes, courtesy of volcanologist Fred M. Bullard. Volcanoes are often referred to as burning mountains, belching forth from their summits flames and smoke and hot cinders. As poetic imagery this may be a satisfactory expression of the drama of a volcanic eruption:

> By turns hot embers from her entrails fly,
> And flakes of mountain flames that arch the sky.
>
> —*The Aeneid,* Virgil

Although the heat in a volcano is intense, in fact no burning in the sense of combustion, as in the burning of wood or fuel, takes place. Some of the most beautiful mountains are volcanoes, but volcanoes are not always mountains, and the volcanic activity does not always occur at the summit. More commonly, eruptions happen along the flanks or sides. The "ash" that we say falls from the eruptive cloud is not the flaky residue of burning but small, disintegrated particles of rock. Finally, notes Bullard, the "smoke" is not smoke but condensed steam, frequently mixed with dust particles until it is dark in color, and the "fire" is the reflection of the red-hot material on the clouds of vapor above the volcano.

Volcanoes can be surprisingly different in form and in the types and intensities of eruptions, but they all consist of a vent or chimney that connects an underground reservoir of molten matter called magma to the surface of the earth. The liquid lava and broken fragments of rock that accumulate around the opening frequently build up to a cone. Some cones are relatively small. Others, such as Mauna Loa in Hawaii, which towers 30,000 feet from the floor of the Pacific Ocean to its summit, are the loftiest mountains on earth. The term volcano properly applies to both the internal plumbing responsible for the volcano's activity and the cone that surrounds the vent.

We often hear the source of the volcano's molten heat referred to as "deep within the bowels of the earth" or "deep within the earth's interior." Perhaps I was unduly influenced by the planet-penetrating odyssey of Professor Lidenbrock and nephew Axel in the Jules Verne fantasy *Journey to the Center of the Earth,* but to me such phrases always convey the visual image of somewhere near the earth's center or at least a sizable portion of the way toward it. But magma chambers that serve volcanoes have nothing to do with the earth's liquid core. They are located in the lower crust or upper mantle of the earth, not all that far beneath the surface when viewed on the planetary scale.

The crust of the earth has about the same thickness in proportion to the total size of the earth as the skin of an apple has to the apple. It is in the lower part of this thin crust or just beneath it that most volcanoes have their origin. The magma source at Kilauea in Hawaii is at a depth of about 40 miles, only a hundredth the distance to the earth's center. The island volcanoes of the circum-Pacific belt have their magma sources at somewhat deeper levels, 75 to 100 miles. This is deep by the standards of humanity's technological reach (our deepest gas and oil wells go about six miles). But it is still a phenomenon of the near-outer layers of the earth.

Magma may be the heat source of volcanoes, but gas is the primary force in producing volcanic eruptions. "Gas," proclaimed pioneer American volcanologist Thomas A. Jaggar, "is the prime mover." The gas is mainly steam, water vapor created when water locked into the underground rocks is heated by the magma. When water changes to the gaseous state, it expands to a thousand times its original volume. It is this explosive expansion that powers a volcanic eruption.

Volcanoes bring violence but they also bring benefit. They have the power to destroy, but also the ability to create.

As landforms, volcanoes provide some of the world's most spectacular and awe-inspiring scenery. Beautiful Fujiyama, sacred symbol to an entire nation. Kilimanjaro, the highest mountain in Africa, towering above the grassy Tanzanian plain,

Eruption of La Soufrière volcano, St. Vincent Island in the Caribbean, on the morning of April 22, 1979. (RICHARD FISKE, SMITHSONIAN INSTITUTION)

a majestic backdrop to the zebras grazing in the foreground. Perpetually snow-capped Popocatepetl, the smoking mountain of the Aztecs, beckoning to all who venture south from the Valley of Mexico. Mount Erebus, the largest active volcano in Antarctica, draped with thick snow and serving a splendid visual welcome to fortunate scientific visitors to the continent. Mount Baker, Mount Rainier, Mount Hood, Mount Jefferson, the series of Cascades volcanoes that dominate the skyline of the Pacific Northwest.

From antiquity, the fertile slopes of volcanoes have been intensively cultivated, their lavas often rich in iron, calcium, magnesium, and other nutrient elements that quickly become transformed into exceedingly rich soil. It is not by coincidence that famous eruptions of the past have had nearby settlements in their path; it is said that at the time of the eruption that buried Pompeii in A.D. 79, Vesuvius was cultivated all the way to its top.

Nearly all oceanic islands owe their existence to volcanoes: the Hawaiian Islands of the Central Pacific, the island arcs of the Western and Southwestern Pacific, the Windward and Leeward Islands of the West Indies, to name a few major chains. Volcanoes are adding new land to existing islands. Kilauea's 1960 eruption added half a square mile to Hawaii. The offshore eruption of Capelinhos in 1957 added nearly a square mile of land to the island of Fayal in the Azores. The island of Surtsey was created south of Iceland by volcanic eruption in 1963.

On a far longer time scale, volcanic actions at the mid-ocean ridges are the birthplace of the earth's crust, creating new ocean bottom to replace old crust consumed at distant ocean margins. "We now think that the creation of the sea floor is volumetrically the most important volcanic process, one that is hidden almost entirely from direct observation by the overlying ocean," note geophysicists Frank Press and Raymond Siever. In the slow but steady dynamics of geological change carried out through the recently confirmed processes of sea floor spreading and plate tectonics, some of that crust will eventually become the new land of continents.

The water of our oceans and the gases of our atmosphere, according to more and more evidence, may have had their origin in volcanic or plutonic (igneous rocks crystallized at great depth) gases issued to the surface from volcanic eruptions, lava flows, and hot springs over vast stretches of geologic time. Thus,

Eruption of Cerro Negro volcano in Nicaragua in 1971. (U.S. GEO-
LOGICAL SURVEY)

volcanoes have helped bring forth from the solid planet the fluids necessary for life on earth.

Eruptions of volcanoes can vary so much from each other that sometimes it almost seems as if wholly different phenomena are at work. At the one extreme are slow, effusive eruptions, in which the lava rises gradually to the surface and overflows the edge of the crater. Gases bubble up and hiss. Sometimes fountains of lava several hundred feet high spray into the air, but the lava flows away like a river, and usually little harm is done. The volcanoes of Hawaii are in this category.

Another variant is the fissure eruption. It does not fit the popular conception of a volcano at all. There is no dramatic mountain, no symmetrical cone. Fluid basaltic lavas ooze up from long, narrow fissures in the earth and spread out over the landscape. The great lava plateaus of the world were created this way. One striking example is the Columbia River Plateau, and adjacent Snake River Plain. Innumerable flows of lava spread out over large parts of what are now Oregon, Washington, and Idaho, covering an area of 200,000 square miles to thicknesses that layer after layer accumulated to as much as 3,000 feet. The volume of the Columbia River and Snake River Plateaus has been estimated to be 60,000 cubic miles. The great flood described in Chapter 5 that created the Channeled Scablands of Southeastern Washington State carved those features out of the pre-existing lava from part of these flows. The Deccan Plateau of India, covering 200,000 square miles, and the Paraná Plateau of Brazil and Paraguay, 300,000 square miles, are other famous examples.

Today, Iceland is the only site where such fissure eruptions are occurring. At intervals averaging, since A.D. 1100, five years, basaltic lava pours out in effusive eruptions from fissures and shield volcanoes. The Icelandic volcanologist Sigurdur Thorarinsson estimates that nearly one-third of the lava produced on earth since A.D. 1500 is to be found in Iceland.

The majority of earth's volcanoes have eruptions of an intermediate type. They yield both lava and explosive fragments and their eruptions can range from relatively benign to disastrously forceful. Many famous volcanoes are in this category including Vesuvius, Vulcano (considered by the ancients to be the location of the forge of Vulcan, the Roman god of fire), and Stromboli (one of the few volcanoes in the world in a state of permanent moderate activity).

An unusual—and in this case deadly—kind of volcanic eruption happened in Zaire in 1977. A system of parallel openings fractured the flanks of the Nyiragongo volcano and in only an hour's time 20 million cubic meters of white-hot lava surged forth. The lava was unusually fluid, due to an abnormally low content of silica. It raced down the volcano's slopes at speeds exceeding 35 miles per hour, overtaking people who might have dodged a more normal, sluggish flow. Seventy Zaireans were killed.

At the far extremes are the explosive eruptions. Tremendous explosions can blow away the side or top of the volcanic mountain. With this sudden release of pressure the rising magma mixes with the expanding gases to form a sort of froth that is ejected with great force as chunks of fragmented solid material called pyroclastics (from Greek words meaning "fire" and "broken"). Pyroclastics range in size from dust so fine it may drift around the earth several times to coarse ash particles to large chunks of rock called bombs. Volcanic bombs typically are about the size of baseballs or basketballs, but some are enormous. Blocks as heavy as 100 tons have been thrown as far as six miles by explosions.

No lava flows forth in these explosive eruptions, because the magma never reaches the surface as a liquid. All volcanic eruptions are potential hazards, but the explosive ones have been responsible for some of the great disasters of history. Three of these explosive catastrophes have forever been etched in memory.

In 1902, Saint-Pierre was a jeweled city of the Caribbean, the largest city on the French island of Martinique, with a population of between 26,000 and 32,000. On the northwest end of the island, its beaches and harbor faced west to the warm Caribbean, and steamers came and went with the commerce of the West Indies. Architecturally it was elegant. One visitor described it as "the quaintest, queerest, and the prettiest, withal, among West Indian cities; all stone-built and stone-flagged, with very narrow streets, wooden or zinc awnings, and peaked roofs of red tile, pierced by gable dormers. Most of the buildings are painted in a clear yellow tone, which contrast delightfully with the burning blue ribbon of tropical sky above; and no street is absolutely level; nearly all of them climb hills, descend into hollows, curve, twist, describe sudden angles. . . . The architecture is that of the seventeenth century, and reminds one of the antiquated quarter of New Orleans."

Rising 4,000 feet above Saint-Pierre to the northeast was the mountain known as Pelée, a volcano that had last erupted in 1856, but with little damage. In April, 1902, Pelée began to come alive again. On April 2, fumaroles were noticed steaming in the upper valley of a river that runs down its flanks to the sea. On April 23, residents at Saint-Pierre noticed a fall of ash and felt a few minor earth tremors. On April 25, there were explosions that sent visible clouds of ash into the air. In the following days a column of steam began emanating from the summit, and the ash falls became heavier. The ash was now beginning to give the city the appearance of winter. Some roads were blocked and businesses closed by the ash, and explosions continued to come from the mountain. "The rain of ashes never ceases," according to the local newspaper, *Les Colonies,* in its May 3 issue. "At about half-past nine the sun shone forth timidly. The passing of carriages in the streets is no longer heard. The wheels are muffled. Puffs of wind sweep the ashes from the roofs and awnings, and blow them into rooms."

By now the populace was alarmed. Refugees from outlying areas on the flanks of the mountain flowed into the city, while many residents of Saint-Pierre began packing their things and leaving for the safety of the capital city of Fort de France and other points to the south of the island. An election was scheduled for May 10, and government officials wanted to stop the panic and keep the people from leaving. An official government commission reported no immediate danger and no reason for fleeing the city. To stop the exodus the governor and his wife came in a gesture of reassurance. They would soon become victims of their own act. Shortly after noon on May 5, a torrent of bubbling mud swept down the valley of the Rivière Blanche, two miles north of Saint-Pierre, at express-train speed, overwhelming a sugar mill at the mouth of the river. All the workmen inside, at least 30, were entombed. They became the volcano's first victims. Now the population was panicked. After particularly violent eruptions on May 6, the governor stationed soldiers on the roads to turn back the flow of refugees. *Les Colonies* contended that no alarm was justified. On May 7, the eve of the catastrophe, the newspaper printed an interview with Professor Landes of the natural science faculty of the Saint-

Pierre Lycée, who had first noted signs of the volcano's renewed activity in early April. Landes scoffed at the public's concern, concluding, in one of the more unfortunate statements by a scientist in history, that "Mount Pelée presents no more danger to the inhabitants of Saint-Pierre than does Vesuvius to those of Naples." The newspaper added its own editorial comment that it failed to understand the panic. "We hope that the opinion expressed by M. Landes in the interview which we published will reassure the most timid."

On May 7 the eruptions continued but in the afternoon came news of the eruption that morning of the volcano La Soufrière, on Saint Vincent, 90 miles away to the south. La Soufrière's eruption was itself a terrible disaster. More than 1,500 persons were killed, and the hot blast from the volcano overturned trees, destroyed homes, and set fire to combustible objects. But ironically, the news of its eruption was a relief to the frightened residents of Saint-Pierre because it was believed that the release at Saint Vincent would ease the pressure inside and below Mount Pelée. How wrong they were!

The rumblings continued throughout that night, but the morning of May 8 dawned bright and sunny. Eighteen ships were

Catastrophic explosion of Mount Pelée on Martinique, May 8, 1902. Drawing was made by a survivor aboard one of the few ships in harbor not destroyed by the explosion. (U.S. GEOLOGICAL SURVEY)

anchored in the harbor, one of which, the *Roraima*, had arrived only that morning. As it had steamed in, its crew beheld the magnificent spectacle of what looked like red flames belching from the mountain. Enormous clouds of black smoke hung over it, and there was a constant muffled roar.

At 7:50 A.M., with no further warning, Mount Pelée blew up. A quick series of four tremendous, sky-splitting explosions ripped out the side of the mountain, and a great cloud of super-heated gas and ash particles raced down its flanks at hurricane velocities. Within two minutes it had overwhelmed Saint-Pierre. Everyone and virtually everything in its path was instantly obliterated. The clock on the tower of the Hôpital Militaire stopped at 7:52 A.M. That was the moment the nearly 30,000 people in Saint-Pierre lost their lives.

Assistant Purser Thompson, on board the *Roraima*, saw it happen:

I saw Saint-Pierre destroyed. It was blotted out by one great flash of fire. . . . There was no warning. The side of the volcano was ripped out, and there hurled straight toward us a solid wall of flame. It sounded like a thousand cannon. The wave of fire was on us and over us like a lightning flash. It was like a hurricane of fire, which rolled in mass straight down on Saint-Pierre and the shipping. The town vanished before our eyes, and then the air grew stifling hot and we were in the thick of it. Wherever the mass of fire struck the sea, the water boiled and sent up great clouds of steam. I saved my life by running to my stateroom and burying myself in the bedding. The blast of fire from the volcano lasted only for a few minutes. It shriveled and set fire to everything it touched. Burning rum ran in streams down every street and out into the sea. Before the volcano burst, the landings at Saint-Pierre were crowded with people. After the explosion, not one living being was seen on land. Only 25 of those on the *Roraima,* out of 68, were left after the first flash. The fire swept off the ship's masts and smoke stack as if they had been cut by a knife.

Sixteen of the 18 vessels in the harbor capsized, and their crews all perished. Only one vessel other than the *Roraima*, the British steamer *Roddam*, stayed afloat. It managed to limp out of the harbor even though more than half the persons on board were lost. As Thompson described it, "It was a dying crew that took her out."

On board the *Roraima*, only two of the passengers, a little girl and her nurse, survived. The nurse gave an account of her experience to volcanologist Jaggar, who soon reached the scene by ship from New York with a group of scientists and reporters. The passengers had been watching the volcano send up smoke when the captain (who perished) announced they were not going to stay any longer than necessary. The nurse went to the cabin and was assisting with dressing the children for breakfast when the steward, who was also a victim, rushed past and shouted, "Close the cabin door—the volcano is coming!"

We closed the door and at the same moment came a terrible explosion which nearly burst the eardrums. The vessel was lifted high into the air, and then seemed to be sinking down, down. We were all thrown off our feet by the shock and huddled crouching in one corner of the cabin. My mistress had the girl baby in her arms, the older girl leaned on my left arm, while I held little Eric in my right.

The explosion seemed to have blown in the skylight over our heads, and before we could raise ourselves, hot moist ashes began to pour in on us; they came in boiling splattering splashes like moist mud without any pieces of rock. . . .

A sense of suffocation came next but when the door burst open, air rushed in and we revived somewhat. When we could see each other's faces, they were all covered with black lava, the baby was dying, Rita, the older girl, was in great agony, and every part of my body was paining me. A heap of hot mud had collected near us and as Rita put her hand down to raise herself up it was plunged up to the elbow in the scalding stuff. . . .

The first engineer soon came and took the nurse and the family to the forward deck. The whole city was one mass of roaring flames. The ship was afire also, but the survivors among the crew managed to put it out.

My mistress [continues the nurse's narrative] lay on the deck in a collapsed state; the little boy was already dead, and the baby dying. The lady was collected and resigned, handed

me some money, told me to take Rita to her aunt, and sucked
a piece of ice before she died.

The destruction of Saint-Pierre was total. What had been a
lovely Caribbean coastal city had now the appearance of ancient
archaeological ruins. No building was left standing. Only the
lower parts of stone walls remained intact, most of them parallel
to the direction of the blast. Three-foot stone walls broadside to
the blast had been sent flying. A 10-foot-long iron siege gun
was moved from its mounting. A three-ton statue of the Virgin
Mary was thrown 50 feet. Heavy trees were uplifted with roots
intact and thrown into the harbor. Sheets of metal were twisted
around posts. Masses of smoking rubble lay everywhere.

The charred and roasted bodies of the city's inhabitants were
found in every conceivable position. Death resulted from the
inhaling of highly heated gases or from burns. In most cases it
seemed to be instantaneous. A family of nine was found seated
around a breakfast table, their hands locked, their faces seared
away. The United States consul in Saint-Pierre, Thomas T.
Prentis, and his wife, were found dead and charred sitting in
chairs facing an open window that looked out upon Mount
Pelée. His daughters' bodies were never located. Prentis had
apparently kept his concerns about the volcano from his family,
but he had told a visitor some months before that he did "not
expect to leave the island alive."

Only two persons in Saint-Pierre did survive. One was a 25-
year-old prisoner, a convicted murderer, in an underground
dungeon. Rescuers did not find him until three days after the
blast. Even though his cell had only one small barred opening
near the top of the door, he was horribly burned on his back
and legs. He recalled how it suddenly grew dark, and then an
intense blast of heat that lasted only a moment left his flesh
burning. This man was later given an official pardon, and he
eventually became a missionary.

The other survivor was León Compère-Léandre, a 28-year-
old shoemaker, who fled on foot to another town after the destruction. He told how he was outside on his doorstep that
morning. "All of a sudden I felt a terrible wind blowing, the
earth began to tremble, and the sky suddenly became dark. I
turned to go into the house, made with great difficulty the three
or four steps that separated me from my room, and felt my arms

and legs burning, also my body." Others came stumbling into the house, writhing in pain. Later he went outside and found in the courtyard "two corpses interlocked; they were the bodies of the two young men who had been with me in the room. Re-entering the house, I came upon the bodies of two men who had been in the garden when I returned to my house at the beginning of the catastrophe. . . . I heard no human cries; I experienced no degree of suffocation, and it was only the air that was lacking to me. But it was burning. There were neither ashes nor mud. The entire city was aflame."

The heat of the blast had softened glass objects, carbonized green juicy fruits, and set wooden ships in the harbor afire. It had not melted copper. Later studies showed that the heat at the point of emission on the mountain was around 1,200 degrees Celsius, or 2,100 degrees Fahrenheit. It would have cooled somewhat by the time it reached the city but nevertheless undoubtedly remained at many hundreds of degrees.

What was this deadly blast of heat and gas? It was a phenomenon never previously identified in volcanic eruptions. It is now known that in volcanoes like Pelée, the lava is of a type that is very stiff and viscous. It tends to seal off the volcano chimney, and gases accumulate until the upper part of the magma column is saturated with them. The explosion expels the highly gas-charred magma. The rapidly expanding gas locked within it causes the magma to shatter into dust particles, and it is this hot ball of gas and exploding particles that descended on Saint-Pierre that day. As it rushes down the slopes, the expansion and compression of the gases being constantly emitted by the fragments of magma give this mixture of dust and gas its great speed and power. The explosions caused by the rapid expansion of the gases continue as the gas moves downward. The mobility of the deadly cloud, it is now known, is created by the self-explosive (gas-generating) properties of the fragments within it. After the disaster, a French scientist coined the term *nuée ardente* (glowing cloud) to describe this phenomenon, and that is what it has been known by ever since. And the type of eruption that launches a *nuée ardente* is today always referred to as Pelean.

I visited Saint-Pierre in 1977, just before the 75th anniversary of the tragedy, and went up on the cloud-covered slopes of Mount Pelée. It is today of course a peaceful scene. Whether the lava dome that now occupies its crater has sealed off the vent and eruptive activity has ended no one can say. The rebuilt town has never achieved the eminence it once held, and now Fort de France is by far the main commercial and shipping center of Martinique. It is hard to imagine the destructive force that burst forth out of the mountain that day. But a visit to the small museum, a memorial to the holocaust, with its molten artifacts and old before-and-after photographs of a city laid to waste, is a vivid reminder of how nature at its most violent can eradicate life with such instant finality.

Horrible as the impact of the Mount Pelée explosion was, the eruption of the Mount Katmai volcano in Alaska 10 years later is generally considered to be the greatest volcanic explosion of the twentieth century. It illustrates how violent events of nature may or may not become disasters depending upon whether people are in the path. In this case, fortunately, the explosion took place in an isolated, sparsely populated area. "Had the Katmai eruption occurred in a densely inhabited region," says volcanologist E. A. Vincent, "it would have constituted a natural disaster far greater than that of Pelée." To borrow an analogy of scale from Press and Siever, had the eruption been centered in New York, the city would have been destroyed, one foot of ash would have covered Philadelphia, and fumes would have reached Denver. Katmai is near the eastern end of the Alaska Peninsula opposite Kodiak Island, and when the top of the mountain blew off and collapsed on June 6, 1912, the sound of the explosion was heard at Juneau, Alaska, 750 miles to the east, and at Dawson, 650 miles to the north across the Alaska Range.

A tremendous incandescent gas-rock emulsion rushed at hurricane velocities out over a broad 12-mile-long valley, knocking over and carbonizing trees and covering every detail of the topography. This ashflow apparently came not from the crater on the mountain top, like a *nuée ardente*, but from fissures within the valley floor itself, the first such case ever demonstrated. The distance and velocities of the flow cannot be attributed to gravity alone, according to Bullard, because the gradient throughout the length of the valley is only a little more than a degree. Liberation of the expanding gases within the particles of the flow powered its advance. Vents left in the thick layer of welded rock fragments covering the valley gave rise to gas and steam for years to come, and it became known as the Valley of Ten Thousand Smokes.

Unlike Pelée's explosion, Mount Katmai's ejected tremendous

quantities of ash into the atmosphere. The events experienced by two ships at Kodiak Island and chronicled by Bullard have, to me, an eerie, nightmarish quality. One was the U.S. Coast Guard cutter *Manning*, under the command of Captain K. W. Perry. It was in the harbor at Kodiak, 100 miles from Mount Katmai. At about 4 P.M. on the day of the eruption, Perry noticed a peculiar dark cloud approaching from the northwest. Soon, coarse gray ash began falling, accompanied by thunder and lightning, and the sky turned dark. Five inches of ash had accumulated on the deck by next morning, and by noon the ash fall resumed. Now everyone was becoming concerned. At 2 P.M., pitch darkness set in. The radio receiver gave forth only static. Through a sleepless night, the crew anxiously awaited dawn. It failed to appear; all sunlight was obliterated. The cloud of falling ash was so thick it was impossible to see a lantern at arm's length. "Sulphurous fumes came at times in the air," recalled Captain Perry, "and many thought and spoke of the destruction of Pompeii." The decks had to be constantly shoveled and sprayed with water "in what at times seemed a vain effort to clear the ship of its horrible burden." On the afternoon of June 8, two days after the arrival of the cloud of night, the ash fall decreased, the sky turned reddish, and objects became dimly visible.

The other ship, the mail steamer *Dora*, had similar experiences. A mail clerk on board, J. E. Thwaites, vividly described the scene: "And now began the real rain of ashes; it fell in torrents; it swirled and eddied . . . Bright clusters of electric lights could be seen but a few feet away, and we had to feel our way about the deck . . . Lurid flashes of lightning glared continuously around the ship, while a constant stream of thunder . . . increased the horror of the inferno raging about us . . . Dust filled our nostrils, sifted down our backs and smote the eye like a dash of acid. Birds floundered, crying wildly, through space and fell helpless to the deck." Nothing could be seen of the sun or the sky or the water, as though the ship were suspended in some strange hell.

An Indian at a fishing camp 30 miles from Mount Katmai wrote a fearful letter to his wife on the third day after the eruption. "We cannot see the daylight. In a word it is terrible, and we are expecting death at any moment, and we have no water. All the rivers are covered by ashes. . . ."

At Kodiak, the total darkness lasted 60 hours. During the

next few weeks, a reddish haze from fine dust in the atmosphere
was observed throughout the world.

The region around the eruption later was designated Katmai
National Monument. Its boundaries have been expanded several
times, and it is now second in size only to Yellowstone National
Park among the areas administered by the U.S. National Park
Service.

The greatest explosion on earth in historic times was the
eruption of Krakatoa in the East Indies in 1883. Eruption seems
hardly the right word. Two-thirds of the island of Krakatoa disappeared in the explosion. Before the upheaval, the land had
risen 400 to 1,400 feet above the level of the sea. Afterward,
there was a great cavity 900 feet below sea level. The effects of
the explosion were seen, heard, and felt literally all around the
world.

Krakatoa was an island arc volcano in the Sunda Strait between Java and Sumatra. (Contrary to the title of the feature
movie made about the disaster, Krakatoa is west, not east, of
Java.) The island itself was uninhabited.

In May of 1883, mild explosive activity began on Krakatoa,
and a column of steam estimated by a German ship captain to
be rising 36,000 feet into the air towered above the island. It
became such an attraction that about 100 persons from the
island of Batavia 90 miles away chartered an excursion boat
and visited it, picnicking on the slopes of the volcano and seeing
a most entertaining show of vapor and fountains of liquid lava.

On the afternoon of August 26, a series of sharp explosions
rocked the island. All that night the explosions continued in a
relentless roar, rattling windows on Java and Batavia like heavy
artillery. Persons all over Western Java were kept awake throughout the night. But all that was just a prelude.

At 10 A.M. on August 27, an explosion the likes of which
the world had not heard since the distant reaches of ancient
times rocked the entire island region of Southeast Asia. In a
sudden, colossal upheaval, the island of Krakatoa had exploded.
The force of the explosion is estimated to have been 26 times
greater than the largest hydrogen bomb ever detonated in underground tests. The volcano's walls had apparently ruptured.
Sea water poured onto the hot magma chamber, and the violent
expansion of hot steam powered the blast.

The sound of the explosion was heard over one-thirteenth the
earth's surface, including Central Australia, New Guinea, the

Philippine Islands, Indo-China, and Southeastern India. On the Southern Indian Ocean island of Rodriguez, east of Madagascar and 2,968 miles from Krakatoa, a coast guard observer carefully noted the character of the sound. It was four hours after the explosion, just the length of time sound waves would require to travel that distance. The police chief on Rodriguez noted that "reports were heard coming from the eastward like the distant roar of heavy guns." In Tavoy, Burma, people listened to the roar. Sheep on the plains of Western Australia were stampeded by the noise. People in Daly Waters, South Australia, were startled. In Borneo, a tribe of headhunters thought an avenging force or evil spirit was coming, and dozens are said to have jumped off cliffs.

The destruction from the blast was almost entirely caused by enormous waves of water, tsunamis (popularly but incorrectly called tidal waves), caused by the collapse of Krakatoa, that first reached Java and Sumatra half an hour after the explosion. Waves as high as 130 feet washed over their coasts. A Dutch warship, the *Berouw*, was carried half a mile inland onto Sumatra and deposited in a forest 30 feet above sea level. The captain of the ship *Loudon* managed to turn the bow directly toward the advancing wave. The ship rode at a high angle up over its crest, then down the other side. A few moments later, the wave consumed a nearby coastal town. Ship engineer N. van Sandick described the sight: "The lighthouse fell in one piece, and all the houses of the town were swept away in one blow like a castle of cards. All was finished. There, where a few moments ago lived the town of Telok Betong, was nothing but the open sea. . . ." Two hundred ninety-five such towns were wholly or partially destroyed, and 36,419 people were either missing or killed, mostly by drowning.

Befitting the greatest volcanic eruption of modern times, the effects were observed worldwide. The pressure wave from the explosion raced around the world, circling the earth four times in one direction, three times in the other. Everywhere, recording barometers monitored its pass.

The enormous load of ash sent hurtling into the air brought days of darkness. At a distance of 130 miles, the darkness lasted 22 hours, and at a distance of 50 miles, for 57 hours. Heavy quantities of ash fell for hundreds of miles, north, west, and south of the island. Ships 1,600 miles away reported the fall of dust three days after the explosion.

The eruption, it is estimated, blew one cubic mile of material to a height of 17 miles, and the dust was carried completely around the earth several times by the high-altitude currents. Soon, areas within 15 degrees of the equator, then gradually the entire earth, were witnessing brilliant glows in the skies after sunset and before sunrise because of the dust particles in the atmosphere. This was a quite controversial scientific question at the time, since little was known of high-altitude circulation.

Wrote the poet Tennyson:

Had the fierce ashes of some fiery Peak
been hurled so high they ranged round the globe?
For day by day through many a blood-red eve
This wrathful sunset glared . . .

In the United States, the glows were first seen at Yuma, Arizona, on October 19, nearly eight weeks after the explosion. On October 30, they were seen for the first time in the Eastern United States. The spectacle that night was dramatic. In both Poughkeepsie, New York, and New Haven, Connecticut, fire engines were called out to quench what seemed to be nearby great fires reflected in the skies. Optical effects produced by particles from Krakatoa were last seen over Europe 2.8 years after the explosion and in Colorado 3.1 years after.

Measurements of the amount of solar radiation reaching the earth's surface show a marked decrease (to less than 88 percent of the average) in 1884 and 1885, corresponding to Krakatoa's eruption. This supports the idea that the low global temperatures of the late 1880s and early 1890s were due to the dust from Krakatoa. The temperature effect wasn't as dramatic as the Year Without a Summer following Tambora's 1816 eruption, mentioned in the previous chapter. Krakatoa's explosion was possibly greater, but the volume of material ejected was not as much as was spewed into the atmosphere by Tambora. Other major volcanic eruptions have also been shown to have temporarily reduced average global temperatures, and episodes of volcanic activity are considered to be one possible factor in influencing climatic change.

The only explosion thought to have exceeded Krakatoa's in intensity since the dawn of human civilization took place one day about 1400 B.C. on an island in the Aegean Sea 70 miles north of Crete. The remnants of that explosion we now call the islands of Santorini, the largest of which is Thera. It was an explosion of unimaginable force, the equal according to one estimate of several hundred hydrogen bombs detonated at once. As did Krakatoa, the 4,900-foot volcanic mountain then collapsed in on itself creating an undersea crater or caldera 1,200 feet below sea level. Fourteen cubic miles of island collapsed, more than three times the volume of Krakatoa's collapse. Multiplying the effects we have seen of the Krakatoa event, we can imagine the magnitude of this cataclysm. Enormous tsunamis radiated out across the Mediterranean with great force.

By far the greatest effect would have been felt on the island of Crete, center of the flourishing pre-Greek Minoan civilization. The tsunamis must have struck the north coast of Crete at great velocity, inundating the whole northern coast 20 to 30 minutes after the volcano's collapse. Estimates for the height of this wave range up to 200 feet. The thick ash fall could have destroyed what remained of the island's crops and ruined the land for agriculture. We now know that the Minoan civilization suddenly disappeared around this time, with traces of its influence thereafter evident at Mycenae in nearby Southern Greece. Many scientists now accept the idea that it was the explosion of Santorini that destroyed the Minoan civilization, or at least weakened it to a fatal degree, although debate on this subject is still going strong. Many believe that this cataclysm may have been what gave rise to the legend of Atlantis recounted by Plato.

Volcanic eruptions have affected history in other parts of the world as well. University of Colorado anthropologist Payson Sheets has proposed that the flowering of the highly classic phase of Mayan civilization in Central America may have been aided by a volcano-caused migration from the highland areas near the Pacific coast to the Mayan lowlands some 2,000 years ago. He and other workers have shown in recent years that a complex and devastating eruption of the now-extinct volcano Ilopango in the mountains of El Salvador may have so ruined the land that it stimulated a migration of perhaps 30,000 persons northward into Guatemala, helping accelerate cultural development of what soon became the Classic Mayan phase. Reconstruction of the events shows that the eruption apparently occurred in three stages. Two of them were incandescent ashflows that rolled across the land and buried villages in their paths as far as 25 miles away. They were followed by an ashfall that uniformly covered the land. The ecological effects, Sheets believes, must have been devastating. Overnight, he says, the lush, tropical vegetation of much of El Salvador must have changed into a white desert. The impact on agriculture and land use was greater than the population's ability to adjust. The archaeological evidence he has compiled indicates that large numbers then migrated to the lowlands, where the Mayan civilization later began to flourish.

Some of the evidence of the ecological effects of a volcanic eruption came from Parícutin. This volcano was born in a farmer's field in the state of Michoacan, Mexico, 200 miles due west of Mexico City, on February 20, 1943. Human eyes (those of the farmer whose land it usurped, Dionisio Pulido, and his wife, son, and neighbor) witnessed the moment of birth, and from virtually then on the volcano has been under regular scientific observation. It is one of only two volcanoes born in North America in historic times (the other was Jorullo, also in western Mexico, in 1759), and it has become a sort of living laboratory for study of the life-cycle of a volcano. Fred Bullard studied Parícutin firsthand in many visits during its nine years of activity. He recounts the story of its birth.

In early February, 1943, a series of small earthquakes was felt in the area. On February 20, while preparing his land for planting, Dionisio Pulido noticed a fissure a foot or so in depth extending through a small hole that had existed in the field for decades. Almost immediately, shaking could be heard, the ground swelled six to eight feet, and smoke or ash began rising from the fissure. The odor of sulphur was in the air, and soon what were described as sparks began spraying in the air. Townspeople came to watch. The ground seemed to be jumping up and down, gurgling sounds came from the hole, and hot stones were being thrown into the air. By the next morning, there was a cone some 30 feet high, and smoke and rocks were being ejected from it with great violence. The cone grew throughout the day, and soon lava began issuing from its base. Mexican geologist Ezequiel Órdoñez reached the scene the evening of February 22:

I was witnessing a sight which few other humans had ever seen, the initial stages of the growth of a new volcano. Tremendous explosions were heard, ground tremors were felt frequently, and a thick high column of vapors with a great

many incandescent rocks could be seen rising almost continuously from the center of a small conical mound then estimated to be 55 meters [180 feet] high. . . .

The cone grew frighteningly fast. At the end of the first week
it was 460 feet high, and its explosions could be heard 200 miles
away. By the end of the first year, it was more than 1,000 feet
high. Its growth then slowed, and it began spewing large quantities of lava from the southwest base of the cone, which soon
destroyed two nearby villages.

Parícutin remained active until March 4, 1952. It was then
1,345 feet above the original surface of Señor Pulido's cornfield
and had covered nearly 10 square miles of land with lava.
Calculations showed that it had emitted an average of 1.1 million metric tons of solid material per day during its active life.

Parícutin was a spectacular sight to those privileged to see it
during its period of activity. "Both by day and by night Parícutin
is a magnificent spectacle," said one observer. By day it gave out
towering, boiling, fleecy masses of steam. "By night, when the
columns of smoke are not visible, the volcano is like an enormous blast furnace, hurling into the air vast quantities of incandescent material which falls in a glowing shower on the
slopes, covering them with a shimmery and ever-changing
mantle of fire as the rocks roll down."

Said another eyewitness, William F. Foshag: "In my opinion,
Parícutin is the greatest show on earth. It is, I believe, as spectacular as Vesuvius ever was, and in its more violent phases it
is better. . . . On August 1, the fireworks became so spectacular that spectators burst into applause. Think of that: people
applauding a volcano!"

Spectacular it may have been, but Parícutin ruined the
countryside over an area 35 miles in diameter and played havoc
with critical human resources. The population of a 300-square-
mile area was forced to relocate. Surface and groundwater flows
were altered. Springs dramatically increased or decreased their
output. New ones formed, old ones dried up. Land was de-
forested, and crops, shrubs, and grasses were ruined. Animals
died from inhalation or ingestion of volcanic chemicals. It has
been estimated that the land around Parícutin will require 200
years to regain normal forest growth and even longer to recover
from the erosional damage.

Parícutin sprang up out of the land, but Surtsey was born in the sea. A submarine eruption in 425 feet of water 20 miles south of Iceland built up a cone that breached the ocean surface on November 15, 1963. For a time, violent explosions threw up fiery showers of magmatic spray as the ocean water came into contact with the fluid basaltic magma.

Volcanologist Sigudur Thorarinsson described the scene: "As we approached, the volcano seemed to redouble its activity. Bombs and pumice flew upward. When darkness fell, the entire cone glowed with bombs, which rolled down the slopes into the white surf. Lightning ripped the eruption cloud with purplish bolts, and thunder cracked above our heads."

As the cone of the new volcano built up high enough to shut out the seawater, the explosive activity diminished and accumulation of lava began. The lava eventually assured the future of the infant island, protecting it from attack by the waves.

A day after its birth, Surtsey was an island 1,800 feet long and 200 feet high. Six weeks later, it had reached a height of 415 feet. By the end of March, 1964, it was a mile-long island reaching 500 feet above sea level. By the time its activity ceased in May, 1967, Surtsey had attained an area of more than one square mile, a new island whose gradual colonization by plants and animals served as a fascinating laboratory for study of the spread of organisms to newly created habitats.

Iceland has been the site of regular volcanic eruptions, but the most catastrophic was the famous Laki upheaval in 1783. It began with fountains of lava bursting from a row of small craters that soon grew into a fissure 18 miles long. For months, lava poured from this fissure in tremendous volumes. During early stages, the eruption was discharging twice as much lava as the Rhine discharges water at its mouth. Two hundred eighteen square miles of land were inundated by 2.9 cubic miles of lava, the largest lava flow observed in historic times. But the worst effects were indirect. Thorarinsson estimates that the explosion released 130 million tons of sulphur dioxide. The air pollution from the volcanic gases stunted the growth of grass over all of Iceland during the summer of 1783. Half the cattle and three-quarters of the sheep on the island died. The sulphurous haze was observed all over Europe and in Africa and Asia. Around Iceland it reduced visibility so much that the nation's fishermen could not put to sea. With so many essential sources of food eliminated, famine spread over Iceland, and nearly a quarter of the island's 50,000 inhabitants died.

The most notable recent eruption at Iceland resulted in a dramatic and resolute campaign of human action to stem the flow of lava. This remarkable effort, two U.S. Geological Survey scientists who observed it later stated, ultimately became the most ambitious program ever attempted by man to control volcanic eruption.

The events began about two in the morning of January 23, 1973, near Iceland's premier fishing port, the town of Vestmannaeyjar on the island of Heimaey. Heimaey is about seven miles south of Iceland and 13 miles north of Surtsey. Less than 1,100 yards from the center of town, a fissure about one mile long opened along a nearly north-south line that completely traversed the island. Fountains of lava spewed from its length. The town was bombarded with volcanic bombs and ash.

Firemen rushed through the streets to wake up the town's residents. One woman looked out the window and saw the grass burning. When she dressed and went outside, she found the ground to be "hot as if it were on fire." The Icelandic civil defense had a contingency plan ready for just such a disaster, and within six hours, making use of everything from fishing boats to coast guard vessels, nearly all Heimaey's 5,300 residents had been evacuated to the mainland.

The volcanic activity soon became restricted to one particular spot along the original fissure, and there a volvanic cone began building. It gained the name Eldfell ("fire mountain"). Its output of lava and pyroclastics was estimated at 131 cubic yards per second. Homes, farmsteads, and public buildings near the rift were being destroyed, either set afire by the glowing lava bombs or overwhelmed by the advancing lava front. When by early February the lava had reached the harbor, officials decided they had to fight the lava flows. The harbor is the best along the entire south coast of Iceland and it serves some of the richest fishing waters in the North Atlantic.

On the advice of Icelandic geologists and geophysicists, a program to cool the lava by spraying it with seawater was put into action. The first limited efforts, using city water, started on February 7, only 15 days after the eruption began. They showed that the spraying cooled the lava enough to cause it to thicken and solidify, thereby slowing its movement.

In early March, a pump ship able to deliver large quantities of water to the site was brought into the harbor, and later that month large pumps brought from the United States were put

Steam rises from the Icelandic island of Heimaey in February, 1973, as rescue workers pump millions of gallons of water over front of molten lava in a successful effort to slow its advance into valuable harbor. (U.S. GEOLOGICAL SURVEY)

into action. Water was pumped directly onto the front of the flow where it met the harbor and also onto the top of the lava. One of the problems was to get water onto the surface of the flow far behind the front. That was solved by networks of branching water pipes put into place with the aid of bulldozers that climbed up onto the hot lava. Nineteen miles of these pipes were eventually installed, and 43 pumps powered water onto the lava.

The water had little effect on a newly drenched section for about a day. But then the flow of water in that area began to slow the lava's movement. The spraying would continue about two weeks at each point. A third of all the buildings in Vestmannaeyjar were destroyed, but the harbor was saved. Later study showed that nearly 8 million cubic yards of water had converted 5½ million cubic yards of molten lava into solid rock. Bore holes showed that the water had caused the lava to cool and solidify 50 to 100 times faster than it would have normally.

Life on Heimaey was seriously disrupted, but the rest of the islanders soon returned, trucked volcanic deposits that had reached the third story of some buildings, and cleaned up their town to where it is once again an attractive place to live and a still vigorous fishing port. But now it is also a tourist attraction and the site of a new geological laboratory. The lava flow added to the island's size, the volcanic rock was used to extend the airport runways, and the tongue of lava that threatened to block off the harbor turned out to be an excellent breakwater. All in all a happy ending to the greatest effort ever attempted to control the flow of lava during an eruption.

It is no accident that Iceland is the most volcanically active land area on the surface of the earth. Iceland, it turns out, is the only place in the world where the planet-girdling mid-ocean ridge reaches above the surface of the sea. And the mid-ocean ridges are where the earth's crustal plates are slowly spreading apart, the gap formed between them filled by magma that wells up from below. But we are getting a little ahead of ourselves.

A look at a map of the distribution of the 516 volcanoes that have erupted in historic time (69 of them submarine eruptions) shows that they tend to occur only in certain places. There is a great belt of volcanoes that extends around the circumference of the Pacific Ocean. It runs up the coast of South and Central America, up through the U.S. Pacific Northwest, down the length of the Aleutian Islands, across to Kamchatka, Japan, the Philippines, through Melanesia and across to New Zealand.

Buildings on outskirts of town of Vestmannaeyjar on Heimaey buried under ash and debris from the eruption of Eldfell. (U.S. GEOLOGICAL SURVEY)

There is another belt across the Alpine-Himalayan zone from the Mediterranean to Southern Asia. In the Atlantic, there is a north-sound band from the Canary and Cape Verde Islands to the Azores to Iceland. There are also some apparently isolated volcanic areas, such as Hawaii. Earthquake activity shows the same kind of distribution. So do the world's youngest mountain ranges.

Through the mid and late 1960s into the early 1970s, an enormous variety of scientific evidence from seismology, paleo-magnetism, heat-flow studies, deep-sea drilling, geology, and even paleontology came together through the efforts of hun-dreds of scientists to explain these distributions. Out of it all came a modern version of the old idea of continental drift but one that did away with the objections that had plagued that theory. The new synthesis explains the distribution of the planet's great mountain belts, ocean trenches, earthquakes, and volcanoes. It shows how the earth's surface is in a perpetual state of change, with spreading apart of the ocean bottoms and creation of new sea floor the fundamental agent of that change. This new synthesis is called plate tectonics, and it is truly one of the revolutionary advances in the history of science. It is often

compared in importance—correctly, I think—to the Darwinian
theory of evolution through natural selection that revolutionized biology.

The upper layer of the earth, the evidence shows, is broken,
like a cracked egg shell, into about 10 large sections called
plates. These plates are about 40 miles thick. (They include
both the crust and a portion of the upper mantle, but for con-
venience they are often called crustal plates.) The plates are
rigid and they are in slow (an inch or so per year) but nearly
constant horizontal motion over the earth, floating, like slabs
of ice, on a weak, partially molten layer of the mantle beneath
them.

In the old continental drift idea, the continents were proposed
to somehow move through the ocean bottom, like a plow through
soil (and that was a major objection to the theory). But in
plate tectonics, continents and ocean bottom alike ride like
passengers on the crustal plates. North America and the western
half of the Atlantic Ocean, for instance, are on the same plate.
Africa is on the same plate as the eastern half of the Atlantic
Ocean. Europe and Northern Asia are on the same plate as
the Northeastern Atlantic Ocean.

These plates spread apart from each other at the mid-ocean
ridges, and that is why we refer to these ridges, where new
material is continually upwelling to be solidified into new rock,
as the birthplace of the earth's crust. Much of this upwelling of
magma is a slow, effusive process, and virtually all of it takes
place deep beneath the ocean, hidden from human eyes.

Except in Iceland. Iceland, as mentioned, is the one place
where the mid-ocean ridge (the part of it beneath the Atlantic
is called the Mid-Atlantic Ridge) rises above the surface to
become land. Iceland is literally a place where the earth's surface is growing, and volcanism, whether mild and effusive or at
times strong and explosive, is the agent of that growth. Iceland
is widening, spreading apart. Its eastern half is moving with the
previously mentioned Eurasian plate, its western half with the
North American plate. The lava that flows up onto the surface as
in the Laki eruption of 1783, and in the countless others before
and since, is the new crust that produces Iceland's growth. The
same thing is happening elsewhere on the mid-ocean ridges,
but most of that activity is unseen except where, as at the
Azores, the tops of the volcanoes have reached the surface, or
where, as was accomplished in 1975 and 1977, scientists go

down in research submarines to observe the process firsthand.

But if plates are spreading apart at one place, they must be coming into contact with each other at other places. That is exactly what is happening. These meetings can be of various kinds, but they all result in events that shape and form the earth as we see it. The Himalayas, for instance, are a place where two plates both carrying continents on their backs (Northern Asia on one, India on the other) collided some 45 million years ago, creating the highest mountains on earth.

The deep trenches around the edge of the Pacific Ocean (the Aleutian, Japan, and Marianas trenches, for example) are the site where the Pacific plate, moving inexorably west and northwest, has come into contact with another plate in the Western Pacific. Here one crustal plate (the Pacific) dips beneath the other (the Eurasian), its lower edge descending at a roughly 45-degree angle several hundred miles into the layer beneath. The descending portion of the plate becomes heated, partly from contact with the warmer temperatures in the mantle, partly from chemical phase changes as minerals in the plate are subjected to greater pressures, and partly from friction. Melted components of this plate, lighter than the surrounding rock, force their way upward to erupt as volcanoes.

The volcanoes on the island arcs of the Western Pacific were formed this way. Similar processes are responsible for the volcanoes along the Java-Sumatra island arc, where the plate carrying the Indian Ocean sea floor has descended beneath the plate carrying Eurasia and the South China Sea. The West Indies volcanoes like Mount Pelée are located where the South American plate thrusts under the small Caribbean plate. The great volcanoes along the west coast of Central America were formed along a line where the small northwestward-moving oceanic plate in the Pacific south of Mexico has thrust beneath the coast. This chain of great volcanoes along the length of Central America can be divided or categorized into some seven different regions, and in 1973 Michael Carr, now of Rutgers University, proposed that the underthrusting plate may be broken into perhaps seven segments, like the fingers of a hand, the differences between each segment responsible for the differences, such as in alignment, in the volcanoes above. Below the Andes volcanoes of South America, an ocean plate is being absorbed into the Peru-Chile trench.

So the volcanoes of the Circum-Pacific Belt have their origin in the heat of battle between two giant slabs of the earth's surface, one forced beneath the other in nonquiet submission. Those along the Central Mediterranean are the products of friction between two plates (the African and Eurasian.) And those of Iceland and the mid-ocean ridges are the fire of crustal separation and crustal rebirth. Those of East Africa have the same cause as well, because along the East African Rift Valley the land is slowly separating, someday to possibly become a new sea.

All this the powerful result of events at the margins of the earth's crustal plates. But what about Hawaii? The Hawaiian Islands are in the center of the Pacific plate, several thousand miles from the nearest plate boundary. Here, the answer may also be drawn from plate tectonics. In the Hawaiian chain, the islands are successively older to the northwest. They seem to have been made in sequence, first one, then the next, the most recently formed also the most volcanically active. The hypothesis still has its detractors, but it appears that these volcanoes may have been formed in succession as the northwestward-moving Pacific plate passed over a stationary "hot spot" in the mantle beneath. In this view, the crustal plate is now in such a position that the island of Hawaii (Mauna Loa and Kilauea volcanoes) lies nearly over the hot spot. The evidence for hot spots is much debated, but for Hawaii, and its volcanoes, at least, the hot spot hypothesis seems to lead the way.

So the volcanoes of the earth, which exhibit their might in such dramatic and fiery fashion, have their origin in subsurface events even more all consuming and awe inspiring. The dynamic earth is not a metaphor. We live on a planet whose surface is in motion, and the volcanoes we both revere and fear are one of the results. And so, we will now see, are earthquakes.

CHAPTER 9

Earthquakes

Until that dreadful day in September, 1978, Tabas was a prosperous trading town, a palm-fringed oasis on the edge of Dasht-e Kavir, the great salt desert of Northeast Iran. It was an ancient city and a historic point, a stop on the route Marco Polo took to China in 1272. It was an agricultural center in an area noted for its dates, grains, and oranges.

But it also was in a land plagued by destructive earthquakes. Since 1962, 30,000 people had died in earthquakes in Iran, the most disastrous one in 1968 in the same province of Khurasan. Eleven thousand six hundred people lost their lives. This one was to be even worse.

It was early in the evening of September 16, 1978, and darkness had just fallen. Some people were fortunate enough to be outside their homes, but most were not. Throughout the region families were sitting down to dinner. At 7:38 P.M. a great earthquake of magnitude 7.7, so strong it was felt over two-thirds of Iran, began shaking the ground with frightening force. Waves of destructive energy radiated across the surface from a point somewhere between Tabas and the city of Ferdous to the northeast.

"I was sitting in front of my house by the pond," said a Tabas man named Hassan. "It was dark. Then all of a sudden I fell to the ground and there was a great roar and screams." His mud brick home collapsed around his family, but they were not hurt seriously. That was the rare exception that night.

Nearly all the buildings in Tabas were built of mud bricks, and virtually all of them crumbled into piles of rubble. Three out of four of the city's inhabitants were buried alive.

Only a few modern institutional buildings such as a bank and two schools were left standing, their fired-brick walls supported by steel frames. In some of the buildings even the windows were still intact amid the scene of total devastation around them. Aerial views telecast to the rest of Iran the next day showed a flattened town—palm trees and one domed minaret joining only a few other structures in standing above the rubble. The city, said one description, "had the appearance of a flattened sand castle."

"The town simply does not exist anymore," said an American reporter at the scene. "It was wiped out in 90 seconds." Entire families were eliminated, crushed under the piles of mud brick. Anyone found alive was likely to be the only survivor from his family. Abbas Abadini, tears streaming down his face, dug through the rubble that was once his home. Somewhere beneath it were his five children. Two young women in the traditional long-flowing chadors still worn in the countryside took out a photograph of their father, an air force captain, who was killed. Of the 20 persons in their family, 16 were killed. Only a brother and the husband of one of the two women survived.

The scenes were repeated at a hundred other villages in the region. Forty of the villages were demolished and 60 badly damaged.

As the rescue efforts continued, the Red Lion and Sun Society, Iran's equivalent of the Red Cross, found its estimates of the death toll going ever upward. In the 1975 census, the population of Tabas was placed at 17,000, and it had grown since then. Only 1,800 residents were still alive. At least 15,200—nearly nine of every 10—inhabitants of Tabas were dead. Throughout the affected area of Iran, the total death toll was officially placed at 25,000.

It was the strongest and most destructive earthquake of 1978. Unfortunately, earthquakes dealing that degree of tragedy have not been any less common in recent years than they have been throughout history. The year 1976, for instance, with considerable justification, has been called the year of the killer earthquakes. The Guatemala earthquake of February 4 killed 23,000. An earthquake in Northeastern Italy near Friuli on May 5 killed 1,000. An earthquake on June 25 in West Irian, the west end of the island of New Guinea, may have killed 6,000. An earthquake and resulting tsunami on August 16 in the Philippines caused 2,000 deaths. And an earthquake near Muradiye in Turkey on November 24 killed 4,000.

But those disasters, as tragic as they were, were dwarfed by

Ground fractures left by 7.3-magnitude earthquake in Khorassan Province, Iran, August 31, 1968, that killed 11,600 persons. The 7.7-magnitude quake on September 16, 1978, that destroyed Tabas and other villages and killed 25,000 occurred in the same area of northeastern Iran. (U.S. GEOLOGICAL SURVEY)

the catastrophic earthquake that struck the city of Tangshan, in Northern China, in the early morning hours of July 28. It was the greatest killer quake in four centuries.

Tangshan was an industrial city of one million people 95 miles east and slightly south of Peking. North China is a region of only moderate earthquake activity. The 1975 earthquake at Haicheng, whose successful prediction by Chinese scientists saved tens of thousands of lives and was heralded worldwide, led to a feeling that the long-term strains accumulated in the area had probably been released. How wrong that proved to be!

Even though Tangshan had had no previous major earthquakes in its immediate vicinity, the city is in the center of a four-sided area outlined by major crustal faults, and the 25-mile-long Tangshan fault passes through it. The city was built on unstable, alluvial soil. Few of its structures were earthquake resistant. At 3:42 A.M. on July 28, the city asleep, a five-mile-long section of the fault right in the middle city suddenly broke. For nearly two minutes the ground shook beneath its inhabitants. It was a magnitude 8.0 shock. In places, the land on the west side of the fault moved five feet northward in relation to the land on the east side. The east block tipped downward toward the north end of the break, upward toward the south end.

In some instances, the ground caved in to form thousands of craters. Trees and crops were bowled over. Some residents reported being catapulted into the air by the force of the shock. Others reported seeing a strange incandescent glow lighting up the night, an apparent observation of the "earthquake lights" occasionally reported in earthquakes.

Over a four-by-five-mile area of Tangshan, the devastation was nearly total. Factories, bridges, railroads, and homes were turned into instant junk heaps. The sleeping citizens of Tangshan were caught beneath the debris of their houses.

In the city of Tientsin, 60 miles to the southwest, Gough Whitlam, the former Prime Minister of Australia, near the end of a world tour, was asleep with his wife on the seventh floor of the Tientsin Friendship Guest House when the shaking began. His was one of the first eyewitness reports of the quake to reach the West. The hotel was a newly built building of modern design. The rooms, he said, were "lunging and tearing." A chest of drawers fell on his wife and hurt her leg. The lights went out and then, Whitlam said, "The hotel was literally split down the middle with about a one-foot gap separating the two parts. We had to walk over the gap going down the corridor. We were then evacuated from the premises in the darkness."

On the same floor was the Australian Ambassador to China, Stephen Fitzgerald. "The building was being thrown in all directions," he said. "It was not just a kind of swaying but it was moving very heavily in all directions, punctuated by extreme jolts which flung me around in the bed. For a time after that, the building swayed in a manner that suggested it was undecided whether or not to fall over, because it would get to each end of the arc and then just kind of teeter there for a while and then swing to the other end and teeter there for a while."

Residents of Peking fled into the streets. By the millions they elected to stay outside rather than risk death in building collapses from aftershocks. Raincoats, oil cloths, umbrellas, tents, sheets, and water culverts were used for days as temporary homes.

In Tangshan, the devastation was complete. The Chinese are traditionally secretive about natural disasters. A long-held view is that they are a mandate from heaven and an omen of trouble for governments. No official disclosure of the death toll was ever made, but estimates of at least 655,000 dead and 780,000 injured are now generally accepted as accurate. That makes it the second worst earthquake in recorded history, next only to the earthquake at Hausien in China's Shensi Province in 1556 that killed 830,000.

A year after the Tangshan earthquake, foreign correspondents were allowed into the city for the first time. Many compared the scene to the devastation in Hiroshima following the atomic bomb. They saw a city still largely unrestored. A few factories were back in operation on the city's outskirts, and some of the railway bridges had been replaced. Much of the heavy machinery necessary to transport coal from the mines in the vicinity was still incapacitated. The survivors were living in makeshift homes fashioned from materials in the debris.

Two years after the disaster, on June 24, 1978, an Agence France-Presse correspondent passing through the city found it to be a shantytown:

The city can be seen from the Peking-Mukden Railway, but is still closed to visitors, and a correspondent was even prevented by the police from getting out on the platform during the few minutes his train stopped in the city. It is again a city of flourishing industry, but its 1.6 million inhabitants still live in white, mudwalled shelters, hardly more than 6 feet high, lit by tiny windows and with corrugated iron roofs held down by stones. The ground is covered with rubble as far as the eye can see, and not one building, apart from a few rebuilt factories, rises above the desolation. Only a few low buildings along the railway line were repaired, shortly after the quake, and some new, low red-brick buildings are visible in the surrounding villages. After the earthquake . . . the authorities gave priority to getting production under way again. The priority was not given to housing inasmuch as an earthquake alert continued during the following months, when 300 secondary tremors occurred.

The Tangshan quake inevitably attracts reference to the 1556 tragedy in Shensi Province which may be not only the worst earthquake but also the worst natural disaster of all time. It struck at five in the morning with a Richter magnitude estimated from 8.0 to 8.3. The area of destruction spanned 500 miles extending over 98 counties and eight provinces of Central China. In the six counties most seriously shaken, the average death rate was 60 percent. It is often reported in the West that the deaths were due to collapse of caves in hills made of loess (thickly compacted windblown dust) in which the peasants supposedly lived, but in fact most of the deaths were caused by the collapse of houses.

In the fall of 1974, a delegation of American seismologists headed by Frank Press, later President Carter's science advisor, visited the area of the 1556 earthquake during a month-long scientific tour of China. They reported that they found the earth-faulting in the area to be "truly spectacular" both on the ground and in photos taken by the U.S. Earth Resources Technology Satellite (ERTS), prints they presented to their Chinese hosts. "Certainly," they said in the report they later wrote, "the area would easily be recognized as earthquake prone . . . even in the absence of historic earthquakes." They also had one other strong impression: "The density of population in the Wei River valley [which flows past Huasien and through the center of Shensi Province] and the construction practices of homes are such that a repetition of the 1556 event would again be a major disaster unless it were accurately predicted and appropriate measures taken."

A quick word about measurements of the severity of earthquakes. The magnitude of the earthquake is a measure of the

Earthquake Magnitude and Expected World Incidence

TYPE OF SHOCK	MAGNITUDE	AVERAGE NO. EACH YEAR
Great	8 or more	1.1
Major	7 to 7.9	18
Large (Destructive)	6 to 6.9	120
Moderate (Damaging)	5 to 5.9	1,000
Minor (Damage slight)	4 to 4.9	6,000
Generally felt	3 to 3.9	49,000
Potentially perceptible	2 to 2.9	300,000
Microearthquake (Imperceptible)	Below 2	600,000+

Source: Earthquake Information Bulletin

Earthquake Magnitude and Expected World Incidence. (EARTHQUAKE INFORMATION BULLETIN)

amplitude, or height, of its seismic waves, roughly the degree of ground shaking. The most widely used scale of magnitude is named after Charles F. Richter of the California Institute of Technology, who devised it. The first important thing to note is that it is a logarithmic scale, meaning that each whole number step represents a tenfold increase in measured amplitude. Thus a magnitude 8 earthquake has an amplitude 10 times as large as a magnitude 7 earthquake, 100 times as large as a magnitude 6 quake, and 10,000 times as large as a magnitude 4 quake.

The energy of an earthquake goes up even faster than amplitude. Each whole-step increase in magnitude represents about 31 times more energy than the preceding number. Thus, a magnitude 8 quake releases 31 times as much energy as a magnitude 7 quake and about 1,000 times as much as a magnitude 6 quake. And it releases about one million times as much energy as an earthquake of magnitude 4. I always find visual analogies helpful. If the energy of a magnitude 3 earthquake is represented by the volume of a tennis ball, the energy released by the San Francisco earthquake (magnitude 8.25) would need to be represented by a sphere with a diameter of 210 feet.

The earthquakes of the great killer year of 1976 took approximately 700,000 lives, probably the world's worst year for earthquake fatalities since that tragic year of 1556. But ironically, there were slightly fewer large earthquakes than average. Waverly Person, a geophysicist with the U.S. Geological Survey's National Earthquake Information Service in Golden, Colorado, noted that in 1976 there were 18 earthquakes of magnitude 7.0 to 7.9, considered "major." The long-term average is 19 per year. An average year in addition brings one "great" earthquake, magnitude 8.0 or higher; 120 "strong" earthquakes, magnitude 6 to 6.9, and about 1,000 "moderate" ones, magnitude 5.0 to 5.9.

Smaller earthquakes are so frequent that nobody keeps track of them all. The National Earthquake Information Service routinely calculates and distributes information on the exact locations of about 6,000 earthquakes a year. But estimates of the total yearly number of tremors of magnitude 2.0 (potentially perceptible) and up range from 300,000 to many more than 800,000. And that doesn't count even greater numbers of smaller "microearthquakes." It is a tremulous earth we live on.

The reason 1976 brought so many deaths and injuries is that most of the major quakes that did hit happened to strike where population densities were high and typical structures were particularly vulnerable.

This illustrates once again that a tragic human disaster requires more than just an intense natural event. The hazardous event brings high death tolls only when it happens in conjunction with large numbers of susceptible people.

A vivid example was the earthquake in Guatemala on February 4, 1976. It was a magnitude 7.5 event, quite strong, but it also unfortunately struck a few minutes after 3 A.M. when families were in their homes asleep. Most of the homes, particularly those west of Guatemala City and in the Motagua River Valley, had walls built of weak adobe mud brick unable to stand much horizontal pressure. They quickly crumbled, bringing the wood beams and tile roofs down on the sleeping people. Broken backs and smashed pelvises were common. Twenty-three thousand persons were killed, 74,000 injured, and a million left homeless.

The survivors were soon seen re-erecting their homes in the same location out of the same weak adobe brick, something that compassionate and sympathetic people can all understand but at the same time lament.

The Guatemala earthquake created the most extensive surface faulting in the Western Hemisphere since the San Francisco earthquake of 1906. The quake caused the ground to break in a continuous, visible, well-defined line extending across Guatemala for 140 miles. The fracture was generally from three to 10 feet across, but in one place it was 30 feet. One long row of trees was offset 10½ feet. Rows of a farmer's field were offset 28 inches. A soccer field had a series of zig-zag rips across it caused by a displacement of three feet. Railroad tracks looked as though a giant had wrenched them sideways in his hand.

Detailed study of this faulting by George Plafker of the U.S. Geological Survey and others produced striking confirmation of some of the basic tenets of plate tectonics theory. It also revealed in dramatic fashion how earthquake-prone Central America is slowly being pulled apart by the inexorable movements of the earth's crustal plates.

As noted in Chapter 8, the earth's crust and uppermost mantle is broken into a series of large 40-mile-thick rigid sections or plates that are in constant relative motion over the softer rock below. The horizontal movements of these plates range from less than one to as much as three inches per year. This brings the plates into contact with each other over long periods of geological time, and where that happens all sorts of massive events can occur. Where plates are colliding head-on in slow, continuous compression, large mountain ranges, such as the Alps and the Himalayas, are squeezed up. Where an oceanic plate descends beneath another plate, large arcs of islands and volcanoes are created, which if near enough a continent, may someday become new land of that continent. Where the edges of two plates are sliding along each other, as along California's San Andreas fault, strong earthquakes are a constant threat. All of these situations produce earthquakes at periodic intervals along the lines of contact as the strain built up through the thickness of the crust by the slow relative plate movements is released. The rock of the crust has only a certain amount of elastic give in it, then it has to yield with a shudder that we feel as an earthquake.

The conceptual revolution represented by the theory of plate tectonics is the result of research by hundreds of earth scientists in the 1960s and 1970s. Although many details are yet to be explained, it allows a wide variety of phenomena to be understood as part of a unified system.

The plate tectonics situation in Central America is complex

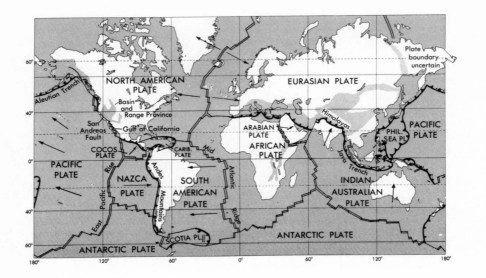

Map of the earth's major crustal plates. Plates are in slow continual motion. Most earthquakes occur along plate boundaries. (ADAPTED FROM WARREN HAMILTON, U.S. GEOLOGICAL SURVEY)

and fascinating. It provides an interesting case study of plate interactions and earthquakes. Central America from Central Guatemala south lies on a relatively small plate that also underlies the entire Caribbean Sea. It is in slow eastward motion in relation to the North American plate, whose southern boundary it is in contact with. On land, the boundary between these two plates cuts generally east and west across Guatemala, and the fault known as the Motagua fault is, the 1976 earthquake showed, its main manifestation. If you were to stand straddling that fault you would have one foot on the North American plate and one on the Caribbean plate. (In the same way, Berkeley seismologist Bruce Bolt points out that where the San Andreas fault cuts northward through a displaced culvert at a winery near Hollister, California, you can stand with one foot on the North American plate and one on the Pacific plate.)

The 1976 Guatemala earthquake happened, Plafker's study showed, when rock along about one-tenth of the entire length of the boundary between the Caribbean and North American plates gave way in response to the forces that over geological time are pressing the Caribbean plate relatively eastward. Along the fault break, the average displacement, or horizontal movement, was four feet. The direction was such that the ground on the south side of the fault moved eastward in relation to the ground on the north side. Plafker called it "a striking confirmation of deductions regarding the late Cenozoic [last 12 million years] relative motion between these two crustal plates that were based largely on indirect geologic and geophysical evidence."

But that's not all. There is more happening than just slippage along the plate boundary. There is geological evidence of differential movement *within* the Caribbean plate in Central America. There is a series of young faults perpendicular to the boundary and south of it in Western Guatemala. And along and near the east edge of the line of great volcanoes that march down the west coast of Central America are geological formations called grabens, blocks of rock that have dropped vertically downward when the crust is pulled apart, releasing its grip on them. Western Central America seems to be being stretched.

The evidence seems to show that a wedge-shaped area of Western Central America that includes Southern Guatemala and Western El Salvador and Nicaragua is caught in a vise. The Caribbean plate wants to move intact eastward in relation to the North American plate. But a third plate, a small one called Cocos, underlies the part of the Pacific Ocean west of Central America. The Cocos plate is moving northeastward, its leading edge descending below the west coastline of Central America, and the force of this movement is pinning down the northwestern corner of the Caribbean plate. It is wedging this corner against the North American plate so that, like a pant leg caught in a door, it cannot move.

The result of all this rather complicated dynamic geometry is that Central America is being torn apart. The eastern part is going on and moving east, but the western coast may be left behind. The plate, Plafker believes, may eventually become "decoupled" along the line of volcanoes. It could, he says, result in the opening of a marginal sea along the volcanic chain. The Gulf of Fonseca, where El Salvador, Honduras, and Nicaragua meet at the Pacific Ocean, may be its start.

Seen in this modern view, Central America has the unfortunate luck to be situated on a strip of land being jostled by interactions of not two but three of the earth's crustal plates. It can be shaken to its core by earthquakes set off by any of four causes: slippage along two plate boundaries, as with the 1976 tragedy; movements along the extensional faults within the Caribbean plate;

downthrust of the Cocos plate beneath the west coast of Central America, which as mentioned in Chapter 8 is also largely responsible for the chain of volcanoes there; and earthquakes set off by eruptions of the volcanoes.

"It's about as bad as you can get anywhere in the world," Plafker says of the perilous geophysical setting of Guatemala and its neighboring countries. It is a seismic time bomb that has gone off many times in the past and will undoubtedly continue to do so in the future.

The irony is that the same complex situation that makes Guatemala, El Salvador, and Nicaragua so susceptible to disastrous natural events is also responsible for their great scenic beauty—their diverse geology and beautiful valleys, mountains, and volcanoes.

Central America's seismic setting is more complicated than most, but unfortunately the somewhat simpler situations of other earthquake-prone areas of the world don't significantly ease their risk.

According to Bruce Bolt, 90 percent of the world's release of seismic energy from shallow earthquakes and virtually all the energy released from deep earthquakes take place in the deep ocean trenches where crustal plates are descending at an angle into the mantle beneath the edge of another plate. Except for areas where plate margins are sliding sideways along each other, as in Central Guatemala or Western California, or where plate collisions are compressing continents, as in Turkey, Iran, or Central Asia, most of the largest earthquakes have occurred in these downthrusting "subduction" regions. Examples are the Alaska earthquake of 1964, the Chile earthquake of 1960, and the great Japan earthquake of 1923.

Virtually the entire circumference of the Pacific Ocean, as mentioned, is bounded by these deep trenches where crustal plates are being consumed. So is the Northeastern Indian Ocean along the curving Sumatra-Java arc. (The Atlantic Ocean has no plate margins at its shores, and that is why Eastern North and South America and Western Africa are relatively free of large earthquakes. The undersea Mid-Atlantic Ridge, which roughly bisects the Atlantic from north of Iceland to below the tip of South America, is a spreading center where crustal plates are moving apart. Moderate earthquake activity occurs all along its length.)

Earthquakes can and do occur along the entire downgoing

portions of these slabs. In fact, seismological studies pinpointing the exact three-dimensional position of the sources of earthquakes provided the most compelling evidence for the existence of these subducting plates. The numerous earthquakes beneath the ocean trenches and island arcs seemed to occur in a particular pattern. Beneath the Tonga arc in the Southwest Pacific, for instance, most earthquake centers were clustered along a narrow zone starting beneath the Tonga trench and dipping westward under it at an angle of about 45 degrees to depths of more than 350 miles. The same thing could be seen under the other prominent island arcs, such as the Aleutians, the Kurils, the Marianas, and Japan. Similar down-dipping planes of earthquakes were also seen beneath Western South America and Central America. Only in such areas were deep earthquakes (down to 400 miles) detected.

Plate tectonics came to the rescue by explaining that this strange situation is a manifestation of the leading edge of the crustal plate angling down into the deeper mantle beneath. Seismological studies can even show in some cases that the earthquakes originating in the upper part of the descending slab are caused by extension, as though the slab's weight is helping pull it down, and that the earthquakes originating in its lower portion are caused by compression, as though the slab has hit bottom.

The seismic tracings show that some of the downgoing slabs are kinked or curved, such as the portion beneath the New Hebrides. In other places, the absence of earthquakes at intermediate depths but their prevalence at shallow and deep depths indicates a stress-free zone or possibly a broken slab. (There's a recent case of a great earthquake that may have been caused by a descending slab breaking away. Caltech seismologist Gordon S. Stewart told the American Geophysical Union in 1978 that the great earthquake off Sumba, Indonesia, on August 19, 1977, possibly the largest since the 1964 Alaska earthquake, may have been caused by a decoupling of the part of the plate descending into the Java trench from the rest of the plate above.)

In other cases, deep earthquakes are absent, apparently indicating that the slab is relatively young and has not yet reached deeper levels. This is the case beneath Central America and the Aleutians. But in no case do earthquakes originate from deeper than 450 miles. Studies by M. Nafi Toksöz and colleagues at the Massachusetts Institute of Technology have shown that the interior of the descending plate remains distinctly cooler than the surrounding mantle until the plate reaches a depth of about 375 miles. It then begins to heat up rapidly, and beyond a depth of 450 miles it can no longer be distinguished as a structural unit. It has become a unit of the mantle. It has become "consumed," the end of the life of ocean floor material that was created at a mid-ocean ridge perhaps thousands of miles away a hundred million years earlier.

Deep, intermediate, and shallow earthquakes occur along the entire length of these subduction zones. Toksöz lists 15 major subduction zones on the earth (several include areas where both collision and partial subduction occur, such as the Himalayan zone). I totaled up the lengths he gives for each of these zones and it comes to 46,250 kilometers, or 28,680 miles, greater than the circumference of the earth. These earthquakes have a lot of territory to happen in.

The greatest United States earthquake along a subduction zone was the Good Friday earthquake of March 27, 1964, in Alaska. Along the entire arc of the Aleutians and the Southern Alaska mainland, the Pacific plate plunges downward and northward. Here, as elsewhere, part of a plate may remain locked into place for centuries while other parts slowly move, then eventually give way with a jolt. Such intermittent thrusting has given the region an active earthquake history.

But the earthquake set off at 5:36 P.M. that day was not average. At magnitude 8.5, it was the strongest earthquake recorded in North America since measuring instruments have been available. It was stronger than the San Francisco earthquake of 1906. In response to strains built up over time, the earth ruptured along an area 500 miles long and 150 miles wide parallel to the Aleutian trench. The sea floor within this area was thrust up an average of 10 feet and in places as much as 30 feet. It was the greatest area of vertical displacement ever measured in earthquake history. (Greater amounts may have occurred elsewhere but have not been observed; the Alaska earthquake was studied extensively and became the best-documented subduction-zone earthquake ever.) Simultaneously, the uplifted terrain narrowed and the coastal part moved as much as 60 feet toward the trench.

These violent submarine land shifts generated large undersea waves, a giant tsunami that began striking the shores of Kenai Peninsula and Kodiak Island. At Kodiak's harbor, the first wave, arriving 34 minutes after the start of the earthquake, did little damage. But the second, an hour after the first, and the third, an hour still later, hit as walls of breaking water. The water rushed up on the shore to levels as much as 30 feet above high-tide levels. Waterfront facilities at Seward and Valdez were washed away, including one pier at Valdez on which a dozen stevedores had been working. A total of 118 persons were killed, mostly by drowning.

At Anchorage, 65 miles from the fault slip, beneath Prince William Sound, strong ground shaking began about 15 seconds after the rocks first broke. The pavement on downtown streets began to come apart, and buildings began to wobble. Along a section of Fourth Street, one whole block gave way, dropping a row of cafes and pawnshops, the street and five cars down to the basement level. "The land had become the ocean, the streets were rippling like waves," exclaimed one woman. "The earth started to roll. It rolled for five minutes. . . . People were clinging to each other, to lampposts, to buildings." The newly built J.C. Penney department store began breaking apart, and the front wall of the building crumbled into giant masses of concrete, one of them crushing a car and fatally injuring the

Collapsed section of 4th Street in Anchorage, Alaska, after the Good Friday earthquake of 1964. The earthquake was the largest in North America since recording instruments have been available. (U.S. GEO-LOGICAL SURVEY)

woman inside. Two teenage girls trapped inside the store's elevator had to be rescued by use of acetylene torches. The control tower at Anchorage International Airport snapped off, killing one of the air controllers. A neurosurgeon operating on victims learned that both his twelve-year-old and his infant son had been killed.

A radio announcer for station KHAR recorded his own reactions to the shaking as it was going on. Sample: "Oooo—oh man! I've never lived through anything like this before in my life! And it hasn't even shown signs of stopping yet, either—ooooeeee—the whole place is shaking. . . . Boy! Let me tell you that sure scared the hell out of me and it's still shaking, I'm telling you. . . . Maa-uhn!—I'm not faking a bit of this—I'm telling you, the whole place just moved like somebody had taken it by the nape of the neck and was shaking it. Everything's moving around here! . . ." His recording was later used to time the duration of the heavy shaking in Anchorage.

All in all, 30 blocks of Anchorage's downtown area were damaged, and many expensive homes in the Anchorage suburb of Turnagain-by-the-sea were demolished, when the 70-foot-high soft clay bluffs beneath them temporarily turned to a liquid state, creating a slide that regressed inland 1,000 feet along one and three-quarters miles of coastline.

When it was over, the total death toll in Alaska was 131, and the damage, which was widespread all over the southern part of the state, was half a billion dollars.

In contrast to the earthquakes caused by downthrusting crustal slabs beneath Alaska and elsewhere around the edge of the Pacific, those in California are a result of relative horizontal movement between two plates. The absence of any subduction zone is attested to by the rarity of California earthquakes deeper than 10 miles. Most are no deeper than three miles. That is no consolation, though. Shallow earthquakes are the most destructive.

The Pacific plate, carrying the small part of California that is west of the San Andreas fault, is moving an average of 2 to 2½ inches a year northward in relation to the North American plate, on which the rest of California and the continent rides. About two-thirds of this movement is taken up by slippage along the San Andreas fault; about one-third, by other structures farther inland. In such situations, the land on either side of the fault system tends to stick together until the strain of the accumulated movement becomes too great.

That is what happened at 5:13 in the morning on April 18, 1906, to cause the San Francisco earthquake. The coastal side lurched as much as 20 feet northwestward along a part of the San Andreas fault 270 miles long, resulting in the most famous earthquake disaster in U.S. history.

The story of this earthquake and the conflagration it ignited has been told many times and I won't deal with it here, except to note a few descriptions of the earliest moments of the quake itself. Police Sergeant Jesse Cook, on his rounds at Washington and Davis streets, had the unique experience of watching it come at him: "The whole street was undulating. It was as if the waves of the ocean were coming toward me, and billowing as they came." John Barrett, news editor of the *San Francisco Examiner*, looked out his window and saw buildings dancing, jiggling, and swaying: "It was as though the earth was slipping quietly away from under our feet. There was a sickening sway, and we were all flat on our faces." Saint Louis brewer Adolphus Busch was in the St. Francis Hotel with his family. The building was "swaying from south to north like a tall poplar in a storm." Said Sam

San Francisco City Hall after the great 1906 earthquake. (U.S. GEO-LOGICAL SURVEY)

Wolfe, who ran out of the Grand Hotel while the quake was in progress, "The street seemed to move like waves of water." J. R. Hand, president of a Los Angeles fruit company, gave a similar description of the hotel itself. "The Grand Hotel tossed like a ship at sea. There was a wavelike motion accompanied by a severe up-and-down shake. The shock was accompanied by a terrific roar that is indescribable." The rest is history. As Jack London, San Francisco's star writer and native son, wrote a few days later: "The earthquake shook down in San Francisco hundreds of thousands of dollars worth of walls and chimneys. But the conflagration that followed burned up hundreds of millions of dollars worth of property. . . . Not in history has a modern imperial city been so completely destroyed. . . . San Francisco is gone. Nothing remains of it but memories and a fringe of dwelling-houses on its outskirts."

If you assume that the plate motions that bring such an earthquake threat to California are mythical or metaphorical, consider the results of these three studies that measured the movement. They were reported in December, 1977, at a meeting of the American Geophysical Union.

One, a traditional geodetic survey, found that points west of the north-south Imperial fault zone in Southern California have moved as much as 12½ feet northward relative to points east of the fault between 1941 and 1975. This is an average movement of nearly 4½ inches a year.

Measurements to a tenth of a billionth of a second of the arrival times of signals from quasars in space at two different locations in California, repeated three years apart, found that the distance between Pasadena and a spot in the Mojave Desert to the east increased by five inches from 1975 to 1977.

An experiment using an orbiting satellite to bounce laser beams between San Diego, on the Pacific plate in Southern California, and Quincy, on the North American plate in Northeastern California, found that the distance between those two points decreased 3½ inches per year from 1973 to 1976.

These direct measurements of plate motion dramatically confirm that the coastal area of California is demonstrably moving northward (northwestward north of Los Angeles where there's a jog in the boundary) compared with the rest of California. The rates of motion are slightly higher than was expected, but that may or may not be significant. The point is that the motions predicted by plate tectonics theory are taking place now. From time to time the strains set up by those differential motions have to give way in violent release. No wonder California is earthquake country!

Not all earthquakes occur along plate margins. The earthquakes of Southeastern China are related to compression between the Eurasian and Indian plates, but the Tangshan disaster in Northeastern China resulted from sideways motion along a fault within the Eurasian plate. This is called an intraplate earthquake.

Surprisingly, two of the strongest earthquakes ever to hit the United States happened not along the plate margin on the West Coast but in the eastern half of the country, far from any plate boundary. These U.S. intraplate quakes pose considerable puzzles.

One was centered near Charleston, South Carolina, but it was felt as far away as Boston, Milwaukee, Cuba, and Bermuda. As it began on the night of August 31, 1886, it stopped the clock in Charleston's public square at 9:51 P.M. The city was left in shambles. Few buildings escaped damage; many were completely wrecked. The medical college, the county jail, and Roper Hospital were almost in ruins. The buildings of Charleston College were almost destroyed; fires set off by the shaking caused destruction of 20 buildings. Sixty persons were killed.

"There was no intermission in the vibration of the mighty subterranean engine," wrote Carl McKinley in the *Charleston News and Courier*. "From every quarter arose the shrieks, the cries of pain and fear, the prayers and wailings of terrified men and women and children . . . The air was everywhere filled to the height of the houses with a whitish cloud of dry, stifling dust, arising from the lime and mortar of the shattered masonry."

In 1978, the U.S. Geological Survey reported on a series of new scientific studies of the earthquake. The most important question was left unanswered. Summarized geologist Paul W. Rankin, coordinator of the studies: "The cause of the earthquake has not been adequately explained."

The quake left no surface faulting. It apparently occurred one to five miles beneath the surface in the crystalline basement rock below the coastal plain sediments. The study did show that earthquakes are continuing within the 1886 quake's area of maximum destruction and at a level higher than before that year. "We may," says the Geological Survey, "still be in the aftershock sequence of the 1886 quake."

A unique feature of many earthquakes in the Eastern United States is the vast size of the areas over which they are felt. Geologic conditions in the eastern and central parts of the country are such that quakes are felt over large distances. This was true of the New Madrid earthquakes of 1811-1812, certainly the most remarkable series of earthquakes ever felt in the United States.

They began in the early morning hours of December 16, 1811. A Scottish naturalist, John Bradbury, gathering samples of North American plant life, was sleeping in a small boat moored to an island in the Mississippi River, 100 miles downstream from the river town of New Madrid, Missouri. He was suddenly awakened about 2 A.M. "by a most tremendous noise." The boat lurched up and down, and the river was suddenly turbulent. "All nature seemed to be running into chaos." Wildfowl were screaming, trees were cracking. The din was horrid. But the worst sound was that of the earthquake itself, "equal to the loudest thunder, but more hollow and vibrating." Soon, the crash of riverbank crumbling into the river added to the cacophony.

This was just the beginning. The shocks continued from December 16 to March 15, and even longer. They were felt over much of the Eastern United States. They destroyed the town of New Madrid, frightened people out of their wits (membership in the Methodist Church in the seven most affected states shot up 50 percent in 1812), and produced a series of remarkable geological effects, some temporary, some permanent. According to seismologist Emil J. Mateker, "The number of shocks, the continuity of the disturbance, the area affected, and the severity of the sequence surpass any recorded earthquake in the history of the North American continent." A valuable new historical study by James Penick, Jr., of the University of Missouri has brought together diverse contemporary descriptions.

The area over which the tremors was felt was indeed extraordinary. In the streets of New York, "people were heard to scream with terror." In South Carolina, "the earthquakes terrified the inhabitants exceedingly," and students at South Carolina College "left their chambers without their clothes" during the first main shock on the morning of December 16. In Richmond, Virginia, people "staggered as they stood." In Savannah, Georgia, they "were made to totter, as if on shipboard." Near Hodgenville, Kentucky, they staggered about "like a drunken man." In New

Madrid itself, people "were thrown on the ground at almost every step."

The earthquakes became a national event. They were felt in Detroit, Quebec, New England, the middle seaboard states, New Orleans, and far up the Missouri River. The area over which they could be felt without the aid of instruments approached one million square miles. There were three sequences of shocks, beginning December 16, January 23, and February 7. St. Louis University seismologist Otto W. Nuttli has studied the quakes extensively. He has estimated on the basis of their effects that these three main shocks had magnitudes of 7.5, 7.3, and 7.8, respectively. But in between, hundreds of other tremors rocked the ground. Some people kept count. Louisville engineer and surveyor Jared Brooks counted 1,874 between December 16 and March 15. He categorized eight as violent, and 10 as very severe. He was one of many persons who built instruments to register the shocks. A pendulum hung in a window in Cincinnati "never ceased to vibrate in nearly five months."

The effects on the ground in the neighborhood of New Madrid were remarkable. Godfrey Lesieur, a young boy at the time, later described some:

The earth was observed to be rolling in waves of a few feet in height, with a visible depression between. By and large these swells burst, throwing up large volumes of water, sand and a species of charcoal, some of which was partly covered with a substance, which by its peculiar odor was thought to be sulphur. When these swells burst, large, wide and long fissures were felt.

The fissures caused great consternation. The "surface of the ground . . . cracked in almost every direction," one observer said. The cracks posed a great obstacle to residents who attempted to run to safety, but many were narrow and shallow. The deepest measured 20 feet. Despite the fears, there is only one documented account of a man falling into one. It was so deep he couldn't climb out, but eventually he managed to crawl out where he found a sloping slide.

Sections of land were sunk, the courses of rivers and streams altered, and lakes and ponds created. Reelfoot Lake in Western Tennessee, 18 miles long and five miles wide, was formed when the land sank. There were also uplifts. One small lake below the river St. Francis was "blown up higher than any of the adjoining country, and instead of water it is filled with beautiful white sand."

Forests were destroyed, trees falling, by one account, "thousands at a time." One estimate said 150,000 acres were destroyed. Many reports noted trees split up the middle, "one part standing on one side of a fissure and the other part on the other." A small island that sank in the Mississippi River left its tree tops sticking up out of the water.

The river was affected most of all. Trees and dirt banks crashing into it produced great turbulence and navigational hazards. Previously fallen trees anchored in the river bottom silt were released to rise to the surface. Dramatic rises and falls of water level were reported. Two small waterfalls were created, their sound loud enough to be heard at New Madrid eight miles away, but they washed away in a few days.

There has long been controversy over reports that for a time the Mississippi reversed its course. One seismologist's study attributed the tale of the river flowing upstream to "hysteria and superstition." Penick agrees that the current reversal has "often been grossly exaggerated and the time involved lengthened from a few hours to a few days." But he says careful study of on-the-spot accounts in contrast to "cumulative" accounts that ignore time sequence does seem to support the reports that for a while on February 7 the river bed rose in at least two places above and below New Madrid to form obstructions that temporarily reversed the current.

What caused the New Madrid earthquakes isn't clear. Bruce Bolt speculates that they may have been produced by "the enormous weight of alluvial deposits" along the Mississippi River system "perhaps in conjunction with intrusions of dense rock thrust upwards in this region." What is clear is that earthquakes of significant magnitude have occurred in the five-state region below Saint Louis for several thousand years—faulting in young rock demonstrates this. The region remains seismically active and unstable. The possible effects of a similar series of earthquakes now that the region is widely inhabited are not pleasant to contemplate.

The hazards put into motion by a strong earthquake can be amazingly diverse. The threat isn't over with the end of the shaking. The tsunami generated by the Alaska earthquake that dealt death and destruction to coastal Alaska is one example. But the same tsunami swept onward out over the Pacific. The Tsunami Warning Center in Honolulu sent out advisory bulletins and warnings. At Crescent City, California, which lies along the great circle perpendicular to the underwater fault that broke at Alaska, the county sheriff received the warning and ordered persons along the coast to evacuate. The first two waves of the tsunami were relatively small. Thinking the danger over, some persons returned to clean up after the minor flooding. Among them were seven persons who re-entered a tavern, including the owner and his wife. Then came a third wave. It was 12 feet high and crashed inland a third of a mile. Thirty city blocks were flooded, and five of the seven persons in the tavern drowned.

The most destructive tsunami of recent history was the one produced by the magnitude 8.5 Chile earthquake in May, 1960. Hawaii had six hours warning, but many persons ignored it. Sixty-one persons at Hilo were killed when the 15- to 35-foot waves arrived. Japan has had long experience with tsunamis (the word itself is Japanese) but no general tsunami alert was issued because it was not known that a tsunami originating so far away could be destructive. One hundred eighty persons were left dead or missing in Northern Japan and Okinawa. Twenty others died in the Philippines. Coastal areas of the United States and New Zealand were damaged, and all towns along the coast of Chile between the 36th and 44th parallels were destroyed or heavily damaged.

Landslides can also be a treacherous earthquake hazard. The magnitude 7.7 earthquake in Peru on May 31, 1970, set off a massive debris avalanche from the glacier-covered 21,860-foot north peak of Huascarán, the highest mountain in Peru. Its power was awesome. Beginning with a sliding mass of glacial ice and rock 3,000 feet wide and about a mile long, it rushed downslope with a noise survivors described as deafening. Everywhere it was accompanied or preceded by a strong turbulent air blast. The ice was partially converted to water by heat and friction. Survivors' accounts suggest that it traveled the nine miles from its start to the town of Yungay in two to four minutes. The trajectories of thousands of boulders weighing up to three tons that were hurled more than 2,000 feet across the Llanganuco Valley indicate that its velocity reached 248 miles per hour. The velocity and volume of this enormous plunging mass enabled it to ride over obstacles such as a 300-to-600-foot-high ridge between the valley and Yungay. There, it obliterated all but a few thousand of the town's 19,000 inhabitants. It went on across the Rio Santa and as much as 175 feet up the opposite bank where it partly destroyed another village. This earthquake-caused avalanche killed more than 20,000 persons—about 40 percent of the tragic quake's total death toll of 50,000. Flash flooding from broken mountain lake basins and from the waters of the Rio Santa pushed into a wave as much as 45 feet high by the avalanche also contributed to the earthquake's death and destruction, which a team of geologists called almost unbelievable. It was the worst natural disaster in the history of the Western Hemisphere.

To most Americans, the archetypal earthquake-caused fire was the 1906 San Francisco blaze. But Tokyo, Japan, has known worse. In 1857, fires that broke out after a massive earthquake destroyed large sections of the city and caused most of the disaster's 107,000 fatalities.

The great earthquake that struck Tokyo and Yokohama on September 1, 1923, set off a chain of events even more incredible. Before the disaster was over, the cities had been visited by typhoon, earthquake, fire, tsunami, tornado, landslides, and rain-caused floods. Known now as the Great Kwanto Earthquake, it struck the Tokyo-Yokohama region at lunchtime when charcoal braziers were being lighted to prepare meals. Hundreds of fires were soon in progress over the city. A rainless typhoon that had been raging in the morning helped fan the flames into uncontrollable conflagration. The earthquake itself, magnitude 8.2, was bad enough. Many of Tokyo's tallest buildings snapped or crumbled. The fires were soon everywhere. Henry W. Kinney, editor of *Trans-Pacific* magazine, managed to escape the blaze and climb to a ridge: "The lurid panorama lay outfolded before us—but it was meaningless. . . . There were no landmarks, no familiar buildings. . . . Yokohama . . . had become a vast plain of fire, of red, devouring sheets of flame which played and flickered. . . . There seemed to be nothing left to burn. It was as if the very earth were now burning."

A tornado, one of a series induced by the heat of the flames, picked up flames from a burning polytechnic school at Kuramaye and scattered them onto the opposite shore of the Sumida River, setting off blazes in the Honjo Ward, where 40,000 persons died. A tsunami rushed in from the bay at Tokyo and carried bodies and more flaming debris into the city. Thou-

sands of landslides struck the Bo-So Peninsula. The inhabitants
of the village of Nebukawa were buried beneath one of them.
For three days the fires raged. Sixty percent of Tokyo and 80
percent of Yokohama were left in ashes. The human toll: 99,331
killed, 43,476 missing—a total of 142,807. Later, heavy rains
came that caused floods and more landslides, one of which
swept a train carrying 200 passengers to the bottom of Sagami
Bay. Seldom if ever has an area been dealt such a diverse and
deadly succession of catastrophic natural events.

The violent energy of earthquakes can produce all manner
of effects. One is the "upthrow" of objects, a consequence of
strong vertical shaking of the ground. R. D. Oldham reported
that during the great Assam, India, earthquake of June 12,
1897, loose stones were tossed into the air "like peas on a
drum." Boulders were tossed upward, leaving cavities in the
ground where they had rested. Posts were reported to have come
vertically upward out of their holes. A splinter of granite three
feet long was thrown 8½ feet. In one place the ground was
torn up "as if a steam plow had passed over it . . . throwing
clods in every direction . . . and in many cases turning the
sods completely over so that only the roots of grass are visible."

In the 1923 Kwanto earthquake, two-foot-wide wooden pillars, former bridge supports buried and forgotten centuries before, rose three feet above the surface. The shaking of the soil
caused potatoes to extrude onto the ground. Large trees sank
into the ground where only their tops were visible. Liquefaction
of the sandy soil was no doubt the dominant factor, Bolt says,
"but the effect of shaking on the soil and potatoes remains to
be explained."

In the San Fernando, California, earthquake of 1971, a fire-
man at a county fire station was thrown out of bed onto the
floor, the receiver of a wall phone was dislodged, and rocks
were thrown off the ground. The building was shifted off its
foundation by four inches, and shingles that had overlapped
the foundation were undisturbed. "The evidence," says Bolt,
"is hard to explain by sliding, but rocking remains an alternative." A 20-ton firetruck inside was moved two to three feet
sideways by the shock. Its brakes were set and no skid marks
were visible. Reports B. J. Morrill: "Marks which appear to
have been made by the right rear tire were found on the door
frame, three feet above the floor. . . . Four feet above the
floor, the hose rack was broken by the rear step of the truck. The

step was bent up while the hose rack was broken downward."

Some reports can be discounted, but, says Bolt, "apparently certain types of objects do separate vertically during an earthquake." This implies that the ground acceleration in the vertical direction during an earthquake can exceed the acceleration of gravity. In only one instance have scientists been able to instrumentally record such an acceleration. It came on May 17, 1976, when the magnitude 7.0 earthquake in the Uzbek, Soviet Union, produced an instrument reading near its source of a vertical acceleration of $1.3g$.

The noises produced by earthquakes can be as strange and unusual as the tremors themselves. In the journal *Nature* in 1951, Frank Kingdon-Ward, an English botanist, described his experience in the great Assam earthquake of August 15, 1950. At magnitude 8.6, it was one of the greatest earthquakes ever recorded. He and his wife, Jean, were in a valley in Tibet about 25 miles from the epicenter. "It felt as though a powerful ram were hitting against the earth beneath us with the persistence of a kettledrum. . . . The din was terrible." Jean Kingdon-Ward described "a deep rumbling noise from the earth itself. . . . Mixed with it was a terrifying clatter, as though a hundred rods were being rapidly drawn over sheets of corrugated iron. The noise was unbelievable, agonizing. Never before had our ears been subjected to such an onslaught of sound." Soon, in her husband's words, "the frightful hammer blows weakened . . . we knew the main shock was over." Then "from high up in the sky to the northwest [as it seemed] came a quick succession of short, sharp explosions—five or six—clear and loud, each quite distinct, like 'ack-ack' shells bursting." Lane quotes John Harpum as explaining that these booms are characteristic of tremors that produce the collapse of underground workings. "I have heard these, and the gunfire description fits perfectly."

Booming sounds have also been heard before earthquakes. In the two weeks preceding the magnitude 7.3 earthquake that killed 4,000 persons in Eastern Turkey on November 24, 1976, booming sounds resembling thunder were heard several times. M. Nafi Toksöz, who interviewed villagers, said the sounds may have been due to small foreshocks. Residents also told of unusual sounds coming from a nearby lake.

The New Madrid earthquakes produced one of the most extensive records of earthquake sounds. Myron L. Fuller catalogued them for the U.S. Geological Survey a century later. One observer described the "roaring and whistling produced by the impetuosity of the air escaping from its confinement" in the alluvial materials. An observer in Tennessee said "a murmuring noise, like that of a fire disturbed by the blowing of a bellows, issued from the pores of the earth. A distant rumbling was heard almost without intermission and sometimes seemed to be in the air." The shocks agitated stones, altogether making a noise "similar to that of the wheels of a wagon in a pebbly road." In Saint Louis, before the tremors, "sounds were heard like wind rushing through the trees but not resembling thunder." In Washington, D.C., the sound was very distinctive and appeared to pass from southwest to northeast.

A report in the *American Journal of Science* told of sounds heard by the people assembled at San Juan Capistrano in Los Angeles County for evening service before the California earthquake of September, 1812, that destroyed the mission: "An unusually loud, but distant rushing sound was heard in the atmosphere to the east and over the water, which resembled the noise of strong wind, but as the sound approached, no perceptible breeze accompanied it. The sea was smooth and the air calm. So distant and loud was this atmospheric sound that several left the building on account of it."

Pressure waves produced by earthquakes can sometimes reach into the upper atmosphere. University of Hawaii scientists showed that a 1968 earthquake in Japan produced detectable effects on the earth's ionosphere. So did the Kuril Islands earthquake of August 11, 1969. Seismic surface waves traveling across the Pacific Ocean launched acoustic pressure waves that apparently traveled almost vertically upward into the atmosphere. These caused the ionosphere 210 miles above the earth to fluctuate vertically by about a mile. These pulsations correlated exactly with the seismic record of the earthquake.

Perhaps none of this should be surprising. Notes William Corliss, who has collected scientific reports of many unusual earthquake phenomena: "A truly great quake is felt globally. . . . Big earthquakes release so much energy that almost all geophysical parameters are shaken a bit."

One of the most striking earthquake-associated phenomena are earthquake lights. Few scientists have worked on this question because most of the reports are made by untrained observers. "Nevertheless," notes John S. Derr, a U.S. Geological

Survey geophysicist who has collected available scientific information about them, "observations have been made for many years, and the existence of earthquake lights is well established." The luminosity occurs in the air close to the ground, generally over certain areas in the earthquake region. Principally they occur during the earthquakes, but they have also been seen before and after them. Sightings occur both on land and at sea and have been reported from as far away as 275 miles.

Despite the paucity of scientific observations, earthquake lights have long been known, as noted by this ancient Japanese hokku:

The earth speaks softly to the mountain
Which trembles
And lights the sky.

The first known investigations of earthquake lights were carried out in the early 1930s by two Japanese seismologists, Torahiko Terado and Inkkiti Musya. Musya collected 1,500 reports of lights from the Idu Peninsula earthquake, which struck at 4:30 A.M. on November 26, 1930. In describing those studies in 1937, seismologist Charles Davison reported:

In most of them the sky was lit up as if by sheet lightning, and nearly all the observers agree in estimating the duration of a single flash as decidedly longer than that of lightning. At one place on the east side of Tokyo Bay, the light resembled auroral streamers diverging from a point on the horizon. Beams and columns of light were seen at different places, several observers comparing the beams to those of a searchlight. Others describe the lights as like that of fireballs. Some state that detached clouds were illuminated or that a ruddy glow was seen in the sky.

The only known photographs of earthquake lights were taken by a Japanese dentist during the Matsushiro earthquake swarm in Japan from 1965 to 1967. They show trees and hills dramatically silhouetted by areas of glowing sky, like sunset. Except these were taken at night. Yutaka Yasui, who has collected and studied these photographs, says the central luminous body is a hemisphere, diameter about 20 to 200 meters (70 to 700 feet), contacting the surface. The body is white but reflections from clouds may be colored. The luminescence generally follows the

Earthquake lights photographed during Matsushiro earthquake swarm in Japan. (U.S. GEOLOGICAL SURVEY)

earthquake and lasts from 10 seconds to two minutes. The glow usually occurs over the summits of hills and mountains, not at the quake's epicenter. Radio interference generally follows, but no apparent associated magnetic effects have been observed. The luminescence occurs frequently at the time a cold front passes.

Yasui believes that ionization in the lowest atmosphere becomes unusually large at the time of an earthquake and causes the luminous phenomena at the place where the electrical gradient is highest.

Earthquake lights have been seen in the United States. The New Madrid quakes produced many reports of "flashes of light" or a red glow in the sky. The earthquake at Santa Rosa, California, on October 1, 1969, produced lights seen extensively over the Santa Rosa area. In 1961, a poultry rancher south of Hollister, California, saw a number of small, sequential flashes from different places on a nearby hillside as the second of two earth tremors started. Derr says this might suggest that sky glows are caused by a large number of small, random-point discharges over part of the epicentral area.

Toksöz says his interviews with villagers in Eastern Turkey

turned up reports of a brightening of the sky the night before a 6.7 magnitude earthquake in Turkey on September 5, 1975. Geologists 150 miles away also noticed the brightening in the direction of the earthquake's epicenter.

Some of the most spectacular earthquake lights ever reported were seen at the time of the great Tangshan, China, earthquake in 1976. They were described to Cinna Lomnitz, a Mexican seismologist who reported accounts of the quake from Peking. The lights lit up the sky in the vicinity of the quake like daylight. They were mainly white and red, and they were bright enough to wake some people up. They were reported as far as 200 miles from the epicenter.

No explanation for earthquake lights has been agreed upon. Geophysicists David Finkelstein and J. R. Powell believe the release of built-up strain in rocks before a large earthquake could generate stress on what is known as piezoelectric (generating electric potential by pressure) quartz in the rocks to produce the luminescences. Another suggestion is that violent low-level air oscillations might transport a space charge that could set up temporary electrical imbalances in the atmosphere. It is a mystery geophysicists would like to solve, because the pre-quake glows might lead to a way to help predict earthquakes.

Animals have long been reported to react strangely before some earthquakes. Prior to one of the New Madrid shocks, John James Audubon was riding his horse in Kentucky when it came to a sudden stop, began groaning, spread out its four legs, and stood stock still. "At that instant all the shrubs and trees began to move from their very roots, the ground rose and fell in successive furrows, like the ruffled waters of a lake." There were other such reports. A horse "refused to proceed, and bracing himself on his legs, stood still." Another report said "bears, panthers, wolves, foxes, etc. side by side with a number of wild deer . . . all seemed animated by a common danger." Toksöz says farmyard animals showed no unusual behavior prior to the 1976 Turkey earthquake, but the barking and howling of dogs a few hours to a few minutes before the quake was widely observed.

Scientists in China and Japan have been the most active in studying earthquake animal behavior. Fish, pheasants, cattle, sheep, dogs, rats, snakes, and other animals have long been valued in China for their abilities to sense earthquake precursors. In the mid-1970s, American scientists began taking the subject seriously. The U.S. Geological Survey convened a conference on the subject in the fall of 1976, concluding that animals apparently can sense some environmental change that precedes earthquakes. Exactly what changes the animals are monitoring when they become restless before an earthquake is not yet clear. Soundwaves outside the range of human hearing, changes in magnetic fields, and other consequences of stress alterations in underground rocks are being explored.

It is fair to say the prime motivation of these studies is not zoological but geophysical. The hope is that animals can tell scientists something about how to anticipate or predict the coming of an earthquake. It is just one of the many possible precursors being examined in earthquake prediction research. And that is one of the subjects we explore next: the forecasting and prediction of severe natural phenomena.

PART II

NATURAL DISASTERS and SOCIETY

CHAPTER 10
Forecasting, Prediction, Warning

A few miles south of Washington, D.C., amid the auto dealers and fast-food outlets of amorphous suburban Camp Springs, Maryland, is a modern but otherwise unremarkable-looking brown eight-story office building. It seems like any of hundreds of other such buildings around the country. A walk around its periphery reveals the ground-floor offices of an insurance company, a realty company, and a mortgage corporation. Just as you are about to decide you are at the wrong place, you come to the main entrance. It bears the words World Weather Building. It is a title fittingly appropriate, if not for the structure, for the activities carried out on the upper floors inside.

For here is where your weather forecast starts. This is the National Meteorological Center, to which stations on land, sea, and in space around the earth continually channel their data on the constantly changing state of the atmosphere. Here these millions of electronic numbers are transformed by computer and the talents of skilled meteorologists into hemispheric and national prognostications of whether tomorrow you are going to have clear skies and warming temperatures or be subjected to the wiles of the darkening storm. It is the forecasting hub of the nation, the nerve center of the never-ending process to monitor the atmosphere and predict how its changes are going to affect you in the coming days.

It is a remarkable process. The initial data come from observations of conditions in at least 10 levels of the atmosphere from the surface up to 100,000 feet provided by 120 nations. All these observations are almost completely exchanged among the nations in less than four hours. Flowing into the National Meteorological Center each day are 50,000 reports from surface stations, 2,500 reports from ships at sea, 2,500 reports of upper-air soundings, 1,200 reports of temperature soundings of the atmosphere by satellite, 1,600 aircraft reports, 600 radar reports, and 100 satellite photographs. That's just the data collection.

The heart of the forecasting process is what scientists call numerical weather prediction. Its development, says NMC director Frederick G. Shuman, "has revolutionized the practice of weather forecasting and has led to gradual improvements in weather services over the past 20 years."

Numerical weather prediction makes use of the largest and fastest computers operationally available. (NMC's IBM 360/195s were too big to move the two miles from their previous location to the newly built World Weather Building in 1974; they were left where they are and connected electronically to the new building.) It is the computer's phenomenal calculating speed that is its great advantage. In numerical modeling, the computer is programmed, in the form of complex equations, with the best understanding science has of how the fluid atmosphere operates—how, for example, a change in temperature at one point affects pressure at another point and how that change in pressure affects winds at the same point and at still other nearby points. These mathematical "models" of the atmosphere are continually being refined. Then, all the up-to-date data from today's most recent observations around the world are fed into the computer, which carries out millions upon millions of calculations to arrive at a forecast of conditions many hours in the future.

The results of these calculations of weather charts for future days are then transmitted to the network of weather forecast offices across the country. Here, meteorologists critically examine the information, modify it if they see fit (here, the individual forecaster's own skills and experience come strongly into play), and adapt it to their own regions' special considerations. Then they prepare the worded forecasts that go out to the general public and specialized users such as aviation, shipping, agriculture, forestry, and pollution control agencies.

It's simple in concept, perhaps, but extremely difficult in execution. For one thing, several billion arithmetical and logical operations must be performed to complete one numerical prediction. Even with the powerful computers, this imposes a practical limit on the models' "resolution"—the minimum separation between geographical points for which conditions are calculated. The model for the Northern Hemisphere, for instance, is limited to a horizontal grid of points 104 miles apart. This gives a three-dimensional mesh of 30,000 points over the hemisphere. (At each point, calculations are made for seven different vertical layers of the atmosphere.) That, to be sure, is a lot of points, but many weather conditions, especially intense local storms, are on a scale less than 104 miles and therefore can be "missed" in the calculations.

At the National Meteorological Center, the main analysis and prediction cycles are carried out twice a day. About an hour and a half after the data are dumped into the computer for processing, out comes a forecast for the weather over the United States and Canada for the next 48 hours. This general forecast is distributed to local and regional National Weather Service offices, who use it in preparing the more specific forecast you're most likely to be listening for on your weather program tonight. It's a product of something called a limited-area fine mesh model, though, and it's limited to 48 hours. Beyond that time, instabilities develop that make this forecast invalid.

Longer-term forecasts and forecasts for the entire hemisphere are then made using another model (seven-layer primitive equation model, for those who like the jargon). They are extended out to 3½ days, then 4½, and then 5½. Three days a week (Sunday, Tuesday, and Thursday) a good sampling of the total data is used in still another model, which in 90 minutes of computer time predicts average general conditions of temperature and precipitation more than a week in advance. This is the basis for the six- to 10-day outlooks that the National Weather Service started distributing at the end of 1977.

It's a far cry from the days before the computer, when forecasters had to tediously plot all incoming data onto charts, spend about an hour analyzing it by hand, then personally prepare the forecast. The only analysis still done by hand at the National Meteorological Center is the location of fronts and the location of the center of storms at sea, deduced from cloud patterns obtained by remote sensors aboard orbiting satellites. Meteorologists can then modify the numerical forecasts to eliminate bad data and make sure the good data get included.

At the NMC, Harry E. Brown, chief of the forecast division's basic weather branch, showed me the last hand-analyzed, hand-

Infrared image from GOES West satellite. The satellites never cease their watch over earth's weather. (NATIONAL ENVIRONMENTAL SATELLITE SERVICE)

charted surface weather chart prepared there. It was for November 4, 1975. It looked, he said, almost like nineteenth-century charts. It was displayed like a museum piece.

On another floor of the World Weather Building is the National Environmental Satellite Service's center for receiving and processing satellite photos from space, another part of the technological revolution that has so changed weather forecasting. Here, every 30 minutes another photograph arrives from each of two sophisticated GOES (Geostationary Operational Environmental Satellite) satellites peering unblinkingly down on the Western Hemisphere from their perch 22,300 miles out in space. They stay in the same location relative to a point below them because at that distance they complete one orbit around the equator in the same time the earth makes one rotation. From the GOES East satellite over South America, a new image of the hemisphere arrives on the hour and half-hour; from the GOES West satellite over the Pacific, on the quarter-hour and three-quarter hour.

You can get a good idea of the splendid view they have if you take an ordinary globe of the earth, about the size of a basketball, and stand three feet away from its surface, directly above the equator. You can see that GOES East, at 75 degrees west longitude above the Colombia-Ecuador border, has an excellent view of the Eastern United States, the Caribbean, and the Western Atlantic. GOES West, at 135 degrees west longitude, has an excellent view of the Western United States and the Eastern Pacific.

Never do these satellites cease their watch over earth's weather. At night, they switch to infrared imaging, probing through the darkness. In case of a problem, duplicate satellites, already in orbit, can quickly take over. When the satellite over the Pacific had to be moved to a position over the Indian Ocean for a global weather research experiment in 1979, it was first replaced by the launch of a new satellite in the summer of 1978.

These satellites have become, in an important sense, the guardians of our planet, 24-hour monitors of our weather, watchdogs against sneak attack by the elements. Because of them, never again will the United States be surprised by a killer hurricane slamming into the coast unexpectedly, as happened in the tragedy at Galveston in 1900. They track the course of large storms over the surface, keep watch on developing weather systems, monitor the movement of frost lines and the temperatures of storm clouds, help chart the winds over the oceans, and even as noted in Chapter 1 sight in on clusters of fierce thunderstorms that may spawn tornadoes. They dramatically bring the weather into the homes of everyone who watches the daily television weather program, visually demonstrating to layman and meteorologist alike the flow of the atmosphere and the interrelated patterns of weather that affect our lives.

The two "stationary" satellites aren't the only ones keeping watch. Weather satellites in north-south polar orbits (where they see a different part of the earth with each of their passes) indirectly take a vertical temperature profile of the atmosphere twice a day. These soundings, like the successive GOES satellite cloud photos that can be used to calculate winds, are particularly useful over the oceans. They are routinely included as data in the numerical prediction models. Like Star Trek's *Enterprise* instrumentally probing a new planet, the polar orbiters' scans also take the temperature of the sea surface. These temperatures are used in the computer to identify areas of surface heating, often important in storm formation over the oceans.

On the fifth floor in the World Weather Building, a bank of 18 minicomputers and associated equipment divides the high-resolution full-disk image of the earth from the geostationary satellites into a variety of images of different sizes, resolutions, and views called sectors. A 4,000-mile square (all of North America) has a two-mile resolution, a 2,000-mile square (two-thirds of the United States) has a one-mile resolution, and a 1,000-mile square (about a quarter of the United States) has a half-mile resolution. The smaller sectors are the electronic equivalent of views through a telephoto lens, increasing the amount of detail visible. The sectorizer superimposes dotted lines representing state and national boundaries on these sector images, then automatically routes them via telephone lines to different parts of the country. They go to half a dozen satellite field service stations, the National Hurricane Center and National Severe Storms Forecast Center, all National Weather Service forecast offices, and to television stations, news media, and universities that have arranged for the equipment and lines. A variety of overlapping views are sent. New York, for instance, can get a close-in view of the Northeastern United States, Atlanta the southeastern states, Baton Rouge the south-central states, Madison the north-central states, Denver the Rocky Mountain and western plains states, San Francisco the far western states, and Seattle the states of the Pacific Northwest.

But the system has more flexibility than that. During severe storm conditions, a human operator sitting at a control console amid this maze of electronic equipment can override the programmed instructions and tell the satellite to produce an image every 15 minutes instead of every 30. (It accomplishes this by eliminating South America from its scan.) This helps forecasters keep close tabs on fast-moving convective storm systems. The satellite field service stations can also call up "floating sectors," moving a sector's position slightly to better encompass a storm system. If hurricane conditions are expected, the sectorizer computer can be instructed to produce any of several types of hurricane-enhancement images from the satellite's infrared-wavelength data. Certain shades of gray representing certain key temperatures in tropical cyclone clouds are thus emphasized. Like a detective dusting for fingerprints, this can make a developing hurricane vividly stand out from the rest of the clouds over the ocean. Another set of instructions can tell the computer to emphasize cold cloud tops and exaggerate the differences between cold and warm clouds. This can make an intense thunderstorm system, with its high, cold cloud tops, seem to jump out at the viewer. Dozens of similar computer enhancements are possible.

As I walk through the NESS satellite control facilities and watch these views of the changing weather flash up onto screens, emerge as photographic prints out of hard-copy automatic printers, and be transformed into time-lapse movie loops, it is hard to remember that only two decades ago no one had ever seen space-eye views of the earth. Now, no longer bound psychologically by the confines of our planet's surface, we all regard them as routine.

The public has been the beneficiary of all the new weather forecasting capabilities. "GOES has become an essential forecasting tool," says George P. Cressman, who recently stepped down as director of the National Weather Service to devote full time to research on numerical modeling. "We can watch storms crossing the Pacific Coast and moving inland and our forecasts are very much improved."

"Both radar and satellites represent vastly improved capabilities for storm detection and warning," say severe storm specialists Edwin Kessler and Allen D. Pearson.

Numerical modeling is not particularly applicable to major local storms, which are often small in size and have short lifetimes, but it has been a boon to weather forecasting in general.

"Contrary to popular mythology," says Cressman, "weather forecasts have improved substantially over the period of numerical weather prediction." He says the accuracy of short-term forecasts (up to 48 hours) is now about 85 percent. And, he says, as the numerical models improve, so do the forecasts. NMC's Shuman gives some details. The greatest success has been in predicting the circulation of the atmosphere 36 hours in advance. In the 20-year period of numerical modeling, that skill has doubled, from 30 percent to 60 percent. The duration of successful circulation forecasts has also doubled, from three days to six days. Forecasting of whether or not there will be precipitation has gradually improved. More difficult is the prediction of how much precipitation will fall. Except for broad storm systems, precipitation usually falls over relatively small areas. That is one thing that makes its accurate prediction for any location tricky. The record shows that the ability to predict accurate amounts of precipitation took a great jump immediately after 1960, when numerical modeling was first put to work on the task, but has not improved much since.

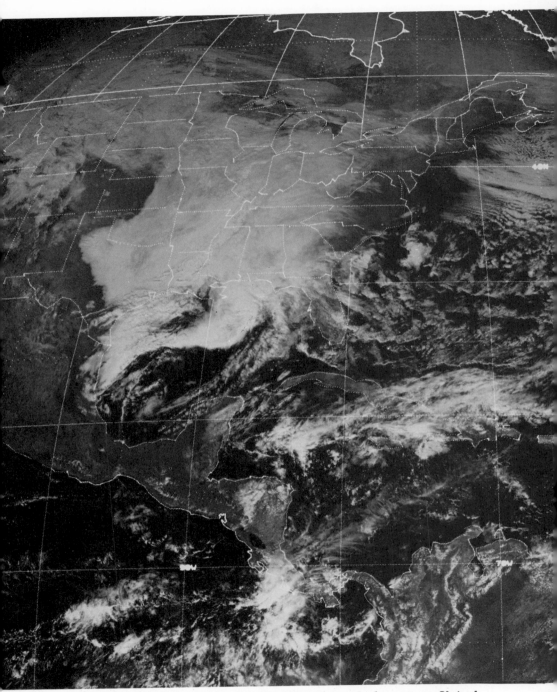

The second of six major snowstorms that struck the eastern United States in early 1978 advances northeastward on January 12. The very last storm in the series was accurately predicted by numerical models. (NATIONAL ENVIRONMENTAL SATELLITE SERVICE)

That is why there was much excitement in national forecasting ranks when the great blizzard of February 6–7, 1978, that brought record snows to Southeastern New England was very accurately predicted by new models at the National Meteorological Center. The new seven-layer primitive equation model, with a much finer 104-mile grid, had been put into operation only in January. It predicted the development of the storm three and a half days in advance. The latest version of the previously mentioned limited-area fine-mesh model, which had been put into operation only six months earlier, consistently produced excellent forecasts of the amounts of precipitation and heavy snow.

Cressman noted that predicting serious winter storms has always been a headache for weather forecasters, but now good progress was being made. He was so pleased by the success of the February, 1978, blizzard prediction accuracy that, as president of the American Meteorological Society, he wrote an editorial in the society's April *Bulletin* congratulating everyone concerned. ". . . The forecasts issued to the public were outstanding in practically every respect. The ability of the science to accomplish this feat is new. Fifteen years ago, such successful forecasts of these extremely rapid developments would have been almost inconceivable. . . . Weather forecasting is coming of age. . . ."

Nature, however, has a way of reasserting its dominance. The George Washington Birthday snowstorm of February 18–19, 1979, was the second worst of the century for the mid-Atlantic coastal states. In Washington, D.C., the snowfall was a record. The fine-mesh numerical model did not anticipate the storm's severity. Neither did subjective forecasts. One meteorologist called the performance of the numerical model in predicting the storm "poor." Another called the forecasts of snow amounts a "big bust." Winter storms still obviously retain their ability to confound even our best efforts at prediction.

Hurricanes have yielded much of their death-dealing potential, at least in the United States, to improved forecasting and warning. Since 1900, hurricane deaths have shown a steady downward trend in the United States even while damage totals have shown a steeper rise. "Thanks to weather satellites, radar, aircraft reconnaissance, and constant improvement in forecast techniques, the U.S. has the best hurricane warning service in the world," says Neil Frank, director of the National Hurricane Center in Miami.

Hurricane forecasters say they can project the path of a hurricane to within a marginal error of 100 miles—an improvement of about 10 percent in the last 10 years. Such improvements have come about mainly because of technological advances that have led to improved monitoring of hurricanes (especially by satellite and by aircraft penetration flights), greater capacity for data processing, and judicious use of statistical models based on growth and movements of past hurricanes. They have not, in the view of Robert H. Simpson, a former director of the National Hurricane Center and now at the University of Virginia, been related to the better physical understanding of hurricanes that has undisputedly been gained in the past two decades. In other words, the better ability to predict hurricanes has been independent of our basic understanding of them.

The problem is that nobody expects any further dramatic improvements. "It now appears that trends in prediction skill have reached a plateau," says Simpson. John Hope, a veteran forecaster at the Miami center, affirms that view: "We think there will be further refinement, but we don't expect any spectacular improvement in the near future." Robert O. Cole, deputy director of the center, agrees that the ability to forecast hurricanes has now leveled off: "We still don't know enough about our atmosphere. Mother Nature has not divulged all her secrets to us."

One of the concerns is that, while the routine hurricane seems fairly predictable, the hurricane that suddenly grows into a major killer is not. Not surprisingly, nearly all the prediction models work best when persistence is a good predictor, when what the hurricane did yesterday is a good indication of what it'll do today. Fortunately, most hurricanes are in that category. But not all are. "Most hurricane-prediction models are better able to predict the run-of-the-mill hurricane than the extreme event," says Simpson. "The principal challenge . . . is to predict dependably the more anomalous movements, the explosive developments, and the heavy precipitation after a hurricane passes inland."

With hurricanes, an even bigger problem now than predicting is ensuring that the people in their path act on that prediction. Here, forecasters get into the difficult problem of human response to disaster warnings. We'll deal with that more in following chapters. For now, it's enough to point out that the number of people living in coastal areas subject to hurricanes has increased rapidly in recent years and that most of these people are new residents who have never experienced a major hurricane. They may not respect it enough to evacuate or take other life-saving action when a warning is issued. That is why Cole says the work of the people at the hurricane center is becoming as much socio-logical as it is meteorological. "The trouble is," says Frank, "too many people think it can never happen to them . . . or they think they can ride it out. Or they have moved here from Tulsa or the Midwest and they think that a hurricane is like a tornado and it will miss them. What they don't realize is that hurricanes can be 50 to 100 miles wide."

A visit to a local National Weather Service forecast office anytime in the past few years has been a last look at the end of an era. Throughout the cenutry, the dominant communications devices have been electro-mechanical and the primary recording medium has been paper. Everywhere there's paper, by the roll, by the carton, by the wallful. Clacking teletype machines and churning facsimile machines continually spew out data and charts on paper. The walls are plastered by clipboards swollen with sheets of torn-off paper. Anytime someone wants a piece of information he has to find it on a piece of paper. From our vantage point on the threshhold of the 1980s, it all has a certain Dickensian flavor, the communications equivalent of the book-keeper sitting on a high stool and filling in amounts on the ac-counts ledger with quill-tip pen.

That's all ending now. Weather service communications are entering the electronics age. Soon all the important data and charts will be stored and disseminated by minicomputer and dis-played on television-like screens, where the local forecaster can, by the push of a button, instantly call up any item or map he needs to better prepare your local forecast. He can zoom in on an area of particular interest. He can bring onto the screen 400 different slides, overlays, and printouts. He can have the com-puter diagram a storm's vertical motion. Forecasters will be freed of much of the paper-handling drudgery that has until now been necessary.

The speed of communications will take a quantum leap. Weather maps will arrive in 15 seconds rather than the 10 min-utes it takes on paper. Messages will arrive at 3,000 words per minute instead of 100. And urgent warnings of a major storm bearing down on your city can be computer-routed in seconds to your radio and TV stations and police and rescue agencies without going through the several previously necessary steps that too often took up precious and costly minutes. It will be an important advance in ensuring that the warning of a tornado, intense wind storm, violent hailstorm, or flash-flood-producing thunderstorms gets to the public before the storm does.

The new system can also help alleviate another sometimes embarrassing and potentially dangerous situation: when the weather changes so fast that the latest forecast is suddenly seriously at odds with the weather outside. This is sometimes due to the ponderous communications process that means the latest forecast is inevitably somewhat stale. But it may also be because the forecaster is too tied up with routine duties to notice the developing divergence between his forecast and the weather. In the new system, the minicomputer at each office will continually compare incoming information about the weather with the predictions of the latest forecast. If the variance becomes too great, it will signal an alarm. A red light on the TV console will begin flashing. For a true emergency, a buzzer can be set off.

I first saw the experimental version of this new "weather office of the future," called AFOS (Automation of Field Operations and Services), demonstrated at the National Weather Service headquarters in Silver Spring, Maryland, in 1974. Tests over the next four years brought about many minor modifications, and in May, 1978, the Pittsburgh Weather Service Forecast Office became the first operational weather service facility to have the AFOS system installed. Installation then proceeded rapidly at other cities. From Portland, Maine, to Portland, Oregon, from Atlanta to Anchorage, from Bismarck to Birmingham, from Albany to Albuquerque, from San Juan to San Francisco, the full system will be operational in 280 Weather Service offices around the country by mid-1981.

Weather Service officials are convinced it will help avoid clogged communications at the time of a great outbreak of severe storms. The steady stream of advisories and warnings sent out during the tornado superoutbreak of April 3–4, 1974, remember, taxed the old communications system at the National Severe Storms Forecast Center in Kansas City almost to its limit. "The teletype system about came apart that night," Allen Pearson, the center's director, recalls. With AFOS, communications during a series of heavy storms should never again come that close to the brink of breakdown.

AFOS may be the weather office of the future, but C. Gordon

Little, a scientist at the National Oceanic and Atmospheric Administration's Boulder, Colorado, laboratories, has a vision of the advanced local regional weather service of the future. If he and his colleagues have their way, areas the size of metropolitan regions such as Washington, D.C., and Denver, in the 1990s will have the most sophisticated, accurate, and tightly focused weather forecasting system ever devised. But let's backtrack a bit first.

Much of the weather that causes destruction of life and property comes from fierce storms of small size and short life spans. We've seen many examples so far. The tornado that roars into the center of a small city. The flood-producing thunderstorm that anchors itself over the upper stretches of a populated river basin. The hailstorm that slices a mile-wide swath of heartbreak through a county's just-ripe wheat and barley. The more populous and developed the area, the more likely tragedy may follow. It is crucial to find better ways of forecasting the duration and paths of these storms over the short scales of distance and time in which they occur.

Numerical weather prediction has become the successful basis for all operational weather forecasting in the time range of 10 hours to 10 days. But severe local storms wreak their havoc over just a few hours or even minutes. Like guerrilla attackers, these storms often slip through the coarse observational grid used in the numerical prediction of national forecasts. They are associated in a statistical way with larger scale, more slowly developing phenomena and thus can be anticipated in a general way.

The national computer predictions alert the forecaster to the possibility of bad weather. But it takes the human input of trained and experienced meteorologists at the National Severe Storms Forecast Center and at local forecast offices in the affected areas to combine the information from radar, satellites, and human spotters and to decide when to issue a severe weather watch or warning. "The synthesizing of this great bulk of imperfect information before issuing a warning is the most difficult, yet the most critical meteorological decision that has to be made today," says meteorologist C. R. Dunn. All this takes time, and —for timely forecasts at the local level—precise, up-to-date local data. Sometimes neither is available.

The real need with fast-developing, fast-moving local storms is for short-term (perhaps 15 minutes to an hour) predictions that are precise enough to specify which sector of the city the thunderstorm will hit, which suburban canyon the flash floods will strike, what the tornado's path will be and exactly when. And then to vividly present this information to the public in a new kind of "real-time" continuously operating communications system that has no time lags.

Such a local forecasting system for the 1990s is the dream of Gordon Little. Little is an urbane, silver-haired, English-educated atmospheric physicist who speaks with reflective excitement of his goal to set up a prototype local weather service using the most advanced technological means to remotely sense the atmosphere. The possibility of doing it is based in large part on recent developments at the NOAA Wave Propagation Laboratory in Boulder, which he heads.

Throughout an area no larger than 125 miles on a side, he would establish a system of sensors now under experimental development that would remotely monitor conditions in the local atmosphere using acoustic, optical, infrared, and radio techniques. Acoustic sensors, for example, that monitor changes in air temperature and wind velocities by changes in sound-wave echoes are being tested. Laser radars can determine the difference between atmospheric water and atmospheric ice, important in monitoring developing thunderstorms.

A technique called microwave attenuation can measure the actual rate at which rain is falling between two distant points. Microwaves bounced off a distant reflector are attenuated, or absorbed, by the rain falling along the beam's path, and the amount of attenuation is a measure of the amount of rain falling. "I think this would be a very reliable and automatic system which would give a continuing average readout of rainfall," Little says. Such instant information about sudden heavy rain is needed to give rapid warnings of flash-flood conditions. "It would have helped immensely in the Big Thompson flood," says Little, whose Boulder laboratory is less than 30 miles from the site of that disaster. An even closer area with a high potential for tragedy if a sudden flash flood should occur is Boulder Canyon, with Boulder and the University of Colorado at its mouth. A 1975 study called the flood problem in Boulder "potentially catastrophic" and even included a case study of a future hypothetical flood caused by torrential rains over Boulder's entire drainage basin. In this "future disaster," a "great wall of water" races down the canyon into the city, flooding municipal buildings, homes, and university housing, ripping out gas lines, washing away electric substations, and claiming 95 lives and causing $43 million damage. It even seriously damages the cluster of research buildings where Little's NOAA laboratory is located, destroying "expensive equipment and irreplaceable research materials." Little says he would like to install a network of microwave beam-paths across high points above Boulder Canyon to help provide early warning against just such a disaster.

Little and other NOAA scientists are developing a plan for a prototype local weather service using a full array of remote sensors from the ground and satellites to provide immediate and detailed meteorological information over an area 200 kilometers (125 miles) square. The data gathered would be plugged in to local (not national) numerical weather models now being developed by a sister laboratory. They would be based on a very fine mesh grid of data points, and would include such local considerations as terrains, valleys, urban heat islands, and lake-shore effects, something national and hemispheric models obviously have to ignore. "The full power of the computer would be applied to this 200-kilometer grid," Little says. The forecasts for the next several hours would be disseminated instantaneously over a dedicated television channel that would use computer-animated graphics to dramatically display weather maps and information visually as well as verbally. Thus the information on a developing storm would go straight to the public without having to be relayed by teletype to radio and television stations and then be read—sometimes with much delay—by announcers.

The prototype system proposed would originally be set up in the Denver area so the NOAA scientists at Boulder could easily monitor and test its accuracy. If it is successful, similar networks would be established in populous areas throughout the nation.

"We can envision supplying data orders of magnitude more dense—a million to a billion times more dense—in time and space than the present system," says Little. It could provide "minute-by-minute, kilometer-by-kilometer" weather information and would be "technologically an enormous improvement. This next generation local weather service would be not an incremental improvement in local weather forecasting but a radical improvement."

The system Little and his colleagues are championing is the ultimate of what weather scientists call "Nowcasting," the timely forecasting and warning of very short-term weather. Computers, satellites, radar (conventional and Doppler), an array of new remote sensors, and new communications like AFOS are all bringing Nowcasting closer to reality.

Take NOAA Weather Radio, as just one more small example. By the end of 1979, the nation will be covered by a network of radio stations that continuously broadcast storm warnings and the latest weather observations and forecasts 24 hours a day, seven days a week. Ninety percent of the population will be within reach of one of the 345 stations. Anybody can receive this information by purchasing an inexpensive very high frequency FM receiver that can tune to the frequencies of 162.40, 162.475, or 162.55 megahertz on which the broadcasts are made. For a little extra, receivers can be bought that either sound a tone or switch the volume to audible levels when a severe weather alert is broadcast, something especially valuable for schools, hospitals, mobile home communities, safety officials, and the news media. The response to NOAA weather radio has been enthusiastic. "This is one of the hottest things we have ever had going for us," says Earl Estelle, program leader for the system. A Nebraska weekly newspaper called it "probably one of the most beneficial systems that the government has ever devised for the taxpayer." It's a simple, low-cost way to obtain continuous weather information and warnings.

From satellites to computers, to radar and other ground-based remote sensors, to AFOS communications systems, to television displays, to NOAA Weather Radio, the technological components of Nowcasting—combined with the talents of skilled meteorologists—are converging toward better forecasts and warnings of storms. "This," says meteorologist Vincent J. Oliver, referring to the array of new techniques, "makes possible the continuous weather watch which is the main ingredient of a successful program of bringing to the public those data and warnings most needed to save life, limb, and property. The weather service of the future is Nowcasting."

Of course, forecasting and warning are only parts of the problem. The public must act on the warnings it receives. When it does, lives are saved. The sharp reduction in tornado deaths during the past two decades has coincided with the growth of efforts to detect and warn of impending tornadoes and to provide public information programs on storms. A vicious tornado that tore through Omaha on May 6, 1975, caused $100 million damage but cost only three lives, as citizens responded to early warnings. But when people ignore the warnings, as happens too often, lives are lost. The "hurricane party" deaths at Pass Christian, Mississippi, during Hurricane Camille grimly demonstrated that. Study of the 1965 Palm Sunday tornadoes revealed that many victims, including 17 in one Mississippi town, had received early warning but could not be persuaded to take shelter. The same problems cropped up with Hurricane Audrey in 1957.

This is why storm experts realize that their job doesn't end with dissemination of the warning. They have to educate the public to the hazards and to life-saving responses. Specialists like Neil Frank of the National Hurricane Center and Allen Pearson—and dozens of others—spend much of their time working to educate the public about storm hazards and warnings. "We must," says Frank, "deal with the consumer—the people— and substitute education for experience. We must become more acquainted with our 'customers' and learn how to stimulate them to action. All too often we have decreed what the customer needed rather than sought to understand his problems. Human behavior is extremely complex—and in some cases even more difficult to predict than the weather—but if our product is to become more effective, we must tailor it to the individual."

Overall, the record is good. The decline of hurricane and tornado deaths in the face of rising damages is one of the triumphs of storm forecasting and warning in the United States.

But the specialists have no illusions. Pearson speaks of the "professional glow of pride on the face of the meteorologist" as he successfully predicts the possibility of a tornado "fading to an expression of shock" as his forecast nevertheless fails to save another town from tragedy. Sirens not sounded. Radio stations not seeing the warnings on the teletype. Mobile homes not tied down. Schoolteachers not trained in what to do. Townspeople failing to take shelter. "It happened last year, and it will again this spring," he laments.

What Pearson says about tornadoes is equally true about the response to warnings of other types of life-threatening storms:

"Certainly the National Severe Storms Forecast Center is going to miss forecasting some tornadoes, and they'll strike without warning. But we hit more than we miss, and we do our best work on the big storms. We'll take things as far as we can, alerting you to possible tornadoes and issuing warnings when they occur. But after that—and before that, too—it's up to you.

As the philosopher George Santayana so aptly said: 'Those who cannot remember the past are condemned to repeat it.' "

In contrast to weather forecasting, earthquake prediction is an infant science. Only in the 1970s has it gained widespread scientific attention and acceptance. Scientists working on earthquake prediction have had a series of ups and downs in the past five years or so. Despite periods of considerable excitement when it looked as though sudden jumps in understanding were at hand, earthquake prediction will undoubtedly have to evolve in the slow and sometimes painful series of successes and failures, tantalizing leads and dead ends, false starts and tedious refining of data that mark all progress in science. In 1978, the Geophysical Predictions Panel of the National Academy of Sciences described earthquake prediction efforts so far as "encouraging" but "rudimentary."

In general terms, earthquake forecasting has long been with us, in seismic maps that identify the long linear belts along which most earthquakes have occurred and can be expected to occur in the future. The theory of plate tectonics has brought a general understanding of why these seismic zones occur where they do to the exclusion of most other areas of the world. So there is a general understanding of why, how, and where earthquakes occur.

But earthquake prediction has far more specific meaning. An earthquake prediction is generally taken to mean a statement specifying the location, time, and magnitude of an impending earthquake within narrow enough limits that life-saving and property-protecting actions can be planned and carried out. All three components—time, location, and magnitude—are necessary for a prediction to be particularly useful. California's advisory panel on earthquake predictions, established in 1975, has even specified a fourth element: a statement of the odds that an earthquake of the predicted kind would occur by chance alone without reference to any special kind of evidence.

Successful predictions of earthquakes have been made. In the United States, Yash P. Aggarwall and Columbia University colleagues predicted a magnitude 2.6 tremor at Blue Mountain Lake, New York, in 1975, two days in advance. James H. Whitcomb and colleagues at the California Institute of Technology predicted a magnitude 5.5 earthquake in Yucaipa, California, in 1974, but it turned out to be much smaller. Donald

A. Stevenson and Pradeep Talwani of the University of South Carolina predicted a magnitude 2.5 event two days before at Lake Jocasse, South Carolina, in 1977. Charles G. Bufe and U.S. Geological Survey colleagues successfully predicted a magnitude 3.2 tremor to occur within a three-month period east of San Jose, California, in 1977. These predicted earthquakes were all small, not quite the ground-splitting, building-crumbling, death-dealing primeval shaking of the earth that most persons have in mind when they discuss an earthquake they would like to have scientists predict.

Just such an earthquake was successfully predicted in China in 1975. It was this life-saving prediction that was heralded by geophysicist Frank Press of the Massachusetts Institute of Technology, then president of the American Geophysical Union, as "one of the major events in the history of geophysics." The prediction brought worldwide scientific attention to the extensive and highly organized Chinese earthquake prediction effort (which makes use of 10,000 full-time workers and 300,000 volunteers) and renewed impetus to earthquake prediction in the United States. The excitement was tempered the next year by the failure of the Chinese to unambiguously predict the Tangshan earthquake that brought death to at least 650,000 persons. But the Chinese had cautioned that in this early stage of this imperfect science, failures should be expected, and in itself the Tangshan disaster doesn't detract from the scientific significance of the success at Haicheng in 1975. It was the first major earthquake to have been accurately predicted anywhere in the world.

The prediction of the Haicheng earthquake was accomplished in four stages, the first going back five years earlier. These stages illustrate that a successful prediction is not a one-shot prognostication but a continuing process, a gradual narrowing of the constraints of time and place of the expected shaking. The first, long-term, prediction was made in 1970, when the Chinese observed that Northeastern China had entered a phase of extensive seismic activity, with the epicenters of the earthquakes apparently migrating northeastward toward Liaoning Province. They intensified their observations, and in June, 1974, issued a midterm prediction that a magnitude of 5 to 6 shock might occur in the area in the next one to two years. This forecast was based partly on a large increase in the numbers of small earthquakes in the first half of 1974. The Chinese had also noticed a gradual but large northwesterly tilting of the land, and a variation in the vertical component of the magnetic field in the area. Something was happening.

Between June and December of 1974, the northwesterly tilting of the Liaotung Peninsula and the geomagnetic anomaly continued. Beginning in December, unusual animal behavior, changes in the levels of water wells, and increases in the amount of radon gas in groundwater were reported in several localities. On December 22, a swarm of medium-small earthquakes hit just northeast of Haicheng. At the turn of the year, the rate of ground tilting slowed, then reversed direction. On January 13, 1975, the State Seismological Bureau issued a short-term prediction that an earthquake of magnitude 5.5 to 6 would occur in the first six months of 1975.

On February 1, small foreshocks began. At 6:39 P.M. on February 3, a foreshock of magnitude 2.4 hit, and during the next 17 hours eight shocks ranging in magnitude from 3 to 4.8 rippled through the ground. These shocks were large enough to be felt, and they alerted the general public to the possibility of a large earthquake. In these first few days of February, the tiltmeter at one geological observatory measured an unusually large change in ground tilt. Citizens also reported changes in the water table and in the quality of the water. At two sites, wells that normally had to be pumped began to flow spontaneously. The water in some cases became muddy. Animals such as geese, deer, chickens, dogs, and rats began to behave so bizzarely that officials were alerted.

The foreshocks on February 3 had been the largest yet. After the large increase in activity at 6:30 P.M., the Shihpengyu Seismic Observatory warned the Provincial Earthquake Office. Half an hour after midnight on February 4, the Provincial Revolutionary Committee was given a forecast of a strong earthquake near Haicheng for later that day.

The word was quickly transmitted to city committees, provincial officials, and other provinces. Emergency meetings were held. Disaster preparedness plans were activated. Emergency shelters were set up. First-aid facilities were erected and medical teams formed. People were evacuated from their homes.

At 7:36 P.M., the earthquake hit. For one to two minutes— an unusually long duration for strong ground motion—the earth trembled. It was a magnitude 7.3 earthquake. A 1,000-square-kilometer area (about 400 square miles) around and including Haicheng in which half a million people lived was subjected to intense shaking. Ninety percent of the existing structures in Haicheng, a city of 90,000, were seriously damaged or destroyed. At Shihpengyu Brigade to the southwest, 88 percent of the houses were destroyed. Had it not been for the predictions, scientists have estimated that casualties might have been as high as 100,000. But few deaths were reported.

"The Haicheng earthquake is not the first but is certainly the largest earthquake to be successfully predicted," says Peter L. Ward, who heads the U.S. earthquake research program for the U.S. Geological Survey. "It is especially significant because the prediction led to major life-saving action."

"The prediction . . . was apparently not based on any single overwhelmingly convincing observation," concluded a delegation of nine American scientists who traveled to China in 1976 specifically to study the Haicheng prediction. "The foreshocks would come closest to fulfilling that role, but we believe that, taken alone, the foreshocks would not have led to an earthquake prediction and subsequent evacuation. The action seems to have been taken as a result of an accumulation of evidence, any one element of which, taken alone, would not have been considered indicative."

The Haicheng success was not an isolated experience. In 1977, Chinese scientists reported at a meeting in Paris that during the previous year they had managed to successfully predict three of the six magnitude 7 earthquakes that struck China that year. A public warning was issued from a few hours to a day before each of the three. Populations were evacuated and, the Chinese said, thousands of lives were saved.

It is important to point out that despite several successes, earthquake prediction research is filled with uncertainties. Peter Ward notes, for example, that the successful Haicheng prediction was preceded by "at least one and perhaps three false alarms where tens of thousands of people slept outdoors overnight in the cold Manchurian winter." In this early stage of the art, difficulties abound.

As the Haicheng experience indicates, earthquake prediction research—whether in China, the United States, Japan, or the Soviet Union—is not an all-eggs-in-one-basket effort. The whole range of possible advance signs, or precursors, is being studied. A dozen or more have been identified. None stands by itself as a conclusive sign of an impending earthquake. But the hope is that if monitoring can identify enough of them, taken together they may lead to a fairly reliable idea of when, where, and how hard a quake will strike.

"The strategy of earthquake prediction," says Robert M. Hamilton, chief of the Geological Survey's Office of Earthquake Studies, "is to deploy large numbers of instruments and to conduct extensive geodetic surveys in order to 'trap' [signs of] an earthquake."

These tell-tale signs hint of an almost bewildering array of possible geophysical changes before an earthquake: uplift, warping, or horizontal shifting of the land surface, variations in the pattern of small-quake activity, changes in electrical resistivity and magnetic fields, changes in the velocities of seismic waves, changes in the gas content of groundwater, alterations of underground water levels, and noticeable effects on animals.

Before the 1974 Hollister, California, earthquake, for instance, three tiltmeters recorded changes in ground tilt six to 10 miles from the epicenter. In the few days before the Gasli earthquake in the Soviet Union in May, 1975, the amount of radon in well water 250 miles away more than tripled. In the years before the 1964 Niigata, Japan, earthquake of magnitude 7.5, the land east of its epicenter uplifted several inches. Before a 1975 earthquake near Oroville, California, the ratio of the amplitudes of the two primary types of seismic waves (P and S) changed.

Seismic stations first in the Soviet Union and later elsewhere have also measured changes in the velocity of the P type of seismic waves prior to some earthquakes. In these cases, the P waves in the area of an impending earthquake decrease by about one-tenth for a time and then increase again to near their normal value just before the main earthquake hits.

What is responsible for all these changes? They are not as mysteriously random as they may seem, although there are enough unanswered questions to keep seismologists busy for years. Here's a possible scenario: After a long period of buildup of elastic strain in the subsurface rocks, they develop cracks in the fault zones that cause the whole volume of rock to swell. As the cracks open, the compressional P waves from small earthquakes elsewhere are hindered in their route to the surface; their velocity is slowed. The dilation of the rocks causes the surface of the ground to rise, radon gas to escape, electrical resistivity to decrease, and possibly the levels of small microearthquakes to change. Eventually, water seeps into the newly opened cracks. The speed of the P waves increases back toward normal, the surface uplift returns to normal, the radon release slows, and the electrical resistivity decreases more. The earthquake then occurs, and all these values change once again.

"Seismic gaps" are another approach to identifying where a major earthquake is likely to occur next. These are areas along a major active fault zone where a large earthquake has not occurred for some time. Seismic strain has been allowed to accumulate. One such seismic gap is along the coast of Southeastern Alaska. Another is in the Assam region of the Himalayas in Northeastern India. This was the site of the enormous magnitude 8.7 earthquake in 1950 that, among other things, caused the extraordinary sounds recounted in the preceding chapter. A similar one hit in 1897. In December, 1977, seismologists K. N. Khattri and Max Wyss of the University of Colorado and National Oceanic and Atmospheric Administration reported that the region's history shows that every major earthquake in the area in the last 150 years has been preceded by a period of few or no earthquakes, and every period of silence has been followed by a major earthquake. The segment of plate boundary between the major earthquakes of 1897 and 1950 in the Assam region has, they say, been "suspiciously quiet since 1950." They can make no prediction, because they cannot say when, but the area seems to be due for a major earthquake and they suggested watching for its signs.

Three scientists working at the University of Texas used the seismicity-gap concept in 1977 to forecast a major earthquake along the coast of Oaxaca State in Mexico. Their published paper received little attention, but on November 29, 1978, a 7.9-magnitude earthquake struck Southern Mexico within a mile of the epicenter they had predicted. The earthquake, which rocked downtown buildings in Mexico City, 300 miles to the northwest, was one of the three or four largest of the past quarter century. The Oaxaca case was a classic example of a seismicity gap. The scientists—Masakazu Ohtake, Tosimatu Matumota, and Gary V. Latham—had noticed a 150-mile stretch of an active fault that had been suspiciously quiet in the past five years. Fortunately, a joint group from the California Institute of Technology and the University of Mexico was aware of the Texas group's forecast and managed to put together a hastily installed collection of portable instruments in the Oaxaca area in the fall of 1978. They obtained a unique set of data about the seismic events leading to the main quake. There was hope such information could refine the seismicity-gap method of prediction. Especially needed is a way to determine when a quake anticipated by the technique might occur.

The seismic-gap method of prediction attracted even more scientific and public attention when on February 28, 1979, a magnitude 7.8 earthquake struck along a part of the previously mentioned gap in Southeastern Alaska. The gap had been identified by Columbia University scientists eleven years earlier, and in June of 1979 the scientists warned that a future great earthquake may occur in the remaining portion of the gap. The Columbia scientists have also issued maps rating various segments of the world's most active earthquake regions for risk according to the seismic-gap method. Areas assigned to the highest risk category (magnitude 8.0 or greater quake expected) were Southern California, South-central Japan, Northern Chile, the west coast of Sumatra, and several places in the Caribbean.

Earthquake prediction research, after many years of back-seat status, now is moving forward rapidly. In 1978, the federal government doubled its earthquake research effort over the amount for the preceding year. The Earthquake Hazards Reduction Act of 1977 established a hazards reduction program designed to make full use of the research results. President Carter sent it to Congress in June, 1978. California, the most earthquake-prone state, has become the most earthquake-instrumented area in the world. Hope is widespread that someday, as with our long-range weather forecasts and our warnings for storms, our citizens will be given reasonably precise advance word of where, when, and how hard the next major earthquake will strike.

"The Age of Prediction is here," says Peter Ward. "Some predictions have been issued as well as some false alarms. It may be a decade or many decades before a proven prediction system is available. Nevertheless, a credible prediction could be issued at any moment, and preparation to respond to such a prediction should begin now."

How will people respond to an earthquake prediction, and what will its effects be? These questions have been worrying disaster specialists. Some scholars, notably Garrett Hardin, have even suggested that the nation would be better off without earthquake prediction. Most others believe that although a prediction has potential for great economic disruption, it also has great potential for saving lives, and, a secondary goal, property. Our earthquake prediction research program is based on that assumption.

The experience in China, with its homogenous population and tradition of public acceptance of government pronouncements, is not directly applicable. Western populations tend not to take disaster warnings as seriously. Research has shown that Americans, independent and curious, have a compelling tendency to want to seek confirmation of a threat before acting upon it, and the precursory signs of an impending earthquake often produce no dramatic threat symbol.

A National Academy of Sciences panel that studied the implications of earthquake predictions concluded: ". . . Securing adequate, constructive responses to earthquake warnings will not be an easy task. Experience with other disasters suggests that warnings may be widely discounted and ignored and that inaction rather than panic flight will be the most common response among the general public. Especially in case of long-term predictions, the remoteness of the threat will impart a sense of unreality. The absence of external signs through which people can confirm that threat with their own senses creates a special problem of credibility."

Nevertheless, the panel stated its hope that judicious and early planning "will ensure a constructive response to the very first prediction of a serious earthquake." It urged that the human capacity to learn from its first experiences with earthquake predictions "not be underestimated."

Ward states the probably dominant view of those who are bringing earthquake prediction nearer. It is part hope, part conviction: "Evidence could be observed at any moment that may save people's lives, and it should not be withheld. Scientists in the field realize that they must immediately provide such evidence with a responsible interpretation to the public. They also realize that there is a finite chance of issuing a false alarm. Furthermore, it is clear that a credible earthquake prediction could, in the worst case, cause more social and economic disruption than the ensuing earthquake.

"Earthquake prediction is a rapidly advancing area of research and development that offers the possibility to save many lives and significantly reduce economic losses if scientists, civic leaders, policy makers, and all citizens are prepared to respond effectively. The time to prepare is now."

CHAPTER 11

Modification

"Why do you want to send the waves upwards?"

"To make it rain. It is the basic principle of the invention I had in mind. . . . By means of the pylon and the reflector I direct waves against the clouds, and I electrify to saturation point the raindrops they contain. When the difference of potential between a cloud and the earth or one of the adjacent clouds is great enough—and this does not take very long—a storm breaks, and the rain descends. The transformation of the desert into fertile country is quite enough to prove the efficiency of the process."

—Marcel Camaret in Jules Verne's *City in the Sahara* (1905)

Humanity has long had the dream of modifying the weather, a longing that far predates the visions even of Verne's fertile mind. We are embraced by the atmosphere, surrounded by its all-encompassing influence. When the storms that carry life-nourishing moisture are too-long absent or the storms that carry life-endangering hail are too-near a threat, we naturally contemplate how nature might be persuaded to alter, for a time, its ways.

Magic and ritual were early recourses. Farmers in classical Greece attempted to prevent hail by burying laurel leaves moistened with menstrual blood in their fields. As long ago as the sixteenth century, people were setting off artillery and ringing church bells in efforts to ward off thunderstorms. Social disputes over the benefits versus drawbacks of modification date back almost as far. The use of guns for hail suppression was prohibited by the Archduchess of Austria in 1750 because neighboring landowners disagreed over the effects of the barrages. Explosives

278

were used over intermittent periods in the next two centuries to try to lessen the power of hailstorms, and after World War II, farmers in Northern Italy began sending rockets into storms above their fruit orchards to attempt to reduce the chances of hail.

History may be rich with examples of people, usually motivated by a degree of desperation, attempting to bring rain or to modify storms. But the scientific beginnings of weather modification date back only a third of a century to 1946 and the laboratory of Nobel laureate chemist Irving Langmuir and associates Vincent Schaefer and Bernard Vonnegut. These pioneer workers at the General Electric Research Laboratories discovered that ice crystals could be induced in certain clouds by adding to them finely crushed dry ice or smoke from the burning of a silver iodide compound.

Clouds may be below freezing temperatures but still have their water in the form of liquid droplets because of the absence of nuclei around which ice crystals can form. Schaefer and colleagues showed that dry ice or silver iodide particles introduced into these supercooled clouds served as ice nuclei. The droplets were converted to ice crystals, which in turn grew into large enough crystals or aggregations to eventually reach the ground as precipitation.

Sounds simple enough, but practical difficulties are great and scientific proof that seeding has the desired effects has been slow in coming—slower than many optimistic scientists might have predicted 25 years ago. Langmuir had aggressively championed the potential of weather modification. Commercial cloud seeders proceeded in full force, but most atmospheric scientists, necessarily more cautious and circumspect, were not able to share the enthusiasm. In the early 1950s, possibly as much as 10 percent of the land area of the United States was under commercial seeding operations at an annual cost of several million dollars. Many of these efforts were based more on aggressive public relations than on professional knowledge and skill. Most scientists considered these programs premature and probably ineffective. Those paying the bills tended to be disappointed by the results, and the level of commercial seeding rapidly dropped off. Scientific programs of research and some commercial seeding operations nevertheless continued. In 1973, a National Academy of Sciences study examined the progress of weather modification and found that despite many advances, the subject was still fraught with uncertainties: "The panel now concludes on the basis of statistical analysis of well-designed field experiments that ice-nuclei seeding can sometimes lead to more precipitation, can sometimes lead to less precipitation, and at other times the nuclei have no effect, depending on the meteorological conditions." The report found that progress had been made, but not as fast as had been expected. It urged increased efforts and support, a call that has not been heeded.

Five years later, neither the requested additional funding nor the hoped-for scientific weather modification abilities had been achieved. Many programs had suffered setbacks.

"In fact," lamented Dean E. Mann of the University of California at Santa Barbara at the 1978 meeting of the American Association for the Advancement of Science, "the lightning suppression program is virtually dead, hail suppression has undergone retrenchment as a result of the limited results of the National Hail Research Experiment, major efforts at hurricane modification have been delayed, and the Great Lakes snow redistribution project has been eliminated. Even the precipitation augmentation program—where the results are most unequivocally promising—has been subjected to major alterations and budget cutbacks."

The difficulty has been both the problem of competing national priorities and the inability of some noted weather modification research programs to show conclusively positive results. Mann refers to the resistance "by practical men of affairs" to a major effort in weather modification "because other priorities intervened," especially when "it is not possible to place an absolute value on weather modification . . . such that it ranks above and below other public investments in science or otherwise."

Weather modification is admittedly uncertain but it is also promising, and many scientists deplore the falloff in support. A 1976 National Academy of Sciences study of weather fluctuations and food stated that an ability to increase precipitation 5 percent to 10 percent over large crop-growing areas would bring gains in agricultural production far exceeding the costs of the modification. Says Mann: "The frustration level is high among those who are optimistic about the public benefits to be derived from weather modification generally and from hail suppression specifically."

The efforts in scientific hail reduction are typical of the difficulties encountered. As we saw in Chapter 4, hail is a hazard of frightening proportions to farmers and agricultural regions throughout large parts of the world. The difference between full or empty pockets for the farmer at the end of the harvest can be 10 minutes of hail, and the economic effects on farming regions and on food prices generally can be enormous. The yearly loss to agriculture caused by hail is estimated to be $775 million in the United States and more than $1 billion worldwide. If some way could be found to cut those losses, agriculture—indeed, all of society—would benefit.

The Soviet Union is one of the most hail-plagued nations. Interest in the United States in hail suppression began in the 1960s on the basis of reports by the Soviets of dramatic success in hail-reduction efforts. Soviet scientists claimed 70 to 95 percent success rates in suppressing hail in the Caucasus region by cloud seeding. By 1972, 2.5 million acres of crops were reportedly under protection in the Soviet Union. The Soviet scientists estimated the benefits exceeded the costs by 10 times. No wonder American scientists and policy planners were intrigued!

The Soviet claims were difficult to evaluate from afar. No independent analyses were available. The Soviets had put the emphasis on operational seeding without a strong program to gain detailed scientific understanding of the responsible processes. The claims had to be treated with caution until more could be learned.

The National Hail Research Experiment was begun in 1972 with the hope that it could test the validity of the Soviet concept. Field experiments carried out in Northeastern Colorado would closely emulate the Soviet approach and try to gain a better understanding of the dynamics of a hailstorm. The practical goals were to determine the potential for using cloud seeding to suppress hail and to learn whether hail suppression could be done operationally.

Aircraft, dropsondes, dual-wavelength Doppler radar, and other sensors probed and monitored hailstorms in virtually every way possible. Potential hailstorms were seeded on a randomly selected basis to provide bias-free samples and "controls." The idea of the seeding was conceptually simple: enough ice nuclei would be introduced into the supercooled portions of the cloud to produce many small hailstones that would melt on their way to the ground, rather than a few large, damaging ones. Complex statistical analyses would sort through the data and hunt for the hoped-for conclusions.

The experiment began on notes of optimism. "Of all the severe storms plaguing humanity," said the program's first scientific director, Guy G. Goyer, "the hailstorm appears to be the most manageable." An earlier National Academy of Sciences report in 1967 had referred to "a wide range of opinion on whether or not hail can be effectively suppressed," but the 1973 update said "there is now more optimism than existed some seven years ago." An American Meteorological Society statement in 1973 referred to "growing optimism."

Amid these hopes, the seeding experiments were carried out during the summers of 1972, 1973, and 1974. Other field work was conducted in the summers of 1975 and 1976, but by then the verdict was clear. A wealth of information on hailstorms and their evolution was gained, as noted in Chapter 4, but the statistical seeding experiment revealed that no significant effect— either suppression or enhancement of hail—could be attributed to the seeding of clouds. The project had not found a way to suppress hail.

The concepts developed in the Soviet Union had indicated that rapid growth of hail occurs in regions of the cloud having especially high contents of liquid water. The U.S. experiment found that this model does not apply, at least not to hailstorms in Northeastern Colorado. Zones of high liquid water content are not common in the Colorado hailstorms and are certainly not necessary for hailstone growth.

So it was back to the drawing boards for the scientists. Official meetings and discussions among those responsible for the program were unanimous in concluding that any renewal of the hail-suppression experiment under a new design could not be guaranteed to bring any better or more significant results than the original design. It was decided to direct scientific efforts for the time being toward obtaining more knowledge of the detailed physics of convective storms.

A broad study of hail-suppression technology carried out for the National Science Foundation in 1977 by a group of 13 scientists gave this assessment: "The current status of hail suppression in the United States can be characterized by lack of physical measurements and understanding of in-cloud processes during hail suppression efforts [and] scientific uncertainty and disagreement as to levels of alterations related to inconclusive experimentation."

Despite these uncertainties, the operational use of hail suppression in the United States continues to grow. One hundred thirty thousand square miles of land were under operational hail-suppression efforts in 1975. The study's evaluation of most of these operational programs showed some evidence of reductions of hail by 20 to 40 percent. But these supposed reductions "are mostly not statistically significant," and "without randomization it is difficult to get conclusive tests and wide scientific acceptance." In other words, it is hard to tell whether these apparent reductions are real or not.

It all has a familiar ring. "The current situation surrounding hail suppression reflects a similar one for rainfall modification five to 15 years ago. The users [agriculturists] and applicators [industry] have joined forces to apply an uncertain technology, while the scientific community does not agree and wants more proof of the preciseness of the technology."

As the lead scientist in that study, Stanley A. Changnon, Jr., said later: "At present there is no established hail suppression technology." And he reiterated the study's conclusion that a properly conducted project might be able to reduce damaging hail throughout the growing season by about 25 percent. But to obtain that capability would require a major long-term federal commitment for a systematic program of research. A minimal level of support, the scientists concluded, would not help. Such a large-scale program of funding and research, frankly, does not seem likely.

Lightning may seem among the most violent and awesome forces of all to control. Several research efforts have nevertheless made experimental attempts. The heavy losses of timber in the Western United States from lightning-caused fires prompted the U.S. Forest Service to develop a program of lightning research in the 1960s called Project Skyfire. It used silver iodide seeding of thunderstorms over Montana from both aircraft and ground-based generators to test whether these additional ice nuclei could reduce the frequency and intensity of cloud-to-ground lightning. One set of results suggested that the number of fire-causing lightning flashes could be reduced, but the tests were not continued to the point where this conclusion could be considered proven. Tests in other parts of the world similarly produced inconclusive results.

The National Oceanic and Atmospheric Administration more recently conducted studies to determine whether the dispersal of long metallic fibers into a thundercloud could change the electrical properties enough to reduce the frequency of lightning. Laboratory experiments indicated that about five pounds of such chaff, containing 10 million fibers, dispersed through a large column of the cloud might produce a "leakage current" adequate to counterbalance the output of current from the storm and therefore suppress lightning. Early results were encouraging, but they too were not carried far enough to be conclusive.

Funds for lightning-suppression research have, as Mann indicated, virtually vanished, so advances in this area cannot be expected very soon. That is perhaps ironic. The new scientific view that occasional forest fires are essential to the long-term ecological health of the forest has somewhat weakened concern about lightning-caused forest fires. But lightning kills more people than either hurricanes or tornadoes, and it causes enormous property damage. And as the lightning-triggered New York City power blackout of 1977 again showed, the susceptibility of society's interlinked technological systems to lightning is growing. Atmospheric scientists who favor further lightning-suppression research say it should be considered a route toward further understanding of the basic electrical properties of thunderstorms.

Not all the weather modification news, however, is discouraging. The most clear-cut success has come not in relieving the hazard of a violent storm but in adding to the benefit of a nonviolent storm. By this, I refer to studies over the past decade and a half that have shown it is possible to use cloud seeding of winter storms over the mountains of the West to increase the amount of snow they produce. No one who has lived in the West can fail to understand the degree to which the continuing need for water affects all life. Much of the West is an area of at best marginally sufficient rainfall. Civilization is dependent upon the flow into rivers, reservoirs, and irrigation systems of meltwater from the snowpack deposited in the high mountains during the winter. Water is the essential fact of life in the West; winter snowfall is its main source.

Years of sophisticated seeding experiments carried out in the Rocky Mountains under the direction of Lewis O. Grant of Colorado State University have shown that it is possible to increase snowfall by substantial amounts when the right kinds of clouds are seeded. First, the scientists developed a physical model of how air flows, how clouds form, and how precipitation develops in the high mountain area of Colorado near Climax where the main experiments were conducted. Using this understanding, they described how seeding should affect winter clouds under various conditions. Then they conducted random seeding experiments. The results were as theory predicted.

On days when the temperature at the cloud tops is between $-20°$ C and $-11°$ C ($-4°$ F and $12°$ F) seeding produced substantially greater snowfall than nonseeding. Seeding of these relatively warm clouds produces the perfect concentration of ice nuclei to increase snowfall. When colder clouds were seeded less snow was produced. This also was expected; seeding under these colder conditions produces an over-seeded cloud whose nuclei are so small that the ice crystals evaporate instead of falling as snow. So the trick is merely to seed those clouds showing the proper temperature range for snowfall augmentation. The studies show that seeding only these clouds can produce seasonal precipitation increases of about 10 to 30 percent.

For sixteen years, the U.S. Bureau of Reclamation carried out its own study of snowfall augmentation in Colorado. The results of this Project Skywater, announced in November, 1977, echoed Grant's 10-to-30-percent precipitation increase for seeding the right winter clouds. And in July, 1978, the new National Weather Modification Advisory Board, established the previous year under the National Weather Modification Policy Act of 1976, used the same figures in proclaiming that 10-to-30-percent increases in accumulations of mountain snow will probably be possible by the early 1980s. Rarely in weather modification has there been such unanimous agreement about the positive value of a particular technique to alter precipitation.

A second major success in weather modification research has been a complex experiment carried out in South Florida throughout the 1970s. Called the Florida Area Cumulus Experiment, it has shown strong evidence that seeding can promote the growth and organization of cumulus cloud systems so that they produce substantially more rain than they would ordinarily. This pioneering work may be the forerunner of a research effort using the same techniques in the 1980s to maximize rainfall for crop production over some important agricultural areas in the Midwest.

The Florida experiment has been carried out under the direction of scientists of the National Oceanic and Atmospheric Ad-

Cumulus cloud over Florida before (top) and after seeding. Cloud grew rapidly after the seeding with silver iodide. (NOAA)

ministration over a 5,000-square-mile trapezoidal-shaped area extending almost the width of the Florida Peninsula south of Lake Okeechobee. The idea has been to use seeding to cause cumulus cloud systems to become more buoyant so that they will grow larger and last longer and therefore produce more rain. This should happen, so the theory goes, through a series of events. Seeding the supercooled convective clouds with silver iodide causes moisture present to freeze into ice crystals. The heat released by the transformation of water to ice invigorates the updrafts. The whole cloud becomes more buoyant, and this causes more air to flow into the cloud system at its base. These low-level inflows interact with each other to cause the clouds to grow larger and merge. This increased organization results in a greater and more efficient processing of the available moisture, which leads, finally, to greater rainfall.

"The whole process relies on manipulation of cloud dynamics," says William L. Woodley, director of the experiment. "If you can manipulate the dynamics of clouds, you are going far beyond rain modification."

Early phases of the work had shown spectacular cloud growth, and experiments on single clouds had shown that more rainfall was produced. But detailed field experiments were necessary to show that the process worked over a broad area.

Each day during the designated experimental periods from 1970 to 1976, instrument readings scanned developing clouds to determine whether they were suitable for seeding. Then a scientist went up in an aircraft to make an on-site assessment of suitability. If both these techniques found the conditions suitable, an experimental day was declared.

The experiment was what scientists call "double blind." In medical research, a patient may be given a drug on one day and not on another day, so that comparison of the results can be made. Often it is advisable not to have the patient know which day is which so that psychological factors don't intervene. On the "not" days, a placebo, or dummy pill identical in appearance to the real thing, is given. In especially tricky experiments, it is also advisable not to have the research physician himself know whether the pill or placebo is given. Otherwise his knowledge might subconsciously influence his analysis of the results. This is called a "double-blind experiment." Neither the physician nor the patient knows at the time whether or not the patient is being administered the drug.

Some sophisticated weather modification experiments function the same way. In this case, on a declared experimental day, an aircraft was sent up into the cloud. According to a randomly selected choice, it then either ejected silver iodide flares or did not. The scientists analyzing the results did not at the time know which. In 1976, the final year of the main experiment, on the designated "no-seed" days the aircraft actually ejected a placebo consisting of 100 grams of fine Mojave Desert sand, so the scientists watching from the ground wouldn't be able to tell the difference. (The sand is known not to affect ice-crystal nucleation.)

At any rate, after all the statistical analyses were completed, it turned out that rainfall was on the average 50 percent higher in the area directly seeded on seed days than on nonseeded "control" days. Over the entire broad target area, rainfall was 25 percent higher on seeding days than nonseeding days. All the results were what scientists call "statistically significant." Furthermore, the scientists often could actually see the clouds growing taller after what turned out to be seeding, and measurements confirmed that.

All in all, say Woodley and colleagues J. A. Jordan and Joanne Simpson, the results "lead to the strong indication" that the seeding increased the area of rainfall. Good scientists are always cautious, and Woodley says the results cannot be considered confirmed until they see whether duplicate experiments being carried out by his group, to be completed in 1979, can reproduce the results. If so, they already have their next goal in sight.

"If the results are confirmed," Woodley says, "then we hope to move into a major agricultural area in the U.S. Midwest." The eventual goal for this kind of weather modification project is to use cloud seeding to increase water supplies for growing crops, and the Midwestern experiment would be the main step toward such practical use in the United States. Already Woodley has a name for the effort, which would be carried out over five years (possibly in Illinois) in the 1980s. It is PACE, for Precipitation Augmentation for Crops Experiment. It would be funded by the National Oceanic and Atmospheric Administration, the National Science Foundation, state agencies, and universities.

"It's going to be an incredibly difficult experiment," predicts Woodley. "And we are going to have to have a very good and honest public relations program with the farmers."

The swirling, mighty hurricane might seem the least likely of all severe storms to yield to weather modification. With its huge rotating wind system hundreds of miles across and its enormous load of heat and moisture, the hurricane releases as much energy through condensation in one day as the United States uses electrically in one year. It's the equivalent of 2,000 one-megaton hydrogen bombs. How in the name of Hunraken could anyone go up against that? Not by direct frontal assault, certainly. No trying to match might with might. No brute force approach. Civilization's puny powers shrink to insignificance before the advance of the hurricane.

Three points to remember, however. One, unlike the tornado, for example, the hurricane is a large, long-lived, and relatively stationary storm. At least it's easy to identify and locate. It's not here one moment, gone the next. Two, to significantly cut its potential for damage as it heads landward, modifiers wouldn't have to destroy it. Merely weakening it a bit would help greatly. Studies have indicated that the savings brought about by weakening *one* land-bound hurricane enough to decrease its damages 10 percent would exceed the costs of 10 years of hurricane modification effort by tenfold. Three, the fundamental physics of a rotating storm system such as a hurricane show a potential way to weaken its winds in a relatively subtle way. The scientific David may have a chance against the meteorological Goliath.

The basic idea behind the United States' hurricane modification research program, Project Stormfury, is simple. It's the same kind of "dynamic seeding" we've already seen in the Florida cumulus experiments. The seeding produces an initial change that the storm then responds to in a series of theoretically predictable events that lead to the desired result. Once these forces within the seeded clouds are stimulated, the hurricane does the rest of the work and—so the theory goes—weakens itself.

The seeding is performed by aircraft high in the cumulus cloud towers just outside the hurricane's eyewall. In other words, just out beyond the storm's main vertical conduit for air, moisture, and energy exchange. As in the Florida experiments, the seeding causes freezing of supercooled water droplets, resulting in release of heat that makes the clouds more buoyant and leads them to develop vertically. These seeded clouds eventually become a new eyewall, replacing the original one. The hurricane eye is thus effectively increased in diameter, and this reduces its maximum winds. This last wind-weakening event is a consequence of the same principle of conservation of angular momentum that governs a spinning ice skater and causes her rotation speed to slow as she extends her arms outward.

This is the theory. The problem is that hurricanes haven't been very cooperative. Since the start of Project Stormfury in the 1960s, few hurricanes have come along that meet all the criteria for being tested. The hurricane needs to be close enough to land to be within reach of seeding or test aircraft based in Miami or Puerto Rico but not so close that the effects of landfall would complicate the work of detecting the effects of seeding. Also, since this is a research program, it's necessary that seeding not be done on any hurricane that is going to reach land; no one wants the scientific effort to get involved in any subsequent hassle about responsibility for damages the storm causes.

To be eligible for seeding, the hurricane must be predicted to be within 700 nautical miles of the operating base (either Miami or San Juan) for at least 12 hours. Seeding cannot be done if the hurricane has more than a 10 percent probability of approaching within 50 nautical miles of a populated land area within 24 hours of seeding.

Only four hurricanes have been seeded in Project Stormfury

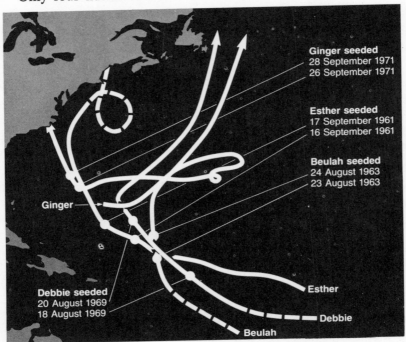

Ginger seeded
28 September 1971
26 September 1971

Esther seeded
17 September 1961
16 September 1961

Beulah seeded
24 August 1963
23 August 1963

Ginger

Esther

Debbie seeded
20 August 1969
18 August 1969

Debbie

Beulah

Tracks of seeded hurricanes. (NOAA)

so far: Esther in 1961, Beulah in 1963, Debbie in 1969, and Ginger in 1971. In all four cases, the changes perceived after seeding fell within the broad range of normal variability of hurricanes. None of them increased in strength.

Debbie, however, showed some intriguing changes after seeding. These alterations, apparently caused by the seeding, have brought hope that hurricane modification may eventually become feasible, if only enough tests on actual hurricanes can be conducted. Hurricane Debbie had maximum winds of 112 miles per hour when it was heavily seeded with silver iodide on August 18, 1969. Five hours after the seedings, its peak winds had dropped to 78 miles per hour, almost to below hurricane force. Also, radar showed its eyewall had expanded, just as theory predicted. No seeding was done the next day, and the storm reintensified. On August 20, its winds were 113 miles per hour, and seeding was resumed. Five hours after completion of this round of seeding, the winds had diminished to 97 miles per hour. This was a 15 percent drop, not as large as the 30 percent decrease on the first day of seeding, but significant nonetheless. Many other measurements further supported the idea that the seeding had affected the hurricane in the way predicted by theory. "The data suggest we did modify the hurricane," said Stormfury's director at the time, R. Cecil Gentry.

Computer studies since then using mathematical models of hurricanes have shown that seeding outside the eyewall does decrease the maximum winds in the model hurricanes. They also show that seeding has little or no net effect on the model storm's track or the net amount of rain it produces. In both the models and the actual hurricanes seeded, the effects are transient, disappearing 12 to 24 hours after seeding.

Following the promising results with Debbie, the Stormfury scientists eagerly awaited another suitable hurricane to seed. None occurred over the experimental areas in 1970, 1971, and 1972. An anomalous storm called Ginger was seeded in 1971, but little new information was gained.

Stormfury's field experiments were discontinued in 1973 until, among other things, new aircraft could be purchased. In the following years discussions explored the possibility of moving the project to the Western Pacific Ocean where hurricanes (there called typhoons) are far more abundant than in the North Atlantic. There the chances of a storm meeting seeding requirements would be better. But the governments of Japan and the

People's Republic of China indicated they would oppose the seeding, and President Marcos of the Republic of the Philippines declined to give his permission. (The Philippines may, however, soon begin their own experimental seeding of typhoons that could hit their shores. The results will be watched closely.)

In 1977, somewhat late for full planning, Stormfury was given the go-ahead to again seed one hurricane in the Atlantic, as a rehearsal for full-scale resumption of seeding operations there. No suitable storm came into the area.

In 1978, plans were readied well in advance. All five aircraft and crews assigned to Stormfury were poised for seeding and monitoring out of either Miami or San Juan any time after August 1. Two of them carried the world's most advanced instrumentation for atmospheric studies. Thousands of pencil-sized pyrotechnic flares by which 500 pounds of silver iodide per seeding would be released into a storm were ready. The designated officials of the National Oceanic and Atmospheric Administration who would weigh a decision to seed a candidate storm were set to quickly swing into action.

All that was needed was a suitable hurricane. It did not come. The October 15 cut-off date came and went. But no hurricane that met the criteria appeared. Hurricane Ella, which had lingered off the North Carolina coast on Labor Day weekend before turning seaward, had come close to the seeding area, but not close enough. Once again the hopes of the Stormfury scientists were frustrated. Said Robert C. Sheets, scientific director of Stormfury-1978: "It is disappointing."

So the Stormfury researchers are in virtually the position they were in 10 years ago. They have one very promising set of results from Hurricane Debbie but still no subsequent field experiments to verify those encouraging signs. "All indications to date are that, yes, we can relieve the maximum winds by 10 to 15 percent by seeding," Sheets said following the 1978 disappointment. But he believes the project needs to seed about 10 more storms to establish that fact to a strong level of confidence, although five might be sufficient if all gave such clear-cut results as Debbie did. But past experience shows that those 10 storms are going to be hard to come by in the Atlantic.

The aircraft used in Stormfury were committed to international atmospheric experiments elsewhere in 1979, so no further seeding is likely until 1980. By then, Sheets says, negotiations in progress with Mexico and Australia may have opened up two new areas for possible seeding operations. Both the Eastern Pacific off Mexico and the ocean areas off Australia are good candidates for seedable storms, and their availability in addition to the Atlantic would greatly increase the opportunities for having storms that meet seeding criteria. Perhaps with the help of those two nations, the problem of the frustrating lack of suitable storms can be alleviated, and the Stormfury hurricane modification hypothesis can then be proved.

But don't put too many hopes on it. The short history of scientific weather modification gives ample reason for caution against over-optimistic expectations.

As if the scientific problems weren't enough, weather modification raises a host of social, political, and legal issues. Fledgling and uncertain science it may be, but those involved in it have learned, sometimes the hard way, that the science and technology of weather modification cannot be conducted in isolation from human considerations. Weather modification efforts, whether research or operational, need to be carried out in a way that meets the approval of the public. The people who are likely to be affected have to be involved in the decisions of whether, when, and where to seed the skies.

The choices are not necessarily easy. A sustained rain that ends a drought may also bring floods. A rain that benefits one farmer may ruin the crops of another. A rainfall that means more power for a hydroelectric company may mean fewer tourists at a nearby area's resort. A heavy snowfall that delights skiers and water management people might not seem so pleasant to mountain valley ranchers with homes beneath avalanche-prone slopes. Additional rain may be welcome; hail is not. A hurricane may bring tragedy; it may also bring much-needed rains. There have been hurricanes whose economic benefits from rainfall greatly exceeded their total damages.

The problem is that not all the consequences of a weather modification program can necessarily be known or controlled. The effects are difficult to predict and they are impossible to limit to precise boundaries. And even when results are reasonably certain, the public perceptions of risks and benefits may differ from those of the scientists or the organization sponsoring the project.

Sometimes the sponsors' attitudes toward the public can make the difference between acceptance or hostility. The National Hail Research Experiment in Northeastern Colorado employed a very open policy of public information and public education and experienced no major opposition. But a commercial hail-suppression program in the San Luis Valley of Southern Colorado provoked intense debate, controversy, legal action, and even violence. It presents an interesting case study of how not to handle a weather modification effort. The program was sponsored by a major beer company which in 1972 told a group of 300 barley producers in the valley that the company's continuing purchase of barley from them was contingent upon their support of the hail-suppression program to protect the company's investment in the crop. But the valley economy was far more dependent on ranching and timber than on barley, and the ranchers and timber interests in the area had not been included in the weather modification decisions. They felt the hail suppression was responsible for the recent lack of needed rains in the area. The exclusion of these interests from most cloud seeding decisions and the failure to negotiate compromises that might have made the operations tolerable to them created an adversary situation. The public debate led to passage of legislation regulating weather modification in Colorado and providing for public hearings prior to granting project permits. The hearings were held, and the permit was granted. Two weeks later a trailer containing $50,000 worth of project equipment was dynamited. In the November general election that year a five-county straw vote was taken, and the citizens voted against weather modification four to one. The results of that ballot, although not legally binding, strongly influenced the state Department of Natural Resources' decision, following a second public hearing in March, to deny a permit for the coming season, and the denial was subsequently upheld in court. This, according to weather modification legal expert Ray Jay Davis, was the first time in litigation that a public vote was considered in reaching a weather modification decision.

An interesting sequel came about in 1975 when the valley's growers decided to sponsor an operational snowfall augmentation project in the mountains to the west in hopes of increasing the water supply to the crops. This time, the project's operator and sponsors invited opponents to discuss the situation and express their concerns. Many of the opponents were the same persons who had fought the hail-suppression project, but a citizens' committee was set up to monitor the operations and the committee was given veto authority to suspend operations at any time. Prior to each seeding decision a committee member was contacted to give clearance, and no major difficulties arose.

This, according to Barbara C. Farhar of the University of Colorado, is the only known instance of an organized opposition agreeing to tolerate a weather modification project after successfully halting prior operations. "These developments were unique in the history of public response to weather modification. The trade-off negotiated between project proponents and opponents —citizen committee monitoring and veto authority in exchange for opponent tolerance of the project—made it possible for the project to function."

Concerns over who has the right to change the weather have also become public issues in states as widespread as Pennsylvania, Texas, California, South Dakota, and Washington. Some persons have proposed federal regulation, but as yet there are no federal licensing or control provisions beyond a requirement to report weather modification activities. About half the states have laws dealing with licensing or regulation of weather modification, but their provisions vary widely and many are considered inadequate.

An example of the potential seriousness of a controversy over the effects of weather modification was a debate arising after the devastating floods at Rapid City, South Dakota, in 1972. Two hundred thirty-eight persons lost their lives in floods caused by up to 14 inches of rainfall in the mountains west of Rapid City. In Chapter 5 we showed how both the Rapid City and the 1976 Big Thompson floods were caused by similar sets of meteorological circumstances. But in the case of the Rapid City flood there also had been an aircraft conducting cloud seeding operations in the area on the day of the big rains. An official report on the flood stated that cloud seeding did not contribute materially to the flood, but weather modification proponents shudder to think of the implications if such a flood ever is the result of a modification effort.

Hurricane modification brings up the same kinds of issues, but on a larger scale. In 1975, a Mexican geography professor accused the United States of having used weather modification in September, 1974, to "artificially detour" away from the United States Hurricane Fifi, which slammed into Honduras, causing widespread destruction and destroying most of the country's corn crop. As we've seen, Project Stormfury seeded no storms after 1971 and wasn't even in existence as a cloud seeding op-

eration in 1974. Yet the accusation points up the kinds of concerns—legitimate or not—that might be raised in the future if a
seeded hurricane does turn toward a populated area and wreak
destruction. In 1965, Hurricane Betsy turned erratically, first toward New Orleans, then back across the tip of Florida, then re-
circling back to Louisiana. The hurricane caused 74 deaths and
$1.4 billion in damage. It was not seeded by the then-fledgling
Project Stormfury. "If it had been seeded," wrote University of
Arizona meteorologist Louis J. Battan, "many people would
have insisted that the sharp changes of direction were caused by
the seeding. . . . Had it been seeded . . . the courts would,
in all likelihood, have been besieged by lawsuits alleging that the
seeding caused the effects and hence that the seeders were responsible for the damage. The thought of such a possibility must
send shivers through the scientists of this project. . . ." Japan,
in contrast, opposed proposals to move Project Stormfury to the
Western Pacific in part because it feared a reduction in the
needed rainfall that typhoons supply.

Operational hurricane modification is still many years away,
but it is not too early to seriously consider the social and legal
implications of such a capability. Who, for instance, ask Robert
G. Fleagle and University of Washington colleagues in their
study *Weather Modification in the Public Interest*, should have
the power to authorize modification in the path of a hurricane,
particularly if the new course results in damage and loss of lives
to an area that would otherwise have remained safe? How can
those affected by a modified hurricane be compensated for their
losses? By whom, if anyone, will those who have been deprived
of rainfall due to the change in its course be compensated? How
will insurance companies react? How will the U.S. government
respond if a modified hurricane causes damage, deaths, or
changes in rainfall in another country?

And once it becomes possible to modify a hurricane, these
issues will not be avoided by deciding that seeding is too risky.
For a decision not to seed will have consequences too. What if a
hurricane that could be seeded is not, and it plows undiminished
into a major populated area?

Such questions have a certain surreal quality, especially when
we remember that progress in weather modification, especially in
modifying major storms, has been slow. But a new technology
with such potentially far-reaching implications must be considered within its human, social, and political context, even though

the implementation of that technology may be years or decades away.

I have always tried to encourage in others a positive outlook on science and technology, believing that the endeavor to understand nature is a noble pursuit that enriches humankind and that the attempt to modify our natural environment for human benefit is also a natural process and an inevitable outgrowth of that understanding. Humankind's first attempts to moderate inclement environmental conditions go back at least to the caveman's first use of fire to warm his habitat against the cold. Weather modification in itself is no more and no less than a natural continuation of that ageless striving to ease the ever-present burden of environmental extremes. If used wisely, the human benefit may someday be significant.

But the record shows that progress will be slow, especially in learning to lessen the violence of savage storms. Far from being a panacea, weather modification will at best bring incremental improvements, marginal gains in the effort to achieve an edge over nature, and accompanying it will be new issues and problems to be faced. Neither the fears of nor the hopes for weather modification should be exaggerated.

The powerful forces of nature are not, as we've emphasized before, fluke events, something apart from the natural order of things. They are the natural consequences of dynamic adjustments of the natural world itself, a manifestation of a quest for balance, an outgrowth of the need for equilibrium. As such they will always be with us, and rather than place undue hope in seeing them somehow diminished by the efforts of science, we should instead treat them with the respect their powers are due, realistically preparing our homes and our cities and our lives for their occasional and inevitable reoccurrence. As Francis Bacon observed, "Nature to be commanded must be obeyed."

CHAPTER 12

How to Prepare for Disaster

I am absolutely convinced that no one should ever become a tornado fatality. But if lives are to be saved, they must be saved days, weeks, and even months ahead of time, not when the storm is bearing down.

—Allen D. Pearson, Director,
National Severe Storms Forecast Center

Violent events of nature may be inevitable; the terrible human toll of natural disasters need not be. From time immemorial, no one has been able to persuade us always to act in our own best long-term interests. With disasters, ignorance of the hazard and fatalism over the consequences are the enemies of survival; a realistic awareness of risk and a determination to take action in advance are the guardians of life.

The equivalent of a city of 250,000 persons die in natural disasters each year. The litany of death and destruction from tornadoes, lightning, floods, hurricanes, blizzards, volcanoes, and earthquakes may create an impression of overwhelming natural force in the face of which human life-saving action is as useless as a rock thrown against the tide or a shout against the wind.

Nothing could be further from the truth. Disasters are not external phenomena, generated by nature and thrust upon the unsuspecting population. They are not acts of nature, or of God, or of any other outside force, whatever be the name. Their mitigation lies primarily not with natural science but with human science and human action.

Natural phenomena don't "cause" disasters, although we frequently say they do. The more modern, and undoubtedly correct, view is that nature, even at its most powerful, is neutral and that disasters result when natural events and human populations intersect, like a collision at a road crossing. Just as it takes two to make a collision, it takes both the human presence and the natural force to make a disaster. A tsunami on an unpopulated coast may be a dramatic event, but it won't be a disaster. An earthquake where human population is sparse and buildings absent may be a noteworthy geological event, but it won't be a disaster. A flood where the floodplain is unoccupied may have environmental effects, but it won't be a disaster. A hurricane that remains at sea far from a populated coast is only a storm, not a disaster. A tornado that skips along the fields between farmhouses may produce a spectacular scare but no disaster.

Yet if the same geophysical events are transferred to a site where human beings live and work, where they have their homes, offices, factories, and schools, this intersection of human works and natural event can bring tragedy.

A disaster, then, is as much a human-caused as a nature-caused happening, and a realistic appreciation of that fact is the first necessary step in reducing the frequency and tolls of disasters. It is not an academic point. If we see the world as full of forces whose potentially hazardous effects are beyond our influence, we will see no purpose in planning action to mitigate those hazards. But if we realize that the hazardous effects are a consequence of our own presence, we can take steps to make our presence less vulnerable. Just as ill-advised human action or inaction helps create "natural" catastrophes, positive human action can help avert them. Some incidence of disaster is inevitable with human occupation of the earth, but wise adjustments and preparations can significantly reduce your own risk. Extrapolated to a whole society, such actions can at least help slow the world rate of increase in disasters as human populations grow and spread into more disaster-prone locales.

It is the knowledge of how much could be done to save life and property—but isn't—that poses such a frustration to those who are involved professionally with hazardous events and calamities. The most productive actions have to be taken long before a tornado funnel slices down out of the boiling cloud, long before the hurricane's atmospheric whirlpool sends coastal palms reeling, long before the wind first whips the snow into the first bitter blasts of the blizzard, long before the dishes in the cupboard rattle in announcement of the earthquake.

Take tornadoes, for instance. Allen Pearson isn't kidding when he says we really shouldn't have any tornado fatalities. He's also under no illusions that that'll ever be attained. "By and large," he says, "complacency seems the order of the day. If you don't think about it, maybe it won't happen, at least to me or my town."

Planning to cut tornado deaths has to begin far in advance. Your child's school should have a tornado plan, and it should be tested through drills. An engineer should survey the building to select the safest shelter area. School bus drivers should be trained in what to do and what not to do. Ask officials at the school whether they have made such preparations.

Does your town have a truly effective warning system, and if not, why not? Yes, it costs money, but all such expenditures are a matter of priorities. The saving of lives and the protection of citizens is theoretically one of the high priorities of government, and that fact should be emphasized to city officials.

Do your local radio stations have the National Weather Service weather wire, and do they conscientiously check it regularly for storm warnings? It costs only a few dollars a day. At the very least, the stations should have a tone-alert NOAA Weather Radio receiver.

Does your local government have a strongly worded ordinance requiring mobile homes to be strongly tied down? Mobile homes are about as dangerous a place as conceivable to be in during a tornado or strong windstorm, and the accelerating cost of conventional housing is turning more and more Americans to mobile homes. More than 30 percent of all new single-family residences are now mobile homes, so their notoriously poor behavior in high winds is not the relatively isolated problem it used to be. It is not enough that manufacturers are required to furnish tie-down attachments with every unit. Like unused seat belts, unattached tie-downs have not been fully accepted (fewer than half of all mobile homes are tied down). But like the unfastened seat belt hanging limp in the wrecked car, the driver smashed against the windshield or the pavement, unattached mobile home tie-downs have a way of silently mocking an owner indifferent to safety. A 1978 report to the Disaster Preparedness Staff of the National Weather Service by wind engineering specialists of the Institute for Disaster Research of Texas Tech

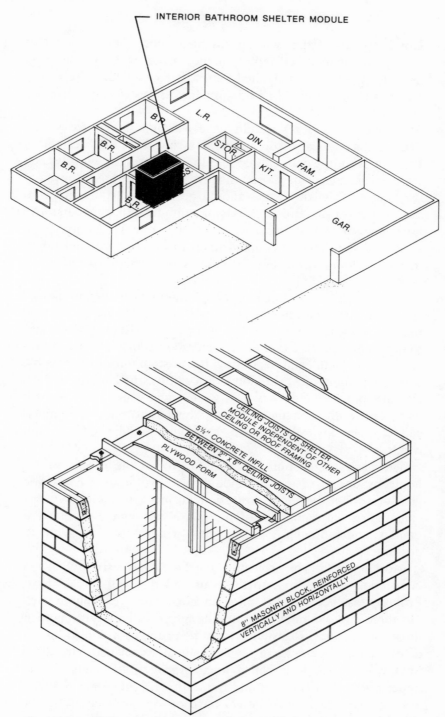

INTERIOR BATHROOM SHELTER MODULE

CEILING JOISTS OF SHELTER MODULE INDEPENDENT OF OTHER CEILING OR ROOF FRAMING

5½" CONCRETE INFILL BETWEEN 2" x 6" CEILING JOISTS

PLYWOOD FORM

8" MASONRY BLOCK, REINFORCED VERTICALLY AND HORIZONTALLY

Well-built in-resident shelters like this can save lives in a tornado.
(DEFENSE CIVIL PREPAREDNESS AGENCY)

University found that windspeeds high enough to cause major damage to unanchored mobile homes occur every few years in almost all areas of the United States. It concluded: "Use of tie-downs should be made mandatory for all mobile homes in the United States."

Mobile home parks should have warning signals for severe windstorms and a structure usable as a shelter (often a recreation room or laundry room can double for the purpose) within quick walking distance. All those who live in mobile homes, even if they have strong tie-downs, should be prepared to evacuate to the shelter or to stronger lodging any time a thunderstorm, hurricane, or tornado warning is issued for their vicinity. Even tie-downs shouldn't be counted upon to provide personal safety to mobile home occupants in winds greater than 70 miles per hour.

We all tend to be fatalistic about the chances of our homes surviving a tornado, but in fact relatively minor alterations during construction can markedly improve the resistance of a house to damaging winds. Good design and good construction can prevent failure and collapse during the vast majority of possible winds, including most tornadoes. Specialists involved in the new interdisciplinary field known as wind engineering have become more and more convinced during the past decade that much can be done to protect houses and other buildings from high winds.

The basic design philosophy is to protect the people in the home by design of a small module within it that can provide nearly absolute personal protection during a tornado or hurricane. Then the remainder of the house is designed so that the damage and economic loss from such winds will be as slight as possible.

Most important in protecting the house is to strengthen the connections of the roof to the wall and the wall to the floor. Properly fastened metal framing anchor plates, available in various three-dimensional shapes and designs, can greatly strengthen those connections. Resistance to uplift of the roof and to lateral deformation (racking) can be economically provided with diagonal wooden supports called knee braces nailed between the upper portions of the wall and the roof. This integrates the roof and wall structure. Such braces have proven architecturally acceptable, very inexpensive, and very easily installed, according to specialists at Texas Tech University. Exterior walls can be diagonally braced with lumber, metal straps, or with plywood sheathing. Roof members can be connected directly to foundations by steel through-tie rods. The connection of walls to roofs and to floors merely by toe-nailing or side-nailing doesn't provide much support against high winds.

More important, of course, than the protection of property is the preservation of life. The 1970s have seen evolution of a new concept for protecting persons in their homes during tornadoes. It involves strengthening a small interior room on the main floor so it can double as an in-residence shelter.

"Until recently," says Ernst W. Kiesling, chairman of the Department of Civil Engineering at Texas Tech University, "most people thought that the forces of a tornado were so awesome that nothing could be done to provide safety above ground economically." The tornado that raced through downtown Lubbock in 1970 provided what Kiesling calls "a $135 million laboratory" in the form of damaged structures. In that tornado and in dozens of others since (the 1974 tornado superoutbreak provided many such examples), it was noticed that often a small interior room such as a closet or bathroom remained standing even though nearly all the rest of the house was in rubble. The concept of the in-residence shelter grew from those observations.

The idea has many advantages. Basements are fine, but their cost is high and homes in many parts of the nation are constructed without them. Outdoor storm shelters pose a risk from flying debris to those who try to reach them too late. An in-residence shelter near the center of the house at the main-floor level permits a family to continue their normal living habits during a severe weather watch, knowing that a safe place is only a few seconds away. And an in-residence shelter can be economically constructed in an existing house. A basement cannot. Unlike the outside storm shelter, the in-house shelter would be a normal part of the house, say a bathroom, walk-in closet, or study.

Two such types of in-residence shelters have been tested at Texas Tech, one for building while the house is under construction, one for fitting into existing houses. Both meet tough criteria for resisting tornado winds and penetration by flying missiles sent airborne by the tornado. They are designed to stand up against the winds and missiles expected in 98 percent of all tornadoes. They are designed, for instance, to stop a 14-foot 2 x 4 board fired at the wall end-on at 100 miles per hour. Both can be built from available, inexpensive materials that can be handled by ordinary building crews. For a small room, say 8 x 8 feet, occupant protection can be provided for between $500 and $1,000 for new houses, somewhat more for existing ones.

In a new house, the shelter is constructed on the slab before the rest of the house is formed. The shelter is not tied to the structure of the surrounding house. A concrete block wall anchored into the floor with reinforcing bars is erected to within half a foot of the height of the ceiling of the surrounding rooms. Reinforcing bars are placed into each of the cavities in the concrete block, and a few inches above the wall the bars are bent horizontally to form reinforcement for the ceiling. The holes in the concrete block walls are then filled with concrete. The roof is formed by a continuous pour of lightweight or conventional concrete.

For an existing house, the wallboard is stripped from the wall. The walls are securely anchored to the floor, perhaps by steel bars and plates. Several layers of steel mesh are attached to the wall studs. Three-fourths-inch plywood goes over that. Then the wall cavity created is filled with either lightweight vermiculite concrete or conventional concrete. The same materials are used for the ceiling. A sliding door has been developed that protects against missile impact. It consists of two layers of three-fourths-inch plywood covered on one side with a sheet of 14-gage or heavier steel. For normal use, an attractive swinging door can be provided.

Someday, such shelters might be mass produced. Factory-built bathrooms with plumbing, wiring, and fixtures already installed and with walls capable of repelling a tornado-hurled missile could conceivably become available as an off-the-shelf item. But until then, homeowners can have their own built. Conceptual designs are available from the Institute for Disaster Research at Texas Tech University or from the Defense Civil Preparedness Agency (now part of the new Federal Emergency Management Agency), which has published booklets describing their design and construction. Design details and inspection should be sought from an architect or an engineer.

"Besides occupant protection, an in-residence shelter can offer, at very little cost, freedom from the anxiety caused by a severe weather watch," concludes Kiesling.

The shelter concept the Institute for Disaster Research has

developed can also be applied to schools. Here, the shelter is conceived as interior hallway protective modules capable of resisting wind forces that occur in 98 percent of recorded tornadoes.

I have stressed the in-house shelter idea partly because it is a relatively new concept that hasn't yet found its way into all the safety literature and partly because it so well emphasizes that by positive advance planning and action you can provide physical protection for yourself and your family against even the high winds of tornadoes and hurricanes.

Incorporating all these wind-proofing features into a new house need not be especially expensive. Kiesling has built several homes in the Lubbock area that have many features to resist strong winds, and he says they add approximately 2 to 4 percent to the initial cost, depending on the size of the house. Features usually include well-constructed prefab roof frames, several types of anchorages, an above-ground storm shelter, blowout panels, wind-resistant fence, and landscaping to redirect wind currents.

One of the biggest problems in gaining public acceptance of these storm-protection measures is to overcome stereotypes about the completely overpowering force of tornadoes and hurricanes. Many people, including engineers and architects, are under the impression that these winds are so strong that there is no use trying to protect against them. Joseph E. Minor, director of the Texas Tech Disaster Research Institute, has been particularly outspoken against such misbeliefs. He refers to the "credibility gap between the known facts about tornadoes and what the practitioner and the public believe."

I've already described, in the chapter on tornadoes, the myth of astronomical windspeeds in tornadoes. References to speeds of up to 500 miles per hour in tornadoes, studies in the 1970s have shown, have no basis in fact. The meager evidence on which such estimates were based has been supplanted by better and more detailed studies that indicate much lower maximum windspeeds. The strongest tornadoes, it appears, have maximum windspeeds of between 200 and 250 miles per hour. Strong, yes, but the point to remember is that only a very small percentage of all tornadoes have windspeeds that high. In fact, in more than 90 percent of all tornadoes the maximum windspeeds are less than those in a moderate hurricane (150 miles per hour). Furthermore, much of the damage in severe tornadoes occurs along their outer periphery where winds are less than 125 miles per hour. So most tornado occurrences are considered to be manageable by using design and construction methods commonly employed in hurricane-susceptible areas.

Minor lambasts reference works that "convey impressions of complete unmanageability where tornadic windspeeds are concerned." The misconception is a barrier to effective action.

"Only a very small percentage of all tornadoes possess windspeeds near maximum values. Appreciation of this point would remove a major hindrance to the acceptance of principles of design for extreme winds on the parts of the practitioner and the public. . . . The popular concepts of astronomical windspeeds must be overturned. Further, the fact that large percentages of tornadoes possess windspeeds that are well within the reach of economical designs must be advanced."

Minor also attacks "a popular concept among laymen and some professionals that the change in atmospheric pressure associated with the tornado vortex is the cause of structures 'exploding' in the face of tornadic activity. While the presence of this change in pressure undoubtedly plays a role in inducing structural failure, popular concepts completey ignore the role of the wind in causing the failure."

Again, this misconception is more than just a scientific point; it hinders effective design. "Most researchers . . . would agree that the atmospheric pressure change effect is not the sole cause of structural 'explosions,' and that actual atmospheric changes are relatively small," says Minor. "This point is important to the principles of tornado-resistant design. We need to remove from the mind of the practitioner the apparent preoccupation with atmospheric pressure change and replace it with a more balanced approach which considers wind and atmospheric pressure change as manageable effects."

The same criticism holds for fatalistic attitudes that nothing can be done to protect against extreme missiles hurled by tornado winds. Many such reports are exaggerations. In any case, as the in-house shelter concept shows, it is possible to design against almost all expected impacts.

"Technical knowledge is available which will enhance the ability of society to cope with nature's most severe weather phenomenon—the tornado," concludes Minor. "Society can learn to live with the tornado."

Hurricanes too pose grave threats that long-range advance

planning in the form of good building design can lessen. What can happen when a hurricane hits a developed area featuring inadequately built housing was dramatically illustrated when Cyclone Tracy hit Darwin, Australia, on Christmas morning of 1974.

Cyclone Tracy originated as a tropical depression over the Arafura Sea 290 miles northeast of Darwin on December 20. Darwin, on Australia's northern coast, is a city of 30,000 and the seat of government for the Northern Territory. In the early morning hours of Christmas Day, the cyclone moved onto shore. Its eye passed directly over the Darwin International Airport, located in the center of the city. The cyclone moved very slowly —only 5 miles per hour—and this kept it over the city for an unusually long time. For more than four hours, winds ranging up to 168 miles per hour raked over Darwin. The northern suburbs had the highest maximum winds, the downtown commercial area the lowest, 110 miles per hour.

Darwin's residential areas were demolished. Eighty percent of its houses were seriously damaged. Only 400 of the original 8,000 houses were reasonably intact and habitable. Fifty persons were killed, and damage to buildings was estimated at $250 million.

This was a rare case in which most damage was from winds alone, rather than from winds and storm surge. Darwin had been hit by cyclones before—in 1878, 1897, 1917, and 1937—but investigation after the Cyclone Tracy disaster showed that most of the housing had nevertheless been built on the traditional approach, using a mixture of intuition and experience and very little engineering input. The problem has since received considerable attention because of the high degree of damage and because more than half of the housing in Darwin was government-owned or government-built.

Many of the houses had been built on high pillars, a concept designed to catch sea breezes while creating open, shaded space beneath. Large windows were common, and most of the houses had corrugated steel roofs.

Ninety percent of the houses lost their roofs, many of which went flying off to crash into the weak siding of adjacent houses. With the roofs gone and the brittle asbestos cement cladding broken, the frames of the houses were greatly weakened. They had been built, it turned out, in such a way that the roofing braced the roof beams, supported the walls, and in general served to tie the structure together. The large windows and lack of internal bracing made the walls very weak. Once the roofs were torn away, the walls were relatively unsupported and could be easily blown down.

Commercial buildings and houses that had been well engineered fared much better. After the cyclone, Darwin established new wind-resistant building codes. Wind-engineered houses were constructed on a tract basis. A whole new philosophy of cyclone-resistant housing design was created.

The Darwin experience may have some lessons for residential construction in the United States as well. Texas Tech's Minor and R. D. Marshall of the U.S. National Bureau of Standards studied the Darwin disaster firsthand. They concluded that "a few design misjudgments and a few oversights in the details of construction were factors in producing a major disaster." Similar deficiencies may well exist in American housing.

"A hurricane of Tracy's intensity at Houston, Miami, or New Orleans may reveal that we in the United States have overlooked a few things in design and construction of housing as well."

After floods, severe winds of all kinds are the greatest cause of disaster in the United States. Property damage alone from strong winds exceeds $500 million a year and is climbing. Yet in our new construction we are building toward more disaster.

"The architectural and engineering communities must act immediately if the current trends in housing construction, which are not reflective of wind-resistant designs, are to be reversed," says Minor. "If such a reversal is not achieved soon, we can expect more of the type of housing-related disaster experienced in Darwin, in Lubbock, in Corpus Christi, and elsewhere along the Gulf Coast."

I have been stressing long-range preparations for disaster because they are too often overlooked. But when a tornado or hurricane bears down on your community, you must take immediate, short-range action as well. A good outfielder or infielder in baseball is always thinking before each pitch, outlining in his mind what he will do if the ball is hit to him under the situation of the moment. You too should think out in advance what you should do in various disaster situations. Know where you should go and what you should do.

Excellent guidelines have been prepared by the National Oceanic and Atmospheric Administration, parent agency of the National Weather Service. A tornado watch means tornadoes are expected to develop. Keep a battery-operated radio or tele-vison set handy, and listen for weather advisories. If you have a NOAA Weather Radio (and if you live in a storm-prone area you should have), keep it on. A tornado warning means a tor-nado has actually been sighted or detected on radar. Seek inside shelter, preferably in a tornado cellar, or steel-framed or rein-forced concrete building of strong construction. Stay away from windows. In homes, a basement offers the greatest safety. If you have no basement or in-house shelter, a small interior room on the lowest floor such as a closet or bathroom may offer good protection. Or lie beneath a sturdy piece of furniture. Keep some windows open but stay away from them.

In an office building, go to an interior hallway on the lowest floor or to a designated shelter. In a shopping center, do not go to your parked car. Go to a designated shelter.

In school, teachers should lead students to a room or hall-way in the interior of the building on the lowest floor. The room should be of framed construction rather than having load-bearing walls whose collapse could bring down the roof. If the tornado is approaching from the southwest, as most do, a cor-ridor that opens only to the north is safest, followed by one opening only to the east. Stay away from classrooms with win-dows facing west and south and from hallways in line with the tornado's direction of travel (they can become wind tunnels for flying glass and debris). But even those hallways are preferable to rooms that open to either side. Stay away from doorways and crouch or lie flat. Cover your head. Do not take shelter in large rooms with free-span roofs such as gymnasiums, cafeterias, and auditoriums. Such roofs frequently fail due to a combination of aerodynamic lifting by the winds and collapse of the walls that support them.

In open areas, move away from the tornado's path at right angles. If there is no time to escape, lie flat in the nearest ditch or ravine.

In the case of hurricanes, as in tornadoes, advance planning and thought can save your life. Realize that the fact that a hurri-cane may not have struck your coastal area for many years does not mean that the risk is necessarily low. And if the area has been in a hurricane before and survived, learn from the lessons of that experience. But do not take an experience with the out-skirts of a hurricane as typical of what might happen if the main central region of a hurricane moves in. Respect its potential.

Every coastal community in hurricane-susceptible areas should have a hurricane-preparedness committee. It should help educate the citizens about risks and necessary preparation, carry out long-term planning, set up emergency shelters, and supervise evacuation and rescue work when necessary. Take part in these community preparedness activities. Keep yourself and your family well informed.

Learn the storm surge history and elevation of your area. Learn safe routes inland and the location of shelters. Trim dead wood from trees. At the start of each hurricane season (June) recheck your supply of boards, batteries, nonperishable foods, and equipment you may need if a hurricane strikes.

Pay close attention to tropical cyclone advisories so you will have maximum time to plan in the event any such storms turn into hurricanes. A hurricane watch is issued for a coastal area when there is a threat of hurricane conditions within 24 to 36 hours. When a hurricane watch is issued, fill your car's gas tank. Check supplies of medicines and emergency provisions. Bring all lawn furniture and other outside objects indoors. Tape, board, or shutter your windows to prevent them from shattering. Wedge sliding glass doors shut to prevent them from lifting. Stay tuned to weather advisories.

A hurricane warning is issued to your area when hurricane conditions (winds of 74 miles per hour or more or dangerously high tides or waves) are expected within 24 hours or less. If your house is sturdy and on high ground and if you are not advised to evacuate, stay home. Board up garage and porch doors. Move valuables to upper floors. Bring in pets. Fill containers, including the bathtub, with water in case you lose your water supply. Turn the refrigerator up to maximum cold. Stay indoors on the downwind side of the house and away from windows.

If you are advised to evacuate, do so. Remember the all-too-frequent tragic instances in which persons needlessly died because they failed to heed evacuation warnings. In general, if you live on the coastline or a coastal island, leave. If you live near a floodplain or a river, leave. Remember that most hurricane deaths are caused by drowning when storm surge, tide, and waves bring abnormally high seas inland, and the torrents of rain bring flash flooding and overflowing rivers.

If you have to leave, don't wait until the last moment. Realize that traffic may be heavy and roads blocked. Shut off your electricity, water, and gas. Leave food and water for your pets.

Take small valuables but travel light. Drive carefully using recommended evacuation routes. Be orderly, cooperative, and helpful.

Do not travel during the hurricane. Flying debris and flood waters make it extremely dangerous. Don't be deceived by the calm eye of the hurricane. It may take an hour or more to pass, but then hurricane force winds will resume.

The building and darkening cumulonimbus clouds that herald a gathering thunderstorm are a signal to the weather-wary of danger. The storm may bring only needed rain and pleasant cooling. But thunderstorms also carry the twin sudden-death threats of lightning and flash floods.

I have already emphasized that lightning is the underrated killer. Yet there is a pattern, and awareness of where lightning is most likely to strike can save your life. Five words can summarize what most to avoid during a thunderstorm: water, trees, metal, electricity, elevations.

Nearly 40 percent of lightning deaths now occur during water activities. Get away from swimming pools, rivers, lakes, or the surf during a thunderstorm. Don't get caught in a small boat. The safest place to be is indoors or inside an automobile. Don't take shelter under an isolated tree. In fact, stay twice as far from an isolated tree as the tree is high. Stay away from open doors and windows, fireplaces, radiators, stoves, metal pipes, sinks, and plug-in electrical appliances. Don't use plug-in electrical equipment such as hair dryers, electric razors, or electric toothbrushes during the storm. Try not to use the telephone or CB radio during the storm. Lightning often comes down through antennas, telephone lines, and electric power lines.

Don't work on fences, pipelines, or structural steel fabrication. Don't use metal objects such as fishing rods and golf clubs. Golfers using metal-cleated shoes are epecially at risk. Do not drive a tractor, especially if it is pulling metal equipment in touch with the ground. Avoid wire fences, metal clothes lines, exposed sheds, and any electrically conductive elevated objects.

Get away from high ground. Avoid hill tops and other high places. Don't stand where you project above the immediate surroundings. Your best bet for shelter out of doors is a canyon, valley, or cave. In a forest, seek a thick, low-lying grove of small trees.

If you are in an exposed situation with a group, say mountain climbing on a high ridge, spread out so that a strike cannot affect more than one person.

If you are in an exposed area and you feel an electrical charge building up—the surest sign is your hair standing on end—lightning may be about to strike. Drop to your knees and bend forward with your hands on your knees. This minimizes the chance of lightning using your body as a conductor. In the past, most safety guidelines recommended dropping flat to the ground in this situation. The World Meteorological Organization's International Commission on Atmospheric Electricity disapproves. It recommends kneeling instead to minimize contact with the ground while still maintaining a low profile. It also recommends against lying in a ditch or hollow where surface water or saturated soil is likely to serve as a conductor.

If lightning does strike a person, attempts should quickly be begun to resuscitate him. Although he may have suffered severe electrical shock and be burned, he carries no electrical charge and can be safely handled. Prompt mouth-to-mouth resuscitation, cardiac massage, and prolonged artificial respiration can often revive a lightning-struck person who appears to be dead.

The same thunderstorm that brings the lash of lightning also harbors the threat of a flash flood. Flash floods now rank as the major killers and destroyers among weather-related disasters in the United States. Agnes, Rapid City, Big Thompson, Kansas City, Johnstown, Buffalo Creek—these are just a few of the hundreds of names associated with major flash flood disasters in the 1970s. The toll is going to continue rising as we occupy flood-prone areas for settlement and recreation.

As with all "natural" disasters, the best preventative is a respect for nature, a realistic assessment of the risk, a degree of humility about the ability of man's works to supplant the inevitable course of natural events.

Long-range organized action is again a necessity. You may not like regulation, but you should support enlightened ordinances and legislation governing the use of areas subject to flash flooding. Support efforts to improve the ability to monitor and detect flash floods. Support community public awareness efforts and warning programs. Place emphasis on encouraging prompt individual response to flash flood threats. Too often warnings to take high ground are ignored until it is too late.

Be aware of the flash flood threat. When heavy thunderstorms come, consider the possibility of flash floods. Any locally intense rain can cause flash flooding. Do not assume that the rainfall where you are is typical of areas at higher elevations. They may have had far greater amounts of rain. Stay closely tuned to weather advisories for flash flood watches or warnings. A "watch" warns of the possibility of flash flooding in a specified area. A "warning" is an announcement that flash flooding is occurring or is imminent. But realize the information on which they are based may not be completely up to date. (The first official flash flood warning bulletin for the Big Thompson flood was issued at 11 P.M., after most of the death and destruction had already occurred.) Be aware of the flood history of your area (before the 1977 Johnstown, Pennsylvania, flood, many residents incredibly were convinced the area was "flood free," despite two previous disastrous floods there). When the warning to evacuate is given, obey it. Don't delay. Don't assume that just because previous floods have not reached the level of your home or location, this one won't. Such complacency too often brings death. If you are in a mountain canyon in imminent danger of flash flooding, don't try to drive down the canyon to safety. As the signs now posted in Colorado's Big Thompson and Poudre canyons warn, climb the canyon's sides to safety.

Do not try to drive your car through water of unknown depth. If your car stalls in water over a roadway, abandon it immediately. Take to high ground. Don't try to move it. Many deaths occur when cars are washed away by rapidly rising water. Do not attempt to cross a flowing stream on foot if water is above your knees.

Be especially cautious at night. Many flash floods occur at night, especially in the eastern two-thirds of the nation, and the danger they pose is harder to see and to communicate.

Flash floods can strike amazingly fast, but proper advance planning and prompt immediate action can make them less of a killer. Don't let your life be washed away in a few moments of foolishness. Respect the danger of flash floods.

Fierce winter storms bring their share of hardship and death too. Winter-wary residents of the snowbelt states know that preparations are necessary at the beginning of each winter. Keep flashlights, battery-powered radios, and fresh batteries on hand. Buy extra stocks of nonperishable foods. Arrange for emergency cooking capabilities (camping stove and fuel). Don't allow heating fuel to get too low. Have the car winterized and keep it fueled. Get the snow tires on. Keep chains handy. Have booster cables.

When the storm hits, stay inside as much as possible. Don't overexert yourself. Don't kill yourself trying to shovel too much snow. Heart attacks are common. In fact, as many people die of heart attacks while shoveling snow as are killed by tornadoes.

When you do go out, dress warmly, with layers of loose-fitting, light-weight clothing. Wear water-repellent, wind-resistant outer garments with a hood.

Travel during winter storms can be hazardous, but proper planning can ease the danger. Keep a sack of sand in the trunk. The extra weight over the rear axles will aid traction, and the sand can be spread over areas of slick ice in front of the wheels. Keep a winter storm kit in the car. It should include blankets, sleeping bags, extra clothing, nonperishable food, shovel, knife, first-aid kit, compass and road maps, flashlights, tow chains, booster cables, tire chains, and windshield scrapers. A CB radio can be useful.

Always check the latest weather information before starting, and stay alert for weather advisories. Travel in convoys if possible. Travel with at least one other person in your car. Plan main and alternate routes in advance, and inform others of those plans. Keep the gasoline tank at least half full.

If your car becomes stranded in a blizzard, do not attempt to walk out. Wait until the storm subsides. It is too easy to become disoriented while walking in a blizzard, and becoming lost while exposed invites death. Stay in your car. Tie a brightly colored cloth to the radio aerial. Be aware of the dangers of carbon monoxide poisoning and oxygen deprivation. Keep fresh air ventilating. Run the motor and heater sparingly, and only with a window on the downwind side open. Do not stay in one position too long. Exercise by clapping your hands and moving your legs vigorously. Keep a dome light on at night to make the car visible to work or rescue crews, and don't let everyone fall asleep at once. If you follow these procedures, your chances of survival are excellent. Remember the experience of the Cleveland trucker in the January, 1978, blizzard who stayed buried in his truck cab for six days and was alive and well when rescued.

As with the other natural hazards, earthquakes can be made less potentially disastrous by early attention to preparations. Emergency supplies should be on hand, especially flashlights, portable radios, canned food, and first-aid kits. Know where and how to turn off your gas, water, and electricity. Check your house and garage for heavy loose objects that may fall and hurt someone during shaking. Heavy appliances should be anchored and bookshelves and cupboards securely fastened to the walls. Have a plan for reuniting your family if they are in different places during an earthquake. Make sure that your school and office has made preparations for earthquakes. Learn about your community's emergency disaster plans.

When an earthquake hits, stay as calm as possible. Realize that the shaking is likely to last no more than a few minutes, usually far less. If indoors, stay there; if outdoors, move away from buildings and power lines. Don't rush into or out of a building; many injuries and deaths occur from objects falling on entryways.

If indoors, stand in a doorway or against an interior wall. Or try to get under a heavy table or desk. Stay away from windows and exterior walls. Do not use matches, candles, or other open flames. If you smell gas after the earthquake, shut off the valve, open windows, and leave. If you are in a moving car, stop and stay inside.

Listen to radio reports and do what is advised. Don't go sightseeing.

But the main hope for reducing earthquake tolls is in long-range planning and coordination at the community and state levels years in advance. Consider the factors that most contribute to large-scale earthquake damage and deaths: Development in the area of an active seismic zone. Overpopulation. Inadequate building codes. Poor workmanship of buildings and houses. Substandard building materials. Construction of buildings on loose soil. Breakage of water lines for fire protection. Fires crossing between closely spaced buildings. Lack of emergency planning and education.

Clearly the mitigation of earthquake hazards is a large, complex task. It is one that deserves broad citizen support and participation. Tough land-use regulations and building code requirements pose difficult economic and political problems. Citizens need to become well-informed on the types of actions that can be and are being done in their community and state, and lend all the support they can to the officials and agencies attempting to carry them out. The same can be said for efforts to reduce the risks of all other types of natural hazards.

The fury of severe storms and the primeval wrenching of the earthquake will always be with us. The disaster that all too often follows need not be.

CHAPTER 13

Our Increasing Vulnerability to Disaster

The date: a few years from now, during hurricane season. The place: just south of Miami, Florida.

A strong, slow-moving, moisture-laden hurricane moves northwest toward the coast. With a central pressure of 925 millibars, it is as intense as such previous memorable hurricanes as Donna (1960), Carla (1961), and Betsy (1965). But it is nowhere near as powerful as the devastating Florida Keys hurricane of 1935, in which 730 people drowned despite relatively low population densities in the low-lying areas affected.

The National Hurricane Center in Coral Gables issues a warning for residents of Key Biscayne, Virginia Key, and south Miami to evacuate. Key Biscayne, a wealthy residential area, and Virginia Key, an oceanographic research center, are about five miles off the coast of south Miami. Both are quite low, elevations ranging from two or three feet to 10 feet, with an average of five feet. The two islands are connected to the mainland by a two-mile-long bridge, the Rickenbacker Causeway, across Biscayne Bay. It is bisected by a drawbridge.

Despite the warning, events conspire to prevent evacuation of the entire population. A large proportion of the residents have never witnessed a major hurricane. They fail to understand the full range of its threats. Fewer than 50 percent of them heed the evacuation order.

Those who attempt to leave encounter a succession of obstacles. A hurricane warning is usually made at least 12 hours before the storm's predicted landfall. But six hours before landfall, the storm surge causes tides to begin rising. Low points on roadways are flooded, and the evacuation is halted. Even before the peak of the storm surge, traffic had been seriously snarled by a combination of congestion, the weather, automobile accidents, and flat tires. Frequent raising of the drawbridge to allow vessels to reach shelter in the Miami River and other points northward further slowed the evacuation. Residents of Key Biscayne and Virginia Key who did not promptly heed the evacuation warning are trapped.

Alternatives are minimal. Small craft can be used to take people to the mainland, but only a handful can be transported at a time and the danger to them mounts as the hurricane approaches. Evacuation by air is not possible due to lack of an airport and the danger of flying helicopters in the high winds. "Vertical evacuation" into the many newly built high-rise condominiums is theoretically possible. But space is limited and many owners resist allowing strangers access to their own private property.

On the mainland, the situation is not much better. The early storm surge catches many residents still preparing to evacuate. The heavy rainfall, high winds and poor visibility make it worse.

The hurricane heads toward landfall at Saga Bay, a newly developed residential area south of Miami. Here, coastal development has greatly increased the potential for disaster. The influx of new housing and residents was stimulated by construction of the West Dade Expressway, connected to Saga Bay by Old Cutler Road. Most elevations range from sea level to five feet. The developers tore out the unsightly and ill-smelling mangroves along the coast which had provided one of the few effective barriers to storm surge. Without them, only a clean sweep of beach greets the storm surge before it washes up on the houses.

Saga Bay residents attempt to evacuate to the expressway and points north by way of Old Cutler Road. But the rains have swollen Black Creek beyond its banks, cutting off the shortest route. Those who make it to the north encounter massive congestion from the automobiles fleeing from Key Biscayne, Virginia Key, and Coral Gables. The intersections of major routes create bumper-to-bumper traffic.

No matter what direction the residents go, the roadway can't handle the traffic. The weather deteriorates further. Visibility in the rain and storm-brought darkness is minimal. Time runs out. They are trapped in their automobiles when the hurricane hits.

Those who have made it to the West Dade Expressway are still not safe. The Palmetto and the North-South (Interstate 95) expressways have major tie-ups as do all northbound streets. Traffic is four times heavier than at rush hour.

The traffic jams in Miami are made even worse by the fact that, except for the expressways, all major north-south arteries in Miami cross the Miami River and have drawbridges. Boats leaving marinas and proceeding up the river in flotillas toward safety require periodic raising of the drawbridges. Traffic becomes more clogged.

More than 10,000 small craft are registered in Biscayne Bay, but no more than 1,000 of them can be accommodated up the Miami River. Turned away, their owners seek shelter elsewhere and many are caught in open water when the hurricane hits.

Much of the flooding hampering evacuation is caused by the network of canals of the South Florida Water Control Conservation Project. The canals, built by the Corps of Engineers to prevent flooding of agricultural land in South-central Florida, flow to the sea through residential communities in Dade and Broward counties. Their construction created high-priced waterfront home-sites. But now the storm surge blocks their flow to the sea, and the heavy rainfall causes them to overflow, blocking streets and causing heavy damage.

The hurricane moves ashore at 15 miles per hour, and its area of maximum winds is 30 miles across. Along its right side, the storm surge is 10 to 15 feet high, and the five-to-ten-foot elevations of Saga Bay, Key Biscayne, Virginia Key, and the coastal mainland are washed over.

The death toll of unfortunate Floridians caught in their homes, cars, and boats is high. Every day more bodies are found, and the count reaches the high hundreds and climbs toward 1,000. The South Florida hurricane long dreaded by those concerned about disaster has hit, and some of the worst fears have been realized. Civilization's vulnerability has again been tragically demonstrated. Not for many years will coastal residents of the United States again take the hurricane threat for granted.

This future disaster scenario is one of several devised several years back by geographer and disaster specialist Gilbert F. White of the Institute of Behavioral Science at the University of Colorado and sociologist J. Eugene Haas, in an assessment of research on natural hazards for the National Science Foundation. This future disaster, like the others they propose, may not be realized this century or it may happen next year. But it contains many elements that illustrate their theme that the nation, despite new technological aids for prediction and warning, is becoming more, not less, vulnerable to catastrophe.

Here are revealed the problems caused by spread of population to disaster-vulnerable areas: the complacency of many new residents not personally familiar with the hurricane threat, the danger caused by concentration of population in areas served by only a few evacuation routes, and the hazards exacerbated by certain kinds of coastal development and well-meant engineering works.

"The United States," White and Haas concluded in their detailed review, "is becoming more vulnerable to catastrophes caused by natural events."

Not only the United States but also most other nations are finding themselves increasingly susceptible to cataclysm. There do appear to be important differences, however, among nations of varying stages of development. Most of the increased risk is due to human presence and actions.

The best and most up-to-date analysis of the world's perils from extreme natural events has recently been completed by three prominent geographers—Ian Burton of the University of Toronto, Robert W. Kates of Clark University in Massachusetts, and Gilbert White—known for their research into the risks from natural dangers. Their study, *The Environment as Hazard* (Oxford University Press, 1978), suggests that the human race may actually be cultivating greater damages and building the groundwork for larger catastrophes in its very attempts to cope with the risk of natural calamities from air, water, and land.

The global toll from extreme events of nature is rising, even in a time of unparalleled human effort to control nature. Damage to property in natural disasters is rising in most parts of the world, and loss of life is continuing or increasing in most poorer regions.

The number of major internationally reported cataclysms has remained relatively constant, at about 30 per year. It may even be slightly declining. But the geographical area struck by them is broadening, and the death tolls have climbed significantly. (Admittedly, the death rates are distorted by the occurrence in the 1970s of the two largest disasters of the century, the Tangshan earthquake of 1976 and the Bangladesh cyclone of 1970.)

Floods are by far the most frequent and do the most damage. Tropical cyclones cause the most deaths.

The cost of natural hazards has now reached $40 billion a year worldwide. About $25 billion is in damage and the rest in the costs of preventing and mitigating disasters. About $10 billion to $15 billion of the $25 billion in damage comes in the form of catastrophic losses.

The human toll of death in disasters is about a quarter of a million persons a year. About half of those deaths occur in major calamities.

The vast majority of the deaths (95 percent), it turns out, occur among the two-thirds of the world's people who live in developing countries. But as might be expected, the economic loss is highest in developed nations. Three-fourths of the absolute global economic loss occurs in the wealthy countries. Yet in personal terms, the people in poorer countries lose a far greater proportion of their wealth; the ratio of loss to income is much higher in the developing countries.

In summary, Burton, Kates, and White find that the global toll of natural disaster rises at least as fast as the increase of population and material wealth, and probably faster. Catastrophies in developing countries may be less frequent but are more damaging and more costly in human lives and relative wealth. In industrialized nations, they are becoming increasingly costly in absolute wealth. In human lives, the equivalent of the population of a city the size of Ann Arbor, Michigan, Charleston, West Virginia, or Montgomery, Alabama, is wiped out each year.

At least three major forces are responsible for this rise in damage. All, you will see, are quite powerful trends in themselves. They are not easily retarded. They are a result of natural and understandable, perhaps even inevitable, social patterns and actions, in much the same way that hurricanes, earthquakes, floods, and tornadoes are a natural and inevitable result of certain geophysical patterns and conditions. They are more the "cause" of the rising toll of natural cataclysms than the extreme natural events we often mistakenly say cause them.

The first is the spread of people. In the first three-quarters of the twentieth century, the population of the earth increased by 2.25 billion—well over a 100-percent increase. Even with the evidence reported by the U.S. Census Bureau in late 1978 that the growth *rate* of world population is finally tapering off, world population is of course still increasing, by about 200,000 people a day. And it is expected to continue increasing well into the twenty-first century. There are simply more people to be caught up in disasters than ever before. Along with the rise in world population has come a rise in material wealth. The statistics are not very good, but one study estimated that the net worth of private households in the world, correcting for changes in monetary value, tripled in 70 years. The average annual increase in wealth amounts to about 3 percent. So there is more property to be damaged or destroyed.

Just as important as the absolute increase in population and property has been their changing distribution. In areas such as the United States, the population has shifted from country and city to the suburbs and exurbs (areas out beyond the suburbs). The outward movement of suburban population stimulated by urban pressures, the mobility of the automobile, and the quest for second homes has brought people into new and unfamiliar surroundings where they are totally unaware of potential risks and how to deal with them. More and more people are moving into floodplains, seismic-risk zones, and coastal areas exposed to hurricane winds, storm surges, and coastal erosion.

Americans inexperienced with tropical storms have moved in large numbers to hurricane-prone coastal areas of the Atlantic and Gulf states. Austrian city dwellers are building country homes in the paths of past avalanches, places mountain people know to avoid. Floodplains have been occupied and used for agriculture since the beginnings of civilization, but people everywhere, including the United States, are now spreading onto them out of a false sense of security created by technological works such as dams and levees. California, where many homes, schools, and businesses are built on earthquake faults and on hillsides subject to landslides, is a prominent example of how the spread of people into areas that are desirable for many other reasons increases the risk of land disaster.

A second influence on the rising toll of damages is the increased potential for catastrophe. A catastrophe is an extreme disaster, one that causes a major dislocation of the orderly processes and social and economic life and requires a long time for recovery. In many countries, the loss of life from natural hazards is declining overall but the loss of life in catastrophes is rising. What it means is that in most years the loss of life from, for example, tornadoes and floods is less than it used to be, but in the exceptional years it is greater. The superoutbreak of killer tornadoes in 1974, during a long-term period of decline in tornado death tolls, is one example of that. The Tangshan earthquake and Bangladesh cyclone are others. Specialists like Burton and colleagues think this trend toward more catastrophes will continue. They give many reasons: the spread of cities, pressures for living space, overconfidence in the ability of technology to control nature, and human and organizational shortcomings in preparing for severe natural phenomena.

The third contribution to rising disaster damages is the expanding hazard in developing countries. As countries develop they seem to make the same mistakes the more developed countries made earlier. In Kingston, Jamaica, new buildings are being constructed on alluvial and unconsolidated soils just as was done earlier in the San Francisco Bay area. In the island nation of Sri Lanka, much of the residential and industrial construction in Colombo in recent years has been on the floodplain of the Kalani River. If the developing countries follow in the Western mold—and all indications are that they will—the disaster potential will continue to increase. Studies have shown that the more a society depends on physical things, the more social disruption results from disaster. Disaster potential rises with economic development; the more successful the developmental process is in other respects, the more likely the losses from natural hazards will rise.

Sometimes the aid industrialized nations give developing countries makes their potential for disaster worse. Many of the Bangladeshans killed in the 1970 cyclone had been encouraged to move into storm-susceptible delta lowlands by the construction of partial protective works financed by the Netherlands and the United States. Sri Lankans mistakenly placed too much reliance on dikes that were built from knowledge gained in England.

You might think that greater technological sophistication acquired as nations develop would ease the threat of disaster. It doesn't necessarily work that way. In fact, Burton and his co-workers say there is little sign that modernization can relieve traditional societies of their high death toll—not in the short run at least. The growth of cities, for example, is alone enough to cause larger losses from floods. But the installation of better communications and roads in rural areas is not enough to bring the degree of safety up to levels enjoyed by industrialized nations. The Bangladesh cyclone was accurately predicted by satellites but that wasn't much help to the isolated delta island farmer with no access to that information, especially when no evacuation effort was mobilized.

Bangladesh, in fact, is an example of a country where the

disaster potential has gotten even worse, not better. Since the 1970 storm, the deadliest cyclone of the century, intense economic pressures are continuing to drive farmers and their families to settle low-lying lands, the government has constructed more protective works that offer a (probably false) sense of security, and relief and rehabilitation efforts have encouraged reoccupation of the same storm-prone lands. The combination of these factors, Burton and his colleagues warn, "is probably setting the stage for enormous destruction and loss of life in future severe storms unless much heavier attention is given to land-use patterns, building design, and warning systems."

The trends in developing countries are not encouraging. "Changes already underway in developing countries," Burton, Kates, and White say, "seem likely, if permitted to continue, to bring increase in economic loss from natural hazards in the modern sectors of the economy, while failing to offset high loss of life in the more traditional sectors." They believe that unless governmental policies curb uneconomic exposure to extreme events (and such policies are unlikely unless the costs are low), year-to-year losses will rise and the disruption from occasional disasters will be greater still.

The potential for catastrophes that interact with each other, one making the impact of the other even worse, is also on the rise. An example offered in the Burton study is an acute drought affecting the Indian subcontinent in conjunction with heavy flooding in China and an earthquake in Japan. Each might worsen the consequences of the other by making demands on world supplies of food and goods and curtailing production.

In industrialized countries such as the United States, several other trends are at work to increase disaster tolls. When material wealth is high, the ability to absorb small losses is greater. People are less likely to suffer much from small losses, so they are prone to put off actions that might avert major disasters, until, perhaps, it is too late. They tend to reach a threshold of awareness about the hazard potential later than do people of less wealth. (On the other hand, people in societies of less wealth may be slightly more aware of the hazard potential but that doesn't necessarily seem to stimulate them to take action to reduce the risk.) This process has an accumulating effect. A large U.S. industry, for instance, can afford to absorb occasional small flood losses to gain advantages of locating on a waterway that might be prone to flood. The industry's location draws new residential construction and small businesses to the floodplain, their owners often unaware of the hazard. The potential for disaster rises.

The growth of mobile homes as an alternative—often the only one many people can afford—to the high cost of new housing in the United States also is an element in the increased risk of natural hazards. Roughly a third of all new home starts are mobile homes, and as I've mentioned earlier they are notoriously susceptible to damage in high winds that afflict at times nearly every area of the nation. The danger is very real. In 1973, for instance, half of all wind-caused deaths in the United States occurred in mobile homes. Mobile home communities are also often located in isolated areas not subject to the usual municipal building zone codes (often these areas are in floodplains as well), and frequently ordinances that do apply are not as stringent as they are for permanent residential areas. With the average cost of a new home in the United States at $55,000 (in 1978) and the high cost of mortgage money, the trend toward mobile homes and the greater potential for disaster they bring will undoubtedly continue.

White and Haas's 1975 study found that for virtually all the natural hazards they studied, the trend for damages was upward. This was true for avalanche, coastal erosion, earthquake, flood, frost, hail, hurricane, landslide, tornado, urban snow, and windstorm. Only for lightning and drought was there no evidence for increasing damage.

Casualties were another matter (their study pertained only to the United States). Over the past two or three decades, the trend in loss of life is upward for earthquake, windstorm, and avalanche. For most other hazards the trend in casualties is downward or stable. The most pronounced of these increasing-damage, decreasing-deaths situations are for tornadoes and hurricanes. This again shows that while major-storm warnings can save lives in an industrialized country having an efficient weather service and good communications, the people's material wealth lies increasingly at risk.

In contrast to the downward trend in deaths, the potential for catastrophe in the United States, White and Haas found, is going up. Here they define catastrophe as a situation in which damages to property, human health, and social structure or processes are so severe that recovery and rehabilitation are long and trying procedures. Six natural hazards have high catastrophe potential: earthquake, flood, hurricane, tornado, tsunami, and volcano. But for all 15 of the hazards they studied except drought, the evidence is that the potential for catastrophe is increasing.

This, they say, applies even to lightning, a hazard usually not associated with catastrophe. Its catastrophe potential, although still low, is rising as airborne electronic systems, interlinked computer systems on which our society increasingly depends, and surface electrical power transmission systems are becoming more vulnerable. The looting and social disruption in the midst of the lightning-triggered New York City blackout of 1977 tragically illustrate that point.

An aspect of natural hazards often neglected in the attention given to deaths and property damage is the cost of adjustments. This is the cost of measures taken by individuals and public agencies to attempt to reduce the hazards. Included are the cost of all direct protection works such as those for erosion- and flood-control, hurricane, landslide, and tsunami. Also included are such things as the extra 5 percent often estimated to be the cost of making buildings resistant to earthquake, floods, or high winds. The installation of lightning rods and mobile-home tie-downs are others.

White and Haas found that in no instance is the annual cost of such adjustments showing signs of decreasing. Costs of adjustments to coastal erosion, landslide, and tornado are increasing at a rapid rate. Adjustments for earthquake, flood, and hurricane are also rising.

A cost not included is the environmental damage caused by engineering works such as dams, levees, drainage systems, and stream channelization meant, at least in part, to lessen the hazard of disasters. Comparison of all the costs versus benefits of these practices is a tricky business, and few such studies have been done.

But what is disturbing is evidence that these procedures often make the disaster potential worse in the long run. As White and Haas say: ". . . A substantial proportion [of the adjustment costs] appear to contribute to the enlargement of catastrophe potential as a result of strengthened reliance upon technological measures."

The classic case of this technological backfire has been with flood control. The Federal Flood Control Act of 1936 initiated a long-term program of federally funded flood-control works such as dams, channel improvements, and levees. There was great optimism that all these well-meant engineering works would reduce the national hazard from flood. But studies by White and other geographers, published in 1958, showed that the net effect of the first two decades of all these unprecedented massive protection efforts, which cost more than $5 billion, was to increase the total national losses from floods. Average annual flood losses rose, and the proportion of losses caused by catastrophic floods increased dramatically.

The construction of large protective works such as dams and levees, it turns out, encourages more and more people to move into the floodplain downstream, thus in the long term compounding the risk. Upstream reservoirs, for instance, stimulated the invasion of a Tennessee Valley floodplain around Chattanooga. Numerous such studies have shown that total reliance on such protection schemes builds a greater potential for catastrophe by inducing a buildup of vulnerable property and causing the people to have a false sense of security and protection. (The same can be said for short-sighted insurance programs that reimburse people for losses without stipulating enlightened measures of hazard mitigation.) A recent example was the Johnstown, Pennsylvania, flash flood of 1977. Many residents thought the dams and levees constructed since Johnstown's earlier flood disasters would protect them from another.

White has long been opposed to what he calls the technological "quick fix" against flood and other natural hazards. An unrealistic dependence upon narrow technological solutions without addressing the human and social considerations that lead people to occupy hazardous areas is, he and his colleagues have felt, counterproductive.

Nowhere have they stated it more strongly than in summarizing their criticisms of most government-supported research on natural hazards:

Research today concentrates largely on technologically oriented solutions to problems of natural hazards, instead of focusing equally on the social, economic and political factors which lead to nonadoption of technological findings, or which indicate that proposed steps would not work or would only tend to perpetuate and increase the problem. In short, the all-important social, economic and political "people" factors involved in hazards reduction have been largely ignored. . . .

It is not a question of more technology or less technology but of technology in balance. (White and Haas, 1975)

The 1978 Burton, Kates, and White study put it bluntly too: "Reliance on a technological approach to hazard control has undoubtedly increased loss in many instances."

White and his colleagues are social scientists, and it's understandable that they feel sociological concerns should be given greater attention. They have, however, devoted much of their careers to better understanding of the human role in natural disasters and thus have a valuable perspective to offer. Some engineers have accused them of a certain amount of bias (one points out that with earthquakes technological solutions are given high marks), but mainly what they are calling for is a greater degree of balance between technological solutions and social and economic considerations. Certainly the two need to go hand in hand.

With floods, the federal government, after three decades of heavy reliance on engineering works, began shifting emphasis in 1966 to a broader mix of adjustments. Now there is a somewhat more integrated approach. There is more emphasis on proving information on flood hazards, curbing federal construction on floodplains, expanding technical advice on floodproofing, improving the national flood-warning service, and research on predicting the kinds of storms that lead to flash floods.

The National Flood Insurance Program now makes flood insurance available to property owners under the condition that their communities adopt floodplain management actions to reduce loss of lives and property. At a minimum the community must review building permits to assure that the sites are reasonably free from flooding, require proper anchoring of structures, require construction materials and practices and techniques that minimize flood damage, and provide adequate drainage for new subdivisions. Relief payments for people and agencies in known hazard areas are contingent upon their having signed up for such insurance and that federal mortgage insurance for houses in the floodplain is taken on insured property. The goal is to provide relief to those afflicted by floods without encouraging unwise new development on floodplains. Translating all this into policy at the local level has been slow and difficult, however, and any gains in reducing flood vulnerability are, at best, slow to become apparent.

The death and damage from flash floods in the 1970s in the United States has hardly been encouraging. Death tolls in the last decade are double those in the previous one, and property damage is running at about a billion dollars a year. As National Weather Service Director George Cressman noted in a call for action in 1978, people are living, working, and camping in floodplains to an extent never seen before.

In its 1978 statement of concern about flash floods, the American Meteorological Society noted that the list of danger spots is growing, that 15,000 communities and recreational areas have been identified as flash flood-prone, and that 85 percent of all Presidential declarations of major disasters are now associated with floods and flash floods.

The U.S. Water Resources Council predicts that unless floodplain management is improved, damage from floods and flash floods in the United States will reach $3.5 billion annually by the year 2000.

So the flood problem in the United States, far from being eased, has dramatically worsened in the 1970s with the spread of urban development and increased mobility of the population, and the forecast is for the degree of hazard to become worse rather than better.

Internationally, the situation is similar. Many countries, large and small, have worsening flood problems. The case of Sri Lanka illustrates that small developing nations often have their flood dangers exacerbated by population invasion and engineering works the same as large industrial giants such as the United States. D. Hewapathirane studied the situation there for his 1977 Ph.D. thesis in geography at the University of Colorado. He found that not only rural people (two-thirds of the island's 13 million people make their living from agriculture) but also city dwellers have faced increased flood risk despite (or because of) heavy government outlays for levees, channel improvements, and dams.

The population has grown rapidly. The trend of expansion has been from the uplands down into the floodplains. Unoccupied land there was available, but at the price of recurrent inundation. This invasion of the floodplain was stimulated not only by population pressures but also by the building of small levees by the British. The temporary protection these levees offered attracted still more people. But when the levees break, the losses are great. The levees furthermore tend to keep water that has flooded fields from draining back into the rivers, thus prolonging flood episodes. All in all, the larger engineering works have given many fields and homes additional protection while causing others to be exposed to longer periods of standing water and more frequent and catastrophic overflow.

"There is growing recognition in Sri Lanka," says the Burton-Kates-White study, "that primary reliance upon engineering works to cope with flood losses is leading to larger losses while protecting selected areas." But the emphasis is still on engineering adjustment, in contrast to the earlier shunning of floodplain, and there seems little short-term hope of improvement.

Rumania, historically subjected to great floods, has been undertaking a comprehensive series of preventative actions since the 1970 floods that affected large areas of the country and caused more than half a billion dollars in damage. Many non-structural measures were instigated, including floodplain regulations, new policies on land and water use, and educational programs. Engineering works are also planned, but they are in conjunction with the other actions designed to lessen the tendency for people to make themselves more vulnerable to floods.

Elsewhere in Europe the outlook is not so good. Europe's largest system of river levees and dikes is in Hungary, but a 1970 flood there along the Danube and a tributary in which 100,000 people had to be evacuated suggests that still worse floods are to come and that the levees will be overtopped. Upstream land-use changes, mainly in neighboring countries, and the tendency for river levels to rise as a result of flood-protection works have made the problem worse. A Great Danube Flood is a possible future catastrophe.

The potential for a hurricane disaster of major proportions has long been building in the United States. Each year storm and disaster specialists become more worried about the consequences of a strong hurricane striking U.S. shores. The continuing rapid buildup along the extensive length of coastline vulnerable to hurricanes, much of it by persons never exposed to the full might of these storms, is the main culprit. Coastal areas are growing more than three times as fast as the rest of the United States. Of the 36 million people now living along the Atlantic and Gulf coasts, approximately 28 million are newcomers in the past two decades. They haven't had the kind of experience with hurricanes that prompts strong local action.

Neil L. Frank, Director of the National Hurricane Center in

Miami, has long been trying to inform and educate people about the increasing risk. In 1974, he wrote an article, "Hard Facts about Hurricanes," attempting to point out the rising danger brought about by the acceleration in coastal development. He referred to "the spectre that haunts every hurricane forecaster," a major hurricane descending upon a densely settled coastal area, evacuation routes inadequate, the population consisting almost entirely of people unfamiliar with the devastating potential of the storm.

Since then the hurricane hazard has only worsened. "It's gotten worse because we've had four or five more years of great development," says Frank. "We are continuing to occupy the coastline in ever greater numbers, and as long as that trend continues, we're going to make the problem worse."

There are many serious trouble spots. "We've known for years that New Orleans is a difficult area. Much of the land is below sea level, and we've got the lake to the north, the Gulf to the south, and the river to the east."

Inability to evacuate exposed residents in time is an awesome worry. "There is Tampa Bay with its offshore islands, the Florida Keys with 60,000 people in residence and only a two-lane causeway out, the New Jersey coast offshore barrier islands, new developments on the North Carolina and Georgia coasts, Hilton Head Island off South Carolina. It's not clear people will be able to get out of these areas."

Frank says a recent definitive evacuation study for the Fort Meyers, Florida, area has shown that it will take 20 hours to get people off nearby populated islands such as Sanibel Island. If one island alone were evacuating, the time might be 10 hours, but merging of evacuation traffic from all the islands increases the time to 20 hours. "And remember, we [hurricane forecasters] have never said we can give more than 12 hours warning of a hurricane striking a particular area. What's going to happen when it takes longer than that to evacuate?" It's not known how many other places are in the same situation. "How many little Sanibel islands tucked along the coastline are we not aware of?" Frank asks.

Offshore islands are hardly the only problem. The southern coast of New Jersey has only one road out, and traffic experts estimate that it can handle about 4,500 cars per hour. Cape May County, at the southern tip of New Jersey, has some 60,000 permanent residents but on a normal summer weekday tourists swell the population to 10 times that number and on a summer weekend the figure may reach one million.

In the Miami area, Frank says, the situation is about as bad as the scenario at the beginning of this chapter indicates. The Saga Bay area hasn't been developed at the rate that had been expected, but evacuation of Key Biscayne, and the problems of boats, drawbridges, and auto traffic are great.

Ironically, the absence of major hurricanes in recent decades along the Atlantic Coast has made the future disaster potential far worse. For example, Broward County north of Miami, one of the fastest growing areas in the United States, has not had a direct hit from a hurricane since 1947. It was brushed by Hurricane Betsy in 1965, but experience with fringe conditions is often worse than nothing because it lulls those who passed through them into a false sense of security, thinking a hurricane isn't so bad after all. It's hard for them to realize that the conditions in the central portion are much worse than those they encountered on the edges. The result of it all is that, in Frank's words, "nearly 90 percent of Broward County's million residents just don't know what a strong hurricane was all about. The weak ones and the fringe experiences have lulled many into a state of apathy." The same can be said for many other coastal areas, among them heavily populated regions such as Long Island, New York. On Florida's west coast, the last direct hit in cities such as Tampa Bay, Clearwater, and Saint Petersburg was in 1921.

"The longer you go away from the last [disastrous] event," Frank notes, "the more complacent people get."

Areas along the West Gulf Coast, in contrast to the Atlantic and Florida Gulf coasts, have had considerable experience in the past two decades with powerful hurricanes. They've gained lessons from Celia in 1970, Camille in 1969, Beulah in 1967, Betsy in 1965, Hilda in 1964, and Carla in 1961 (a period during which not one severe hurricane struck the East Coast of the United States).

Nevertheless, coastal development has been rapid and the disaster potential is great. In the Galveston-Houston area, for instance, there has been enormous population growth (Houston is now the nation's fifth largest city), continuing oil development, and erection of the NASA space complex. The 17-foot storm wall built after the Galveston Island hurricane catastrophe in 1900 provides some protection, but even that, Frank says, could be topped by the storm surge of a strong hurricane.

But what about satellites? Haven't they at least eased the threat of surprise from a hurricane? To only a certain degree, says Frank, who quickly adds that he's a great believer in the value of satellites for identifying storms. But he points out that with a hurricane, satellites are an observing tool, not a forecasting tool, and they "don't tell you where it's going to go." It's a mistake for people to take too much comfort from the capability of satellite imagery, he says. The problem still exists of predicting where the hurricane will hit in time to get all the people evacuated. And all the evidence indicates that that is not always going to be possible.

"If the right hurricane comes along next summer at the right place," Frank says, "we could have a real disaster."

What, if anything, can be done? Coastal development has brought millions of additional people into areas of exposure to hurricanes, but there is little point in focusing merely on stemming the tide. The attraction of coastal living, especially in the warmer (and more hurricane-susceptible) latitudes, is perfectly understandable. As Frank says, it's a great life-style. Neither he nor most others who speak out about the dangers are against coastal development in itself. The need is to carry out development with more wisdom, more awareness of the risks, more humility in the face of the forces of ocean and atmosphere that inevitably will bring the seas onshore, the only uncertainty being time and place.

It's a problem of awareness and of local governmental action. Well-thought-out hurricane-preparedness plans at state, county, and local levels are essential. The folly of building on too-low coastal land has to be emphasized by education and regulation, and escape routes have to be planned and, if inadequate, built. Vertical evacuation into high-rise buildings needs to be explored. The advantages of coastal living bring also risk to life and property, and that lesson has to be learned. Complacency is the prelude to disaster. "If people go there to live," says Frank, "let's make sure they are aware of the problem and let's do something about it."

The American Meteorological Society's 1976 statement of concern about the hurricane hazard concluded: "If we do not initiate ways of informing our coastal communities of the hurricane problem, Mother Nature will impose her own education program, which is swift and severe."

After floods and tropical cyclones, earthquakes are the most prevalent type of natural hazard worldwide. The world spread of population and the artifacts of civilization into seismic zones continues to bring increased danger.

In the United States, much attention has been given to the earthquake hazard in California, but the seismic risk in the eastern half of the nation has until recently received little visibility. Here, where population densities are high, the problem is compounded by enormous scientific uncertainty over the causes of Eastern U.S. earthquakes and by crustal properties that cause eastern earthquakes to be felt over large areas. Major eastern earthquakes may be relatively infrequent (even that we can't say for sure because of the geologically short historical record), but their disaster potential may be high.

The New Madrid earthquakes of 1811–1812, which created many unusual phenomena and were felt over the eastern two-thirds of the country, fortunately happened when the five-state Mississippi Valley area most strongly affected was still relatively unpopulated. Since then, cities such as Memphis have been built on seismically unstable surfaces. Development throughout the eastern and central parts of the country has given little attention to earthquake-resistant building methods. While the nation's costliest natural disaster has been tropical storm Agnes in 1972, which caused $4 billion in damage, White and Haas estimate that the cost of a recurrence of the New Madrid earthquakes today could reach an incredible $100 billion.

Growing population and increasing urbanization have made the nation more susceptible. Well over 70 million people live in the two highest-risk seismic zones. As White and Haas point out, perhaps more than any other geophysical hazard, major earthquakes are likely to produce almost complete social disruption in modern urban areas. All the life-supporting technologies of a city both above and below ground (streets, bridges, viaducts, train tracks, subways, electrical power, telephone, teletype, fuel lines, water supply, sewer) may be shattered, and quick repair of below-ground life lines is almost impossible. Deaths and injuries may be high. Survivors will suffer physical and psychological hardship. Family and community life patterns will be altered for months by physical and economic dislocation.

Earth scientists are virtually unanimous in their feeling that a large or great earthquake somewhere in California is inevitable. The question here also is when and exactly where. The phenomenal growth of California since the last great quake in 1906 makes almost certain that no matter where it happens, death and destruction will be high. The San Fernando earthquake of 1971, magnitude 6.6, was only moderately strong, yet 65 people died and damages totaled $439 million. Several hospitals were heavily damaged and an earthen dam whose failure would have put 80,000 people in extreme danger almost gave way. Detailed studies have shown that the next major earthquake in Los Angeles could kill more than 12,000 persons. If a major dam broke, the figure could be doubled.

California's Joint Committee on Seismic Safety has estimated that under certain conditions an earthquake in San Francisco of magnitude 8.0 (about an eighth the energy released in 1906) and lasting a minute could cause property damages in the range of $30 billion. This would amount to about one-third of the total annual personal income in the state. Losses from declines in production, wages, salaries, profits, rents, and taxes would make the total economic loss catastrophic. And casualties might reach 350,000 dead and injured. Other, more modest, scenarios envision 2,000 to 10,000 dead, 40,000 injured, and $6 billion to $7 billion in damages. Either way, the prospects are not appealing.

The greatest earthquake-fire disaster of the century devastated much of Tokyo and Yokohama in 1923, with 370,000 buildings destroyed and the loss of 142,000 lives, yet many experts consider that region to be even more vulnerable today than it was then. The charcoal pots which when tumbled started the fires of 1923 have been replaced by oil and gas stoves and houses are generally better constructed, but otherwise the disaster potential has worsened in many ways.

There has been enormous flow of population from the rural areas of Japan into the city, and now Tokyo is the world's most populous city, with five times as many residents as at the time of the Great Kwanto Earthquake. The city is full of storage facilities for gasoline, oil, liquefied gases, and chemicals. High-voltage electric lines cut across residential areas. Eighty percent of the city is still crowded with wooden houses. They are so close together the potential for rapidly spreading fire is great, and many of the streets are too narrow for fire engines. Twenty-five square miles of the city are below sea level, highly vulnerable to storm surge and tsunami.

Paradoxes are plentiful, one researcher notes. A new steel mill has been built on landfill reclaimed from Tokyo Bay, where, only a few feet above sea level, it is subject to earthquake, tsunami, flood, and typhoon. Yet six anti-disaster open spaces to serve as refuge from fire are being built at enormous expense in a 10-year project in the highly vulnerable Kota area of Tokyo. They are ringed by fireproof high-rise buildings to shield the area from fire, and the buildings are surrounded by a canal system, making the whole thing reminiscent of medieval castles.

Such dramatic actions are essential because studies have estimated that a recurrence of the 1923 earthquake in Tokyo could result in as many as half a million casualties if it happened on a winter evening with high winds.

My friend and colleague John H. Douglas recently spent a year on a study fellowship in Japan, living in Tokyo. His observations of conditions and his interviews with disaster-prevention researchers confirm the great vulnerability of the metropolitan area to disaster. He was in a high-rise building in Tokyo on January 14, 1978, that began swaying from an earthquake along the Izu Peninsula, 75 miles southwest of Tokyo. As he put it: "The little group around me—and the rest of the 14.5 million people in the Tokyo-Yokohama area—breathed a sigh of relief: this wasn't 'The Big One.' " For a great—magnitude 8.0 or higher—quake in Central Japan south of Tokyo is expected by scientists in the coming years. It even already has a name—the Great Tokai Earthquake. (Controversial statistical studies also indicate the possibility of a great earthquake in Tokyo itself between 1979 and 1992.) The Izu Peninsula quake at magnitude 7.0 wasn't it, but it nevertheless started 110 landslides, swept a bus off the road, crushed houses, and buried some people alive. Twenty-five persons were killed and $20 million in damage was reported.

Two members of the Tokyo Metropolitan Government's Disaster Prevention Council later said that if the Izu quake had been centered closer to Tokyo, the city would have been decimated. A scientist said that the expected Great Tokai Earthquake would produce the same degree of shaking in Tokyo as that felt on the Izu Peninsula from the landslide-triggering Izu quake.

The Japanese have become the world leaders in earthquake engineering, and much progress has been made in designing buildings that will "give" but not collapse during the shaking. But application of this new knowledge is still in the preliminary stages. Besides, the greatest damage is likely to come from secondary effects of fire, floods, and landslides. "Fragile Blossom" is more than a political and social metaphor when applied to Japan, Douglas reports. And he quotes a scientist as saying he cannot predict all the effects of a major earthquake on Tokyo, "but I'm afraid."

The examples in this chapter are meant to emphasize the reality of the increased vulnerability of much of the world's population to disaster, and especially to the extreme form, catastrophe. Burton, Kates, and White refer to the "bewildering array of environmental threats having catastrophic potential" that are appearing "on the world scene with increasing frequency."

As the planet's population grows and spreads out into ever more vulnerable areas, as works of humans are erected in hazard-prone areas where formerly only nature presided, as the increasingly interdependent links of civilization expose us all to danger when one of the links is broken, as we grow away from a harmony with land and nature that respects the force and inevitability of extreme natural events, we place ourselves in the path of immense hazards and bring the threat of disaster down on ourselves.

CHAPTER 14
Responses to Disaster

Our views about how people react in disasters are heavily conditioned by the dramatized fiction of motion pictures, television, and radio, and by on-deadline news accounts of actual disasters in newspapers and broadcasts. Perhaps more than any real disaster, the response to the fictional landing of Martian invaders in the New Jersey countryside during Orson Welles's famous radio dramatization of H. G. Wells's *War of the Worlds* has indelibly imprinted on our minds certain images of what happens when people are suddenly confronted with a horrible event. The impression we have of the human response to that broadcast is vivid: mass confusion, panic, and flight. Disaster, so it would seem, whether natural, man-made, or brought by fictional aliens from another world, brings us to fits of irrationality, where panic supplants reason, normal codes of conduct fall apart, and disorder prevails.

What we really know about human response to disaster, however, doesn't always fit such glib portrayals. In fact, much of what behavioral and social scientists have learned about human behavior in disasters runs counter to the impressions most of us have. Not always, of course, but often enough to require that we question some of the stereotypes we may hold. Often what's lacking is an accurate sense of proportion, a need to realize that although some people may have behaved in an unusual or exotic way that gained public attention, the large majority of others may not have. A study of the events surrounding Welles's *War of the Worlds* dramatization, for example, found that 84 percent of his audience were not even disturbed by the broadcast. That is a quite high proportion, hardly in accord with the image we have of mass panic. Yet this event more than any other in the last half-century is the one most often cited as an example of panic behavior.

Well then, how do people behave in disaster? What does happen when flood, tornado, earthquake, hurricane, or blizzard hits? We've encountered many examples of human actions in the face of disaster so far in the pages of this book, but what kind of generalizations can be made?

Over the years at least five major scientific programs of research have been organized to explore these questions, which have fascinated man for millennia and been the ingredients of drama from playwrights of classical Greece and Elizabethan England to the filmmakers and writers of today. The earliest two were the National Opinion Research Center project at the University of Chicago (1950–1954), and the Disaster Research Group of the National Academy of Sciences (1952–1963). Following them came the Disaster Research Center of Ohio State University (1963 to present), the Program of Collaborative Research on Natural Hazards (University of Chicago, Clark University, University of Toronto, 1967–73), and the Research Program on Technology, Environment and Man of the University of Colorado's Institute of Behavioral Science (1970 to present).

The scholars in these research programs have attempted to get beneath the headlines and 30-second television spots to obtain a deeper understanding of the human and social responses to disaster, one free of speculation and of the problems often necessarily inherent in news accounts prepared in the excitement and tragedy of the moment. Where the news media have to move on to other things after the event has ceased being a major news story, the behavioral researchers can come in later and take advantage of the perspective of time in following the people, groups, and communities caught in tragedy through the stages of post-impact response and reconstruction following disaster and carrying out systematic inquiries into the events leading up to it.

Disaster researchers usually divide the events of a disaster into five or six different intervals, from long before it begins to long after it is over, but for simplicity I'll combine them into three: before, during (the emergency period), and after.

The stage for disaster, I have frequently emphasized, is set by human actions and inactions long before the storm breaks, the flood hits, or the earth shakes. A lot has to do with acceptance of risk and our perceptions of the degree of that risk. Every human activity from swallowing a pill to crossing the street has a certain amount of risk associated with it, and we are continually making choices based on our assessment of that risk. If we perceive it small and the benefits large then we are likely to tolerate it in order to gain the advantages sought. That is the kind of choice-making that allows people to decide to settle on floodplains, high-seismic-risk zones, and hurricane-susceptible coasts. (Sometimes the benefits accrue to one group, the risks to another, such as when a developer builds houses in a likely flood area and sells them to newcomers unaware of the flood threat.)

Every person's and every group's perception of that risk is likely to be different. The level of peril itself may change, but even if it does not, the perception of that danger can change. And perception of that risk often depends on our prior experience with disaster.

That is why, ironically, it often takes a disaster to get people to prepare for (the next) disaster. This has been documented many times, and it seems to be true whether you are talking about individuals or governments. Gilbert White and Eugene Haas note that the great proportion of changes in federal legislation on natural hazards follows within a few months or a year of a major disaster. "The record for federal flood control legislation since the great Mississippi flood of 1927," they add, "mirrors in an exact fashion the occurrence of severe flooding in the preceding year." The San Fernando earthquake of 1971 prompted new awareness of the earthquake peril in California. The legislation that eventually led to the Disaster Relief Act of 1974 was initially stimulated by the Agnes, Buffalo Creek, and Rapid City flood disasters of 1972 (the "Year of the Floods"). It then bogged down into very slow progress until 1974, when suddenly it was speedily enacted following the concerns raised by the superoutbreak of 148 tornadoes on April 3–4 of that year. "Instances in which changes occur independently of crisis situations are few," conclude White and Haas.

Communities that have experienced disaster are better able to cope with a future one. When a tornado hit Jonesboro, Arkansas, in 1968, the town had no preparedness plans. Afterwards, spotter networks, educational programs, disaster drill procedures, an emergency operations center, and a warning communications system were set up. When another tornado hit Jonesboro in 1973, deaths and injuries were greatly reduced even though the property damage was six times higher than in the 1968 twister.

This is true of floods too. "After a flash flood has occurred," says Frank Makosky of the Little Rock, Arkansas, National Weather Service Forecast Office, "it is relatively simple to interest a community in a flash flood plan designed to buy time for precautionary measures."

As disaster researcher Charles E. Fritz has pointed out: "The most highly organized preparation exists in communities and societies that have repeatedly and recently experienced the same kind of disaster."

Of course, certain caveats are necessary. The previous disaster must indeed have been recent. The lessons wear off fast. Although a recent flash flood spurs action, "If one tries to stimulate interest in a vulnerable community five years after the last flash flood," says Makosky, "one often runs into a wall of complacency—especially if the plan calls for the expenditure of local time and money." Also, it appears that the previous disaster experience usually promotes needed action only if there is feedback in which specialists provide advice on how to improve community preparedness. If not, improvement does not always follow. And sometimes a particular type of disaster will direct attention and resources to lessening its effects next time to such

Topeka, Kansas, residents dash to shelter as tornado approaches, June 8, 1966. (TOPEKA-CAPITAL JOURNAL PHOTO FROM AMERICAN RED CROSS)

a degree that funds may be diverted from preparing against another type of disaster just as hazardous. A community may be so preoccupied with lessening the flood threat that it ignores the need to inspect buildings against the dangers of an earthquake.

I've already noted how people who have had experience with only the fringes of a hurricane are often led to underestimate the full force of such a storm. Similar cases in which a person's experience with a hazard can lead to false perceptions of the actual risk happen with floods. Some longtime residents of the Big Thompson Canyon didn't take the flash flood threat seriously the night of July 31, 1976, because they had experienced previous high-water levels which had not threatened their homes. But the flood that came roaring down the canyon that night brought 240 times the average flow of water and almost 10 times the greatest quantity ever before recorded. Experience was a false guide. Many residents of Rapid City failed to understand the flood threat there the night of June 9, 1972, for the same reasons.

Recent exposure to an extreme natural event also sometimes causes people mistakenly to assume that the possibility of its happening again soon is thereby reduced. This is called the "gambler's fallacy." Just as the 50-50 odds of turning up heads on the next flip of a coin are not changed by having flipped heads the five previous times, the risk of a major storm or flood in the coming year is not reduced by the fact of its occurrence in the past year. (Yes, lightning does strike twice in the same place.) An event that is random has the same probability of occurrence one year as it did the previous year.

This may seem obvious, but the terminology of 25-year, 50-year, or 100-year floods contributes to the confusion. A 25-year flood may statistically be expected to occur once in 25 years, on a long-term average, but that doesn't mean such floods can't and won't happen only a few years apart, or even in back-to-back years. On the Housatonic River in New England, two floods estimated to have a probability of once in 100 years took place during the same summer of 1955. Nevertheless, many people, subconsciously at least, tend to be victims of the "gambler's fallacy" and assume that a severe flood or snowfall signals a period of respite.

Long-time residents of rural areas seem to have a far more realistic view of the risks of natural hazards than do people who live in urban areas or former city dwellers recently moved to the countryside. Burton, Kates, and White point out in their study that it is not uncommon to hear people who live in a hazardous place—especially if it's a large urban area—claim that there is no special peril there. Or they may be aware of the threat of the natural hazard but not consider it a danger.

This, they say, seldom happens with farmers. Farm people tend to be keenly aware of the natural hazard risk. This undoubtedly is because they live closer to the land and their livelihood depends upon realistic thinking about such matters. City dwellers, in contrast, often have legitimate worries of other kinds of risk—traffic, crime, pollution—which may overshadow their awareness of natural hazards and cause them to underestimate their likelihood.

People respond to warnings of specific imminent hazards in such diverse ways that the warning process is far more complex than it may seem. For one thing, even though people may be listening to the same warning, everybody hears different things. We all have selective perception. Second, people respond on the basis of how what they hear stimulates them to behave. Third, people are stimulated differently depending on who they are, whom they are with, or who and what they see. These three simple principles, summarized by disaster researchers Dennis S. Mileti, Thomas E. Drabek, and Haas in their attempt to codify what social science research has learned about human response in disaster, go a long way toward explaining why problems so often come up. They show why those responsible for issuing strong storm and flood warnings are constantly being reminded that it's not enough just to put a warning out. Everyone is going to perceive it and act on it (or not) somewhat differently, and the task of warning is not just to send a warning "out there" but to make sure that it is understood and acted on properly.

As E. L. Quarantelli, director of Ohio State University's Disaster Research Center, says: "There is a tendency to think of disaster warnings in technological and/or mechanical terms, such as radio or siren soundings. . . . Warning should be thought of primarily as involving psychological functions and social structures."

Certain types of behavior can be counted upon. Widely acknowledged is that people seek independent confirmation of a disaster warning. They try to gain additional information beyond that contained in the original warning. The warning is more likely to be believed if there is some visible evidence of the danger. A tornado warning heard on the radio is likely to send the listener to his or her window or yard to check the sky. A flood warning often sends people to the river banks to see for themselves. (Flash floods are sometimes intractable to warning for this reason; the heavy rains that cause them are often too far up-river or up-canyon to yield any first-person sign of danger to the people living or camping downstream. Scientists see an even worse problem with any future warning of an imminent earthquake because there is no way the citizen can see for himself any evidence of an impending major quake, unless foreshocks are felt.)

It is natural to seek supporting information. Different things affect the level of need. Research shows that people seek confirmation of warnings received over the mass media more often than they do for warnings received from a more personal process, such as from a neighbor or an official. Although independent confirmation is usually sought for the first warning, a second warning often seems to serve as confirmation of the first. So repeating warnings are important. Families that are united at the time of warning are less likely to seek confirmation of the threat than are families that are separated. People who have been in disasters before are more likely to go through organizational channels in seeking further information than are persons without disaster experience. The closer the person is to the place where the disaster is expected to hit, the more sources of information there are for confirmation and the more likely he is to hear confirming warnings by word of mouth.

Whether people believe the warning or not depends on many things as well. As with preparedness, past experience is a guide. If a person's past experience is that a warning was indeed followed by the predicted violent natural event (especially if it resulted in a disaster), he is more likely to give credence to the next warning he hears. On the other hand, if, the last time he heard a warning, nothing noteworthy happened, he's less likely to believe in the next warning. (It is this natural inclination that gives severe storm forecasters fits. A certain amount of "overwarning" is necessary and inevitable when dealing with difficult-to-predict events. It is preferable, at least, to "underwarning." But the family or community that evacuates on the basis of a hurricane warning only to have the storm fizzle or turn away at the last minute is going to give less credence to a future warning even though the warning issued for the first storm may have been totally justified. Those involved in planning for a future earthquake-prediction capability are similarly concerned about this "crying wolf" problem.)

Belief in the warning is also related to who is issuing it. The general finding of most research is that people are more likely to believe warnings from official sources such as the police, state patrol, or fire department. Warnings delivered in a personal manner, such as a policeman or neighbor coming to the door, are usually more effective than those communicated by an impersonal medium, such as the radio. (Sometimes, however, even personal warnings are ineffective. In the Big Thompson flood, state patrolmen individually warning residents to take high ground occasionally found their pleas unheeded and in the Rapid City flood the personal pleas of the mayor at the riverside were ignored by many. These behaviors, however, were probably related to the previously mentioned absence of physical signs of the hazard downstream from the source of the threat.) If people see other people around them heeding the hazard warnings, they are more likely to respond than if not. If a person is with a group of his peers, he is less likely to respond to the hazard warning than if he's with his family. (Apparently, there can be peer pressure to underestimate the hazard or scoff at the danger.) And certainly, people are more likely to believe in the warning and respond to it if they believe the danger being warned against is a likely occurrence. This causes problems with very unusual or extraordinary events (the Big Thompson flood is again an example) in comparison with those deemed more common (a flood on the Mississippi, a tornado in the Midwest, a moderate earthquake in California). And as subsequent warning messages, whatever form they may be in, give more precise times and locations, add information about actions to take, clear up earlier ambiguities, and become consistent with other sources of information, the more likely people are to believe in and heed them.

Even under the threat of disaster, people behave in ways that are mainly extensions of their normal, everyday behavior. Exotic, unusual, highly unpredictable behavior is the rare exception. Far more common is conduct that fits the threat into normal, everyday patterns of behavior. Advice given during disaster warnings that would require people to act in ways distinctly different from their normal tendencies thus may not be only futile but misguided. The positive corollary is that warning advice is more likely to succeed when it takes into consideration normal human impulses and finds ways to direct those inclinations toward the desired action.

"Ways ought to be explored to take advantage of everyday behaviors, rather than to try to force persons to act in 'unnatural' ways, contrary to routine habits and impulses," suggest Quarantelli and colleague Verta Taylor. The example they give is the often-heard advice to stay off the phone during disaster situations.

"The 'public' is frequently urged not to use some channels of communications, such as the telephone, at times of collective trouble. Such admonitions, all the evidence indicates, are useless. People will use the phone since that is a normal, everyday habit. Instead of trying to stop the impossible—people calling one another at times of community stress—ways ought to be found to take advantage of such calls so as to improve the dissemination of warning messages."

It is clear from the evidence I've already mentioned that people seek confirmation of warnings, and it seems also true that at times of danger people feel a great need to share their feelings and available information with friends and loved ones. So it is hardly surprising that a first impulse on hearing a disaster warning is to jump to the telephone. Anyway, as Quarantelli says, it may be a good way to spread the news, especially when you remember the fact that warnings are taken more seriously when delivered in a personal way.

Quarantelli is a professor of sociology at Ohio State as well as co-founder of the Disaster Research Center, the first of its kind in the world. Along with many colleagues, he has been trying for years to counteract numerous myths and misconceptions that have grown up about how people respond in disaster situations. In 1972, he and sociologist and co-founder Russell R. Dynes wrote an article in *Psychology Today* entitled "When Disaster Strikes (It Isn't Much Like What You've Heard & Read About)" seeking to point out the many misunderstandings surrounding the subject. He says now that the myths still persist, despite additional findings by researchers studying the abundant crop of disasters throughout the 1970s, most all of which reaffirm the previously stated views.

The most prominent myth of all is that when disaster strikes, people will panic. It's just not true, says Quarantelli, and there is much social science research to back him up. Mass panic, hysteria, irrationality, and widespread disorganization are seldom found. In fact, human beings usually act in quite controlled and reasonable ways during disasters, adapting to the suddenly changed circumstances better than might be expected.

"Basically," Quarantelli says, "people respond much better to extreme stress than they've been given credit for. Most problems during disasters get handled relatively well. Most people don't sit around wringing their hands. They do what they have to do. They check through the rubble. They get the injured to hospitals."

This seems to be true around the world. Disaster researchers in Japan, Australia, and Italy have recently been coming independently to the same conclusions. Quarantelli refers to the situation as one of "astounding high agreement."

"Most persons confronting natural disasters do not suddenly become wildly disorganized and irrational," says Thomas Drabek, a University of Denver sociologist. "In immediate danger they may flee, but that hardly justifies the stereotype."

Readers of news reports often confuse orderly evacuation from the site of an impending disaster such as a hurricane or flood with mass fleeing in panic. Controlled withdrawal, not merely an escape from danger but movement toward a goal, is more common than panic, researchers Nicholas Demerath and Anthony Wallace reported as long ago as 1957. Images of thousands of people running in terror before the onrushing wall of water are more the stuff of fiction than fact, disaster researchers say. In fact, the problem more often is just the opposite. People tend to stay at the scene of danger. They remain almost too calm. They resist evacuation. Even when mass evacuations are carried out, and people by the thousands leave, more often than not the majority stay behind.

The largest evacuation in American history came with the threat of Hurricane Carla in 1961. There was four days' warning of a clearly recognized threat, and more than half a million people left their homes along the coasts of Texas and Louisiana. Yet, points out Quarantelli, the majority of the residents stayed behind. A study by Harry E. Moore and co-workers showed that 35 percent remained in their own homes and an additional 22 percent stayed with friends and relatives. Despite this fact and evidence that most who did evacuate did so orderly, several newspaper headlines declared: "MORE THAN 100,000 PERSONS FLEE IN NEAR PANIC." This, Quarantelli says, is an example of

Evacuation of Hurricane Betsy victims in New Orleans. (AMERICAN
RED CROSS PHOTO BY R. VETTER)

the mistaken assumption that all flights are disorganized. In fact,
no fatalities resulted from the evacuation. There were few traffic
accidents. In contrast to the every-person-for-himself image,
people evacuating often help others get away. Evacuations are
very much family-centered. Drabek's study of response to the
1965 Platte River floods in Denver found that 92 percent of the
families who left their homes in the face of the threat left together.

Panic flight, although rare in a natural disaster, does occasionally occur. Several studies have shown that three conditions
contribute most critically to panic (defined as acute fear coupled
with flight or attempted flight): when the danger is immediate
and strikes with little or no warning, when the victim believes
escape routes are closing, and when the victim feels extremely
isolated.

Few clear-cut cases of panic involving more than three or
four persons have been documented in recent decades, according to Quarantelli. In the famous case of the Cocoanut Grove
nightclub fire in Boston in 1942, in which 491 persons perished,
Quarantelli says the evidence clearly suggests that most of the
occupants did not panic. Many persons were asphyxiated before

they had a clear idea of the danger and many others managed to find alternate escape routes. Study of the Beverly Hills, Kentucky, supperclub fire of May 28, 1977, reveals little evidence of real panic, he says, despite some news reports to the contrary.

We note often in works of fiction and occasionally in actual fact of instances in which officials faced with warning the public of a possibly dangerous or unsettling future event decide to withhold information about it for fear of causing mass panic. After the Soviet nuclear-powered satellite Cosmos 954 crashed to the earth in Canada in January, 1978, there was speculation that had officials who knew about its imminent demise told the public about it in advance, great fear and panic might have been unloosed. Quarantelli feels that's a misguided concern, a return to the "panic myth." Far better to be open with the public so the people can have an accurate idea of the risk. Fear of panic just isn't that valid a concern, he says, re-emphasizing that people generally respond well to warnings of disaster and other risky events. In fact, the decision not to disclose information is dysfunctional; it undermines public confidence in the future actions of the agencies responsible for the decision.

When disaster does hit, the victims usually respond actively to help themselves and their families. They don't wait around for authorities to come tell them what to do. They seldom lapse into a helpless daze or passive wandering. The impulse for survival takes over. Patterns of self-reliance and informal mutual aid come to the fore.

When help is needed, victims seek it first from family, friends, and neighbors. Small groups such as local church organizations are turned to next followed by police and social welfare groups. Quarantelli and Dynes report that people tend to turn to impersonal disaster-relief organizations such as the Red Cross or the civil defense for aid only as a last resort. (A possible exception is large-scale floods in which nearby relatives and friends are also affected.) During the evacuation of 80,000 people during the threat of dam break after the San Fernando earthquake, for example, fewer than 7 percent sought housing aid from public agencies. Fewer than a quarter of the people who evacuated from Hurricane Carla went to public shelters. Fifty-eight percent went to homes of friends or family members.

Time and time again this pattern is repeated. Disasters tend to bring families together to share the burdens they must face. Says Drabek: "Like funerals, christenings, and weddings, disasters appear to be events wherein kin are expected to re-establish networks that may remain in varied degrees of dormancy for long periods of time. If separated, nuclear family members will try hard to unite; once together they tend to stay together."

Those not injured in the disaster also naturally seek first to help members of their own family, if nearby. Only after the immediate needs of nearby family members, close friends, and neighbors are looked after do nonvictims turn to the problems of others.

Once that point is reached, however, the behavior of those not directly affected toward those who are tends to be very generous and altruistic. As Drabek summarizes: "Being a nonvictim appears to generate a strong desire to help. . . . Persons learning of a nearby disaster tend to be curious, wonder about kin and friend involvement, and very likely will go to the scene. Once there, they seek ways to help, and if a helping role can be assumed they will exhibit altruistic behaviors that, upon retrospect, even they may find surprising."

A study by Morgan Martin found altruism, affection, cooperation, and group solidarity to be the prevalent characteristics in disaster situations. Helping is usually carried out without regard to usual social barriers such as differences in social class, race, and age. These differences suddenly become less relevant.

Those who need medical aid are usually attended to relatively quickly whether or not any formal disaster-relief help is available. A study of a tornado in Flint-Beecher, Michigan, found that the people in the devastated area were able to get from two-thirds to three-fourths of the 927 casualties to hospitals within three to four hours with almost no aid from formal organizations. In fact, only about a fifth of the people ever came into contact with official disaster agencies. This small proportion is typical of most disasters. Hurricane Betsy in 1965 brought about one of the largest relief efforts in the history of the American Red Cross, yet, Quarantelli points out, only about 34,000 of the 178,000 families who suffered some degree of loss received Red Cross aid.

Still, Quarantelli emphasizes, organization and prior planning are important. "The efficiency and effectiveness of any response is dependent on planning by organizations." Organization is needed to mobilize resources and coordinate efforts. "You can have the best-trained citizens in the world, but if you can't get a major piece of equipment or don't know how to deal with a par-

ticular situation, it's not going to be of much use." This is especially relevant in certain kinds of "technological" disasters such
as the wreck of a tank car containing toxic chemicals.

The need of nonvictims to help in some way can be quite
intense. When they do help, they feel they've contributed something useful. When they are unable to help, they feel left out
and frustrated. The clearer their role is, the better off they are.
A study by James B. Taylor, Louis A. Zurcher, and William H.
Key of community response to a tornado found that nonvictims
have a great "tension" to do something. If they had some means
to help, they quickly plunged into the task, but if they didn't
they became frustrated. A study by W. C. Menninger found
that, once assigned to any kind of job, the individual felt some
relief. Menninger also found that, during the crisis, the groups
of workers seemed somewhat exhilarated.

What about trained people such as police or firemen or doctors who have valuable skills and whose jobs require them to
participate in rescue and relief operations, sometimes to the
neglect of their own families? Don't they sometimes have a
tendency to abandon their official tasks during disasters to assist
their own families? There have been reports of this "role conflict," but many of them don't seem to stand up. A study by
Gilbert White of response in three disasters found that not a
single person abandoned ongoing disaster work to be with his
family. And Quarantelli says his center's interviews with more
than 4,500 members of agencies in more than 150 disasters,
plus reports on the behavior of thousands of relief workers,
have failed to turn up one instance in which a person left an
important emergency-related post out of anxiety for his family.

Another concern that seems often to be exaggerated is looting.
Fears of looting are almost automatically raised as soon as the
dust from a disaster settles. We all have images of near-empty
commercial and residential areas pillaged by gangs of looters in
the aftermath of disaster. These concerns are reinforced by news
reports almost invariably mentioning that officials have sent in
special police or soldiers to prevent looting, thus tending to emphasize the certainty of the threat. Often, Quarantelli says, this
is simply the political thing to do to avoid future accusations
that the contingency wasn't anticipated. When looting then
doesn't occur it is often attributed to these wise preventative
actions rather than to the possibility that looting wouldn't have
taken place anyway.

Quarantelli says the Disaster Research Center has found few documented cases of looting in disasters in the United States. And people seem to have a perception of much greater looting than actually can be proved to have taken place. It is always important to distinguish reports from actual incidences. Quarantelli says both his earlier studies and his center's study of the Xenia, Ohio, tornado disaster found that a great majority of disaster victims (60 to 70 percent) said they had heard *reports* of looting, but the figures dropped drastically (to 8 percent or less) when asked if they *knew* of actual incidents. In the month following Hurricane Betsy, major crime actually fell 26 percent. Burglaries and thefts were down.

After the collision of an airliner and another aircraft over San Diego on September 25, 1978, in which 144 persons died, a report circulated of looting at the crash site. The San Diego chief of police was disturbed enough by this rumor, which he said couldn't be traced, to write to a national newsmagazine: "There is absolutely no evidence that any looting occurred at the crash site or in the immediate vicinity."

The flagrant looting that took place in Harlem during the 1977 New York City blackout undoubtedly will reinforce the stereotype of looting's high prevalence during urban vulnerability. Yet obviously a blackout is not a typical "disaster," and the antisocial behavior observed that evening is not necessarily typical anyway, either of that blackout or of others. The 1965 New York City blackout resulted predominantly in feelings and actions of camaraderie and even festivity. Other urban areas have had the same kinds of experience. My wife and I were living in New York during the 1965 blackout. The main impression that has stuck with us is one of remarkable openness and sharing. It was a break from the routine, a dramatic event we were all experiencing and enjoying together.

Quarantelli further emphasizes that, public impression to the contrary, martial law has never been declared in any American disaster. Those who say otherwise are often confusing local emergency powers given police by city officials—often to control crowds—with martial law.

What about the psychological and mental health legacies of disaster? Don't the human tragedies that disasters bring result in widespread mental suffering and acute long-term emotional disorders? That emotional illness followed disasters was long the conventional wisdom. One study in the 1950s projected that 12 to 25 percent of the population struck by catastrophe would exhibit bizarre behavior, hysteria, anxiety, and psychoses. An additional 75 percent would be dazed, stunned, apathetic, passive, or otherwise exhibit symptoms of shock that had been dubbed the "disaster syndrome." But the "myth of madness" began to change in the early 1970s following studies of such disasters as the San Fernando earthquake, and the floods of tropical storm Agnes and Rapid City. What really changed the thinking was an extensive major study of the mental health effects of the powerful tornado that struck and devastated Xenia. Here was a disaster that might be expected to bring out the most severe pathological problems: 33 dead, 1,200 injured, 20 percent of the residential housing destroyed and 25 percent damaged, and half the jobs in town temporarily lost. News reports speculated about possible outbreaks of insanity. Mental health workers expected the worst.

Four hours after the twister, the Disaster Research Center had a field team in Xenia initiating an 18-month study of the short- and long-term psychological effects of the disaster. What they found was surprising. Sociologist Verta Taylor, then co-director of the center, reported the results in 1977: "The study found that there was an extremely low rate of serious mental illness, if any at all, as a consequence of the tornado. On the contrary, it concluded that a large percentage of the people had extremely positive reactions to the disaster. Eighty-four percent claimed that their experiences had shown them they could handle crises better than they had thought; 69 percent reported that they felt they had met a great challenge and were better off for it. A year and a half later, there were still few cases of severe pathological disturbances as a direct result of the disaster."

Mental health professionals who had predicted widespread emotional disorganization reported no cases of hysterical breakdowns or loss of contact with reality at the peak of the emergency. In fact, agencies that provide treatment and hospitalization of serious psychiatric problems reported that the demand for their services declined.

The field research teams carried out two surveys of the victims' own perceptions of their psychological well-being; one, six months after the disaster, the other, a year later. They found that only 3 percent of the population reported feeling at any time after the disaster that they might have a nervous breakdown. Only 1 percent had considered suicide in the aftermath.

Only 3 percent said they drank more afterwards, and 7 percent said they drank less. (The State Department of Liquor Control confirmed that alcohol consumption went down significantly after the disaster.)

Social relationships seemed to be improved, not worsened. Two percent said their relationships with family and close friends were worse, 27 percent said they were better. Three percent found their marriages less satisfying, 28 percent found them more so. Marriage and divorce rates were unchanged.

The near-absence of serious psychological disorders such as those that might require psychotherapy does not of course mean that the victims of the Xenia tornado suffered no emotional or psychological problems. As Taylor reports, many victims did show signs of stress and had trouble adjusting. Fifty-eight percent said they considered their emotional state to be good or excellent after the disaster, but 33 percent said only fair and 9 percent said poor. About half the population said they had been more nervous or excited and half said they had been depressed at some time. More than a quarter had had trouble sleeping (consumption of tranquilizers and sleeping pills jumped after the disaster). Juvenile delinquency rose, probably a symptom of both adjustment problems by young people and the loss of recreational opportunities. Even a year and a half after the tornado, four of ten people reported an overall increase in problems in everyday living.

Yet overall, the people of Xenia showed far greater emotional resiliency than had been expected, considering the degree of suffering and disruption they had undergone. What accounts for this resiliency, and why did 98 percent say they felt the city would be a better place to live in in the future as a result of the tornado?

Other natural disasters have produced the same kind of reaction among the people in the afflicted community. Taylor points out—as have Quarantelli and Dynes with earlier tragedies —that disasters often bring about heightened morale. People who have been caught up in disasters have shared a common experience. Their suffering has not been in isolation. They have had to take strong and immediate actions to cope with the problem. They have set aside normal activities to help themselves and others. The veneer of routine, often petty, daily concerns that separate us from our inner selves and from others has been stripped away. In taking necessary positive, mutual action, people have downplayed their suffering and revealed to themselves that they can accomplish much under difficult circumstances. The result is both a sense of accomplishment and an increased sense of community that helps offset the personal losses.

A year after the Xenia tornado, much of the town had been rebuilt. The determination, pride, and cooperation of the townspeople had paid off. Said one woman: "Selfishness disappeared for a time in Xenia. That and a feeling that this storm just wasn't big enough to ruin us are what made it all possible."

(The one prominent exception to the absence of severe mental disturbances from disasters in the 1970s was the Buffalo Creek dam break in West Virginia in 1972, in which 125 people died and 4,000 were left homeless. Lawyers won settlement for the "psychic impairment" the survivors had suffered. The disaster was hardly typical, however, says Taylor; nearly every family lost at least one member, and the entire mining community was nearly obliterated culturally and socially as well as physically.)

"What our research into collective stress situations indicates," concludes Verta Taylor, "is that mental health is a dynamic state. . . . It is re-energized by doing and acting and responding to challenges. . . . The world and its triumphs and tragedies must be confronted each day, and the way we respond to them deeply affects our psychological self-image. Perhaps the experience of coping with and mastering the many personal crises associated with disaster might even enhance a person's well-being."

The boost in community spirit often displayed in disasters helps explain another sometimes-noted response: aversion to outside help whether it's needed or not. This doesn't always happen, of course, but sometimes the people of the afflicted community gain such a feeling of pride in their mutual efforts against the challenge that they feel they want to go it alone. As Quarantelli and Dynes put it: "Townspeople often see Red Cross and government rescue teams as impersonal, unsympathetic, cold, and insensitive to local problems and issues. The victims feel that it is their disaster and they do not want outsiders coming in to take credit for the work done during the emergency period." This despite the fact that disaster experts give groups such as the Red Cross high marks for their humane efforts.

Communities often see visits to the scenes of disasters by prominent political figures in the same light, assuming the prime motivation to be personal publicity, not a sincere desire to assist.

Elderly patients being carried to safety in flooded Wilkes-Barre, Pennsylvania, during the floods of Hurricane Agnes. (PHILLIPS BUT-LER PHOTO FROM AMERICAN RED CROSS)

Every major disaster brings an outpouring of clothing, food, and supplies sent by generous persons to the scene. The greater the disaster, the more generous the response. But contrary to popular impression the need for additional food and clothing is usually not especially great. (It's a rare disaster, notes Quarantelli, that catches everyone running around naked.) Supplies arrive in far greater quantities than can be used, and often a large proportion of the materials are unneeded, inappropriate, and unusable. (Among items sent to survivors of the 1972 Managua, Nicaragua, earthquake were toys, winter clothing, and frozen TV dinners.) Their arrival requires people to attend to them and causes extra congestion at the disaster site. Still the "cornucopia" response seems almost inevitable. It seems to be a way for people away from the disaster to fulfill their need to "do something."

All in all, people and communities usually perform not only better than we have been lead to expect by the popular mythology of total human and social collapse during disaster; they react better than they themselves expected they could. As Quarantelli says, most people caught up in disaster compare their response with that of the myth of people breaking down and thus see their positive, effective actions as unusual and extraordinary. They often refer to themselves as having "risen to the occasion." It's true, but it shouldn't be surprising. As Quarantelli and Dynes concluded: "The reality suggests that human beings are amazingly resilient in the face of adversity. Perhaps heroism is not the wrong word to describe disaster behavior."

Two caveats about everything I've said so far about human response to disaster: First, the vast bulk of social and behavioral research on disasters has been done in modern, industrial, urban societies. The research findings I've described are solidly grounded only in such societies as America, Western Europe, and Japan. Chances are most will apply to other kinds of societies as well, but that can't be said for certain. Second, while studies of disaster show that people bear up rather well under disasters, they also show that organizations that respond to disasters often are the weak links in the response. In some extreme cases, the organized effort to provide help and assistance sometimes is more socially and psychologically disruptive than the actual physical disaster itself. Improvements in preparedness and response to disasters will have to come through improving disaster organizations.

The emergency period of a disaster, in which the people and community have had to cope with the immediate problems caused by the destruction and by the injuries and deaths, ends after a few days or weeks. Further search and rescue operations are called off, emergency feeding and housing efforts are terminated, and the principal streets are now free of rubble. Some semblance of normality returns, but with it comes the end of that period of euphoria created by people working urgently together in common, immediate tasks. Stories of each others' actions, often heroic, have now been told and retold. The drama is over, the news reporters have now gone on to other things, and people must now look to the future.

New problems and conflicts may arise as people and communities previously caught up in the needs of the moment now have to make decisions about restoration and reconstruction. Differences of opinion about future courses of action may develop. People who a few days earlier were spontaneously and efficiently attending to their immediate needs now find themselves faced with insurance forms, regulations of long-term disaster relief, bureaucratic procedures, and in general a return to the more formalized, rigid patterns of normal life. All these annoyances seem amplified; frustration and bickering are common. Some may experience temporary dejection and depression. People's natural frustrations at having to depend to a certain degree on disaster-relief organizations may cause them to be overly critical of the agencies' performances. Those who try to help often are now criticized, and this may cause them to resort to less individualized, more bureaucratic procedures. Impatience and hostility are common. All in all, the contrast with the earlier mood of cooperation during the emergency period is often quite stark.

The decisions that have to be made necessarily involve organizations. City governments have to decide courses of action in rebuilding. Cities, like the people who comprise them, are amazingly resilient. Damage often turns out to be only about half that initially estimated, and in all but the worst disasters, more of the city remains intact than has been destroyed. The issue is almost never whether to rebuild—that is usually a foregone conclusion—but exactly how and under what new kinds of guidelines.

History shows that cities survive the destruction and disruption of major disasters, except in rare cases, where there is total destruction. The last significant urban place that failed to totally rebuild was Saint-Pierre in Martinique, following its destruction by the explosion of Mount Pelée in 1902. Specialists in disaster response find it hard to envision a city failing to rebuild following a natural disaster. A city is far more than just an assemblage of buildings and businesses. It is a center of life and economy and culture, and it has a symbolic value to the citizenry often far more important than is realized.

Sociologist J. Eugene Haas and Clark University geographers Robert Kates and Martyn J. Bowden recently completed a study of how cities recover from disaster (*Reconstruction Following Disaster*, MIT Press, 1977). They conclude that this symbolic value of the city to its residents and the region argues strongly for the reconstruction of a disaster-struck city. It accounts for the persistence of cities despite whole series of disasters. And it shows, they feel, that it is futile for specialists to attempt to persuade residents to rebuild their city in a less hazardous place. The relocation of a city following a disaster is extraordinarily rare. The last time it happened was the relocation of Antigua, Guatemala, following the earthquake of 1773. The compulsion to rebuild, restore life to the way it was before the disaster— and almost always in the same place—is obviously very strong.

All kinds of new issues come up, however. Should regular decision-making procedures or extraordinary ones be used in choosing courses of action for the city? Should land-use regulations and building codes be changed to make resettlement less hazardous? Should rebuilding take advantage of the chance to make the city more efficient and more attractive? Should property holders receive compensation or financial assistance? And how should it all be financed?

Decisions on such issues aren't easy. They all have negative as well as positive consequences. After the Rapid City flood, the city decided to turn the heavily damaged area into open space, a "floodway" to reduce future disaster possibilities. Undamaged homes as well as those damaged by the flood were condemned. The owners of the untouched homes had to find homes elsewhere. They were "relocation" victims.

There is always the realization that rebuilding after a disaster is a chance to make the city better than it was. Ideally, everyone wants to have the city become a more efficient and pleasant place, to provide fuller services, to reduce the vulnerability to future hazards. That's the ideal. But all that requires extensive planning, discussion, and debate, and it's usually accomplished only at the price of much time. It is generally successful only if a broad community consensus can be reached quickly. Warns the Haas-Kates-Bowden study: "Comprehensiveness of study, flexibility of planning, and innovativeness of design are all purchased in heavy post-disaster coin, a high cost in precious time and anxious uncertainty. . . . If too much time is taken to study, design, or administer, if the changes proposed are overly ambitious, or if the plans are grandiose and lead to uncertainty, conflict and further delay, then failure follows. The plans are not executed."

They point out that a city's residents already have a plan for the new city indelibly stamped in their minds: the way it was before. And if there are too many delays in implementing new plans, people and businesses are going to proceed to reconstruct as best they can, plan or no plan.

After the 1972 earthquake in Managua which destroyed much of the business district and left three-quarters of the 420,000 residents homeless, the question first arose of whether to move the city out of the hazardous earthquake zone. That was quickly answered in the negative. Then broad, comprehensive planning to rebuild the city in ways to reduce the earthquake risk was begun. But it was a year before the plan became public and another year and a half before the first preliminary plan for rebuilding the downtown core area came out, during which time no downtown reconstruction was permitted and tropical vegetation took over. The people couldn't wait. As a consequence, the city grew in a haphazard way, out on its periphery. Small businesses moved into former residential areas. In the absence of a quickly resolved plan, rebuilding was carried out through a series of private decisions by individuals and businesses, whose goal naturally is to return to normal as quickly as possible. The city's character was diminished from that envisioned in the too-much-delayed master plan. People were bitter about the uncertainties. The pace of recovery was badly handicapped.

Such examples of the problems cities encounter in recovering from a disaster lead Haas, Kates, and Bowden to a series of suggestions for disaster-struck cities: don't assume private individuals, businesses, and builders will delay their decisions about rebuilding until new policies are developed. (They won't.) Begin reconstruction planning as early as possible. Remember that despite everyone's ideals and best efforts to reshape the city,

Survivors at Ferdows, Iran, bury their dead following the severe 1968 earthquake. (AMERICAN RED CROSS)

fundamental change is unlikely. Past trends will usually be accelerated. Don't assume all temporary housing will be temporary. Do use every reasonable opportunity to make the city safer, but don't make invulnerability the ultimate objective. And, perhaps, most important of all: "When tempted to delay an important decision, don't."

How long does it take a town or city to recover from disaster? The study led by Haas divided recovery into three overlapping periods following the emergency phase: restoration (patching up structures and returning life and business to some semblance of normality), replacement reconstruction (rebuilding the city and its activities to predisaster levels), and commemorative, betterment, and developmental reconstruction (basically, making the city better than it was). Each of these periods lasts about 10 times as long as the one before. The emergency period lasts a few days or weeks, restoration a few months, replacement reconstruction several years, and betterment reconstruction 10 to 20 years. Of course, quick or slow decisions can speed or delay the process at any phase.

Cities heavily hit by disaster, including war, seem to be able to recover a 10-percent loss in population caused by disaster in about three years or a 50-percent loss (as happened to Messina, Italy, in a 1908 earthquake) in seven years. But the previous strength of the city or community has much to do with it. Trends before the disaster are accelerated, the Haas study found. Rapidly growing cities recover from disasters rapidly. Stable, stagnant, or declining cities recover slowly or decline may even accelerate.

The pace of recovery may be slow or fast, but it is frequently hampered by still another aftermath of disaster: the need to place blame, to find scapegoats. The search for scapegoats is typical of nonnatural disasters such as fires, airplane crashes, cave-ins, dam failures, building collapses, and the like, but it also is sometimes seen in "natural" disasters when people realize with benefit of sharp hindsight that better awareness of the hazard and different early actions and decisions might have lessened the danger or even averted the disaster. This personalizing of blame is a way to work off anxieties and frustrations and all the natural feelings of guilt, horror, and shock that go with disasters. It also is sometimes seen as a route toward reducing the hazard in the future, especially if some form of punishment can help bring about necessary changes. So the assessment of guilt may have its psychological and practical purposes, but one thing is clear: the search for *who* rather than *what* caused the disaster can be counterproductive. The search for individuals to blame can, and often does, divert attention from the more fundamental causes of the disaster. Furthermore, news of the punishment administered can create an illusion that corrective action has been taken when it hasn't. Thus the firing of a flight controller who by some different action might have prevented a mid-air collision may make the victims' relatives feel better and give everyone a sense the incident is closed. Yet it doesn't necessarily reduce conditions of heavy air traffic or compensate for the absence of on-board collision-warning devices that may be the more basic cause of the accident. The hazard may still be the same. A flood, earthquake, or hurricane may be followed by inquiries into why forecasters didn't provide better warnings rather than into the more fundamental and complex issues of why people were occupying vulnerable floodplains, seismic-risk zones, or coastal areas in such large numbers and what might be done about it.

The response of people to natural disaster mirrors the whole range of human characteristics that make human beings such complex and fascinating creatures. Some of the actions and reactions in the face of disaster seem predictable; others strike us as surprising even though they shouldn't.

If you and the community you live in have managed to avoid significant natural disaster, you are fortunate. More than likely the very absence of disaster experience has led you and your townspeople to underestimate the degree and diversity of natural hazards. If a warning of imminent disaster is issued, each person will interpret and act on it somewhat differently. If a flood, earthquake, tornado, or other major storm does strike your community, hindsight, always a sharper perception than foresight, will quickly detect ways the degree of tragedy might have been reduced. It's very possible this will then stimulate actions to lessen the chance of its happening again. It's a foible of human nature that it sometimes takes disaster to provoke awareness of disaster.

If you, your family, and neighbors are caught in a disaster, you more than likely will find yourself and those around you behaving with a high degree of positive action, even courage. You won't panic in the face of the danger. You won't lapse into a helpless daze. Despite the devastation and tragedy, you and they will quickly respond to the needs of the injured, calling on resources hidden within you to do whatever has to be done. Long-unused skills and abilities will emerge to help. You'll feel a special sense of togetherness with your family and friends, and you'll voluntarily assist relief workers in sifting through and clearing the debris. You'll feel a need to help in any way you can. Throughout, the feeling of pride and near exhilaration in together facing a horrible challenge and doing what had to be done will help compensate for the feelings of loss and violation. Afterwards you and your neighbors will express surprise at how well you all managed in the grip of such adversity.

If you have suffered personal loss you will experience all the grief that goes with human tragedy, but you will not be suffering in isolation, and the survivors will gain strength through that common bond and through the generous efforts and aid of others.

Your loss may not be personal, but the devastation and suffering around you may provoke initial fears of the future and understandable depression. Yet, the human spirit is resilient, and there is little likelihood of any deep-seated psychological damage. You may even eventually view it all as a positive experience.

You and your community will feel an enormous compulsion to rise, Phoenix-like, from the ashes of destruction, and return life to normal as rapidly as possible. Recovery and reconstruction will be difficult, filled with contentions and divergent views that contrast with the clear goals and cooperation during the emergency. Yet the rebuilding of the community will proceed, perhaps with a greater wisdom and humility toward the capacity of nature for sudden violence, but nevertheless with an inevitable determination to restore the conditions that made it home. The human will to make the best of adversity will prevail.

CHAPTER 15

Disasters and the Future

The violent forces of nature that we associate with disasters have helped shape the history of our planet. Some, such as lightning and the gas-spewing volcanoes, may even have played a role in the development of life. Eons before humans made their appearance in these recent moments of planetary history, severe thunderstorms, hail, tornadoes, floods, hurricanes, blizzards, earthquakes, and volcanic eruptions periodically shattered the calm—merely extreme extensions of the normal ebb and flow of the natural elements.

They are nature's way of reattaining balance from momentary imbalance, stability from temporary instability. They are not some aberration of nature but a fundamental part of the workings of nature. As such, it is futile and misguided to lament their emergence or to wish for their dissolution.

Our wisest course is to understand, appreciate, and respect them. From understanding comes control of fear. Said Lucretius, who first championed a realistic view of natural forces more than 2,000 years ago: "As children in blank darkness tremble and start at everything, so we in broad daylight are oppressed at times by fears as baseless as those horrors which children imagine coming on them in the dark. This dread and darkness of the mind cannot be dispelled by the sunbeams, the shining shafts of day, but only by an understanding of the outward forms and inner workings of nature."

Natural forces bring tragedy, it is true. But we should not forget that they can also bring benefit. Thunderstorms and hurricanes bring life-giving rain. Floods bring fertile lowland soil. Volcanic action has produced much of the earth's surface. Heavy winter snows lay a protective blanket over cropland and create solid reservoirs that months later melt to alleviate our thirst

and irrigate our farms. Earthquakes, whose violence is otherwise unwelcome, have at least taught us virtually everything we
know about the deep interior of our planet.

With them also is aesthetic beauty. The boiling drama of a
building thundercloud. The brilliant forked flashes of nighttime lightning. The organized symmetrical whirl of the hurricane. The towering majesty of the snow-capped volcanic cone.
The pristine cleanliness of the snow-covered countryside.

To think of the severe natural forces only in terms of tragedy
is to shortchange our full understanding of nature and of our
place in it. The events of nature are neutral. They have no
human purpose, good or bad. They have happened countless
times in the past, and they will forever be with us in the future.

What has changed is the spread of people over the planet,
with greater numbers occupying hazardous zones. That too
seems to be an irreversible trend. And that is why we will
always have natural disasters. In our technological age, we
somehow assume that the potential for catastrophe should be
diminishing when in fact it is not. We think our works can
protect us against nature, when in fact they have led us to
live in less harmony with the natural world, to remove ourselves from the natural cycles of nature, and to live under a
false sense of security that all too often is shattered by sudden
natural violence. Our increasingly interdependent world is becoming more susceptible to natural disaster, not less.

It is sad to have to recount the conclusion of geographers
Burton, Kates, and White when they look ahead to the future
of disasters: "It will be appreciated that a reduction in disaster
potential cannot be achieved easily and that further increase in
the incidence of disaster is the probable 'wave' of the next
decade. . . . The forces propelling the world toward more and
greater disasters will continue to outweigh by a wide margin the
forces promoting a wise choice of adjustments to hazard. There
is hope for a safer environment, but it cannot be achieved easily
or soon."

There are a few bright spots. More and more, at least in the
highly industrialized countries, the toll in disasters is in high
property damage, not in lives. Property damage will continue
to escalate rapidly, to catastrophically high potentials, but the
human tolls of deaths and injuries may be reduced despite the
increasing populations susceptible to natural hazards.

In the United States, communities are generally better prepared for disaster than they were 20 years ago. There have been improvements in planning and preparedness. There is much greater sensitivity to the problems of mitigating the hazards and lessening the risks. There is increasing awareness that a broad range of adjustments is necessary.

Yet no one is under the illusion that the potential for tragedy has been alleviated. The scenarios of future disasters loom ominously, ghostlike, ahead, awaiting only the unfortunate collision of severe natural event and dense, vulnerable population to become transformed from conjecture to cold, hard reality.

A strong hurricane striking Miami or New Orleans or any other low-lying, difficult-to-evacuate area might, disaster specialists warn, leave a greater human death toll than the 6,000 who died at Galveston in 1900. The next great California earthquake poses a potential for disaster that summons up numbers almost too awful to contemplate. Tokyo lies exposed to the triple threat of earthquake, tsunami, and fire (to say nothing of typhoon and storm surge) that could bring greater tragedy than the six-figure-fatality catastrophe of 1923. The Bay of Bengal will always be funneling tropical cyclones onto highly susceptible populations. Volcanoes, their fertile slopes attracting people to live and farm in their shadow, lie in temporary, deceptive repose, and where and when the next one will violently erupt we cannot say for certain. Many of the same features that make these areas dangerous also make them attractive places to live. The social forces that drive toward disaster are not easily slowed or diverted.

The violent forces of nature will always be with us. When they intersect large numbers of vulnerable people, we will have disasters. Realistic awareness and wise planning can lessen the hazard and must be encouraged. But they cannot eliminate it. The headlines for the next disaster await only the exact time, place, and number of victims. It is unfortunate, but true. Our best hope is for the wisdom to understand the risks and for the determination to plan our lives and communities so that we reduce, not increase, the chances of the next violent natural event turning into a natural disaster.

BIBLIOGRAPHY

This is a selective bibliography. I've listed only books and articles I consulted in preparing *The Violent Face of Nature*. The emphasis is on relatively recent works. To readers seeking a more exhaustive list of earlier references, I recommend Lane's book, which has a 44-page bibliography, current through 1965.

American Meteorological Society. "Flash Floods—A National Problem." *Bulletin American Meteorological Society* 59 (May, 1978): 585.

American Meteorological Society. "The Hurricane Problem." *Bulletin American Meteorological Society* 57 (August, 1976): 996–7.

American Seismology Delegation. "Earthquake Research in China." *EOS,* Transactions American Geophysical Union 56 (November, 1975): 838–81.

Anthes, Richard A., Hans A. Panofsky, John J. Cahir, and Albert Rango. *The Atmosphere.* 2nd ed. Columbus, Ohio: Charles E. Merrill, 1978.

Bailey, J. F., J. L. Patterson, and J. L. H. Paulhus. "Hurricane Agnes Rainfall and Floods, June–July 1972." Professional Paper 924, U.S. Geological Survey, Reston, Va., 1975.

Barnes, Stanley L. "Severe Local Storms: Concepts and Understanding." *Bulletin American Meteorological Society* 57 (April, 1976): 412–19.

Barton, Allen H. *Communities in Disaster.* Garden City, N.Y.: Doubleday & Co., 1969.

Battan, Louis. "Killer Storms." *1972 Encyclopedia Britannica Yearbook of Science and the Future,* pp. 115–127.

———. *The Nature of Violent Storms.* Garden City, N.Y.: Anchor Books, Doubleday & Co., 1961.

————. *Weather*. Englewood Cliffs, N.J.: Prentice-Hall, 1974.

Bickham, Jack M. *Twister*. Garden City, N.Y.: Doubleday & Co., 1976.

Big Thompson Canyon Flash Flood of July 31–August 1, 1976. Natural Disaster Survey Report 76-1. National Oceanic and Atmospheric Administration, Washington, D. C., 1976.

The Big Thompson Disaster. Loveland, Colo.: Lithographic Press, Inc., 1976.

Boffey, Philip M. "Investigators Agree N.Y. Blackout of 1977 Could Have Been Avoided." *Science* 201 (15 September, 1978): 994–998.

Bolt, B. A., W. L. Horn, G. A. Macdonald, and R. F. Scott. *Geological Hazards*. New York: Springer-Verlag, Rev. 2nd Ed., 1977.

————. *Earthquakes: A Primer*. San Francisco: W. H. Freeman and Company, 1978.

Brown, Harry E., and David A. Olson. "Performance of NMC in Forecasting a Record-Breaking Winter Storm, 6–7 February 1978." *Bulletin American Meteorological Society* 59 (May, 1978): 562–75.

Brown, Rodger A., ed. *The Union City, Oklahoma, Tornado of 24 May 1973*. NOAA Technical Memorandum ERL NSSL-80, National Severe Storms Laboratory, Norman, Okla., 1976.

Brown, Rodger A., Leslie R. Lemon, and Donald W. Burgess. "Tornado Detection by Pulsed Doppler Radar." *Monthly Weather Review* 106 (January, 1978): 29–38.

Bullard, Fred M. *Volcanoes of the Earth*. Austin: University of Texas Press, 1976.

Burton, Ian, Robert W. Kates, and Gilbert F. White. *The Environment as Hazard*. New York: Oxford University Press, 1978.

Calder, Nigel. *The Weather Machine*. New York: Viking Press, 1974.

Changnon, Stanley A., *et al*. *Hail Suppression: Impacts and Issues*. Final report, Technology Assessment of the Suppression of Hail. Urbana: Illinois State Water Survey, 1977.

Committee on Atmospheric Sciences. *The Atmospheric Sciences: Problems and Applications*. National Academy of Sciences, Washington, D.C., 1977.

Committee on Atmospheric Sciences. *Severe Storms: Prediction, Detection, and Warning*. National Academy of Sciences, Washington, D.C., 1977.

Committee on Atmospheric Sciences. *Weather & Climate Modification*. National Academy of Sciences, Washington, D.C., 1973.

Committee on Climate and Weather Fluctuations and Agricultural Production. *Climate and Food*. National Academy of Sciences, Washington, D.C., 1976.

Conrad, Andrée. "Beyond the Panic Principle: Disaster and the

American Imagination." *Book Forum* Vol. IV No. 2, 1978, pp. 204–54.

Corliss, William R. *Handbook of Unusual Natural Phenomena.* Glen Arm, Md.: The Sourcebook Project, 1977.

Cornell, James. *The Great International Disaster Book.* New York: Charles Scribner's Sons, 1976.

Cowen, Robert C. "Founding Our House Upon a Rock." *Technology Review* 80 (October/November, 1977): 8–9.

Cressman, George P. "A Notable Forecasting Achievement." *Bulletin American Meteorological Society* 59 (April, 1978): 370.

Davies-Jones, Robert P., Donald W. Burgess, Leslie R. Lemon, and Daniel Purcell. "Interpretation of Surface Marks and Debris Patterns from the 24 May 1973 Union City, Oklahoma Tornado." *Monthly Weather Review* 106 (January, 1978): 12–21.

Derr, John S. "Earthquake Lights." *Earthquake Information Bulletin* (May-June, 1977): 18–21.

Douglas, John H. "Waiting for the 'Great Tokai Quake.'" *Science News* 113 (29 April, 1978): 282.

———. "Forecast of Mexican Quake Accurate, but Ignored." *Science News* 114 (9 December, 1978): 404.

Drabek, Thomas E. "System Shock: Immediate Responses Following Impact." In *Human Systems in Extreme Environments* by D. S. Mileti, T. E. Drabek, and J. E. Haas. Institute of Behavioral Science, University of Colorado, Boulder, 1975.

Drabek, Thomas E., and E. L. Quarantelli. "Scapegoats, Villains, and Disasters." *Trans-Action* 4 (March, 1967): 12–16.

Dunn, Gordon E., and Banner I. Miller. *Atlantic Hurricanes.* Baton Rouge: Louisiana State University Press, 1960.

Dynes, Russell R., and E. L. Quarantelli. "Helping Behavior in Large-Scale Disasters." Preliminary Paper 48, Disaster Research Center, Ohio State University, Columbus, 1977.

Eberhart, Jonathan. "Apollo 12: More Footsteps on the Moon." *Science News* 96 (22 November, 1969): 470–72.

Edgar, B. C. "Global Lightning Distribution at Dawn and Dusk for August-December 1977 as Observed by the DMSP Lightning Detector." Report No. SSL-78(3639-02)-1 Space Sciences Laboratory, The Aerospace Corporation, Los Angeles, 1978. *Journal of Geophysical Research*, in press.

Edinger, James G. *Watching for the Wind.* Garden City, N.Y.: Anchor Books, Doubleday & Co., 1967.

Fairbridge, Rhodes, ed. *The Encyclopedia of Atmospheric Sciences and Astrogeology.* New York: Reinhold, 1967.

Fairbridge, Rhodes W., ed. *Marvels and Mysteries of the World Around Us.* Pleasantville, N.Y.: Reader's Digest Association Inc., 1977.

Farhar, Barbara C. "Hail Suppression Efforts in the United States." In Changnon, Stanley A., et al., Hail Suppression: Impacts and Issues. Final report, Technology Assessment of the Suppression of Hail. Urbana: Illinois State Water Survey, 1977.

Fendell, Francis E. "Tropical Cyclones." Advances in Geophysics Volume 17, 1974, pp. 1–100.

Fleagle, Robert G., James A. Crutchfield, Ralph W. Johnson, and Mohamed F. Abdo. Weather Modification in the Public Interest. Seattle: University of Washington Press, 1974.

Follin, J. W. Jr., E. P. Gray, and K. Yu. "The Connection Between Cosmic Rays and Thunderstorms." (Abstract) EOS 58 (December, 1977), p. 1220.

————. "Cosmic Ray Influence on Cloud Dynamics and Global Circulation." (Abstract) EOS 59 (April, 1978), p. 285.

Frank, Neil L., and S. A. Husain. "The Deadliest Tropical Cyclone in History?" Bulletin American Meteorological Society 52 (June, 1971): 438–44.

Frank, Neil. "The Hard Facts About Hurricanes." NOAA Magazine 4 (July, 1974).

Frazier, Kendrick. "California's Shifting Crust: Slip Sliding Away." Science News 112 (17 December, 1977): 404.

————. "Earthquake and Avalanche: Peruvian Disaster." Science News 98 (1 August, 1970): 94.

————. "Mapping Lightning by Satellite." Science News 112 (17 December, 1977): 408.

————. "The Search for a Way to Suppress Hail." Science News 99 (20 March, 1971): 200–202.

————. "The Shifting, Stretching Crust of Central America." Science News 110 (9 October, 1976): 234–35.

Frisch, Joan Vandiver. "Lightning: A Search for the Source." NOAA 7 (January, 1977): 8–9.

Fuchs, Sir Vivian, ed. Forces of Nature. New York: Holt, Rinehart and Winston, 1977.

Fujita, T. Theodore. "Anticyclonic Tornadoes." Weatherwise 30 (April, 1977): 51–64.

Fujita, T. Theodore, et al. "Photogrammetric Analyses of Tornadoes." In Peterson, R. E., ed. Proceedings, Symposium on Tornadoes, 1976.

Fujita, T. Theodore, and Horace R. Byers. "Spearhead Echo and Downburst in the Crash of an Airliner." Monthly Weather Review 105 (February, 1977): 129–46.

Gelman, Woody. Disaster Illustrated. New York: Harmony Books, 1976.

Geophysics Study Committee. Geophysical Predictions. Geophysics Research Board, National Academy of Sciences, Washington, D.C., 1978.

Golden, Joseph H., and Daniel Purcell. "Life Cycle of the Union City, Oklahoma Tornado and Comparison with Waterspouts." *Monthly Weather Review* 106 (January, 1978): 3–11.

Gould, Stephen Jay. "The Great Scablands Debate." *Natural History* 84 (August-September, 1978): 12.

Guillen, Michael A. "Lava Flow Causes 70 Deaths." *Science News* 111 (18 June, 1977): 388.

————. "Tangshan Quake: Portrait of a Catastrophe." *Science News* 111 (18 June, 1977): 388.

Gurka, James J. "Satellite and Surface Observations of Strong Wind Zones Accompanying Thunderstorms." *Monthly Weather Review* 104 (December, 1976): 1484–93.

Haas, J. Eugene, Robert W. Kates, and Martyn J. Bowden, eds. *Reconstruction Following Disaster.* Cambridge, Mass.: MIT Press, 1977.

Haicheng Earthquake Study Delegation. "Prediction of the Haicheng Earthquake." *EOS* 58 (May, 1977): 236–72.

Hamilton, Warren. "Plate Tectonics and Man." *Annual Report Fiscal Year 1976* U.S. Geological Survey: 39–53.

Harpum, John. "Energy Scale." Appendix C in *The Elements Rage* by Frank W. Lane. Philadelphia: Chilton Books, 1965.

Herman, John R., Richard A. Goldberg, and Jay R. Herman. "Thunderstorm Triggering by Solar Activity." (Abstract) *EOS* 58 (December, 1977): 1220.

Hindley, Keith. "Learning to Live with Twisters." *New Scientist* 75 (4 August, 1977): 280–82.

Hoxit, Lee R., and Charles F. Chappell. "Tornado Outbreak of April 3–4, 1974: Synoptic Analysis." NOAA Technical Report ERL 338-APCL 37 Environmental Research Laboratories, Boulder, Colo., 1975.

Hughes, Patrick. *American Weather Stories.* Washington, D.C.: U.S. Department of Commerce, 1974.

Illingsworth, Anthony. "Charging Up a Thunderstorm." *New Scientist* 78 (25 May, 1978): 504–6.

Jennings, Gary. *The Killer Storms.* Philadelphia: J. B. Lippincott, 1970.

Justice, Alonzo A. "Seeing the Inside of a Tornado." *Monthly Weather Review* 58 (May, 1930): 205–206.

Kessler, Edwin. "Recent Developments in Tornado Research." In *Proceedings, Symposium on Tornadoes,* Richard E. Peterson, ed., Texas Tech University, Lubbock, Tex., 1976.

————. "A Storm's Incalculable Energy." *Natural History,* April, 1966.

————. "Tornadoes: State of Knowledge." *Journal of the Structural Division, Proceedings of the American Society of Civil Engineers* 104 (February, 1978): 352–57.

————. "Tornadoes." *Bulletin of the American Meteorological Society* 51 (October, 1970): 926–36.

Kiesling, Ernst W., Kishor C. Mehta, and Joseph E. Minor. "Protection of Property and Occupants in Windstorms." Paper presented at the American Society of Civil Engineers National Convention, Dallas, Texas, April 29, 1977.

Kiesling, Ernst W., and David E. Goosby. "In-Home Shelters from Extreme Winds." *Civil Engineering* 44 (September, 1974): 105–107.

Krafft, Maurice and Kata. *Volcano.* New York: Harry N. Abrams, Inc., 1975.

Lane, Frank W. *The Elements Rage.* Philadelphia: Chilton Books, 1965.

Lee, Albert. *Weather Wisdom.* New York: Doubleday, 1976.

Ley, Willy. *On Earth and in the Sky.* New York: Ace Books, 1967.

Ludlum, David. *Early American Hurricanes 1492–1870.* Boston: American Meteorological Society, 1963.

————. *Weather Record Book.* Princeton, N.J.: Weatherwise, Inc., 1971.

Maddox, Robert A., L. R. Hoxit, C. F. Chappell, and F. Caracena. "Comparison of Meteorological Aspects of the Big Thompson and Rapid City Flash Floods." *Monthly Weather Review* 106 (March, 1978): 375–89.

Markson, Ralph. "Solar Modulation of Atmospheric Electrification and Possible Implications for the Sun-weather Relationship." *Nature* 273 (11 May, 1978): 103–9.

Mehta, Kishor C., Joseph E. Minor, and James R. McDonald. "Interim Guidelines for Building Occupant Protection from Tornadoes and Extreme Winds." TR-83A/Defense Civil Preparedness Agency, Washington, 1975.

Mileti, Dennis S., Thomas E. Drabek, and J. Eugene Haas. *Human Systems in Extreme Environments: A Sociological Perspective.* Program on Technology, Environment and Man, Monograph 21, Boulder: Institute of Behavioral Science, University of Colorado, 1975.

Minor, Joseph E. "Applications of Tornado Technology in Professional Practice." In Peterson, R. E., ed., *Proceedings, Symposium on Tornadoes,* Texas Tech University, Lubbock, Tex., 1976.

Minor, Joseph E., and Richard D. Marshall. "Cyclone 'Tracy': Implications for Residential Construction?" Unpublished paper, 9 pages, undated.

Mogil, H. Michael, Marjorie Rush, and Mary Kutka. "Lightning—A Preliminary Reassessment." *Weatherwise* 30 (October, 1977): 192–99.

Moore, Gerald. "The Town That Wouldn't Die." *Saturday Evening Post* December, 1975.

Murchie, Guy. *Song of the Sky*. Boston: Houghton Mifflin; Cambridge: Riverside Press, 1954.

Nash, Jay Robert. *Darkest Hours*. Chicago: Nelson Hall; New York: Pocket Books, Wallaby Editions, 1977.

National Geographic Society. *The Powers of Nature*. Washington, D.C., 1978.

Nuttli, Otto W. "The Mississippi Valley Earthquakes of 1811 and 1812." *Bulletin of the Seismological Society of America* 63 (February, 1973): 227–48.

Orville, Richard E. "Bolt from the Blue." *Natural History* 86 (June-July, 1977): 66–73.

―――. "Electricity in the Sky." *Encyclopedia Britannica Yearbook of Science and the Future* 1976: 155–165.

Panel on Public Policy Implications of Earthquake Prediction. *Earthquake Prediction and Public Policy*. Advisory Committee on Emergency Planning, National Academy of Sciences, Washington, D.C., 1975.

Penick, James, Jr. *The New Madrid Earthquakes of 1811–1812*. Columbia, Mo.: University of Missouri Press, 1976.

Peterson, R. E., ed. *Proceedings, Symposium on Tornadoes*, Texas Tech University, Lubbock, Tex., 1976.

Plafker, George. "Tectonic Aspects of the Guatemala Earthquake of 4 February 1976." *Science* 193 (24 September, 1976): 1201–8.

Press, Frank, and Raymond Siever. *Earth*. San Francisco: W. H. Freeman and Co., 1974.

Purdom, James F. W. "Some Uses of High-Resolution GOES Imagery in the Mesoscale Forecasting of Convection and Its Behavior." *Monthly Weather Review* 104 (December, 1976): 1474–83.

Quarantelli, E. L. "Panic Behavior: Some Empirical Observations." In *Human Response to Tall Buildings*. Stroudsburg, Pa.: Dowden Hutchinson & Ross, Inc., 1977.

Quarantelli, E. L., and Russell R. Dynes. "When Disaster Strikes (It Isn't Much Like What You've Heard & Read About)." *Psychology Today* 5 (February, 1972): 66–70.

Quarantelli, E. L., and Verta Taylor. "Some Views on the Warning Problem in Disasters as Suggested by Sociological Research." *Preprints, Tenth Conference on Severe Local Storms*. Boston: American Meteorological Society, 1977.

Rankin, William H. *The Man Who Rode the Thunder*. New York: Prentice-Hall, 1960.

Roberts, Walter Orr. "We're Doing Something About the Weather." *National Geographic* 141 (April, 1972): 518–55.

Schwartz, Glenn E. "The Day It Snowed in Miami." *Weatherwise* 30 (April, 1977): 50.

Schwarz, Francis K., *et al.* "The Black Hills-Rapid City Flood of

June 9-10, 1972." Professional Paper 877, U.S. Geological Survey, Reston, Va., 1975.

"Severe Local Storms." Papers presented to the U.S. House of Representatives Subcommittee on Environment and the Atmosphere at a special review session of the AMS 9th Conference on Severe Local Storms, Norman, Okla., 23 October, 1975. *Bulletin American Meteorological Society* 57 (April, 1976): 398–435.

Simpson, R. H. "The Complex Killer." *Oceanus* 17 (Spring, 1974): 22–27.

————. "Hurricane Prediction." In Geophysics Study Committee, *Geophysical Predictions*. National Academy of Sciences, Washington, D.C., 1978.

Singhal, Ramesh P. *How to Save Your Life and Home from Natural Disasters*. New York: Pagurian Press, 1977.

Snow, Edward Rowe. *The Fury of the Seas*. New York: Dodd, Mead & Co., 1964.

"Solar Weather Cycles Could be Electric." *New Scientist* 11 (May, 1978).

Stewart, George R. *Storm*. New York: Random House, 1941.

Stewart, Gordon S. "Implications for Plate Tectonics of the Aug. 19, 1977, Indonesian Decoupling Normal-Fault Earthquake." (Abstract) *EOS* 59 (April, 1978): 326.

Sullivan, Walter. *Continents in Motion*. New York: McGraw-Hill, 1974.

Sutcliffe, R. C. *Weather & Climate*. New York: Norton, 1966.

Sutton, Ann and Myron. *Nature on the Rampage*. New York: Lippincott, 1962.

Sutton, O. G. *The Challenge of the Atmosphere*. New York: Harper Brothers, 1961.

Tan-Schnell, Suan N., and Russell C. Schnell. "Tea Litter: A Prolific Source of Ice (Hail?) Nuclei." (Abstract) *EOS* 59 (December, 1978): 1086.

Taylor, Verta. "Good News About Disaster." *Psychology Today* 11 (October, 1977): 93.

Thorarinsson, Sigurdur. "Surtsey: Island Born of Fire." *National Geographic* 127 (May, 1965): 713–26.

Toksöz, M. Nafi. "The Subduction of the Lithosphere." *Scientific American* 235 (November, 1975).

Trotter, Robert J. "Unraveling a Mayan Mystery." *Science News* 111 (29 January, 1977): 74.

Tufty, Barbara. *1001 Questions Answered About Storms and Other Natural Air Disasters*. New York: Dodd, Mead & Co., 1970.

Turman, B. N. "Detection of Lightning Superbolts." *Journal of Geophysical Research* 82 (20 June, 1977): 2566–68.

Uman, Martin A., *et al*. "An Unusual Lightning Flash at Kennedy Space Center." *Science* 201 (7 July, 1978): 9–16.

Vann, W. Pennington, and James R. McDonald. *An Engineering Analysis: Mobile Homes in Windstorms.* Institute for Disaster Research, Texas Tech University, Lubbock, Tex., 1978.

Viemeister, Peter E. *The Lightning Book.* Garden City, N.Y.: Doubleday, 1961.

Wagner, A. James. "The Record-Breaking Winter of 1976–77." *Weatherwise* 30 (April, 1977): 65–69.

Walker, George R., Joseph E. Minor, and Richard D. Marshall. "The Darwin Cyclone: Valuable Lesson in Structural Design." *Civil Engineering* 45 (December, 1975): 82–86.

Ward, Delbert B. "Wind-Resistant Design Concepts for Residences." TR-83/Defense Civil Preparedness Agency, Washington, 1975.

Ward, Peter F. "Earthquake Prediction." In Geophysics Study Committee, *Geophysical Predictions.* National Academy of Sciences, Washington, D.C., 1978.

Weigel, Edwin P. "Lightning: The Underrated Killer." *NOAA* 6 (April, 1976).

———. "NOAA Weather Radio." *Weatherwise* 31 (August, 1978): 147–51.

———. "Some New Ideas About Tornadoes." *NOAA* 5 (July, 1975).

White, Gilbert F., ed. *Natural Hazards: Local, National, Global.* New York: Oxford University Press, 1974.

White, Gilbert F., and J. Eugene Haas. *Assessment of Research on Natural Hazards.* Cambridge, Mass.: MIT Press, 1975.

Williams, Richard S., and James C. Moore. "Man Against Volcano: The Eruption on Heimaey." (Booklet) U.S. Geological Survey, Reston, Va., 1977.

Wilson, J. Tuzo, ed. *Continents Adrift and Continents Aground.* (Readings from *Scientific American.*) San Francisco: W. H. Freeman and Co., 1976.

Woodley, W. L., J. A. Jordan, J. Simpson, R. Biondini, and J. Flueck. "NOAA's Florida Area Cumulus Experiment Rainfall Results: 1970–1976." *Journal of Applied Meteorology* in press.

Working Group on Earthquake Hazards Reduction. *Earthquake Hazards Reduction: Issues for an Implementation Plan.* Office of Science and Technology Policy, Executive Office of the President, Washington, D.C., 1978.

Wrightson, R. A. "The Wild Winter of 1976–77 in New York State." *Weatherwise* 30 (April, 1977): 70–75.

Wylie, Evan McLeod. "The Blizzard of '88: How Bad Was It, Really?" *Yankee* 42 (March, 1978): 86.

Young, Louise B. *Earth's Aura.* New York: Knopf, 1977.

Newspaper accounts from the *New York Times*, the *Los Angeles Times*, the *Washington Post*, and (for the Big Thompson flood in

Colorado) the *Loveland Reporter-Herald*, *Greeley Tribune*, and *Denver Post* have also proved valuable. Several wire service reports from the Associated Press, United Press International, Reuters, and Agence-France Press also supplied information.

INDEX

Abernethy, James J., 59
AFOS system, 264, 268
Aggarwall, Yash P., 270
Air Force Geophysics Laboratory, 75
Air parcel, 31
Air Weather Service, 75, 76
Airline disasters, 28, 37, 85
Alaska, 203, 232–234
Aleutian trench, 232
Aleutians, 230, 231
American Association for the Advancement of Science, 280
American Geophysical Union, 97, 271
American Meteorological Society, 129, 282, 328, 332
American Red Cross, 349, 354
Anchorage, Alaska, 234
Antigua Guatemala, 258
Arc line clouds, 41
Ashfall, Krakatoa, 206
Ashflow, 203, 208
Assam earthquake, 243, 244
Assam region, 275
Atlantic hurricanes, origin, 165
Atlantis, 208
Atmosphere
    mathematical models, 254
    monitoring process, 253
    remote sensing, 266
    unstable, 30–32
Atmospheric models, 255
Atmospheric pressure change, 306
Audubon, John James, 248
Australia, storm seeding, 293
Automation of Field Operations and Services (AFOS), 264, 268
Avalanche, earthquake-caused, 242
Azores, 216

Bacon, Francis, 297
Baguio, 146
Ball lightning, 91–93
Battan, Louis J., 296
Bay of Bengal, 366
    cyclone, 154–156
Big Thompson Canyon flood, 134, 266, 313
    damage to canyon, 128

damage to property, 127
findings of study, 133
rainfall, 120
warnings unheeded, 341, 344
Blizzard, definition, 167
    Donner party, 185
    formation, 186
    New Hampshire coast, 182
    New York City, 179
    Ohio, 178
    prediction accuracy, 261
    snow removal, 174, 175
    snowfall records, 179
    survival story, 178, 179
    wind-chill temperatures, 171
Blizzard of 1778, 184
Blizzard of 1888, 185, 186
Blizzard of 1978, Wisconsin, 177
Blue Ridge Tornado, 56
Bolt, Bruce, 228, 230, 240
Borland, Hal, 100
Boulder Canyon, flash floods, 266, 267
Bowden, Martyn J., 358, 359
Bradbury, John, 238
Bradford, William, 148
Brandenburg Tornado, 47, 48, 54, 56
Bretz, J. Harlen, 136
British Meteorological Office, 92, 117
Brook, Marx, 93
Brooks, Jared, 239
Brown, Harry E., 255
Browning, Keith A., 117
Bufe, Charles G., 271
Buffalo blizzard, 171, 172, 174
Buffalo Creek dam break, 354
Bullard, Fred M., 190, 203, 204, 209
Burgess, Donald W., 75
Burton, Ian, 319–322, 328, 341, 365
Byers, Horace, 35, 39, 54, 114, 116

California earthquakes, 333
    disaster potential, 334, 366
    plate motions, 236
Cape May County, 330
Capelinhos eruption, 193
Caribbean plate, 217, 228, 229
Carr, Michael, 217
Catastrophe potential, U.S., 324

Catastrophic events, 242
  deadly succession, 243
  global toll, 320
  interacting, 323
Central America, 227, 228, 231
Changnon, Stanley A., Jr., 105, 108,
  109, 283
Channeled Scablands, 136, 195
Chappell, Charles F., 132, 133
Char Jabbar, 155, 156
Charleston earthquake, 237
Chesapeake Bay disaster, 24
Chile earthquake, tsunami, 241
China, earthquakes, 15, 222, 223
  prediction, 222, 271
China, flood damage, 142
Cirrus clouds, 24, 186
Cities, disaster-struck, 357
  rebuilding, 358, 359
Clark Fork Canyon, 137
Cline, Isaac M., 143, 144
Cloud electrification, 93
Cloud parcel, 34
Cloud seeding, 279, 287
  Soviet Union, 281
  winter snowfall, 284, 285
Coastal area growth, 321, 329
Cocos plate, 229, 230
Cold fronts, 36
Cold season of 1816, 188
Cold seasons, volcanic dust, 188, 189
Cold wave, south Florida, 170
Cole, Robert O., 262
Columbia River Plateau, 195
Columbus, Christopher, 147
Committee on Natural Disasters, 57
Compère-Léandre, León, 201
Conrad, Charles, 87
Continental drift, 215, 216
Corliss, William, 245
Corps of Engineers, 318
Cosmos 954 crash, 248
Cressman, George P., 128, 259, 328
Crete, tsunamis, 208
Cumulonimbus clouds, 30, 31, 35, 42,
  133, 311
  daughter cloud formation, 114
  ionizing radiation, 44
  rotary formation, 156
Cumulus clouds, 24, 34, 114
Cyclone disasters
  Bangladesh, 15, 154–156, 322
  Bay of Bengal, 154–156
  Tracy, Australia, 307

Dade County, crop damage, 170
Dams and levees, 321, 326, 328
Danube, levees and dikes, 329
Davis, Ray Jay, 294
Davison, Charles, 246
Death toll, annual, 79, 80
Death toll reduced, 365
Demerath, Nicholas, 346
Depauw Tornado, 54, 46
Derr, John C., 245
Developing countries, 322, 323
Disaster potential, 323, 365, 366
Disaster Preparedness Staff, 300
Disaster relief agencies, 349, 356, 357
Disaster Research Center, 338, 342,
  345, 351, 352
Disaster Research Group, NAS, 338
Disaster vulnerability, 316–336
Disaster warnings, human response,
  262, 263, 277, 348
  psychological and social, 342, 343
  selective perception, 342
Disasters, human response, 337–363
  community, 350
  family members, 349
  mental health effects, 352–354
  social relationships, 353
  use of telephone, 345
Disasters, technological, 350
Doppler, Christian, 74
Doppler radar, 74, 75, 96
Douglas, John H., 335, 336
Drabek, Thomas E., 342, 346, 348
Drought cycles, Western U.S., 43, 44
Dunn, C. R., 265
Durward, J., 92
Dynes, Russell R., 345, 348, 353, 356

Earth tremor predictions, 270
Earthquake causes, 229, 230
Earthquake hazards, 240–243, 333
  safety measures, 314, 315
Earthquake Hazards Reduction Act,
  276
Earthquake lights, 245–248
Earthquake magnitudes, 225
Earthquake noises, 244, 245
Earthquake precursors, 248, 249, 272–
  274
Earthquake prediction, 249, 270
  areas of highest risk, 276
  Haicheng, China, 222, 271, 272
  people responding to, 276
  seismic gap concept, 275, 276

social and economic disruption, 278
  successful, 270, 271
Earthquake-fire disaster, 334
Earthquake-prone areas, 229, 230
Earthquakes, 226
  California, 234, 333–336, 366
  Central America, 228
  China, 15, 222, 237, 271
  death toll, 219, 220, 223, 226
  deep and shallow, 230, 231, 234
  Eastern U.S., 238, 333
  energy release, 14
  frequency of strikes, 13
  island arcs, 231
  maximum depth, 231
  ocean trenches, 231
  pressure waves, 245
  source of energy, 14
  subduction zones, 232
  Tangshan, China, 222, 237, 271
  Turkey, 248
  U.S. intraplate, 237
  vertical acceleration, 244
Earth's crust, 191, 216, 227
East African Rift Valley, 218
Edgar, Bruce C., 98
El Salvador, 230
Electrical storm, typical, 77
Emergency disaster plans, 315
Energy release, earth's interior, 14
Environment as Hazard, The, 319
Environmental Data Service, 175, 179
Estelle, Earl, 268
Estes Park flash flood, 122–126
Evacuation disaster, Miami, 316–318
Evacuation study, Fort Myers, 330
Evacuation warnings, 310
Evacuations, 346

Farhar, Barbara C., 295
Federal Disaster Assistance Adminis-
    tration, 129
Federal Emergency Management
    Agency, 304
Federal Flood Control Act of 1936,
    325
Ferguson, Edward, 41
Few, Arthur, 94
Finkelstein, David, 248
Fitzgerald, Stephen, 223
Flammarion, Nicholas Camille, 85
Flash flood creation, 133, 134

Flash flood disasters
  Big Thompson Canyon, 119
  eyewitness reports, 122–126
  major killers, 312
  population density, 135
  similarities, 132
Flash flood warnings, 313
Flash-flood-prone areas, 129
Flash floods
  death toll, 129
  earthquake-caused, 242
  Kansas City, 135
  nocturnal, 132
  preparedness, 340
  property damage, 129
Fleagle, Robert G., 296
Flood control, 325–327
Flood disasters, steady rise, 139
Flood Insurance Administration, 129
Flood warnings, disregarded, 131
Floodplains, 13, 321, 329
Floods
  eastern Washington State, 136, 137
  Hurricane Agnes, 140
  Johnstown, Pennsylvania, 119, 134
Florida Area Cumulus Experiment,
    285
Florida cold wave, 170
Florida Keys, 330
Flora, S. D., 59
Follin, J. W., Jr., 45
Frank, Neil L., 261, 269, 329, 331
Franklin, Benjamin, 87
French Academy of Science, 92
Fritz, Charles E., 340
Froissart, Sir John, 103
Fujita, T. Theodore, 29, 48, 54, 63,
    71, 73
Fujita-Pearson Tornado Intensity
    Scale, 54
Fujiyama, 191

Gainesville tornadoes, 67
Galveston hurricane of 1900, 143–146
Galveston-Houston area, 331
Gambler's fallacy, 341
Gasli earthquake, 274
GATE, 165, 166
General Electric Research Laborato-
    ries, 279
Gentry, R. Cecil, 291
Geophysical changes, 274
Geophysical Flood Dynamics Labora-
    tory, 162

Geophysical Predictions Panel, NAS, 270
Geostationary Operational Environmental Satellites (GOES), 256–259
Glacial Lake Missoula, 136, 138
Global Atmospheric Research Program (GARP), 165
GOES East and West, 40, 256–259
Goyer, Guy G., 282
Grabens, 229
Grand Coulee canyon, 137
Grant, Lewis O., 284
Great Hurricane of 1780, 150
Great Ice Age, Marmes site, 136
Great Kwanto Earthquake, 242
Great Lakes snowstorms, 171, 175
  snow redistribution, 280
Great Plains
  hailstorms, 109
  squall lines, 36
  thunderstorms, 114
Great Spokane Flood, 136
Guatemala, 230
Guatemala earthquake, 220, 226, 227
Guin tornado, 47, 49, 54, 56
Gulf of Mexico, 61, 163
Gurka, James J., 42
Gust front, 41

Haas, J. Eugene, 318, 324, 325, 339, 342, 358, 359, 361
Haicheng earthquake, 222, 271–273
Hail Alley, 108, 109, 113
Hail damage, 48
  animals killed, 104
  annual U.S. toll, 109, 110
  crop destruction, 102, 110, 118
  homes and automobiles, 111
Hail drifts, 112
Hail formation, 112, 113
Hail suppression, 280
  magic and ritual, 278
  operational programs, 283
  San Luis Valley, 294
  seeding experiments, 282
  Soviet Union, 281
  testing Soviet mode, 113
Hail-producing weather, 108
Hail-prone region, world's, 107
Hailstones, 112
  downdraft velocity, 116
  fallspeed velocity, 114
  growth process, 113, 117
  killing, 102–104
  shapes, 105
  sizes, 107, 109
Hailstorm, monitored, 281
Hailstorm cross-section, 116
Hailstorm description, 100, 101
Hailstorm frequency, 108
Hailstorm structure, 114
Hailstorms
  four-day multi-state, 111
  historical, 103, 104
  network of sensors, 113
  property damage, 111, 112
  supercell storms, 117, 118
Hailstreak, typical, 112
Hail-tea plantation link, 108
Hamilton, Robert M., 274
Hardin, Garrett, 276
Hartford Civic Center, 177
Hawaiian Islands, 193, 218
Heimaey, island, 212
Hewapathirane, D., 328
Himalayas, 217
Hollister, California, 228, 274
Hoover, Herbert, 139
Hope, John, 262
Hot spot hypothesis, 218
Houses, wind damage, 307, 308
Hurricane, 146
Hurricane Agnes, 15, 140, 160
Hurricane Anita, 163
Hurricane Betsy, 296, 351, 359
Hurricane Camille, 153, 160, 269
Hurricane Carla evacuation, 346, 348
Hurricane Debbie, 291, 292
Hurricane Diane, 160
Hurricane Ella, 292
Hurricane eyewall, 157, 158, 289
Hurricane Faith, 160
Hurricane fatalities, 153
Hurricane Fifi, 295
Hurricane forecasting, error, 262
Hurricane formation, 151, 157
  African connection, 165, 166
Hurricane Ginger, 152, 160
Hurricane Ginny, 160
Hurricane Group, NOAA, 163
Hurricane hazard, 316–318, 330
  potential U.S., 329
Hurricane modification, 280, 289, 290, 295
Hurricane paths, erratic, 160
Hurricane prediction, 262

Hurricane preparedness committees, 310, 332
Hurricane simulations, 166
Hurricane speeds, 159
Hurricane warnings, 257, 295
Hurricane-force winds, 151
Hurricane-resistant design, 307, 308
Hurricanes, 148, 263
  average rainfall, 152
  direct observations, 164, 165
  flying weather stations, 163
  Galveston, Texas, 143
  lowest pressure recorded, 159
  New England, 148, 149
  New Spain Flota, 147
  safety guidelines, 308–310
  storm surges, 152–154
  warm eddies, 165
  weather patterns, 166
  West Indies, 150
  wind intensification, 157
Hwang-Ho River, China, 141

Iceland volcanoes, 195, 216–218
  eruption control, 211–214
Ilopango volcano, 208
Infrared imaging, 257
Institute of Disaster Research, 57, 300, 304
Insurance programs, 326
International Commission on Atmospheric Electricity, 312
Ionizing radiation, 44
Ionosphere, pulsating, 245
Islam, M. Aminul, 154
Island arcs, 193, 217, 231

Jaggar, Thomas, 191, 200
James River flood, 141
Jamestown hurricane of 1609, 148
Japan
  earthquake engineering, 335
  Project Stormfury, 292, 296
  typhoon rainfall, 151
Java-Sumatra island arc, 217
Johnstown flood, 134, 313, 326
Joint Committee on Seismic Safety, 334
Jonesboro Tornado, preparedness, 339
Jordan, J. A., 288
Journey to the Center of the Earth, 191

Kansas-Missouri floods, 140

Kates, Robert W., 319, 321–323, 328, 341, 358, 359, 365
Katmai National Monument, 205
Keller, Will, 67
Kenya hailstorms, 107, 108
Kessler, Edwin, 58, 259
Key, William H., 350
Key Biscayne, 316, 317, 331
Khattri, K. N., 275
Kiesling, Ernst W., 303
Kilauea, 191, 193, 218
Kilimanjaro, 191
Kingdon-Ward, Frank, 244
Kingston, Jamaica, 322
Kinney, Henry W., 242
Knight, Charles and Nancy, 107
Krakatoa eruption, 205–207
Krehbiel, Paul R., 93
Krishnamurti, T. N., 166
Kwanto earthquake, 243
Kuril Islands, 231, 245

Lake Erie storm, 172
Laki eruption, catastrophic, 211, 216
Landes, M., 197, 198
Landslides, 241, 243
Lane, Franklin W., 79
Langmuir, Irving, 279
Latham, Gary V., 275
Lava flow control, 212, 214
Lava plateaus, 195
Lee, J. T., 43
Lightning, 77
  death toll, 15, 79, 80, 85
  death-to-injury ratio, 83
  forest and oil fires, 86
  freakish, 84
  frequency, 13, 99
  global view, 98
  intracloud, cloud-to-ground, 96
  radio triangulation, 94
  regions of highest activity, 98
  safety guidelines, 311, 312
  South Africa, 94
  Southern Hemisphere, 98
  worldwide, 79, 97
  zeppelin crash, 85
Lightning bolts
  Apollo 12, 87
  heat-generated, 90
  New York City blackout, 86
  survival, 83
Lightning charge temperature, 94, 95

Lightning flashes
  cloud-to-cloud, 91
  cloud-to-ground, 93, 94, 96
  geographic concentration, 97
  global frequency, 99
  intracloud, 96
  Kennedy Space Center, 96
  sources of, 94
  step leaders, 89
Lightning formation, 96, 97
Lightning hazards, 325
  CB radio, 82
  livestock, 84
  trees, 81
Lightning mythologies, 87
Lightning suppression, 280, 283, 284
Lightning rod, 88
Lightning superbolts, 97
Little, C. Gordon, 265, 266
Lomnitz, Cinna, 248
Looting, 350, 351
Los Angeles, earthquake potential, 334
Louisville tornado, 52
Lubbock Tornado, 65, 303
Ludlum, David M., 111

Maddox, Robert A., 132
Magma chambers, 191
Magma sources, 190
Makovsky, Frank, 340
Managua earthquake, 356, 359
Mann, Dean, 280, 284
Markson, Ralph, 45
Marshall, R. D., 308
Martial law, 351
Martin, Morgan, 349
Mateker, Emil J., 238
Mather, Cotton, 149
Mather, Richard, 148
Matsushiro earthquake swarm, 246
Matumota, Tosimatu, 275
Mauna Loa, 191, 218
Mayan civilization, 208
McDonald, James R., 65
Menninger, W. C., 350
Mesocyclone, 62, 74, 75
Messina earthquake, 360
Meteorologists, 265
Miami area, 316–318, 366
Microwave attenuation, 266
Mid-Atlantic Ridge, 230
Mid-ocean ridges, 216
Midwest

hailstorms, 109, 111
rainfall maximization, 285–288
Mileti, Dennis S., 242
Miller, Joseph A., 65
Minicomputers, 263, 264
Minoan civilization, 208
Minor, Joseph E., 65, 305, 308
Mississippi Valley, 139, 333
Mobile homes, 56, 178, 300, 302
Monticello Tornado, 56
Moore, Harry E., 346
Moore, Willis L., 64
Morrill, B. J., 243
Motagua fault, 228
Mount Erebus, 193
Mount Katmai explosion, 203, 204
Mount Pelée, 196–202, 217, 358
Murchie, Guy, 89
Musya, Inkkiti, 246

National Academy of Sciences
  earthquake predictions, 277
  weather modification, 279, 280, 282
National Center for Atmospheric Research, 107, 113, 117
National Climatic Center, 183
National Earthquake Information Service, 226
National Environmental Satellite Service, 42, 256
National Flood Insurance Association, 131
National Flood Insurance Program, 327
National Hail Research Experiment, 113, 117, 280, 293
National Hurricane Center, 258, 261, 269, 316, 329
National Meteorological Center, 253–255, 260
National Oceanic and Atmospheric Administration (NOAA), 41, 74, 108, 117, 129, 153, 162, 266, 267, 275, 284, 288
National Opinion Research Center, 338
National Science Foundation, 282, 288, 318
National Severe Storms Forecast Center, 46, 58, 64, 258, 264, 265, 269
National Severe Storms Laboratory, 43, 68, 75, 94, 96
National Transportation Safety Board, 29, 37

National Weather Modification Policy Act of 1976, 285
National Weather Service, 75, 80, 152, 170, 255, 258, 263, 300, 328, 340
Natural disaster, definition, 14
Natural disasters
  annual death toll, 298
  assessment of guilt, 362
  outlook for reduction, 364
  worldwide cost, 319–336
Natural forces, benefits, 17, 364, 365
Nature of the Universe, The, 87
New England Blizzard, 181
New England Hurricane, 149, 159
New Hebrides, 231
New Jersey coast, 330
New Madrid earthquakes, 238–240, 244–247
New Orleans, 330, 366
New York City blackout, 86, 284, 351
Nicaragua, 230
NOAA Weather Radio, 268, 309
Nowcasting, 267
Numerical modeling, 259, 261
Numerical weather prediction, 254
  human input critical, 265
  local, 267
  satellite data, 257
Nuttli, Otto W., 239
Nyiragongo volcano, 196

Oaxaca State, Mexico, 275
Obey River Tornado, 56
Ocean trenches, 231
Office of Earthquake Studies, 274
Offshore islands, 330
Ohio River Valley floods, 140
Ohtake, Masakazu, 275
Oklahoma storms, 96
Oldham, R. D., 243
Oliver, Vincent J., 268
Ordoñez, Ezequiel, 209

PACE, 288
Panic behavior, myths, 338, 346, 348
Paraná Plateau of Brazil, 195
Paricutín, birth of volcano, 209, 210
Pearson, Allen D., 46, 54, 63, 65, 73, 259, 264, 269, 300
Penick, James, Jr., 238
Perry, K. W., 204
Person, Waverly, 226
Peru earthquake of 1976, 241
Peru-Chile trench, 217

Plafker, George, 227
Plate tectonics, 193, 215, 216
  Central America, 227–229
  descending slabs, 231
  motions measured, 334, 336
  North American plate, 228, 234
  Pacific plate, 217, 218, 228, 232
  vertical displacement, 232
  volcanoes, 218
Plutonic gases, 193
Popocatepetl, 193
Population increase, 320
Powell, J. R., 248
Precipitation augmentation, 280, 285
Precipitation Augmentation for Crops Experiment, 288
Precipitation prediction, 259
Press, Frank, 193, 224, 271
Pressure waves, 206, 245
Priestley, Joseph, 88
Proctor, David, 94
Program of Collaborative Research on Natural Disasters, 338
Project Hailswath, 114
Project Nimrod, 30
Project Roughrider, 43
Project Skyfire, 283
Project Skywater, 285
Project Stormfury, 289–292
Proni, John, 165
Pulido, Dionisio, 209, 210
Purcell, Daniel, 70, 71
Purdom, James F. W., 41
Purdy, Hugh, 119
P-waves, 174, 275
Pyroclastics, 196

Quale, Robert C., 183
Quarantelli, E. L., 342, 345–351, 353, 356

Radon, well water, 274
Rain damage, 37, 160
Rainfall, 120, 130, 152
Rainfall augmentation, 285–288
Rainfall measurement, 266
Rankin, Paul W., 237
Rankin, William, 38
Rapid City flood, 129–131, 295
Rapid-scan radars, 95
Reconstruction Following Disaster, 358
Red Cross aid, 349, 354
Reed, Richard J., 166

Research Program on Technology, Environment and Man, 338
Rhode Island hurricane, 150
Rhodes, James A., 278
Ribbon lightning, 91
Richter, Charles F., 225
Richter scale of magnitude, 225
Rocky Mountains, 61
    cloud seeding, 284
    flash floods, 119
    hail activity, 109
    thunderstorms, 34
Rust, W. David, 94, 96

Safety precautions
    blizzards, 314
    earthquakes, 314, 315
    electrical charge, 312
    flash floods, 312
    house construction, 302, 303
    hurricanes, 309, 310
    in-residence shelters, 303, 304
    lightning, 311
    mobile homes, 300
    schools, 309
    wind damage, 307
    winter storms, 313, 314
Saint Louis Tornado, 66
Saint-Pierre, 196, 199–201
San Andreas fault, 227–228, 234
San Fernando earthquake, 243, 334, 348, 352
San Francisco earthquake, 225, 235–236
Sanibel Island evacuation, 330
Santa Rosa earthquake, 247
Santorini explosion, 207, 208
Sargasso Sea, chilled, 175
Satellite Field Services Station, 41
Satellite imagery, 332
Satellite photographs, 256
    earth-faulting in China, 224
Satellites
    Air Force DMS Flight 2, 98
    Air Force Vela, 97
    ATS-3 satellite, 46
    ERTS, 224
    GOES-West, GOES-East, 40, 256
    hurricane paths from, 156
    polar orbiters, 257
Saturn 5, lightning bolt, 87
Saylor Park Tornado, 54
Schaefer, Vincent, 279
Schnell, Russell C., 108

Sea floor, volcanic process, 193
Sea-floor spreading, 215
Seismic gaps, 275, 276
Seismic zones, 270, 321, 333
Severe Weather Watches, 48
Shakespeare, William, 148
Sheets, Payson, 208
Sheets, Robert C., 292
Shuman, Frederick G., 254, 259
Siever, Raymond, 193
Silver iodide, 179, 287
Simpson, Joanne, 288
Simpson, Robert H., 262
Sioux Falls Tornado, 64
Snake River Plain, 195
Snow shoveling, 314
Snowdrifts, 172, 173, 178, 181
Snowfall augmentation, 284, 285, 294
Snowfall, records, 168, 175, 177, 181
Snowstorm
    forecasting and formation, 186
Snowstorms, lake effect, 171
Solar flares, thunderstorms, 45
Soufrière eruption, 189, 198
South Fork Dam break, 134
Sri Lanka, 322, 328
Stevenson, Donald A., 271
Stewart, Gordon S., 231
Storm surges, 152–155, 310, 316
Storm systems, monitoring, 258
Storm warnings, response, 269
Storms, local, 265
Stout, G. E., 109
Stromboli, 195
Subduction zones, 232
Sullivan, Roy C., 83
Sumatra-Java arc, 230
Sumba earthquake, 231
Summer storms, 94
Sun Belt states, 183
Sunspot cycle, 44
Supercell storms, 36, 117, 118
Surtsey, Iceland, 193, 211
Susquehanna River flood, 141
Szymanski, Edwin W., 96

Tabas, Iran, 219
Talwani, Pradeep, 271
Tampa Bay, 330
Tanner Tornadoes, 54, 56
Taylor, James B., 350
Taylor, Verta, 345, 352–354
Taylor, William L., 96

Tempest, The, 148
Tennessee Valley floodplain, 326
Terado, Torahiko, 246
Thorarinsson, Sigurdur, 195, 211
Thunder, 79, 90
Thundercloud, charge in, 88
Thunderhead, glider into, 37, 38
Thunderstorm, typical, 26, 27
  cell, 35
  penetrations, 43
  photographs, 40–43
Thunderstorm Project, 39, 114
Thunderstorm Research International
    Program (TRIP), 96, 97
Thunderstorms, 14, 27, 28
  Black Hills, South Dakota, 130, 131
  conditions creating, 24, 30, 32
  downbursts, 29
  downdrafts and updrafts, 39
  electrical properties, 44
  flash flood creation, 133
  flash flood threat, 312, 313
  flying rules, 39
  frequency, 13, 24, 27, 31
  geographical incidence, 27
  gust fronts, 42
  hail generation, 112
  Midwest, 34
  pilots' experiences, 37–39
  research instruments, 39, 40
  Rocky Mountains, 34
  southeastern U.S., 21–24, 77
  squall lines, 36, 37
Thwaites, J. E., 204
Tientsin hotel, earthquake, 222
Toksöz, M. Nafi, 231, 244, 247, 248
Tokyo, 334, 366
Tokyo-Yokohama earthquake, 242
Tonga arc, 230
Tornado
  center, look into, 67, 68
  detection, 76
  formation, 62
  frequency, 13, 61
  funnels, 62, 70
  intensity scale, 54
  life cycle, 70
  superoutbreak of 1974, 46–61, 264–
    303
  vertical paths, 56
  vortex, 75, 306
  warnings, 74, 75, 269
  windspeeds, 58, 305
Tornado-resistant design, 306

Tornadoes, 15, 63, 73
  airborne debris, 64, 65
  American Midwest, 61
  anti-cyclonic, 73
  Birmingham, Alabama, 37
  deaths and damage, 54
  effects on buildings, 59, 60
  flame-induced, 242
  mathematical probability, 64
  maximum pressure drop, 66
  mobile homes, 56
  multiple hits, 64, 67
  multiple-vortexed, 73
  preparedness in schools, 53, 59, 61
  preventing fatalities, 300
  protecting houses, 302–304
  safety guidelines, 308, 309
  suction vortices, 71–73
  Tri-State of 1925, 47–54, 64, 66
  Union City, 65, 68, 70, 75
  U.S., geographical areas, 63
Tropical cyclone, 146, 151, 310
  Bangladesh, 15, 322
Tropical storms, 151, 165
Truly, James, 179
Tsunami Warning Center, 241
Tsunamis, 241
  Crete, 208
  Kodiak harbor, 232
  Krakatoa explosion, 206
Turman, B. N., 97
Typhoon, 146, 151
  death toll, 154
  seeding, 291

Udall, Kansas, 67
Union City Tornado, 65, 68, 70, 75
U.S. Bureau of Reclamation, 285
U.S. Fish and Wildlife Service, 104
U.S. Forest Service, 283
U.S. Geological Survey, 226, 227, 245,
    273
U.S. Water Resources Council, 328
U.S. Weather Bureau, 64, 143
Uzbek earthquake, 244

Valley of Ten Thousand Smokes, 203
Van Sandick, N., 206
Vela optical sensors, 97
Verne, Jules, 191
Vertical evacuation, 317, 332
Vesuvius, 195
Vicksburg, Mississippi, 139

Vincent, E. A., 203
Virginia Key, Florida, 316, 317
Volcanic bombs, 196
Volcanic dust, 189
Volcanic eruption control, 212
Volcanic eruptions, 14
  gas, 191
  global temperatures, 207
  oceanic islands, 193
  pressure wave, 206
  submarine, 211–215
  variants of, 195
  Zaire, 195
Volcanic explosions, 196–207
  Krakatoa, 205–207
  Mount Pelée, 197, 202
Volcanic soil, 193
Volcanoes, 14
  active, 13
  belts of, 214, 215, 217
  deceptive repose, 366
  formation, Central America, 217
  map of distribution, 214
  mid-ocean ridges, 218
  misconceptions, 190
  most spectacular, 191
  Pacific Northwest, 193
  Parícutin's birth, 209, 210
  plate processes, 216, 217
  Tambura, 189
Vonnegut, Bernard, 279
Vulcano, 195

Wall cloud, 70
Wallace, Anthony, 346
War of the Worlds, 337
Ward, Peter L., 273, 276
Wasatch National Forest, 84
Washington, D.C., 141, 176, 177
  snowstorm of 1979, 261
Water-graupel-snow mixture, 95, 96
Wave Propagation Laboratory, 266
Weather changes, 43, 44
Weather chart, hand-analyzed, 256
Weather forecasting, 253–270
  electronic communications, 263
  longer-term models, 255
  numerical, 254–265
  short-term accuracy, 259
  very short-term, 267
Weather modification, 278–297
  barley producers, 294
  commercial seeding, 279

Florida Area Cumulus Experiment, 285
  public response, 295
  risks and benefits, 293
Weather Modification in the Public Interest, 296
Weather radars, 74
Weather Radio receiver, 300
Weather service, local, 267
Welles, Orson, 337
Wells, H. G., 337
West Dade Expressway, 317
West Gulf Coast, 331
Whitcomb, James H., 270
White, Gilbert F., 318, 319, 322, 324–328, 339, 341, 350, 365
Whitlam, Gough, 222
Willy-willy, 146
Wilson, C. T. R., 44
Wind-amplified cold, 167
Wind-caused deaths, 324
Wind-chill temperatures, 171, 172
Wind-proofing, 305, 308
Wind-resistant building codes, 308
Wind-shear conditions, 28
Windsor Tornado, 56
Windspeeds, tornadic, 58, 59, 305
Winter of 1816, 187, 188
Winter of 1977, 174–176
Winter of 1978, 182, 183
Winter storms
  New England, 179, 180
  North Pacific, 97
  predicting, 261
  preparations for, 313
  travel during, 314
Winters, U.S., harshest, 168, 183, 184
Winthrop, Governor, 148
Woodley, William L., 287, 288
World Weather Building, 254, 256, 257
World weather changes, 45
World population growth, 320
Wyss, Max, 275

Xenia Tornado, 47–54, 65, 351–354

Yasui, Yutaka, 246, 247
Year of the Tornado (1973), 64
Year Without a Summer, 187, 207
Yungay, Peru, 241, 242

Zurcher, Louis A., 350